Obecní dům
KANT

The exhibition is held under the auspices of VÁCLAV HAVEL, President of the Czech Republic.

JAN KOTĔRA

1871 – 1923

THE FOUNDER

OF MODERN

CZECH

ARCHITECTURE

MUNICIPAL HOUSE / KANT / Prague 2001

< 1
Jan Kotěra, 1910
> 2
Fishing, postcard photograph, 1915

Architect Jan Kotěra

VLADIMÍR ŠLAPETA

There are only a few figures in Czech modern art as legendary as the architect Jan Kotěra. In his lifetime, Kotěra had already become a symbol of the spirit of modernity in Czech fine art culture of the beginning of the 20th century, a symbol later cultivated by his students and collaborators from the Mánes Association of Fine Artists. Nevertheless, one could say that we are still awaiting the true unveiling of this legend. Since Kotěra's sudden and early death on April 17, 1923, his work has been shown only on three occasions, and always in times unfavourable for its reception.

The first showing was a retrospective exhibition at Obecní dům[1] (Municipal House) in Prague in January 1926, the second an exhibition of drawings at the National Technical Museum in 1944,[2] and the last an exhibition in the Mánes Association gallery in 1972,[3] later transferred to the House of Art in Brno.[4] The exhibitions were accompanied by extremely modest catalogues, the first two without illustrations. At the beginning of the year 1926, the time of Kotěra's first retrospective exhibition, the complex process of cleansing architectural expression of the influence of Rondo-Cubism and Civilist Dutch brick architecture, and orienting it towards white Constructivism and Functionalism, had just ended; thus the dialogue regarding Kotěra's work came somewhat late, especially for the youngest generation. We can sense this in the commentary of Karel Teige,[5] who stated that *"our modern architecture is doubtlessly already beyond the reach and direct influence of Kotěra's work, for his individual pieces are already outdated and cannot be our guide and ideal"*.[6] The exhibition of drawings at the National Technical Museum[7] – as with the Obecní dům retrospective organised by Zdeněk Wirth – no doubt aimed to draw attention to the national values of Czech architecture in those difficult times. However, it did not really have a strong impact. Finally, the 1972 exhibition at Mánes came during

---

1   Jan Kotěra (1871–1923). Prague – Obecní dům, January 1926. The exhibition was opened on 6 January 1926.
2   Architectural drawings of Jan Kotěra. Exhibitions on the works of Czech architects. National Technical Museum in Prague, 19 December 1943–30 April 1944.
3   Marie Benešová – Jiří Štursa – Jana Guthova – Jiří Vasiluk, *Jan Kotěra*. Exhibition catalogue. Prague, 1972.
4   For the Brno "revival" of this exhibition, see: Bohuslav Fuchs, *In margine uměleckého odkazu Jana Kotěry*. Dům umění města Brna 1972.

5   Karel Teige, "Posmrtná výstava Jana Kotěry", *Stavba* IV, 1925–26, pp. 90–93.
6   Ibid., p. 93.
7   See note 2.

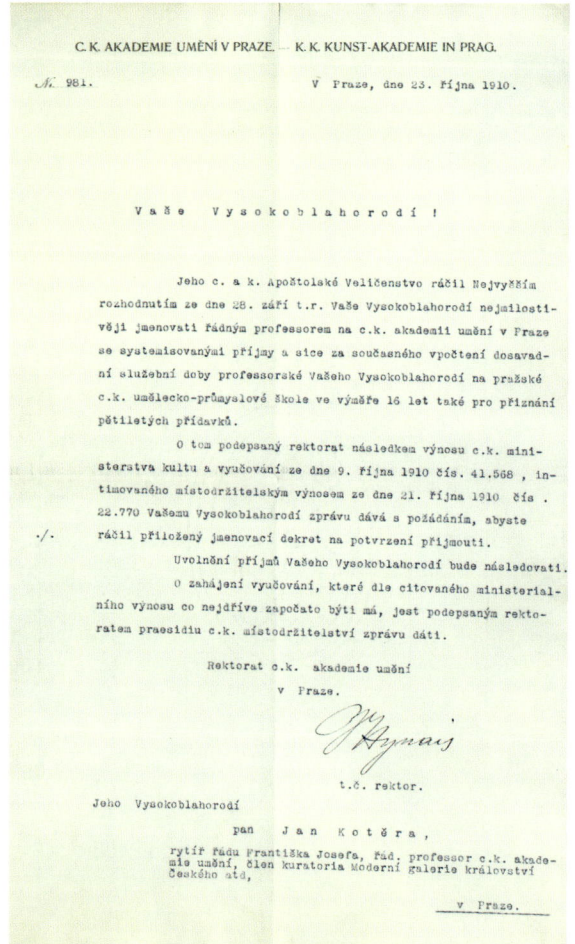

a period of cultural decline and international isolation, at the very moment when increasing interest in the legacy of Josef Maria Olbrich, Josef Hoffmann, Adolf Loos, Hermann Muthesius, Peter Behrens, Hans Poelzig and others could have opened up the possibility of comparing the work of the leading figures of this generation.

If we disregard texts from periodicals, or publications that are difficult to find, there is nothing else for the public to rely on but the short biography by K. B. Mádl published in 1921, on the occasion of Kotěra's 50th birthday,[8] and the remarkable book by Otakar Novotný, *Jan Kotěra and His Time*,[9] published, however, more than 40 years ago. This is why, for younger generations, Kotěra is a remote legend, a leading figure who was once highly cherished by two generations of his students but is now linked only to his few completed projects in Prague, the museum in Hradec Králové, and National House in Prostějov.

Otakar Novotný was the last to attempt to elucidate the work of Jan Kotěra in the wider context of local and international architecture, and dealt venerably with this task in the context of his own era. However, Novotný's monograph was completed at the beginning of the 1940s; it was only expanded and revised in 1958. While research into Kotěra's work has not made any substantial progress since that time, except for monographic studies of three of his buildings, National House in Prostějov,[10] the City Museum in Hradec Králové[11] and Tomáš Baťa's villa,[12] there has been growing interest since the 1970s in the work of his friend and fellow student, Jože Plečnik. The two exhibitions of Plečnik's work, in the Centre Pompidou in Paris in 1985,[13] and ten years later at Prague Castle,[14] came as the result of the rise of postmodern and contextual thinking in architecture. They contributed to the 'discovery' of this Slovene architect, until then unknown to the Western world. The exhibitions on Czech Functionalism[15] and Cubism[16] have, since the middle of the 1980s, brought the legacy of both generations of Kotěra's students into the context of European historiography, while the work of the initiator and driving spirit of Czech Modernism has remained in the shadows. However, with certain good will, the homage to Plečnik and Kotěra's students could be understood as a challenge to stir interest in a new interpretation of Kotěra's legacy, a task that is both needed and relevant in an international context.

Kotěra's personality, which emerged from the new Czech cultural environment at the very end of the 19th century, was in many ways unique and specific. He grew up in a Czech-

---

8   Karel B. Mádl, *Jan Kotěra*. Jan Štenc, Praha 1922.
9   Otakar Novotný, *Jan Kotěra a jeho doba*. SNKLHU Praha 1958.
10 Vladimír Šlapeta – Pavel Marek, *Národní dům v Prostějově*. OKS Prostějov 1978; second enlarged edition 1980, third edition 1987.
11 Rostislav Švácha, "Poznámky ke Kotěrovu muzeu", *Umění* XXXIV, 1986, pp. 171–179.
12 Pavel Zatloukal, "Baťova zlínská vila", *Architekt* XXVII, 1991, p. 4 – Pavel Zatloukal, "Baťova zlínská vila", *Zlínský funkcionalismus*, Státní galerie Zlín 1993, pp. 58–61.
13 *Josef Plečnik – architecte*. Centre Pompidou, Paris, 1985.
14 *Josip Plečnik – architekt Pražského hradu*. Praha 1995.
15 Vladimír Šlapeta, *Czech Functionalism 1918–38*. AA London 1987.
16 Alexander von Vegesack (ed.), *Der tschechische Kubismus*. Vitra Museum. Weil a. R. 1991.

< 3
Appointment as professor at the Academy of Fine Arts, 1910
> 4
Postcard sent to Josef Hoffmann from Plzeň on 24th of November 1897

German family, with a Czech father who was a drawing teacher, and a German mother; he was raised in German schools, first in Ústí nad Labem and then in a state technical college, the School of Engineering in Plzeň.

He came to Prague only after his graduation in 1890, at a time when independent Czech culture began to develop there more rapidly. In Prague, Kotěra completed his apprenticeship in the architectural design studio of his distant relative, the engineer Freyn, and found himself in the proximity of Baron Mladota of Solopisky. The two men recognised his talent and became patrons for his further studies at the Academy of Fine Arts in Vienna, beginning in 1894. This was the very moment when a new professor and an advocate of modern architecture – Otto Wagner – took up his post there. At the time of his Prague intermezzo, from 1890 to 1894, Jan Kotěra witnessed the Jubilee Exhibition in Prague's Stromovka park in 1891, no doubt also the Ethnographic Exhibition in 1895 (where apparently he first became acquainted with young Dušan Jurkovič), and the Exhibition of Architecture and Engineering that took place three years later. During his studies in Vienna, inspired by English examples and by Viollet-le-Duc, he designed a project for the reconstruction of the Mladota family castle in Červený Hrádek, yet at the same time followed the activities and advancement of professor Friedrich Ohmann and the latter's transformation from the Baroque tradition to Secession, without the slightest notion that he was soon to become Ohmann's successor at the School of Applied Arts.

The precondition, and only qualification for his succession, was Kotěra's success at Wagner's school. With his sojourn in Vienna, and as part of his teacher's chosen circle, Kotěra gained a European perspective at a time when Wagner's architectural work was rapidly reaching its creative peak. In Wagner's studio, at the time of Kotěra's studies, there was a young graduate of Baron von Hasenauer (Wagner's predecessor), the Opava-born Josef Maria Olbrich, while Josef Hoffmann – son of the mayor of Brtnice near Jihlava – studied there in his senior year. Olbrich and Hoffmann invited their younger Czech colleague to the "Siebener Club",[17] the debating club which became the seed of the Viennese Secession and *Ver Sacrum* magazine, which was also to publish Kotěra's work.[18] His immediate circle included the painters Koloman Moser, Max Kurzweil and the editor Leo Kainradl, all of whom had experienced a long sojourn in Italy. Occasional participants in the discussions of the "Siebener Club" included architects Josef Urban, Max Fabiani, Friedrich Pilz and Friedrich Kick. Hubert Gessner studied in Kotěra's year, and Jože Plečnik in the following year.[19] Kotěra's friendship with Plečnik was to last until the end of his life. In 1896, after a three-year sojourn in the United

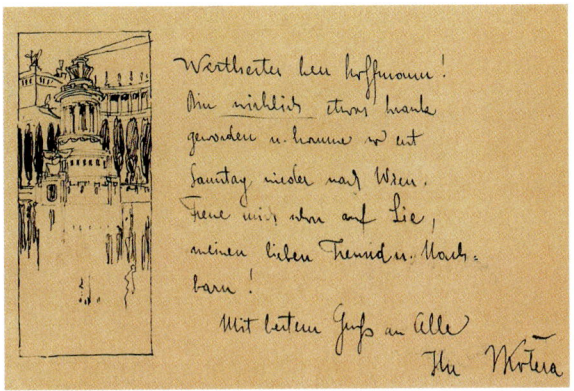

---

17 Otto Maria Graff, *Die vergessene Wagner-Schule*. Wien 1969. – Eduard Sekler, *Josef Hoffmann*. Residenz Verlag, Salzburg 1982.
18 *Ver Sacrum* I, (1898), p. 25.
19 Marco Pozzetto, *Die Schule Otto Wagners* 1894–1912. Anton Schroll, Wien 1980.

< 5
Study for a monument, 1908

States, Adolf Loos returned to Vienna and started his journalistic campaign in the *Neue Freie Presse*, which Kotěra of course followed. In Vienna, Kotěra met Loos, who was once Hofmann's fellow student at the Industrial Design School in Brno.

Within his teaching environment, and in dialogue with his younger fellow students, as well as colleagues of his own generation, Kotěra's artistic views were quickly being formed, influenced on the one hand by Wagner's modernism, and on the other by Italian oriented Neo-Classicism, the aftermath of which was felt at the Viennese Academy. Kotěra himself later characterised this period thus: *"In 1894, he [Wagner] was appointed professor at the Academy of Fine Arts, and in this year began the second phase of his artistic activity, as well as an entirely new period in the architecture of Vienna. The school of architecture [...] enjoyed the best reputation. At the end of the last century, Hansen, Schmidt and Hasenauer taught here. The school was an unrestricted platform where free art was fostered [...] This is why it was understandable that the new professor's appointment created a furore in the artistic world and among the citizens of Vienna [...] His former buildings were received with both enthusiasm and resistance. His gentle taste, broad philosophy and individual approach were widely recognised. It was known that his colleagues and assistants, whom he wisely chose from the best of the young generation, had an influence on the formal elaboration of his projects. What was not yet known was the force of his organising talent, which radically influenced the development of all artistic concepts after his appointment to the school. This great, absorbing organisational characteristic of his predestined him for leadership of a large group. He was an 'inventor' who firmly and impeccably governed over the school, his 'studio' and his artistic friends. He used them as tools for the realisation of his ideas and plans [...] the theoretical essay "Moderne Architektur"*[20] *[...] constituted his own and the generation's credo for a long time to come. In its essence, it contains a requirement for the building's form to match its purpose. He implemented the theory consistently in his entire oeuvre, by accentuating or even exposing the building's construction core, restricting the building's mass to the most essential framework, and treating the materials in accordance with their own nature. This often led him to extremes – he was always radical, both in his beliefs and in his actions. He stirred and provoked, young people rushed to him – as air rushes into a vacuum – and it is in the liberation of spirit that his main importance lies. The talented people that worked on his projects had great influence on the formal aspects of his work, the more so as Wagner prided himself greatly on the draughtsmanship of his architectural plans. [...] Many outstanding talents emerged from his school – Slavs, which explains the fact that the movement which linked itself to the personality of the master carried within itself many virtues originating in the Slavic character. [...] Personally, he was extremely shrewd, logical and – egoistic. However, his temperament and wit brought him closer to his friends and students"*.[21]

In Wagner's studio, Kotěra acquired a broad European perspective, a generosity and an organisational capacity,

---

20 Otto Wagner, *Moderne Architektur*. Wien 1894. – Czech edition: Otto Wagner, *Moderní architektura*. Jan Laichter, Praha 1910.
21 Jan Kotěra, "Otto Wagner". *Volné směry* XIX, 1916–18, p. 230.

characteristics that Prague needed. During the three-year course, Wagner always presented his students with tasks that an architect would face during his career, those that an architect might come across, and finally, large-scale tasks which one most likely would not encounter. In the case of Kotěra, the latter category included projects for a church and for the royal baths, and his final school project, the design of an ideal city at the entrance to a future Calais-Dover tunnel. He conceived each of these works in the fading spirit of Neo-Classicism.

In 1896, Kotěra won the Füger award for his projects, as well as a special school award. One year later, for his final project, he won the prestigious Prix de Rome, including a scholarship to Palazzio Venezia in Rome. One year before Kotěra, Josef Hoffmann won this prize, a year after him, Jože Plečnik.

The sojourn in Rome, incorporating journeys across Italy, which Kotěra undertook from February to June 1898, completed his apprenticeship and supplemented his Viennese experience at the heart of architectural events with an examination of the legacy of the Antiquity and Renaissance.[22] In his Rome sketches, Kotěra researched the eternal problems of architectural composition – the harmony of slender campaniles and the "roof landscapes" of Italian cities, the monumental études of Cestius' pyramid, the Antique temples of Paestum and Girgenti or the motifs from Pompeii, which he captured in masterfully executed drawings. However, as noted by Josef Šusta, who was – together with the painter Knüpfer – one of the principal members of the Czech community in Rome, Kotěra drew in his sketch-books the *"stylised contours of fragile spring blossoms"*, while in his *"general nature the will to achieve severe monumentality struggled with an innate lyricism"*.[23] This polarity between monumentality and lyricism was to accompany Kotěra through his entire oeuvre.

Jan Kotěra presented the artistic outcome of his journey at a successful exhibition of drawings in the Topič gallery. Then in Vienna, with a youthful self-confidence, he negotiated by himself– although doubtlessly with the support of Otto Wagner – his succession to Friedrich Ohmann's post.

---

22 "Z dopisů Jana Kotěry z Itálie roku 1898". *Stavitel* V, 1924, pp. 65–67.
23 Josef Šusta (commemorative introduction), "Z dopisů Jana Kotěry z Itálie". *Umění* IV, 1931, pp. 113–128, 269–275, 313–316, 356–359. – A collection of Kotěra's drawings from Italy and the Riviera illustrates Karel B. Mádl's article, "Příchozí umění". *Volné směry* III, 1899, pp. 120–150.

< 6
M. H. Baillie Scott, Blackwell, hall interior. England, 1897–1900
> 7
Harrison C. Townsend, Whitechapel Art Gallery in London, 1900

Whereas Karel B. Mádl, in his farewell to Ohmann,[24] characterised Ohmann's Prague period as an episode of lasting influence, Josef Chochol saw this occasion with a much more critical eye: *"After the completion of an artistically significant era, characterised at its best in the building of the Czech National Theatre, both Prague and Bohemia entered into an artistic vacuum. The prolific talents and strong figures disappeared, leaving the field open to mediocrities".*[25] Despite the fact that, in literature, the struggle for Modernism had been fervent since the Czech Young Wave, architecture still lacked a figure who could take on this task. Writing about the *"changing of the guard"* at the School of Applied Arts, when Kotěra succeeded the Lvov-born Friedrich Ohmann, Chochol noted that, as an architect, Ohmann did not belong to *"the beginning of an era which so intensely feels its duty to draw all it needs for its art from itself and not from the past. [...] As luck would have it, Ohmann was called to the capital of the old declining monarchy"*, whose *"breakdown was already imminent"*, whereas *"Kotěra was called to a discontented and animated Prague, the centre of a small but persistent nation that never lost hope".*

In Jan Kotěra, the first Czech emissary of Otto Wagner – an undesired emissary as far as the then architectural and professional establishment was concerned – Prague won a youthful, energetic and cosmopolitan figure, able to take upon himself the responsibility for a modern orientation in architecture and the visual arts, and to set – in the sense of Jirasek's motto about *"opening windows onto Europe"*[26] – international standards for it. Kotěra assumed his missionary task immediately and with great vehemence. With the organisational talent inherited from his professor, it was soon felt that *"in him, a new force is rising in Czech architecture, needed as badly as air is for breathing, if it is not to wallow in artistic conservatism long overcome in other places. He returns home [...] as an architect who, with the confidence of a man with absolute belief in his salvation, lives and works within modern times."*[27] Most likely with the

---

24 Karel B. Mádl, "F. Ohmann v Praze". *Volné směry* IV, 1900, pp. 181–186.
25 Josef Chochol, "Jan Kotěra". *Časopis československých architektů*. XXII, 1923, p. 165.
26 Otakar Novotný, "Úvod k členské výstavě S. V. U. Mánes 1932". *Volné směry* XXIX, 1932, pp. 248–250.
27 Karel B. Mádl (see note 23), p. 120.

<> 11
Mácha's villa in Bechyně, 1902–1903

builds simple, yet pleasant wooden promenade arcades, in harmony with the environment and the landscape. Despite this apparent refusal to take on popular pseudo-forms and superficial buildings, the architect in fact draws abundantly from the means at hand, and this is where his strength lies, this is why his work becomes so dear to us, for it bears a physiognomy that is natural, typical of the country and of the nation". In his early residential buildings, Kotěra followed similar principles, making an effort to link the tradition of local folk architecture with the design of the English cottage. This is how he conceived F. Trmal's villa in Strašnice, designed in 1902–03, as well as the sculptor Stanislav Sucharda's villa in Bubeneč some three years later, while in the case of Tonder's villa in St Gilgen, which ends the first phase of Kotěra's residential works, he attempted *"with exquisite taste [...] to bring together*

the Salzburg cottage with the Czech and English equivalent".[39] On the contrary, in his first urban houses, Kotěra employed the popular Baroque, successfully combining it with fine Secessionist ornamentation and, more importantly, with a modern understanding of metropolitan proportions. This is true of his first building in Prague, Peterka's house from 1899–1900, where he could not, however, influence the groundplan,[40] as well as the project for the house "U Nováků"[41] created one year later which only remained at the design stage. In both projects, he designed a large-scale, two-storey glazed parterre. For his Regional Authorities building in Hradec Králové, he applied similar design principles, only on a smaller scale, influenced in a certain sense by the early Viennese works of Josef Maria Olbrich.

Led by the powerful example of Otto Wagner, Kotěra, right at the beginning of his time in Prague, published his conceptual statement "On New Art"[42] in which he declared his support for the Wagnerian theses that architecture is founded on *"the modelling of space – that is, on creating function in accordance with the local conditions and needs (climate, culture, customs) – on the construction of this space with the means at hand (materials and technical knowledge) – and finally on the embellishment, ornamentation, carried out with our innate feeling for natural beauty. [...] Purpose, construction and location therefore represent the moving force – the form is their consequence"*, while stressing that *"each movement not founded on purpose, construction and location, is utopian"*. Soon afterwards, again in Wagnerian spirit, he published a collection of articles entitled *My Work and That of My Students*.[43] Although Wagner personally was not truly satisfied with the publication[44] – Kotěra was aware that he had not *"as yet reached the goal"* he had set himself[45] – the introduction does reveal the ideas and energy

---

39 Otakar Novotný (see note 9), p. 35.
40 Pavel Janák, *Sto let nájemného domu*. Praha 1931.
41 Jan Kotěra, *Práce mé a mých žáků*. (German version: *Meine und meiner Schüler Arbeiten*.) Anton Schroll, Wien 1902.
42 Jan Kotěra, "O novém umění". *Volné směry* IV, 1900, p. 189.
43 Jan Kotěra (see note 41).
44 Otakar Novotný (see note 9).
45 Jan Kotěra (see note 41).

< **12**
Charles R. Mackintosh, Hill House in Kilmacolm, Scotland, 1900–1901
<< **13**
Frank Lloyd Wright, own house and studio in Oak Park, Illinois, entrance to the studio, 1889
> **14**
Peterka's house in Prague, detail of the façade, 1899–1900

he began to apply in his teaching of architecture. *"Artistic education should first of all strive to achieve the following goal: to awaken the student's own personality, to support with all means possible the development and cultivation of his own individuality. Therefore, an art school teacher does not force the language of his own works onto his students, and his artistic and educational influence does not deviate from the boundaries set by the basic principles of certain artistic views and beliefs. This teacher knowingly puts a limit on the influence of his own individuality by preferably using the spoken word, adding only the most necessary comments through drawing; at the same time, he avoids as much as possible demonstrating the origins, realisation and phrasing of his own ideas."*[46] In 1910, Kotěra transferred this concept of education, which he introduced at the School of Applied Arts, to the Academy of Fine Arts, where it was later successfully applied by both his successors on the architectural throne, Josef Gočár and Jaroslav Fragner. The first phase in the development of Kotěra's work reached its peak in 1905–07, with the architect's most extensive work of the period, National House in Prostějov. While the "national" tone in his work culminated in the early 20th century, in his design for the exhibition in St Louis at the beginning of 1904, Josef Chochol noted that already at this time *"subtle signs of transition and future development"*[47] began to show in Kotěra's work, with his emotional delicacy and lyricism maturing into more serene, more monumental forms. In Prostějov, Kotěra divided the entire architectural problem into three basic functions, clearly manifest both in the groundplan and in the volumetric composition: the corpus of the theatre, the incorporation of the restaurant and conference hall, and finally the club house area. With his very individual sense of space, the architect situated the house on the eastern edge of the historical town. The asymmetrical segmentation of mass reflects the three main functions of the building, and while it was still created in a Secessionist spirit, it did not lack a solemness, heralding the architect's future development towards a more rational concept of architecture. The building, which differed greatly from other Czech architecture with a similar function, such as the Prague Vinohrady Theatre, or

46 Ibid.

47 Josef Chochol (see note 25), p. 165.

Municipal House, met with a favourable response not only in the local architectural journals[48] but also abroad; various views of the interiors were published by the Editor-in-Chief of *Moderne Bauformen* magazine, Paul Klopfer.[49]

Kotěra's early period was concluded with the appealing decoration, colour and choice of materials of the interior of the Arco coffee-house, created in collaboration with František Kysela. The picture of this period would not be complete without mention of Kotěra's intimate sepulchral architecture, including the many brilliant free sketches in this genre which display Kotěra's innate subtlety and refinement of style. Latent experience from the Italian sojourn also survived in them, together with reflections of Classical and Renaissance traditions; in these intimate études, the architect tested the abstract effects of three-dimensional forms.

No matter how strongly Kotěra's work in this early period differed from the rest of Czech architecture, it won response only in the fine arts' circle of the Mánes Association and in a small circle of private clients; not even the support of such figures as František Xaver Šalda or Jaroslav Kvapil,

48 *Styl* I, 1908–09.
49 Paul Klopfer, "Professor Jan Kotěra – Prag". *Moderne Bauformen* X, 1910, pp. 441–446.

< **15**
Regional Authorities building in Hradec Králové, 1903–1904
> **16**
My Work and That of My Students, A. Schroll, Vienna 1902
>> **17**
Jan Kotěra (seated in the middle) at the School of Applied Arts, c. 1901

or very probably the group from the Masonic lodge, was enough. Neither was the international reception of his work: Kotěra remained ignored and underestimated by the architects from the Czech Technical College circle, and large commissions passed him by.

The beginning of Kotěra's next creative period brought indications that this situation could change. It was a period inspired by travel: first of all to the United States, from February to June 1904, and later on to Holland and England, in 1905 and 1906. The journeys opened up new horizons. Despite the fact that all we know about the American journey is that he undertook it with Josef Urban, the head of the School of Applied Arts[50] – we do know that he travelled first to Bremen, then took a boat to New York. Although he most likely did not have the opportunity to visit Chicago – he was certainly following developments in the work of Louis Sullivan and especially Frank Lloyd Wright, both of whom he had introduced in *Volné směry* four years earlier. This was happening at a time when the Larkin Building in Buffalo was created, and Wright was making headway from the 'Prairie Houses' of the Mid-West to more monumental architecture, expressing the spirit of American industrial civilisation at the time of its prosperity. It is also possible to speculate that Kotěra's design of the exhibition in St Louis gave rise to a series of meetings with important figures,

50 Josef Urban moved to the States before the First World War and became established there mainly as an experimental stage architect. See: *Theatres by Joseph Urban. Theatre Arts.* New York 1929. In Czechoslovakia, see: Lubomír Šlapeta, Nová škola pro sociální výzkum od Josefa Urbana, New York. *Stavba X*, Praha, 1931–1932, 1, pp. 8–9.

<> 22
City Museum in Hradec Králové, main façade, 1909–1913

side has a glazed winter garden and terrace, while an elongated pergola and alcove were positioned along the western border of the grounds. The entrance is asymmetrically accentuated by the elevated vertical corpus of the stairwell. Displaying a truly modern sense, Kotěra achieved an ascetic and asymmetrical composition of the house, its residential role conceived in a highly functional manner, in which Teige saw the Central European transformation of Wright's family house. As the house also became the seat of the School of Architecture at the Academy of Fine Arts, with all of Kotěra's students spending their apprenticeship years there between 1910–23, the villa became for them an icon of Czech modern architectural thought.[62]

For Karel Teige, Krejcar's friend from *Devětsil*, an even more significant project was the house of publisher Jan Laichter, which Kotěra designed and completed parallel with his own villa. This house, built on a vacant site at the edge of Rieger park, is a combined publishing house and luxurious flat for the owner, with a number of rental flats on the upper floors. Already this combined function was more acceptable for Teige than Kotěra's own simple upper-middle class villa. Moreover, Teige appreciated the main façade for its truthful expression of the building's main functions; he characterised the two buildings – the architect's own villa and Laichter's house – as works which were *"genuinely modern and of a worldly spirit, which anticipate many of the further developments in international architecture. In their value and modernity, they may be placed alongside the more recent works of Oud or Dudok, built some ten or fifteen years later"*.[63]

Whereas in his practice as an architect Kotěra had but few occasions to develop an apartment house typology,[64] the commission to design a workers' housing colony for railway employees in Louny provided him with an opportunity

to comment on the topical question of the garden town. Kotěra became familiar with this type of architecture during his journeys to England, and, in the case of the workers' housing colony in Louny, he encouraged Czech architects and urban planners to focus on it as well. This interest was followed by the move of the Karlsruher Gartenstadtgesellschaft travelling exhibition to Prague and Hradec Králové in 1910, as well as the founding of the Czech Association for Garden Towns.[65]

In the Louny housing colony Kotěra attempted to create widely applicable, standard types of buildings with economical groundplans, using a rather traditional architectonic form. By 1919, a significant part of the colony was finished, whereas other plans for colonies in Zlín and Králův Dvůr, which the architect began working on during the First World War, remained only insubstantial fragments. Nevertheless,

---

62 Jaromír Krejcar published plans for this building in the Czech avant-garde almanac *Život* II, as an example of Czech modern architecture. According to the testimony of F. M. Černý, in 1924 Josef Gočár's school of architecture was still situated in the rented rooms of Kotěra's villa.

63 Karel Teige (see note 59), p. 47.

64 Possibly only with the exception of Laichter's house and the family house on Mickiewicz street in Hradčany where the family of T. G. Masaryk lived after its completion and during the First World War.

65 Vladimír Zákrejs, J. Blažej, Alois Kubiček, Ottokar Fierlinger etc. became the main advocates of the concept of garden towns. – In 1911, Loos' student Rudolf Wels published *Zahradová města*. Knihovna Čas, no. 56, Prague 1911. *Garden Town exhibition*. Prague "New Town Hall", Linhartské square. Organised by the Czech Association for Housing Reform and the Association of Czech Towns. Foreword by the architect Ladislav Blažej, undated.

< 23
City Museum in Hradec Králové, staircase, 1909–1913
> 24
Specialised Education Pavilion at the Chamber of Trade and Commerce Jubilee Exhibition in Prague, in collaboration with K. Göttlich, inner courtyard, 1908

with these experiments Kotěra began a quest to find solutions for this important issue in the first half of the 1920s, later developed in the work of Gahura in Zlín and in a series of "white-collar" colonies built in Czech towns soon after the Czechoslovak Republic was created.[66] This came as a result of the new Republic's insistence on the social mission of its planning and housing policies.[67]

Kotěra's interest in purely functional solutions is inherent in, among others, the uncompleted project for a primary school in Králův Dvůr near Beroun (1908), designed in an asymmetrical, almost "Functionalist" style.

In his second, most creative period, Kotěra sought other options alongside the civilism of exposed brick architecture: he attempted to find a unity between modern and classical architecture. At the time, many other major architects of his generation were inclined towards a certain Neo-Classicism – Josef Maria Olbrich at the close of his career in Düsseldorf, and Josef Hoffmann, in whom this tendency reached its peak in the Austrian pavilion for the 1914 exhibition of the Germand Werkbund in Cologne. Neo-Classicist tendencies were also evident in Hans Poelzig's Four-Dome Pavilion at the 1913 exhibition in Wrocław, and finally in Peter Behrens' German Embassy building in St Petersburg. Kotěra, inspired it seems by West Bohemian spa architecture and the Mediterranean spirit he absorbed during his time in Italy, gave his spa hotel project Peppina Villa in Opatija a lofty, elegant, almost Empire-style character, in which the main residential building with its loggia contrasted with the terrace and oval glazed pavilion. The still unpublished alternative sketch indicates that Kotěra had been prepared to offer a much more modern, almost Constructivist design, which was probably not accepted by the prospective owner.

In this period, Kotěra turned to the Neo-Classicist Empire style on more than one occasion, as testified by the attractive pavilion stalls built at the head of the bridge in Hradec Králové, the Vojáček monument in Prostějov (dated just after the Opatija project), the reconstruction of the Bianca villa in Bubeneč, the interior of the Palm garden within the extension of the Grand Hotel in Hradec Králové, the unrealised projects for a spa building in Grad and the Savings Bank in Hradec Králové. All these projects bear witness to the architect's originality

[66] Stavitel library in 1921 published a collection of Kotěra's designs for garden towns entitled: Jan Kotěra, Dělnické kolonie, with an article by Raymond Unwin "Stavba měst" translated by Kamil Roškot. Raymond Unwin received an honorary doctorate at the German Technical University in Prague. – The Czech version of the book by Ebenezer Howard, Zahradní města budoucnosti, was published in Prague in 1924 by Vesmír publishing house, with commentaries by O. Fierlinger, A. Kubiček and O. Cmunt.

[67] Pavel Janák, "Hmota či duch". Styl V (X), 1924–25, pp. 170–174.

ARCHITECT JAN KOTĚRA   31

32　ARCHITECT JAN KOTĚRA

< **25**
Reconstruction of Bianca villa, detail, sketch, 1910
<< **26**
Charvát's villa in Vysoké Mýto, 1909–1911
> **27**
Kotěra's own villa in Prague-Vinohrady, studio of Kotěra's school, 1908–1909
>> **28**
Kotěra's own villa in Prague-Vinohrady, garden façade, 1908–1909

and inclination towards a Mediterranean architectonic temperament.

On the other hand, in the case of the new Ratboř castle, the first sketches signalled a similarly light Empire spirit, yet Kotěra ultimately became enmeshed in a somewhat schematic Neo-Classicism, which resurfaced several times in his work just before the First World War, as his project for the Epilepsy Institute in Libeň in Prague shows. Here, the architect was obviously searching for his own point of reference in the Cubist period, a style with which he was willing to identify only regarding abstract sculptural disposition.

In 1912, journal *Styl* featured Antonín Engel with an article entitled "Public Buildings in Prague",[68] a strong critique of the contemporary building policies of the Czech metropolis. He noted that the buildings of the National Theatre and the Rudolfinum by Josef Zítek represented the last significant initiatives in Prague, and since that time only Josef Fanta's new railway station *"displays a certain eloquence and a genuine struggle for new form"*.[69] In conclusion, he stated that *"the Municipal House and the new town hall represent the pure catastrophe of Czech official architecture"*.[70] Jan Kotěra was the principal victim of this official building policy.

Isolated at the time of his arrival in Prague, when he alone initiated the fight for a new Czech architecture, he was again isolated at the culmination of his creative endeavours. *"With jealousy and pettiness, so typical of the provincial petty-bourgeoisie, obstacles were continually placed in Kotěra's way which required tremendous energy to overcome, energy which he could, if the circumstances were more favourable, have used for the realisation of his ideas [...] Under the influence of these circumstances, against which he was bound to struggle all his life [...] the greatest Czech architect, predestined to create monumental works which should have documented for centuries to come the supra-European level of Czech modern architecture – had less opportunity to build than any mediocre building entrepreneur"*[71] – the bitter words of Jaromír Krejcar. Even his submission for the 1911 competition to design Koruna Palace in Wenceslas Square went without response; according to Otakar Novotný, it was one of his purest works whose spacious framework, with a two-storey glazed parterre and passageways, masterfully captured the metropolitan character of the palace and its function. At the beginning of the 1920s, after Josef Gočár and Stanislav Sucharda had presented their Bílá Hora sepulchral mound in the first volume of the newly-founded journal *Styl*, and especially after the 1909 competition for the Old Town Hall, Kotěra's students and colleagues began to work independently, searching for a new starting point in Cubist architecture. In his conceptual treatise "From Modern Architecture to Architecture", Pavel Janák outlined his vision of future developments *"in which artistic thinking and abstraction will change after*

---

68   *Styl* IV, 1912, pp. 30–37.
69   See note 68, p. 34.
70   Ibid., p. 37.

71   Jaromír Krejcar, "Jan Kotěra". *Stavba* II, 1923, 2, p. 4.

< 29
Laichter's house in Prague-Vinohrady, version, model, 1908–1912

functionality takes the lead; it will move on in its effort to achieve a three-dimensional form and a three-dimensional realisation of architectural ideas. This is fully in accordance with the creative energy accumulated by present developments, which is now strengthened and able to penetrate deeper into architectural issues. It will also reach deeper into the mass, and extract form from its depths."[72]

Although Kotěra kept in touch with his students' Cubist movement, he accepted it with considerable reserve. The architect, who had great intuition for finding an adequate form appropriate to its function, must have found it difficult to come to terms with the idea that an *a priori* Cubist form should dominate architectural endeavour. This is why he experimented cautiously with Cubism, more in a decorative than an architectonic sense. We can see the reflection of the Cubist movement in Kotěra's work in the commercial and residential building owned by music publisher Mojmír Urbánek, known as the Mozarteum, created in 1911–13, the beginning of the artist's last creative phase. Kotěra ingeniously achieved the plasticity of the main façade, whose longitudinal window on the first floor is borne by Jan Štursa's caryatids, through constructive means: the four-storey exposed brick façade is modelled in such a way that each storey front recedes by 7.5 cm. This plasticity is further accentuated by fluting, which intensifies with each storey and frames the entire façade, itself ending in a stately tympanum.

The well-rounded, serene architecture of the Mozarteum indicates the architect's ability to search, amidst the monumental problems he addressed, for a harmony between modern and classical architecture. The competition projects for the Austro-Hungarian Bank (1911) and the Royal Palace in Sofia (1912) do display certain traces of Cubist detail, yet they remain Neo-Classicist in their essence. In the Lemberger Palace in Vienna, completed just before the outbreak of the First World War, the Cubist detail fulfils only a secondary, decorative role. Finally, even for the General Pension Institute in Prague, situated on Rašínovo embankment, Kotěra reticently applied Cubist details in the bevelled forms of the pillars between the windows, in the window frames and in the decorative treatment of the main and side façades, giving the otherwise rather academic edifice a more plastic form. He was only able to fully identify with the Cubist concept when he approached fine art, namely architectural sculpture. Such was the case in the joint project for the monument to Jan Žižka, created with Jan Štursa, in which he illustrated an ability to intuitively and spontaneously resolve a monumental sculptural task.

Kotěra's indefatigable effort to advocate Czech modern art led to a series of exhibitions in prominent galleries abroad (the last one in Munich in 1913 was reviewed in England[73]). He also contributed to the founding of the independent Czech Union of Applied Artists in the winter of 1913. This led to the participation of the Union in four halls of the Austrian pavilion at the Werkbund Exhibition in Cologne in 1914. Otakar Novotný[74] was entrusted with the task of creating the design. Arguably, Jan Kotěra devoted his greatest attention and energy to the project for the university buldings of the Faculty of

---

[72] Pavel Janák, "Od moderní architektury – k architektuře". *Styl* II, 1910, pp. 105–109.

[73] *The Studio* LX, 1913, pp. 236–237.
[74] Otakar Novotný (see note 9), p. 61. – Vladimír Šlapeta, "Svaz českého díla – Der tschechische Werkbund", in: Astrid Gmeiner – Gottfried Pirhofer, *Der österreichische Werkbund*. Residenz Verlag, Salzburg 1985, pp. 191–207.

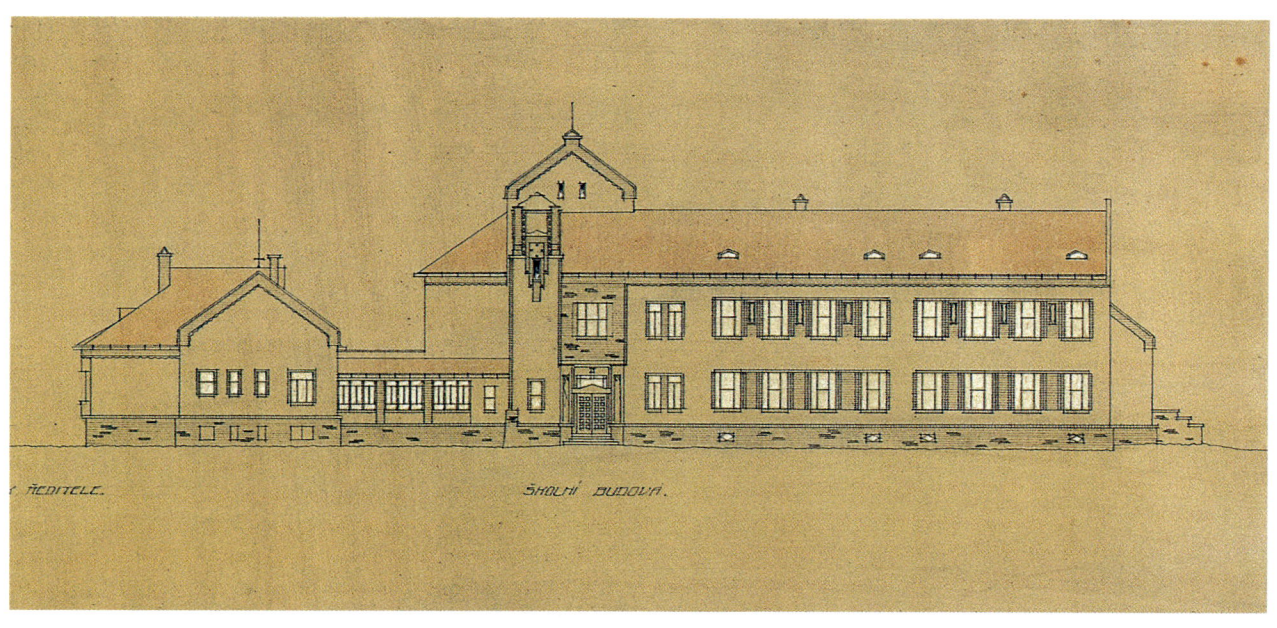

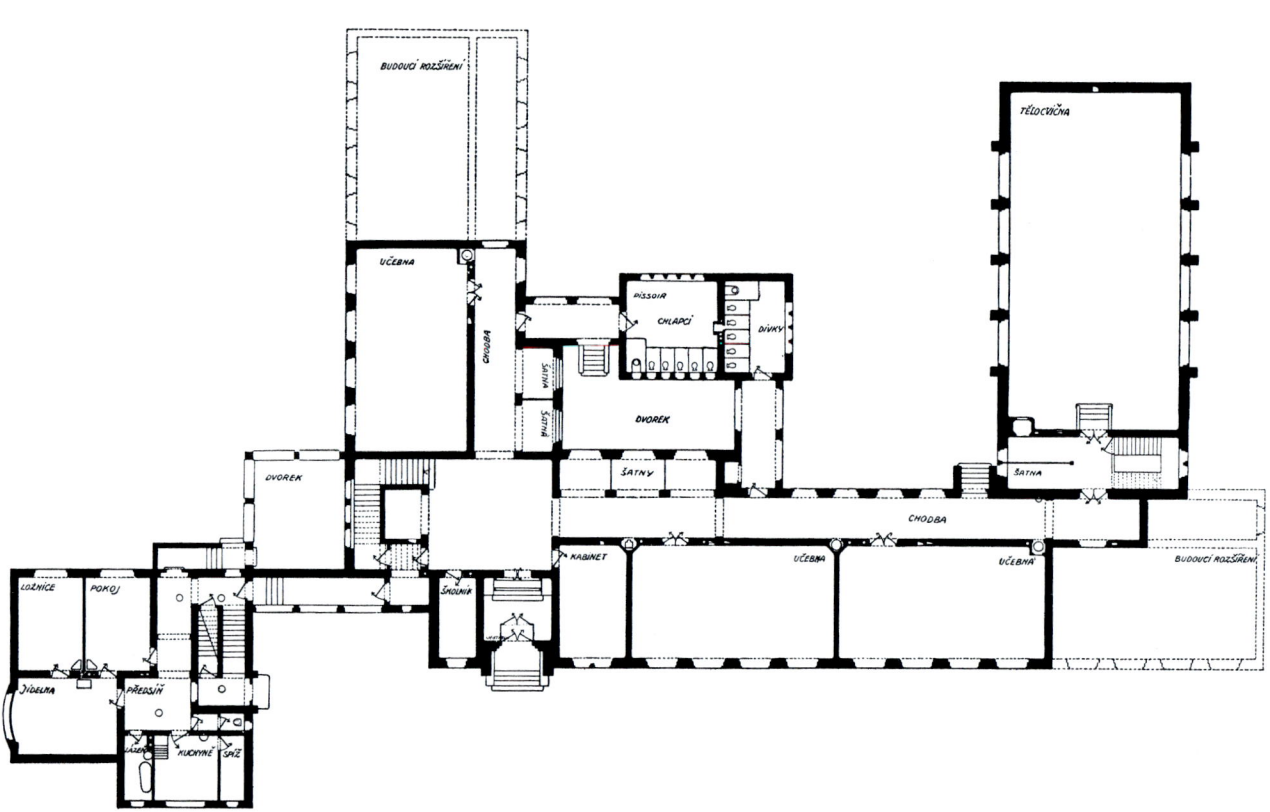

< **30**
Design for a primary school with an apartment for the headmaster in Králův Dvůr near Beroun, façade, 1908
<< **31**
Design for a primary school with an apartment for the headmaster in Králův Dvůr near Beroun, groundplan, 1908
> **32**
Design for the Peppina Villa hotel in Opatija, version, detailed drawing, 1909

Law and Theology at Czech University of Charles-Ferdinand. He prepared the first design in 1907. Identical to one from 1909, this design was derived from the concept of the City Museum in Hradec Králové. The third design, created in a rather Neo-Classicist tone, met with the opposition of Ferdinand d'Este, successor to the throne, who demanded that the project be re-designed in the Baroque style. Kotěra did not comply; it was only at the very beginning of the War, on December 15, 1914, that he delivered his reworked project. Soon after, it was approved by the Ministry in Vienna.

However, the War halted the completion of the project and, in 1920, Kotěra had to present his project again for a competition organised by the Ministry of Public Works. He won the competition once again, but the project was completed only after Kotěra's death, and with certain changes, including its location (the Czech University was originally planned for the opposite side of Mikulášská, today Pařížská, avenue).[75]

"A look at his work from the War period arouses only pity. One tomb after another, war memorial after war memorial, one military graveyard after another – this was his repertoire. In addition, if we are correct in our numbers, projects for two new houses and one reconstructed family home, Baťa's newly renovated library in Zlín, and finally the façade of a farm building in Telč are the result of four years of activity undertaken by an architect approaching his 50th birthday, at the height of his creative powers"[76] – this is the survey of Kotěra's War period described in Otakar Novotný's book. Tombstones and war memorials gave Kotěra an opportunity

[75] Jan Kotěra, "Data k projektu budovy pro právnickou a theologickou fakultu české univerzity". *Styl* II/VII, 1921–1922, p. 93, pp. LIX–LXXVIII.
[76] Otakar Novotný (see note 9), p. 62.

to reconcile himself with the Cubist era, which he did with an originality of his own. In the Hácha tombstone, in the war memorials in Slaný and Nové Hrady, and finally in the 1917 sketches for a mausoleum, the nobility of his early works seemed to have come to life once more, in a more serene Cubist tone, always with the masterful placement of sculptural works within the architectural framework that was so typical of Kotěra. Even in so prosaic a task as the renovation of the warehouse in Telč, he manifested an ingenuity of form and the harmony of Cubist novelty with the existing building.

In the few family houses which he designed during the War, it seems that the architect was searching for a way back to the Czech country house rooted in local traditions. In this, he continued to evolve the ideas from his early period. However, his work emanated greater experience and serenity, notable in the clear layout and higher standards of the projects he undertook. In this case, the roof was designed in harmony with the landscape, and the architect endeavoured to bring the building and garden closer together.

All his life, Jan Kotěra advocated Czech nationalist ideas – even in the war period when, in May 1917, he negotiated the participation of Czech fine artists in the Czech writers' call for national independence;[77] yet the creation of the independent Czechoslovak Republic brought him unexpected disappointment. On the 1st of January 1919, in *Socialistické listy*, he was accused of being a toady of Vienna. This attack on his person, together with the shameful affair surrounding the University buildings commission, the consistent intrigues and tensions at work, affected Kotěra deeply, especially as he was by then already tired, embittered and ill: after two decades of struggle for a new Czech culture, he was as isolated as ever when national inde-

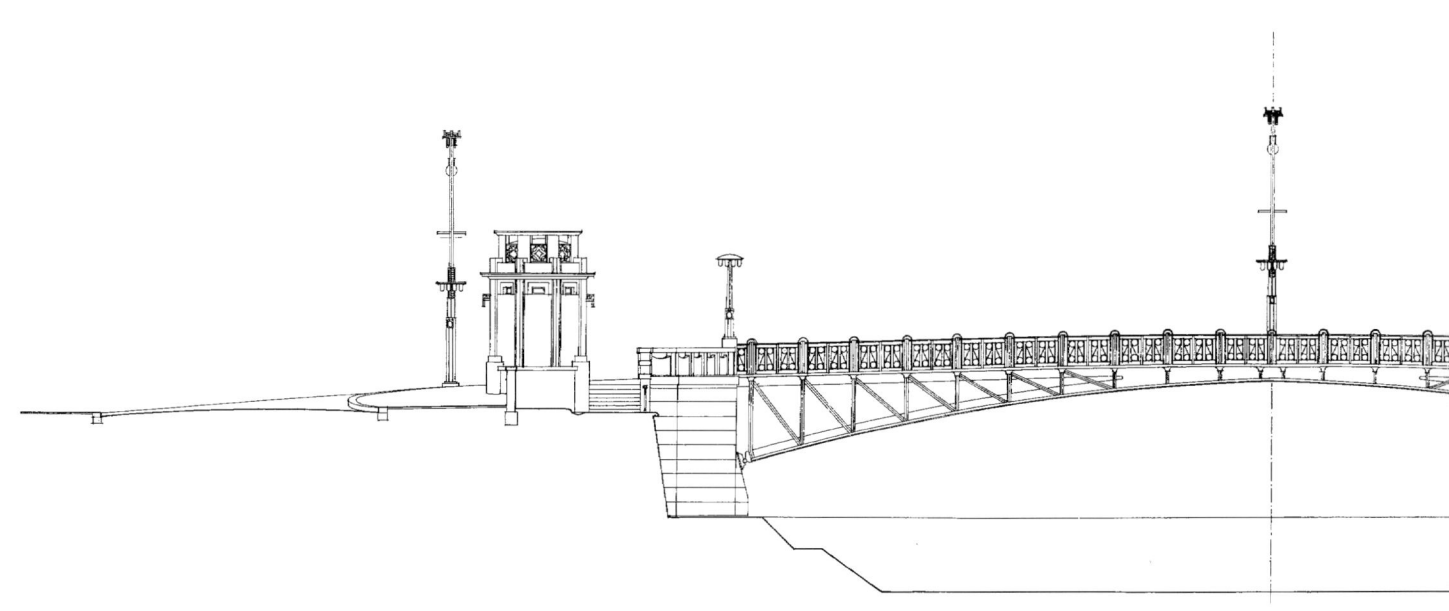

[77] See the letter from Jan Kotěra to *Socialistické listy*, dated *c.* 2 January 1919. Private ownership.

> **<> 33**
> Adaptation of the bridge in Hradec Králové, longitudinal section, 1910

pendence finally came. *"I encountered the most distressful time [...] after the revolution. It is a well known fact that the essence and scope of an architect's work is not granted sufficient appreciation from the uninitiated; it is also well known how natural it is that only so few individuals understand the intensity and exertion our work requires"*,[78] wrote Kotěra. In this bitter frame of mind, he withdrew from public life.

At the beginning of the 1920s, his powers rapidly declining, Kotěra created only a few noteworthy projects. They included a competition entry for the Prague Credit Bank, the design of Můstek in Prague – achieving a considered, serene form which created a gateway to the Old Town, or the vaguely Cubist structure of the Vítkovice ironworks in Bredovská street. An unrealised project for the apartment of President Tomáš Garrigue Masaryk in Hradčany in June 1921 remained faithful to the Neo-Classicist spirit of Mandelík's new castle in Ratboř. The completed back gable of Mandelík's sugar refinery, hitherto overlooked in the context of Kotěra's work, was modelled in the same spirit. The last important project, a rural villa, the summer residence of the publisher Jan Štenc in Všenory, was a compact, intimate work with which this "teacher of living standards"[79] symbolically completed his series of Czech residential buildings. This series occupied Kotěra throughout his professional life.

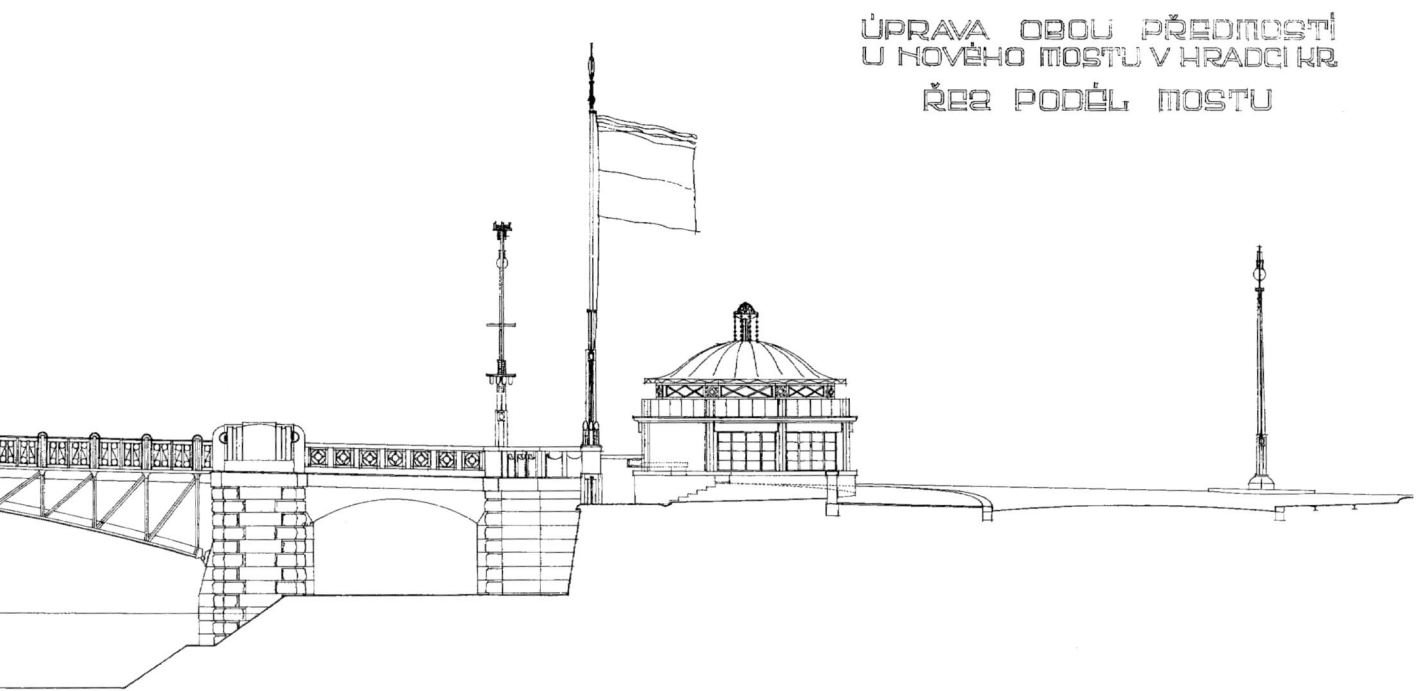

[78] Jan Kotěra (see note 75), p. 93.

[79] Pavel Janák, "Učitel bydlení". *Výtvarná práce* III, 1924, pp. 169–182.

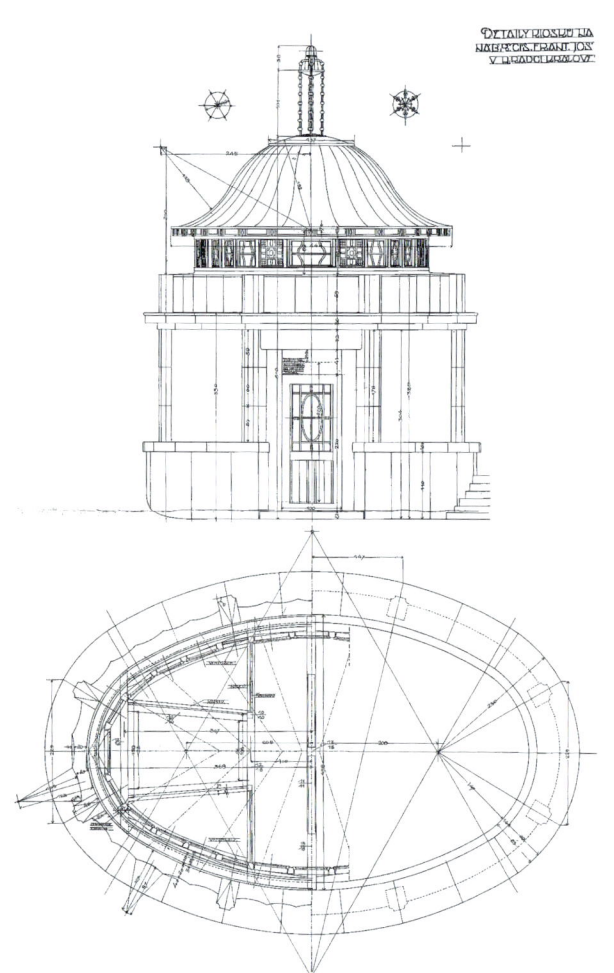
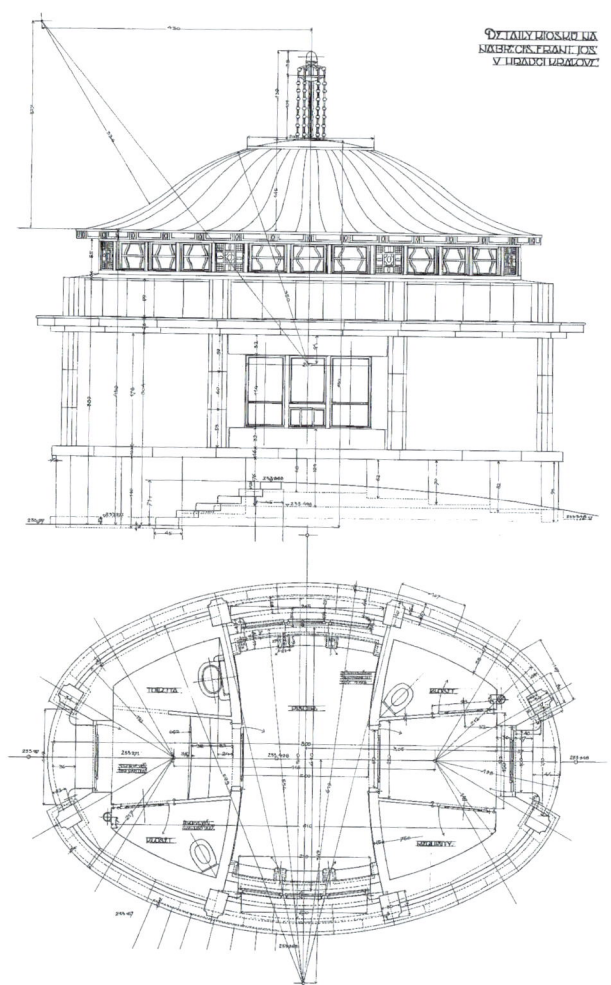

ARCHITECT JAN KOTĚRA

< **34**
Adaptation of the bridge in Hradec Králové,
façade and groundplan of the kiosk, 1910
< **35**
Adaptation of the bridge in Hradec Králové,
façade and groundplan of the kiosk, 1910
<< **36**
Kiosk at the front of the bridge in Hradec Králové, 1910
> **37**
Vojáček memorial in Prostějov, study, 1910

With these buildings the architect addressed *"the ordinary people, their requirements and their need for privacy, intimacy and modesty"*.[80]

In 1921, the Munich-based magazine *Baumeister*[81] once again presented a work by Kotěra – the Specialised Education Pavilion from a 1908 Prague exhibition. Jože Plečnik had left Prague for good, moving to Ljubljana to set up an architectural school there. That year, Josef Hoffman was appointed a member of the Prussian Academy of Arts in Berlin, as was another architect of Kotěra's generation, Hans Poelzig, the following year; also in 1921, Peter Behrens became the successor to Otto Wagner at the Academy in Vienna. Plečnik, Hoffmann, Poelzig and Behrens all saw an increase in their creative activities in the 1920s while Kotěra, who died suddenly on the 17th of April 1923, aged 51, was not granted such a destiny.

Kotěra devoted his last remaining energy to his students. With unfailing intuition, he selected the best talents for his school. *"A genuine friend of youth, Kotěra as an educator always enjoyed its intensity, its fantasy untamed by life, left to burst freely in abstract compositions, often in poetic subjects, and then he would gradually coax it towards the solution of specific problems. Leaving the students absolutely free in their development as individuals, he strove only to lead them towards a harmonious attitude to life, with which they were later to create their work [...] Did he teach? No, he educated. He educated first of all the modern man. This is the secret of his school and its vitality, that it never produced epigones, neither voluntary nor those forced into epigony, as other schools did; instead it created a joyful workplace for a handful of young people, in which Kotěra set the tone not as a professor but as a true leader of the young group."*[82] He also enabled his students to start their careers by mediating their first commissions and upholding the quality of their projects among architectural jurors.[83]

Kotěra's own work remained fragmented. It is an open question which direction it would have taken, and how it would have reacted to the social and technological changes of the inter-War period. His task was assumed by two generations of his students, of whom Josef Gočár and Otakar Novotný,

---

80 Some 20 years later, these houses found a true continuation in the work of Karel Honzík. See: Karel Honzík, "K otázce lidové architektury". *Architektura* III, 1941, pp. 89–100. – also in Hlasná Třebáň by Lubomír Šlapeta. See: Tomáš Pospěch, *Hranická Architektura 1815–1948*. Hranice 2000, p. 64. – also in Bohuslav Fuchs, etc.

81 *Der Baumeister*. Munich 1921.
82 Jaromír Krejcar (see note 71), pp. 4–7.
83 According to the testimony of F. M. Černý, in the competition for the extension and reconstruction of the Micha Palace for the Czechoslovak Sokol Organisation (1921), Jan Kotěra left the jury meeting in protest against the low evaluation of Josef Štěpánek's project.

< 38
Competition entry for a spa building in Grad, sketch, 1911
> 39
Competition entry for the Savings Bank in Hradec Králové, perspective view, 1911

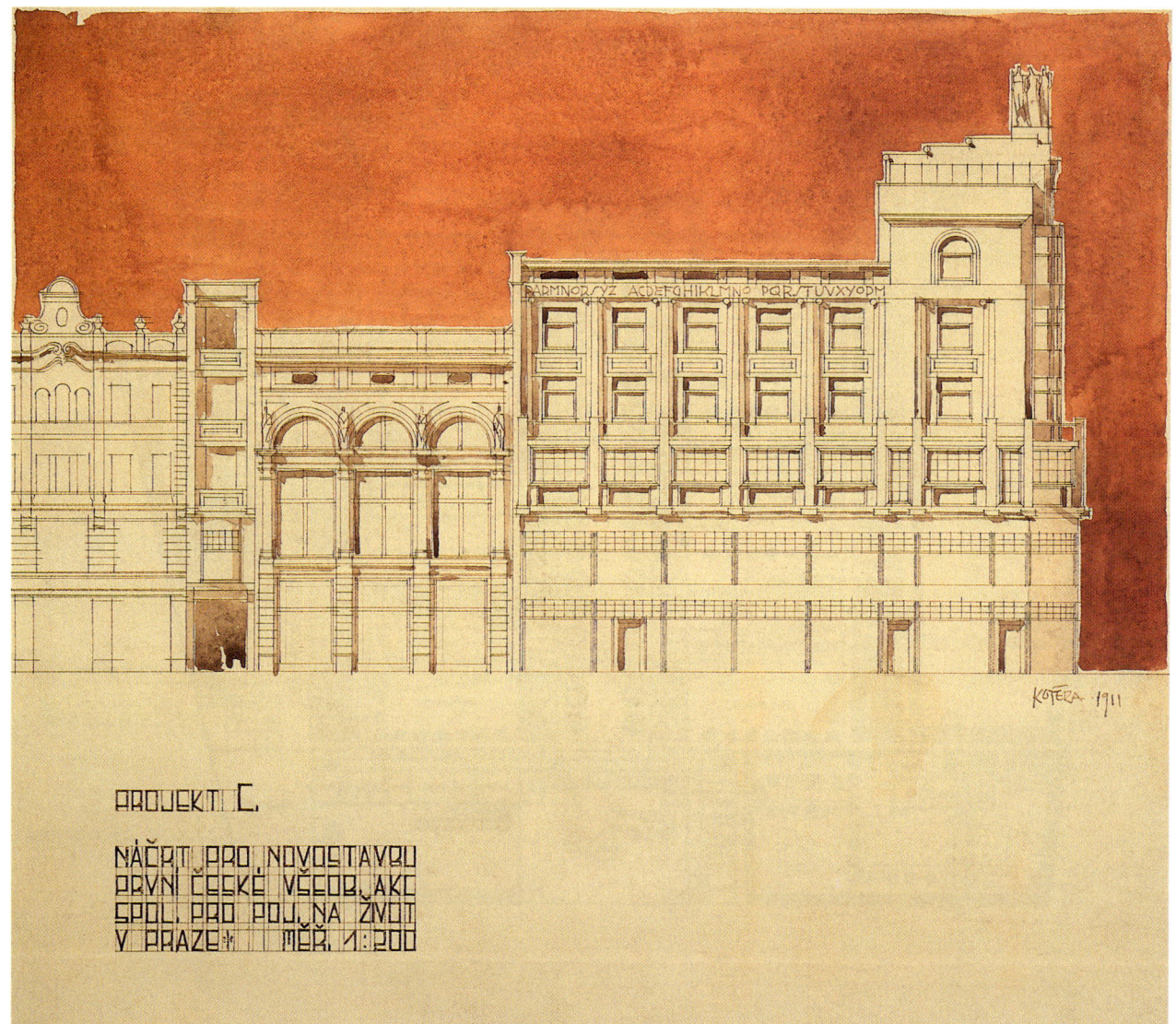

< **42**
Competition entry for a multi-purpose building for the *Koruna* insurance company in Prague, sketch of the façade facing Na Příkopě street, 1911

48 ARCHITECT JAN KOTĚRA

< **43**
Design for the waterworks in Třeboň, sketch, 1912
< **44**
Design for the waterworks in Třeboň, sketch, 1912
> **45**
Excursion to Říp, from the left: O. Novotný, Z. Wirth, (4) J. Kotěra, c. 1912

50 ARCHITECT JAN KOTĚRA

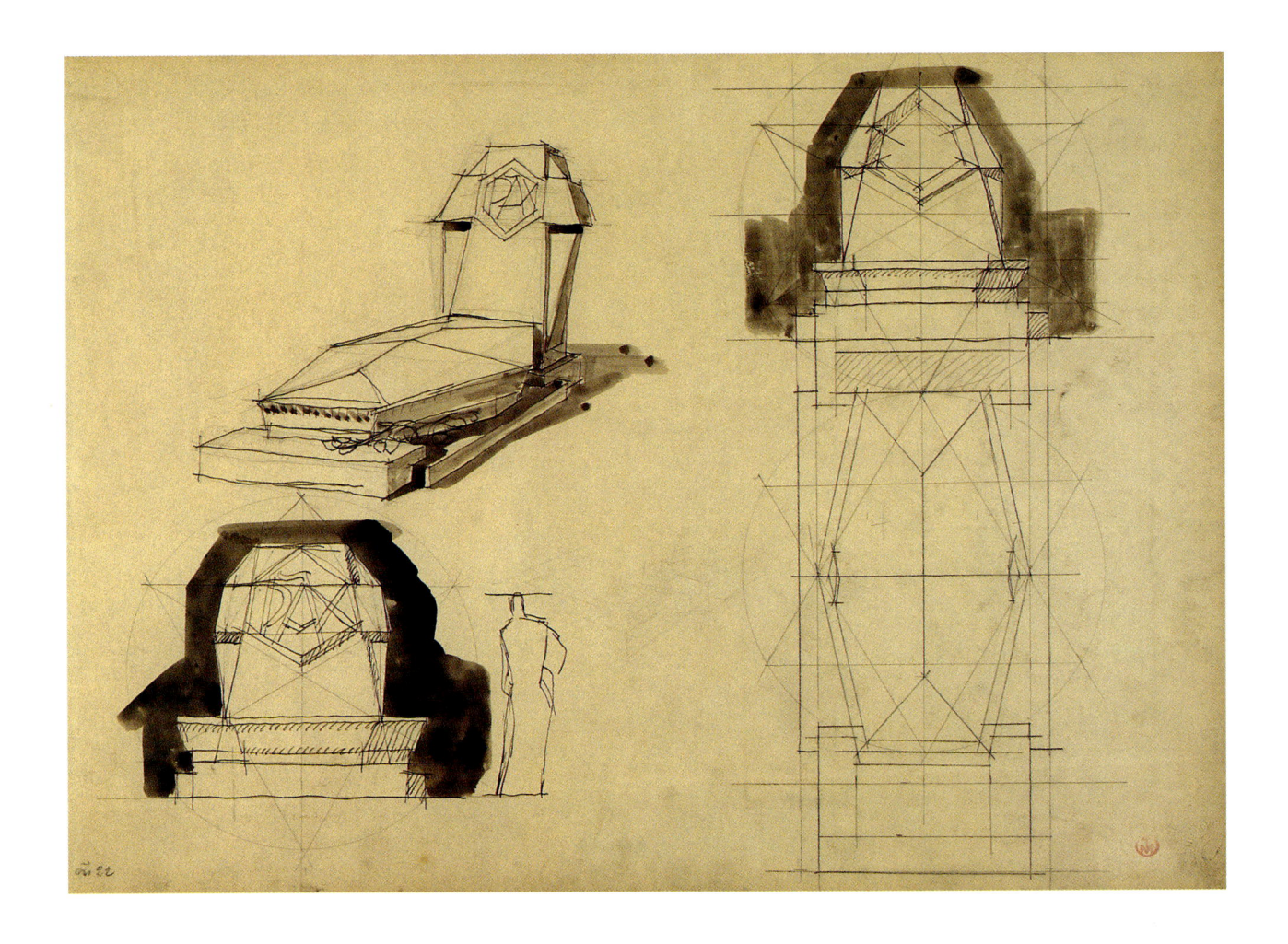

< **46**
Boat house, undated
<< **47**
Design for Hácha tomb, version, 1915
> **48**
Design for the adaptation of the cooperative warehouse façade in Telč, 1917

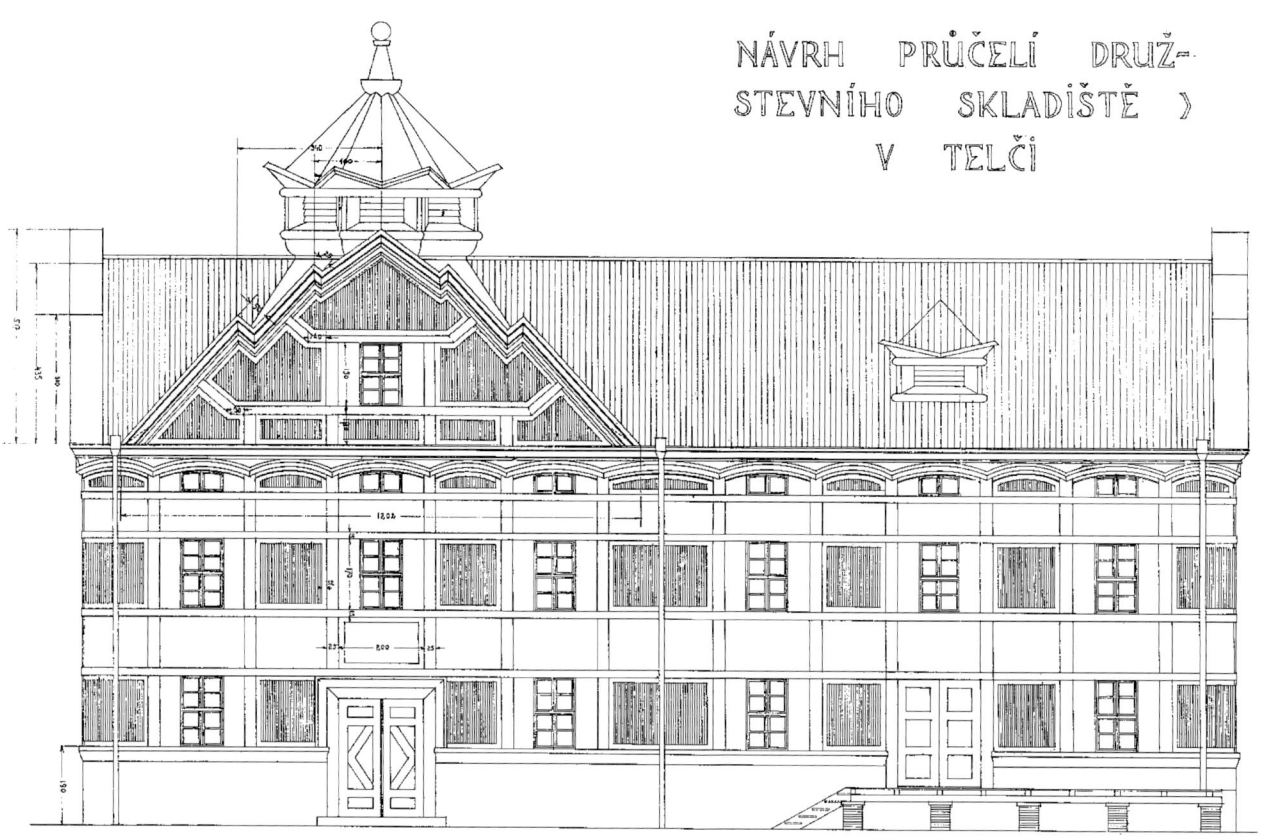

52 ARCHITECT JAN KOTĚRA

< **49**
Law and Theology Faculty in Prague, first project,
hall – drawing, 1907
<< **50**
Law and Theology Faculty in Prague, first project,
façade – drawing, 1907
> **51**
Competition entry for the Prague Credit Bank
at Na Můstku in Prague, 1921

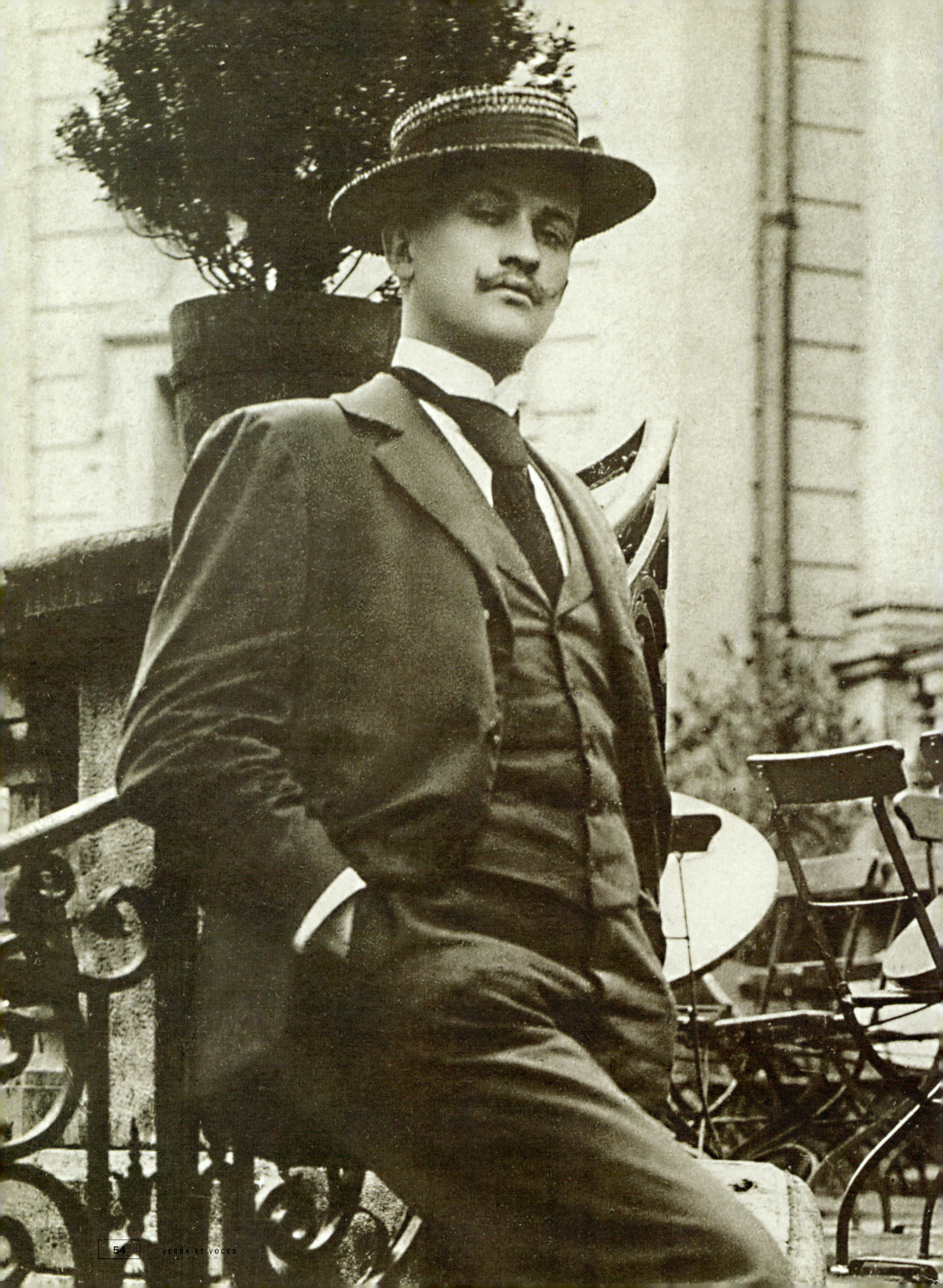

< 52
Jan Kotěra, 1898
> 53
Gottfried Semper, *Der Stil in den technischen und tektonischen Künsten, oder Praktische Aesthetik. Erste Band. Textile Kunst.* Frankfurt am Mein, 1860

Verba et Voces

Jan Kotěra in the Realm of Ideas
and Social Relationships

JINDŘICH VYBÍRAL

At the turn of the 20th century, Czech fine art culture was experiencing a period of profound change. The majority of the Czech artistic community renounced historicism and academic conventions and welcomed the strong attraction of society's new sense of "modernity". The movement had a relatively clear programme, as witnessed by the number of articles and statements published in *Volné směry*, yet there was a considerable lack of charismatic leaders who could put these ideas into action.[1] This was the role bestowed upon Jan Kotěra. His friends expected him to be the creative figure of European standing in Czech architecture, the man who would lead it out of provinciality and away from the schemes of late historicism.

In the following study we will examine to what extent Kotěra fulfilled these hopes. In doing so, we will not search for the answer in his architecture, but in the often elusive delicate threads of ideas and social relationships. Instead of a formal analysis, we will delve into cultural history, instead of "monuments" we will seek clues in the "documents". This will shift our point of view. The first part of the study will deal with Kotěra's views on architecture, the second will focus on the social roles that an architect fulfilled in Czech culture, while the third will examine Kotěra's legend.

The Architectural Thinking of Jan Kotěra

As a young man, with little else behind him but school work, Kotěra suddenly became the most dynamic figure at the School of Applied Arts and the Mánes Association. As a member of the Mánes committee, he participated in the publication of the journal *Volné směry* in 1899 and then spent three years as its Editor-in-Chief. The journal published photographs of Kotěra's works, as well as his drawings and vignettes. It was to be expected that the versatile artist would sooner or later present a written statement about his work. Kotěra published his statement in the 1900 volume of *Volné směry*. While in the past Czech architects had written historical treatises or technical reports, in his article "On New Art" this leader of the young generation spoke about the main aims of his architecture and the trends of modern architecture in general. He expressed his views on the relationships between purpose and form, structure and decoration, the ratio of the local to the international, the old to

---

[1] Cf.: Roman Prahl – Lenka Bydžovská, *Volné směry*. Praha 1993.

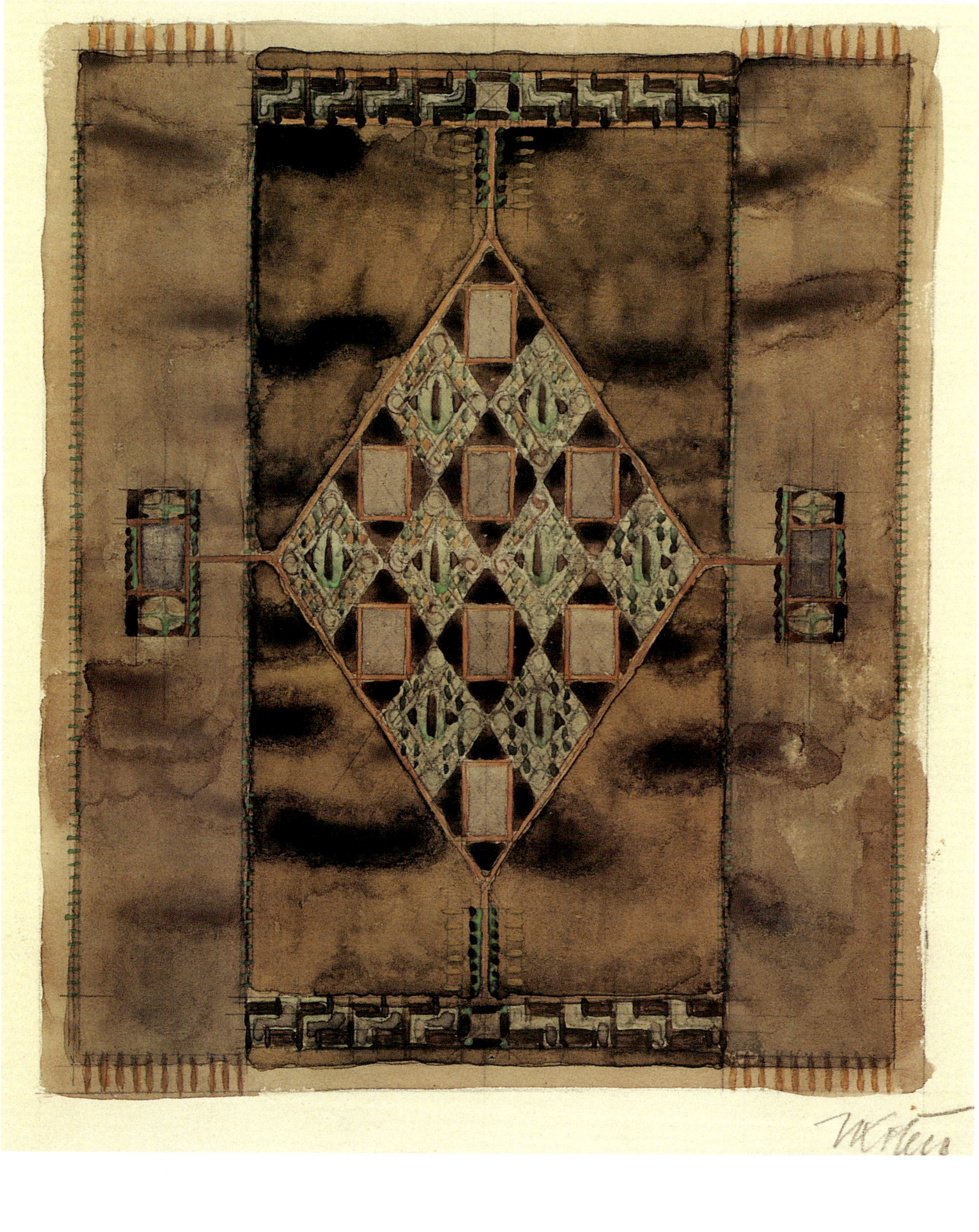

< 54
Carpet design, undated
> 55
Self-portrait with brother, postcard, 1896

the new. He did this not as a scholar but by presenting the main principles of Wagnerian "Modernism"[2] from the position of a practising artist.

In the article's introduction, the architect mentioned the *a priori* "*aim-ideal of a certain time and its belief*", "*the truth of a period*", which governs all spheres of public life and "*naturally moves into art, as it does into all spheres of culture, and its overlap causes a certain change there*".[3] Kotěra's thought implies a certain belief in objective laws which an artist must obey in his work. The new form arises from the joint effort of a few great artistic personalities; however, it does so not as a sovereign artistic gesture, in the way in which Conrad Fiedler or Alois Riegl imagined, but through the "*creative grasp and formulation*" of objective facts. The change of form, according to Kotěra, is provoked by "*a change in lifestyle and morality, which poses new tasks for the artists*".[4] The basis of his thinking apparently lay in a Hegelian notion of art as the manifestation of a worldly spirit and a belief in teleological progress.

Despite the fact that it sprang from philosophical idealism, using our contemporary terminology, Kotěra's theoretical position could be referred to as realism. In the debate on whether realistic needs were to be placed before artistic ideals or vice versa, the architect gave priority to essence before representation. The function of architecture, according to him, lies "*in the first place in the constructive modelling of space, and only in the second in adornment*".[5] The order of these roles is later reflected in the relationship between the two fundamental elements of architecture, "nucleus–space" and "surface–embellishment". Kotěra borrowed these elements from his teacher, Otto Wagner, yet there is no doubt that their prototype was Karl Bötticher's contrast between the structural and the artistic form, *Werkform* and *Kunstform*. This outstanding 19th century theorist understood the coverage and enclosure of space as the bases of architecture, and the visual scheme as the way to symbolically bring the architecture to light.[6] In a similar manner, for Kotěra, "*the first two represent truth itself, and the last is an expression of this truth*".[7] This is more to the effect that the decoration, in the sense of Gottfried Semper's "theory of cladding", was not supposed to be a mere accessory to the structural system, itself of secondary importance, but rather an extension of it. "*In new art, embellishment will only take up the function that is relevant to it: to divide and support the clearly, constructively expressed mass.*"[8] Kotera's insistence on the differentiation between the decorative and the constructive form also originates in Semper's thought. On the other hand, when the architect expressed his resistance to 'imitation' materials, his formulations revealed Ruskin's influence: "*I cannot therefore like it when a straight traverse construction is*

---

2   Jan Kotěra, "O novém umění". Volné směry IV, 1900, pp. 189–195.
3   Ibid., p. 189.
4   Ibid.
5   Ibid.
6   Cf.: Hanno Walter Kruft, *Geschichte der Architekturtheorie*. München 1991. – Werner Oechslin, *Stilhülse und Kern. Otto Wagner, Adolf Loos und der evolutionäre Weg zur modernen Architektur*. Zürich 1994. – Mitchell Schwarzer, *German Architectural Theory and the Search for Modern Identity*. Cambridge, Ma. 1995.
7   Ibid., p. 190.
8   Ibid., p. 194.

and I am so certain about the correctness of my way towards it that I shall not step away from this path under any circumstances." Kotěra finally referred Naděžda Kramář to a text from *Volné směry*, providing her with a short résumé: *"As each period in the past had its own style, as well as creative artists working in it; this also applies to the new era, and the artists can and should express themselves using their own language [...] We have advanced in everything, that is to say our time has truly created its own world, in the arts as in all branches of science. Should architecture be the only copycat of all?".*[28]

Unfortunately, not even this truly unique document provides sufficient evidence of Kotěra's artistic quest and the interior logic of his development. Other articles by the architect provide us with only a hint of this. The text about Jože Plečnik, very refined in its style, testifies most of all to the genuine friendship among fellow students from Wagner's school. But the appreciation with which Kotěra writes about Plečnik's identity with the spirit of Classical and folk art also shows his fine observation of the two substantial sources from which modern architecture drew its inspiration after the end of the Secessionist interlude, and which deeply marked Kotěra's own work. In his description of the characteristics of Plečnik's Slavic originality, which he set against the superficial sparks of fashion in Viennese architecture, we can sense Kotěra identifying at a significant level. *"The soul could feel the breath with which it all breathes, all that represents the very heart of his art and which has so much in it that is Slavic: a certain harshness, sometimes even bitterness in the essential thought, and lyricism, at times a certain softness, in the slender execution of the form."*[29]

In his article on the architecture of Luhačovice, Kotěra juxtaposes in a similar way the traditional villas, *"the caricatures of village architecture, typical creations of our entrepreneurial guilds"*, with the architecture of Dušan Jurkovič, which is *"so truly creative and original"*.[30] What Kotěra valued most of all in the work of the famous Moravian architect was its organic harmony with the landscape, its natural relationship with folk architecture, and its respect for the modern considerations of function and construction. We can sense John Ruskin's or Alfred Lichtwark's ideas here. However, in his arguments, their metaphors are buried in Impressionist descriptions and emotional eulogies, which lower the entire essay to the level of a propagandist commentary on the published photographs.

In 1902, the Viennese publisher Anton Schroll published both a Czech and a German version of Kotěra's publication *My Work and That of My Students*.[31] By presenting his architecture alongside the works of his students from the School of Applied Arts, Jan Kotěra adopted the practice of Wagner's

---

[28] National Museum Archive, Legacy of Dr Karel Kramář, letter from 9 January 1903 (inv. no. 23 5336–23 5340).

[29] Jan Kotěra, "Jože Plečnik". *Volné směry* VI, 1901–02, pp. 91–98, here p. 98.
[30] Jan Kotěra, "Luhačovice". *Volné směry* VIII, 1904, pp. 59–60, here p. 59.
[31] Jan Kotěra, *Práce mé a mých žáků, 1898–1901*. Wien – Praha 1902.

< 67
Caricature of the Mánes artists, c. 1902
> 68
Self-Portrait, 1916

secure the path of progress".[89] According to Mádl, Kotěra did not act, create, only for himself, but rather *"fulfilled the longing and requirement of the new era"* or – in a yet more colourful image – he listened to the *"hum of modern requirement"*.[90] In a similar manner, the other songbirds of Kotěra's heroicsm emphasised in him the characteristic of the predestined, the chosen one. *"His works proved that he was destined to create a new school, our modern architecture."*[91] Kotěra was simply a spirit *"destined for a difficult and important mission"*.[92]

Kotěra's myth was the story of *"eternal youth"*,[93] the myth of awakening, resurrection and creation, the victory of light and life – only in its beginnings linked with the Secessionist revolt. At that time, the hero Kotěra *"leads the young artistic phalanx which, with the vigour of victorious youth, cuts down and breaks the rotten idols of historical academism, opens wide the dusty windows of the academic studios and rips the theatrical costumes off the models stiffened in the poses of Libuše's prophetesses and the gestures of privileged kings, to hungrily descend on their nakedness, burning in a flood of the Sun's radiance"*.[94] In its conclusion, Kotěra's story slips from spring into autumn, a tragic autumn. The hero is betrayed by fate and sacrificed. *"Destined for great edifices"*,[95] he was not given adequate work, so he made up his own architectural tasks or created toys for his children. The artist, who *"walked through life with his head held high"*, who – as in heroic novels – *"was virile, blameless and loyal to the truth"*,[96] now had to pay for his extraordinary abilities with suffering: he encountered incomprehension and malice in a profane world, which prevented him from fulfilling his mission. *"And evil destiny takes pleasure in its spitefulness. A quarter of a century ago it opened for the great artist a door into the world, spoke variously of human happiness – and now it let him die doubting justice"* – these were the words with which Otakar Novotný joined Jan Štursa and Antonín Matějček in their tragic choir.[97] However, the hero's death is not an irreversible event, for in mythical practice, it is followed by the belief that he will return from the dead and enter a new life; in the same way, in Kotěra's suffering, we can sense the archetype of the ritual sacrifice which redeemed the final victory of modern architecture. In the successes that followed, Kotěra "the eagle" rose from the dead as a Phoenix.

---

89 Karel B. Mádl (see note 83), p. 6.
90 Karel B. Mádl (ibid.), pp. 16 and 7.
91 Ladislav Machoň, "Jan Kotěra padesátníkem". *Národní listy* 18 December 1921.
92 "Za Janem Kotěrou" (see note 82).
93 Josef K. Říha (see note 74), p. 1.
94 Jaromír Krejcar (see note 82), here p. 4.
95 Ibid.
96 Antonín Matějček (see note 73).
97 "Pohřeb Jana Kotěry" (see note 72).

This study was created as part of the project "Die böhmische Architektur der 2. Hälfte des 19. Jahrhunderts", with support from the Alexandr von Humboldt Foundation in Bonn.

72 KOTĚRA'S VIENNESE PERIOD: SEMPER, WAGNER, PLEČNIK

Jan Kotěra 1890

< 69
Design for a church, college work, 1896

Kotěra's Viennese Period: Semper, Wagner, Plečnik

DAMJAN PRELOVŠEK

The extensive written documentation on Kotěra's architecture does not really tell us enough about the influence the Viennese school had on his artistic development. The authors usually limit their research to the architect's Prague period and discuss his works in the context of the relevant analytical writing of the time. This would apply also to Otakar Novotný.[1] As one of Kotěra's first students, Novotný had an opportunity to truly "feel the spirit" of the Viennese Academy of Arts, from which Czech modern architecture arose, yet in his book from 1958, Novotný did not ascribe any particular importance to this residue of the old Habsburg rule. The 1950s was a period when the pressing issues were of a rather different nature and Novotný was forced to justify his own approach to Modernism. In other words, in this supplement I will try to elucidate that part of Kotěra's architectural career which fills the period between his studies at the School of Engineering in Plzeň and his later professorship in Prague. The turning point had a double implication: Kotěra both uprooted himself from the German environment of his youth, and crossed over from engineering to architecture, a discipline which, at the time, harboured great national ambition. Without Wagner, Kotěra would surely not have achieved his mission.

The available materials seem to present young Kotěra as a diligent student of the Plzeň School of Engineering and an excellent draughtsman with artistic ambitions.[2] The system of professional education in Austria was at an enviably high level at the time, comparable to similar English or French institutions. After several years' experience with the engineer Josef Freyn, Kotěra left for Vienna to study with Otto Wagner who, after the death of Karl Hasenauer, had taken over one of the two departments of architecture at the Viennese Academy of Fine Arts. At his very first lecture, Kotěra could hear the new professor's prophetic words about artistic creativity which must, Wagner claimed, take into consideration the needs, knowledge, means and advantages of the present.[3] This was Wagner's declaration of war against historicism. However, he allowed his students to use the old decorative forms, applying them in a fresh light. For the young Kotěra, this lecture opened up a whole new aspect of architecture, one that he knew only superficially from Prague. These prophetic words were to remain part of him for the rest of his life. Furthermore, he found other fellow countrymen at the Academy, prepared to follow Wagner's architectural reform with the same zeal. Joseph Maria Olbrich from Silesian Opava, four years older than Kotěra, had finished his studies under Hasenauer. However, Wagner employed this exceptionally talented draughtsman in his private studio immediately after his graduation. Olbrich had a strong influence on the students. He had travelled to Italy and visited parts of the North African coast, which gave him a much broader outlook in comparison with the others. He was also extremely well-educated in the sphere of historical ornamentation, and solved monumental tasks with an

---

1   Otakar Novotný, *Jan Kotěra a jeho doba*. Praha 1958.
2   Kotěra's drawings, college works and lecture notes from his youth are kept in AA NTM in Prague. I would like to thank architect Petr Krajči for the opportunity to look through them.
3   Wagner's introductory lecture at the Academy of Fine Arts from 15 October 1894, printed in: Otto Antonia Graf, *Otto Wagner*, I, *Das Werk des Architekten 1860–1902*. Wien – Köln – Graz 1985, p. 249.

enviable ease. Similarly, Josef Hoffmann, born in Brtnice in Moravia, spent most of his studies in the class of *"the Makart of architecture"* – as the Viennese called Hasenauer – and was intently perfecting his rendering of Italian Renaissance before joining Wagner in 1894.

Kotěra's technical knowledge was not inferior to that of Olbrich and Hoffmann, yet he lacked their wider knowledge of the imperial capital's architecture. With the construction of its circular boulevard, Vienna was expanding to become an important European metropolis. Kotěra was still more engaged on the Czech architectural scene. This was especially true at the beginning, when he worked on the neo-Gothic reconstruction of Červený Hrádek castle for his patron, Baron Mladota of Solopisky. This commitment diverted him from the radical struggle to establish new art forms. Kotěra was also less revolutionary than some of his fellow students – one of them being Leopold Bauer from Silesia, Wagner's first successor at the Academy. His more placid nature kept him from the extremes which later led Bauer, a fervent advocate of their professor's avant-garde ideas, to side with Wagner's opponents. With his knowledge and talent, the attractive Kotěra quickly won respect among his fellow students. For the Slovene Jože Plečnik he doubtlessly represented a centre around which the entire school should evolve.[4]

Let us return to the year 1894, when the 53-year-old Wagner, at the peak of his creative career, broke the bonds of the past and set off along the path of Western European reformers. His journeys to Paris, which he undertook each year, made him increasingly aware that a new time was approaching for architecture. Wagner had been preparing for this radical change for a long time, however, what definitively inspired him to start promoting modern architecture in Austria was his professorship, as well as commissions for two prestigious, highly technical tasks – the regulation of the Danube canal and the Viennese underground metro system. This crucial decision was based partly on practical considerations. In the period of important public commissions for the Viennese Ring, he endeavoured to design a monumental palace there, but was unsuccessful. Above all else, Wagner was a practical man. As a new professor, he needed theoretical foundations on which he could base his teaching. He acquired these foundations from Gottfried Semper, an architect of great authority in German-speaking countries, especially in Austria where he worked on prestigious imperial commissions.

Wagner and Semper were votaries of different times. Semper, in his enthusiasm for the natural sciences in the first half of the 19th century, sought an analogous system of values in architecture.[5] Wagner took from Semper only what he needed for his daily practical activities. He reproached Semper for underestimating the role of construction in the development of architecture, whereas he, himself, promoted persuasive slogans and gave his students practical directives. Insecure as he was on the theoretical level, he invited his best educated colleague at the time, Max Fabiani, to stay with him for several days, during which time they discussed all the relevant issues. Then Fabiani apparently wrote the actual text of *Moderne Architektur*,[6] which

---

[4] Plečnik's letter to Kotěra from 18 April 1898. Plečnik's letters are kept in AA NTM. Vladimír Šlapeta was the first who helped me access them, for which I am very grateful.

[5] H. Laudel, *Gottfried Semper. Architektur und Stil*. Dresden 1991, pp. 50–57.

[6] According to Max Fabiani's testimony. See: N. Šumi, „Pismo Maksa Fabianija iz leta 1955" (Letter by Max Fabiani from 1955), in: *Zbornik za umetnostno zgodovino, nova vrsta XXVII*, Ljubljana 1991, pp. 121–122.

< 70
Červený Hrádek, castle reconstruction, 1894–1896
> 71
Wagner's school trip to Munich, 1897,
from the left: F. Matouschek, F. Dietz von Weidenberg, A. Ludwig, L. Müller, J. Kotěra, A. Hackl, R. Melichar (?), J. Plečnik, K. Liderhaus, S. Karasimeonoff (?)

became the bible of Wagner's school and was reprinted a number of times. In Kotěra's article "On New Art"[7] from 1900, we can still recognise the principal ideas from this book. We could also add that, in his interpretation of the proper use of material according to Wagner and Loos, Kotěra repeated, almost verbatim, Semper's rule that wood could bear all colours except its own, otherwise it would not look genuine.[8]

Wagner's combative slogans found fertile ground with his students. However, in everyday life at the Academy, revolutionary activity was far less sensational. Wagner did not need any zealots contemplating new art. He needed industrious and talented draughtsmen, able to modify old forms to fit new requirements. He also encouraged his students to think in terms of the surface area (*"tafelförmige Ausbildung der Fläche"*) and emphasised a clear division between the constructional and decorative parts of the buildings. In all other respects, he allowed their imagination to take its course. Wagner's main contribution to the development of architecture did not lie in substantial change, as we often read, but in the modernisation of the old. In his architecture, the ornament served as the votary of the new era, and became functional once more – a fact completely overlooked by the zealous Adolf Loos, for example. Wagner's

---

7   Published in: *Volné směry* IV, 1900, pp. 189–195.
8   See note 7, p. 194.

ornamental forms continually acknowledge the construction, they emphasise its technological idiosyncrasies and accompany movement in space. At the same time, they are symbols of modern technology. Wagner had the capacity to focus the efforts of his colleagues and students into a single stylistic current and, in doing so, he accelerated the transition from historicism to modern architecture and created an impression of sudden, revolutionary change.

Wagner's style was not founded on Semper's speculations about the four "pre-materials, four "pre-techniques" and four architectural "pre-elements" that were at the core of the German scholar's teaching.[9] Instead, it was Semper's "cladding theory" that proved useful in Wagner's evolutionary concept of architecture.[10] Wagner's school was mainly focused on the search for a refined understanding of the material. This followed on from the idea that knowledge of the Antiquity underlies all architectural forms. Semper stressed the key importance of ceramics and textiles. During his exile in England, he had an opportunity to observe how particular elements of ornamentation emerged in different Classical communities, and how they were transformed with the adoption of new materials. His involvement with the World Exhibition in London in 1851 convinced him that contemporary architecture could no longer utilise construction materials to their full advantage, that it violated them through a mechanical transition of forms. For this reason, he suggested a return to the untainted sources of ancient art, an idea that became one of the main principles of Wagner's teaching.

According to Semper, a rich collection of ornaments could be gathered from the immeasurable chain of metamorphoses, from the "pre-object" (with the typical "pre-ornament"), to

---

[9] See H. W. Kruft, *Geschichte der Architekturtheorie*. München 1986², p. 359.
[10] See: Damjan Prelovšek, *Jože Plečnik 1872–1957*. New Haven – London 1997 (chiefly the chapter "Semper's principle of cladding", pp. 7–11).

< 72a
Jan Kotěra, J. Plečnik (from the Munich trip), 1897
<< 72b
Jan Kotěra, J. Plečnik (from the Munich trip), 1897
> 73
Viennese Academy college pass, 1894

the final result. Each material should add its own quality to this general morphological "treasure house" of ornamentation. What allows proper use of these decorative elements in a new context is the true understanding of their original meaning. Semper's scientific theory stimulated in Wagner's students, who lacked appropriate knowledge of Classical archaeology, a sense of intuition rather than intellectually justified reflections on the Antiquity. It enabled them to re-shape established ornamentation and accommodate it to suit new materials – iron, aluminium or concrete – in the firm belief that they were following the eternal law of artistic creativity.

Semper saw the beginnings of organised human dwellings in the nomadic tents of Asia Minor. The wealth of ornament in the woven carpets was to provide a source of designs for modern façades and interior decoration. Wagner literally transferred Semper's idea to architecture, treating the main façade of the building as a large stretched fabric, with window openings cut into it. Wagner used Semper's findings on the laws of ancient ornamentation for his own decorative work. The basic principle was founded on its balanced position in relation to movement.

According to Semper's interpretation, this problem had been solved in ancient times by framing the individual ornamental sections, or by accentuating their centre. Wagner would use two side pylons and finish the "frame" with a sharply projecting roof. Thus, he would define the surface proportions of his façade, dividing it almost graphically into separate segments. A series of Semper's analogous accounts and speculations on the Antiquity helped to gradually remove historical elements from the façades – projections, attics, moulding, window frames, protruding portals, sculptural decoration – and to compose the façade's surface according to new principles. Wagner's free interpretation of Gottfried Semper's ideas also promoted a whole new range of materials for the façade facing. In this, he was setting the standards for modern Viennese architecture at the turn of the 20th century. He also provided an opportunity for a non-conventional play of different patterns and encouraged their re-definition. Nor should we forget the presence of the fashionable Belgian and French vegetative motifs true to Art Nouveau, traits of which found their way into Wagner's classroom where far too many different ideas were sparked for the students to be able to master them all.

Kotěra's Urbánek house in Prague is a good example of the depth of Wagner's influence on him. It was built long after the young architect's apprenticeship years in Wagner's studio, after he had already mastered a series of different styles, including the folk architecture revival, Dutch exposure of masonry and Cubism. It seems that, whenever he was unsure how to proceed, Kotěra returned to the safety of Wagner's façade scheme, the large frame with panelling, which he would recreate in his own style. If we disregard the lower part of Urbánek's house – where the sculptural decoration recalls Fabiani's design for the Artaria Cartography Institute at Vienna's Kohlmarkt – and the triangular attic at its top – a tribute to the new wave of European Neo-Classicism – the central part of the building corresponds entirely to Wagner's interpretation of Semper's rule of eurhythmics.[11] Kotěra artfully combined a gradual thinning of the walls with gradated vertical and horizontal partition elements. He broke up the overall surface area within the large frame into a network of rectangles surrounding each of the windows, while the brickwork above them was fashioned into small curtains. With the brick exposed, the façade as a whole gave an impression of fabric. The no-

---

11 Gottfried Semper, *Der Stil in den technischen und tektonischen Künsten, oder Praktische Aesthetik*, 1st edition, Frankfurt am Main 1860, p. XXVII.

< 74
Viennese Academy college certificate, 1896
> 75
Otto Wagner, design for the Berlin cathedral, 1891

tion of a frame with inserted panelling was inspired by the joiner's trade and was very popular in Vienna in 1900. We will find parallels in Olbrich's drawings of bedroom furniture,[12] in Hoffmann's period furniture designs, in the work of Plečnik and many others. The idea of a collection of crossbeams is very similar to the fluting on the Classical columns, which again became fashionable after the Secession.

Unlike Wagner's other students, Kotěra left Vienna and returned home immediately after graduation. At home, he remained informed about architectural progress in the imperial capital. Nevertheless, the culture of Slavic Prague bound him in its circle so tightly that he stopped participating in the victorious march of Wagner's art which, at the turn of the 20th century, had acquired a characteristic unity and had become synonymous with the avant-garde. Kotěra completed his studies in 1897, when the new movement was just beginning to gain a clear profile. Yet without the contribution of his generation – which prepared the ground for modern forms and looked for ways to apply Semper's principles in practice – there would not have been the success that followed. This was a time of passionate discussions about the theoretical bases of architecture, which led to the publication of Wagner's *Moderne Architektur*. It was a period of dialogue, which later generations of students did not experience. From Vienna Kotěra travelled to Italy, where he came into contact with the Classical style, which removed a lot of Wagner's influence. When he later settled in Prague, Kotěra no longer involved himself so much with the formal problems of Wagner's ornamentation and experimentation with new materials.

Wagner's classical projects for large public buildings and apartment houses provided a source for modern Viennese architecture. Each of these types contained in itself a series of typical combinations of decorative features – projections, pylons, colonnades, cupolas, rustic ornaments, fountains, vases, sculptures, and all the other architectural elements from the Renaissance and Neo-Classicist stylistic repertoires. *The Artibus* – Wagner's ideal project from 1880, was the most telling example. It had all the characteristics of his repertoire. It was a synthesis of his favourite architectural and town planning models, transferred to an ideal Italian marine landscape. His models included St Charles' Church in Vienna by Fischer of Erlach, Place de la Concorde in Paris, Semper's Viennese court museum buildings, and the like. All of them had the dust of the Makart era on them, which even young Wagner could not shake off. The task Wagner then consigned his students was to formally simplify or rework the given models, without interfering with their established type. However, their early college projects – including Kotěra's – indicate that their teacher

[12] *Ideen von Olbrich*. Stuttgart 1992, (reprint of 2nd edition from 1904), pp. 89, 108, 109.

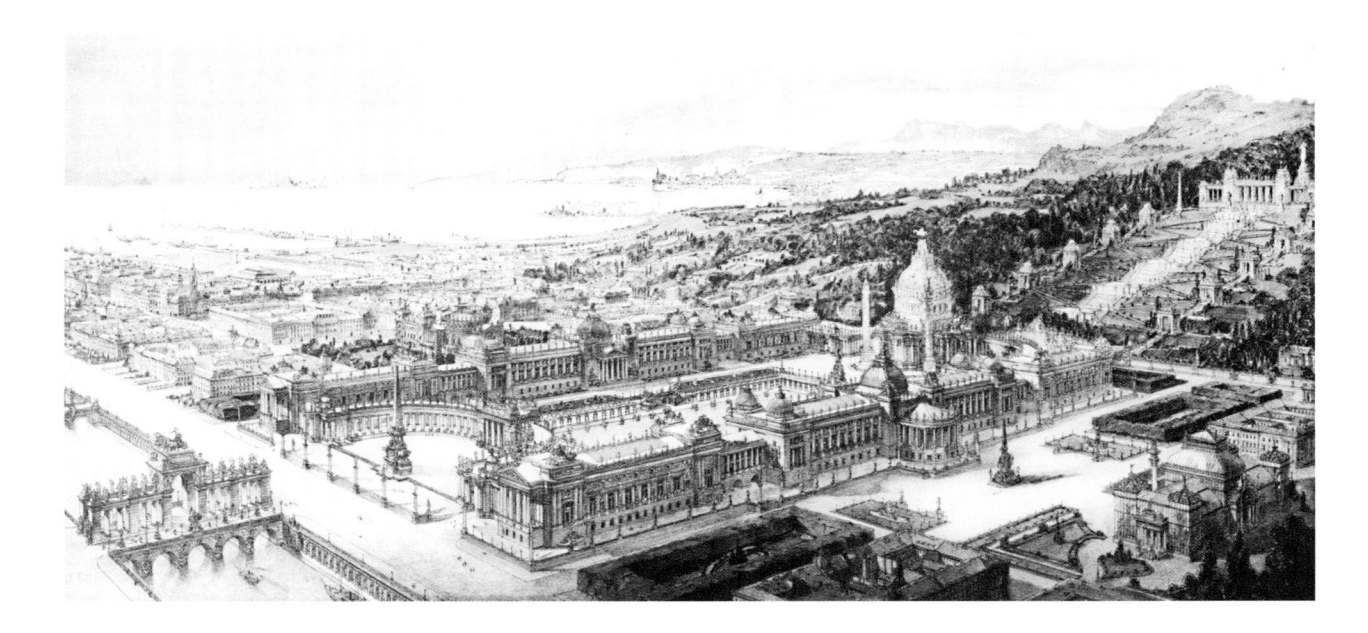

even encouraged them to bring together the maximum of both decoration and partitioning of the façade.

In his second year, Jan Kotěra won two academic awards. He won the Füger medal for his project for the royal baths,[13] and a special school award for designing a parish church.[14] The church was a large central hall in the shape of a Greek cross, with an antechamber on one side and extending into the presbytery on the other. In the spirit of the moral imperative of truth in architecture, Kotěra made an apparent effort to harmonise the interior of the building with its exterior. He carefully separated the construction parts from the decoration, and attempted to give them an expression of quality dictated by the specific material used.[15] We can trace the direction of Wagner's teaching – how indebted it was to Semper's work – from Kotěra's short description of the project. Kotěra's church was designed according to Wagner's ideal of a central space with a triumphal arch at its entrance, with two lower bell towers. But what most compelled the young architect was the dome motif. His professor's unconventional design for the new Berlin cathedral in 1891 featured a transparent iron dome resting on large segmented windows. This idea greatly inspired Kotěra in his own quest. Using Wagner's underground metro stations in Vienna as a model, Kotěra designed a steep pavilion roof with a lantern, set between four pylons, and placed a large segmented window on each of its four sides.

In the latter half of the 1920s, Wagner's school focused on the dome as a chief compositional theme. Kotěra's 1897 drawing for the so-called "Painted" house in Plzeň,[16] for example, has a dome identical to that included in Wagner's design for the imperial pavilion of the Viennese underground metro. Many variously stylised elements of historical ornamentation characterise Kotěra's church design, as well as his subsequent college works. On the other hand, his skilful draughtsmanship, perhaps not entirely coincidentally, brings to mind Ohmann's style of drawing.

Underneath the drawing of the church's perspective, Kotěra added a decorative band of stylised heads of saints, which a year later, in a similar manner, inspired Olbrich to complete the presentation sheet for Wagner's project for the new Academy of Fine Arts in Vienna.

---

13 *Der Architekt* II, 1896, p. 47 ("Aus der Wagner Schule"). The original drawings are deposited in AA NTM.
14 See note 13, pp. 47 and 50. The original drawings are deposited in AA NTM.
15 *Der Architekt* III, 1897, p. 47.
16 *Der Architekt* V, 1899, plate 19.

< **76**
Otto Wagner, *The Artibus* – an ideal project, 1880
> **77**
Ideal project for the royal baths, college work in the studio of
O. Wagner, 1896

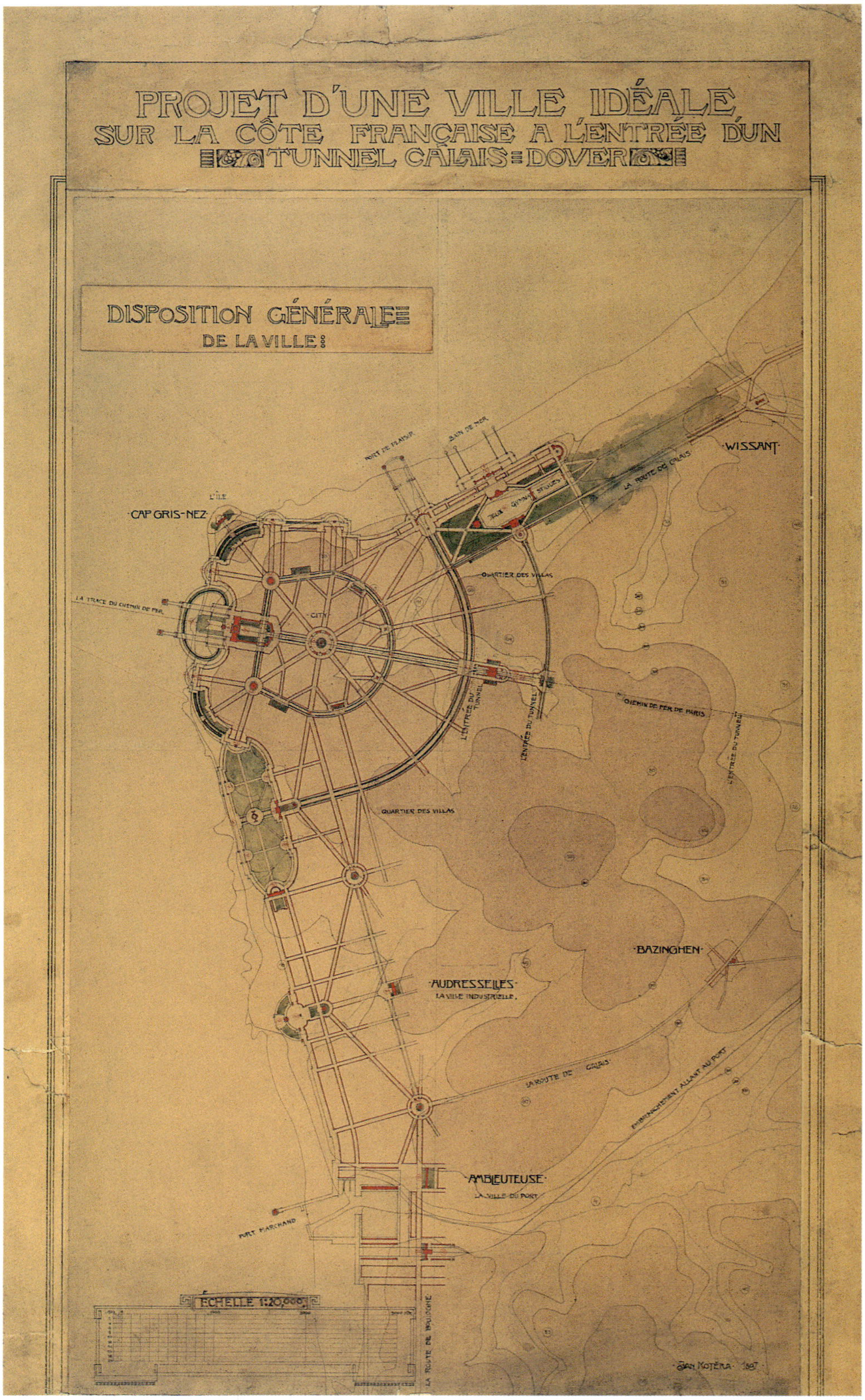
PROJET D'UNE VILLE IDÉALE
SUR LA CÔTE FRANÇAISE A L'ENTRÉE D'UN
TUNNEL CALAIS-DOVER
DISPOSITION GÉNÉRALE
DE LA VILLE
CAP GRIS-NEZ
WISSANT
QUARTIER DES VILLAS
QUARTIER DES VILLAS
CHEMIN DE FER DE PARIS
BAZINGHEN
AUDRESSELLES
AMBLEUTEUSE
PORT MARCHAND
ECHELLE 1:20,000
LA ROUTE DE BOULOGNE

< 78
Ideal project for a city at the entrance to a future Calais-Dover tunnel, graduation project in the studio of O. Wagner, general layout, 1897
> 79
Ideal project for a city at the entrance to a future Calais-Dover tunnel, graduation project in the studio of O. Wagner, 1897

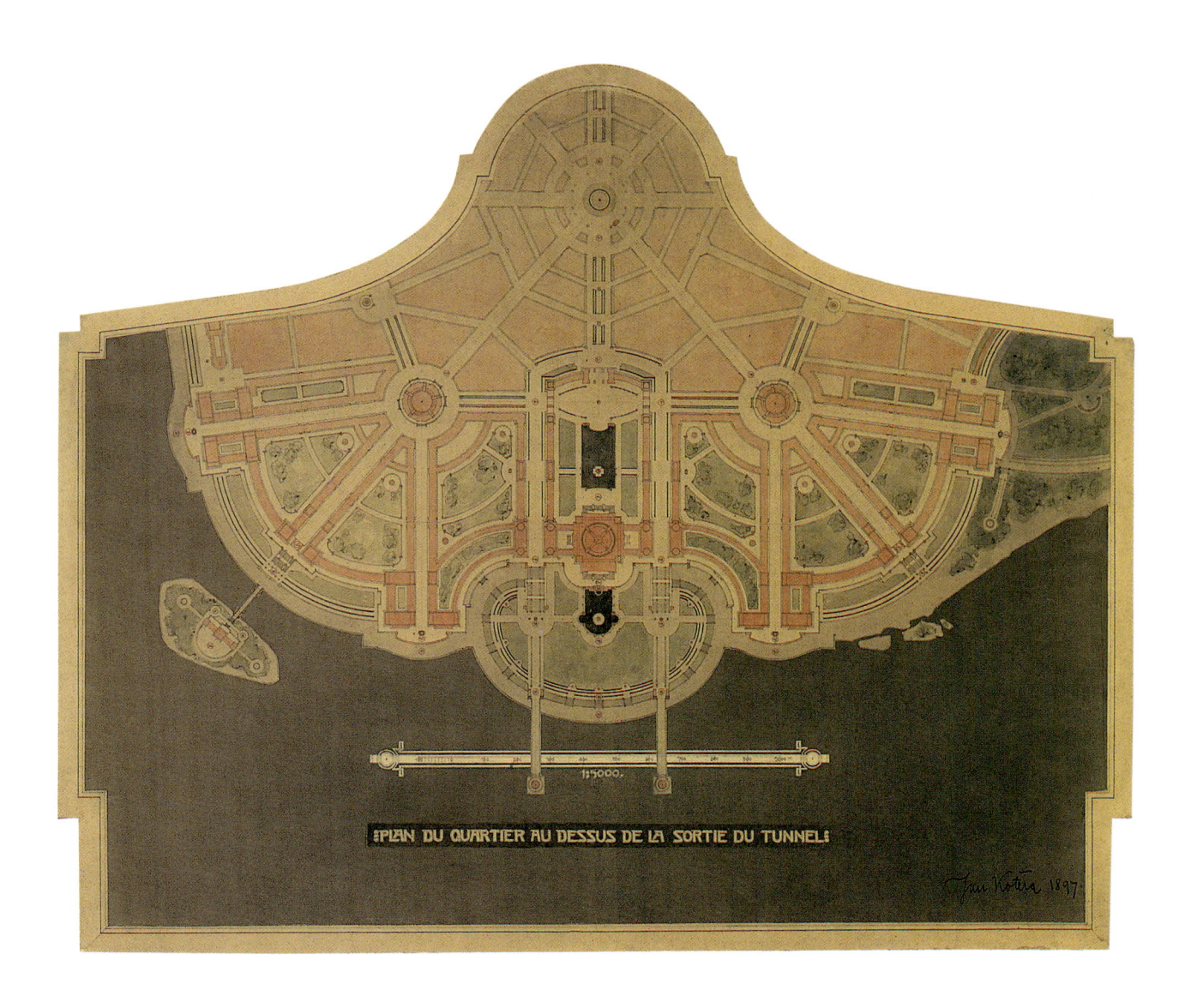

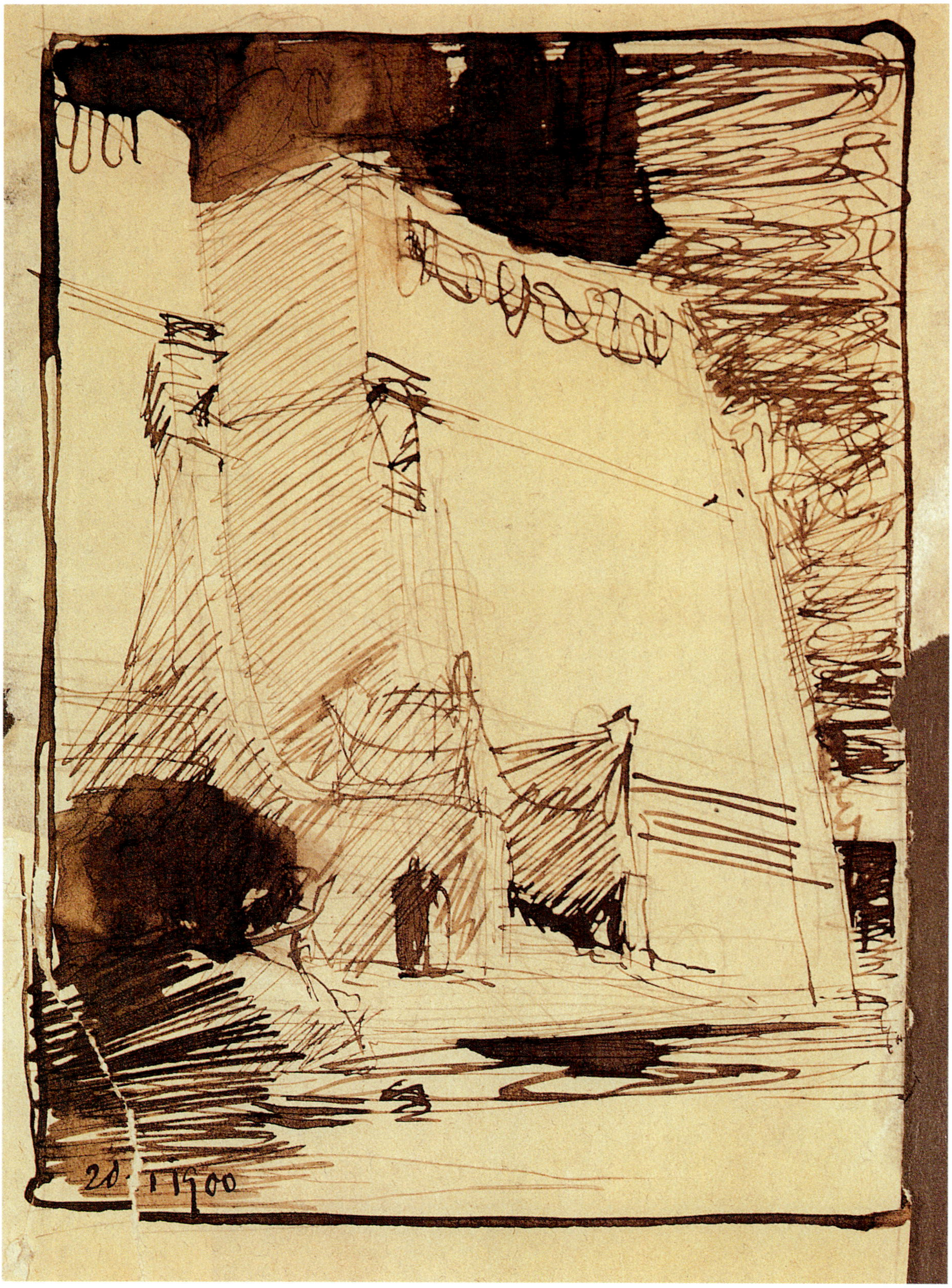
20. 1 1900

< **80**
Sketch of a monument, 1900
> **81**
Jože Plečnik, sketch of a church, 1899

Soon after, Kotěra took part in the school competition for the Füger medal. Here, his fine sense for the building's disposition was even more tangible. The project for the royal baths provided him with an opportunity to experiment with a whole palette of historical ornaments, while still adhering to his teacher's functional demands. He designed the main building of the baths as a large cube with simply partitioned façades. In the spirit of Semper's teachings, he constructed the low pent roofs attached to the lateral wings as a provisional, "textile" addition to the solid stone edifice. There is little of the true Secessionist style in Kotěra's drawing. Its influence is limited to a small number of painted or mosaic rectangular panels. Contrary to the Art Nouveau fashion coming from Western Europe, Wagner encouraged his students to decorate clearly framed geometrical surfaces, so that their desire for ornamentation would not exceed the building's structural parts themselves.

Kotěra completed his studies in Vienna with a typically utopian project – a whole new city envisaged at the entrance to a tunnel under the English Channel.[17] Wagner borrowed the practice of setting such tasks, aimed at firing the students' imagination, from the teaching programme at the Parisian École des Beaux-Arts. This is perhaps why Kotěra's project resembles more an outline for a Baroque castle garden than a model of Sant'Elia futuristic urbanism. It does not differ substantially from his royal baths of the previous year. Its exalted architectural theme corresponded more with visions of the forthcoming 1900 World Exhibition in Paris than with a truly modern city. A central palace with a dome and rich sculptural decoration – monuments, pools, large areas of foliage, avenues flowing into a circular square – and everywhere an omnipresent, obsessive symmetry. This was the highest domain of his urban utopia at the end of the 1890s. After he returned to Prague, he never had an opportunity to put any of it into practice.

As a professional architect, Kotěra was rarely engaged in urban planning. His competition design for the Ministerial buildings at Petrské embankment in Prague and the unfinished housing colony for the state railway employees in Záběhlice were the only projects where he could use his Viennese training in this particular field. For his workers' housing colonies in Louny, Zlín and elsewhere, Kotěra preferred to look for inspiration in the modern English garden town. He

---

17 The situations, groundplans of the city and the view from the sea are kept in AA NTM. The project was published in: *Der Architekt* III, 1897, aus der Wagnerschule MDCCCX-CVII, p. 17 and partly in: *Volné směry* III, 1899, p. 141.

remained true to Wagner's teaching in his designs for large monumental palaces, however, they chiefly remained on paper. The 1912 competition for the Royal Palace in Sofia[18] is a telling example. Despite Neo-Classicist and Cubist elements, its central part still resembles Wagner's abovementioned plan for the Viennese Art Academy which had a dome, obelisks and a canopy in front of the entrance. In the Neo-Classicist atmosphere prior to the First World War, all the creativity that once characterised the works of young Jan Kotěra and his fellow students became rigid and heavy and lost its original sparkle.

After his return to Bohemia, Kotěra never again had the opportunity to build these large edifices he had prepared with Wagner. The situation in Prague clipped the wings of his fantasy and drew him closer to everyday tasks – apartment blocks, department stores and suburban villas. Before we comment on some of these in the context of Kotěra's Viennese education, let us take a look at Kotěra's journey to Italy, undertaken at the very end of his studies. Kotěra did not belong to the generation of architects who documented old monuments with rulers in their hand, practising and learning from the peculiarities of the various styles in order to copy them more faithfully. He walked along the Apennine peninsula with a feeling of self-confidence, without starched prejudice; he judged for himself the artistic value of what he saw.[19]

His sketches from the journey are almost without exception lyrical records of the Mediterranean landscape, or brightly coloured views of towns and monuments. If we disregard the monolithic dome of Theodoric's Mausoleum in Ravenna – which was one of the favoured archetypes of Wagner's school and left traces also on Kotěra[20] – he hardly used any of the visible motifs or elements from this journey in his later work. It also seems that he was more impressed by Classical than by the more recent Italian architecture, with which he was familiar from leafing through the popular Letarouilly album[21] which Wagner used at the school. He liked to immerse himself in the spirit of Classical art, as illustrated by his *Temple to Eros and Psyche*.[22] It is not a work oriented towards architecture but an idyllic drawing, created while admiring Classical sculptures in the museums and galleries of Rome. He imagined the sculptures in a shaded thicket of luxuriant cypresses, in a characteristic Italian landscape with a lake and massive rocks in the background. This sojourn in the Mediterranean region granted Kotěra his creative breakthrough. His fear of vacant space, which in the past forced him to divide up decorative elements on the façades, entirely disappeared. We can still sense the appeal of the smooth

---

18 Otakar Novotný (see note 1), plates 248–251.
19 See Kotěra's letter to his family from Rome, from 6 April 1898, in "Z italských dopisů Jana Kotěry". *Umění* (Štenc) IV, 1931, p. 356. – See also: Jindřich Vybíral, "Čeští architekti v zemi zaslíbené", in: Josef Kroutvor a kol., *Cesta na Jih. Inspirace českého umění 19. a 20. století*. Exhibition catalogue, Praha 1999, p. 116.
20 For example his sketch from 1898 *Hrobka vojevůdce*, published in *Volné směry* III, 1899, p. 135.
21 P. Letarouilly, *Édifices de Rome moderne ou recueil des palais, maisons, églises, couvents et autres monuments public et particulier les plus remarquables de la ville de Rome*. Paris 1840–1857. The book was recommended as a teaching aid by G. Semper.
22 *Volné směry* III, 1899, p. 124.

< **82**
Architectural sketch, postcard, 1897
> **83**
Friedrich Ohmann, Corso coffee-house, 1899

Mediterranean sun-baked walls on some of his drawings from 1898.

The façade of Peterka's house on Wenceslas Square in Prague was Kotěra's first solo work. At a time when the monarchy's capital struggled for new façades, Kotěra was searching for a way to free himself from acquired strategies and find an expression of his own. His subsequent turn to the Belgian-French variation of Art Nouveau, almost the exact opposite of the smooth and geometrical Viennese Secession, came as a natural reaction. Plečnik adopted almost the same approach for his first professional project, Langer's villa in Hietzing.[23] It is a well known fact that Peterka's house had its source in Victor Horta's 1893 Maison Tassel in Brussels,[24] particularly in the use of the oriel.

The composition of Peterka's house is otherwise extremely Viennese. However, the architect linked the lower floors with large shop-windows, which he rounded at the top, thus relieving them of the strict rationality of Wagner's designs. The softly profiled rustication ends in the middle of a floor, as if its stripes were section of columns. The façade has more historical reminders of this kind, which indicate Kotěra's effort to address the local architectural tradition. The wavy motif above the two raised side sections of the façade is especially typical. It recalls the façades of the houses Italian master-builders created in Bohemia and Moravia during the Renaissance. Another design, with which Kotěra and his fellow student from Vienna, Adolf von Infeld, entered the 1897 competition to design Živnostenská Banka in Prague,[25] uses pillars adorned with decorative vases, with alternating panels of garlands and semi-circular motifs. Two years later, in his design for Peterka's house, Kotěra used all these elements again, only this time he rendered them in a Secessionist spirit. The new Viennese mode is most discernible in the wrought ironwork and simple plant decoration in stucco, while the two human figures next to the balcony on the upper floor contradict Wagner's concept of architectonic sculpture.

In the following years, Kotěra focused more on folk architecture. He avoided the Viennese method of breaking up the surface of the wall with an ostensible covering of thin layers of plaster, and returned to the steep saddle roofs with

[23] Damjan Prelovšek (see note 10), pp. 43–46.
[24] Rostislav Švácha, *Od moderny k funkcionalismu*. Praha 1995, p. 53.
[25] *Der Architekt* III, 1897, pp. 21–22, plate 45.

88 KOTĚRA'S VIENNESE PERIOD: SEMPER, WAGNER, PLEČNIK

< > 84
Stage design for *Rusalka*, 1901–1902

KOTĔRA'S VIENNESE PERIOD: SEMPER, WAGNER, PLEČNIK

< **85**
Stage design for *Rusalka*, 1901–1902

richly decorated wooden gables. He used these elements both in the exhibition pavilion for the Mánes Association in Prague which he designed in 1902, and the family villas which followed. The question remains to what extent can one speak of a Viennese influence when reflecting on Kotěra's work. There is certainly a parallel with Josef Hoffmann who in 1900 started publishing sketches of country houses from his native Moravia.[26] It reflected the fashion of emulating rural architecture which spread to Vienna from England and led to hybrids involving a mix of local and foreign, and modern and traditional. Its essence was the dominant belief in the high living standards of the English. Hoffmann's villas at Hohe Warte in Vienna, created as a response to the weary Secessionist aesthetics of Olbrich's artists' colony in Darmstadt, became very popular in the Austrian part of the monarchy. Some of Kotěra's works, such as Trmal's, Mácha's or Sucharda's villas, or even the original Mánes pavilion, were all inspired by Hoffmann.

This outline of Kotěra's early work would be incomplete without mention of the Slovene Jože Plečnik, whose friendship left its strong mark on the architect's oeuvre. Plečnik was only a month younger than Kotěra and had great artistic talent. Nevertheless, he came to Vienna from a different environment, both patriarchal and provincial. He was a building joiner by trade, with experience in the furniture industry. He joined Wagner's school in the same year as Kotěra, but encountered problems from the beginning. Due to a lack of sufficient technical literacy, he was not able to complete the given tasks. This motivated him to spend whole days at the drawing board, in an attempt to make up for lost time. In fear that he would be swallowed up by the Viennese metropolis, he grew strongly attached to his home. His first successes imbued him with a certain confidence, but he was to oscillate between vanity and self-pity for a long time. He felt inferior to Czechs and their culture, which was a result of his Slovene pan-Slavic upbringing. Being a very withdrawn young man, he respected Kotěra for being Czech, yet this respect grew into friendship only in their senior college year. Plečnik admired Kotěra's work and encouraged him to reach for the highest creative goals possible. He commented thus on Kotěra's project for the "Painted" house in Plzeň: *"I do admit that it is not a great stylistic achievement; however, it is temperamental and brilliant […]".*[27] In a similar manner, he listened to and respected his friend's opinions on artistic matters. He later shared Viennese news with Kotěra, and often invited him to visit. In 1900, he travelled to Prague for the first time, and met with leading figures of the Mánes Association.

Plečnik was among those of Wagner's students who most faithfully followed their teacher. However, unlike his fellow students, he was unenthusiastic about the technical advances of his time. He did not long for the new fashionable forms that filled the pages of art magazines, but devoted himself to reworking the classical architectural ornament. In the process, his artistic taste was polished to a truly unique virtuosity. Lacking sufficient education to resist Semper's hypotheses, he faithfully followed the theoretical work of the German master, and enriched the style of Viennese Secessionist architecture with his own ideas. He eliminated

---

26 For example the title page of the article on Hoffmann's architecture from *Ver Sacrum* magazine, 1900.

27 Plečnik's letter to Kotěra from Rome, 17 April 1899. AA NTM.

was not identical with Classical forms.²⁹ It is worth taking a look at Kotěra's formulation of Plečnik's Slavic expression. Kotěra defined the efforts of his friend – in which he partly also believed – by stating that Plečnik was trying to achieve *"a certain harshness, sometimes even bitterness in essential thought, and lyricism, at times a certain softness, in the slender execution of form"*. Plečnik believed that feeling was more important in architecture than the actual forms. He believed that the strength of Slavic art lay in its somewhat bitter lyricism, and tried to convince Kotěra to work in a similar spirit. During the spring exhibition at the Viennese Museum of Decorative Arts in 1901 which, among others, showed works from the Prague School of Applied Arts,³⁰ Plečnik wrote to Kotěra: *"I am not overpraising, the people simply could not part with your altar space.³¹ They observed and admired absolutely everything, and with such interest, with such respect. It was impressive. I was sad when I left, and deeply ashamed of my nation [...] Maybe you will one day turn away from church architecture but, believe me, this will be your misfortune. It will be the beginning of your decline. Success will come quickly. But every success is a sign of decay. Self-reliance doesn't strengthen character. You will lose your bitterness, your depth and love for the truth. You will devote yourself to the art of the lady's*

the heterogeneous character from new designs and artistically refined them.

Kotěra's views of modern architecture were much broader, but the architect highly valued Plečnik's morphological endeavours. What is more, he was convinced of Plečnik's genius. When he joined the editorial board of *Volné směry*, Kotěra wrote a long article about Plečnik²⁸ and started to build the path which would lead to Plečnik's later successes in Bohemia. In the spirit of Semper's teachings, he pointed to Plečnik's desire to embrace the spirit of the Antiquity, which

---

28 Jan Kotěra, "Jože Plečnik". *Volné směry* VI, 1902, pp. 91–98.
29 In his article "Vorläufige Bemerkungen über bemalte Architektur und Plastik dei den Alten" (Gottfried Semper, *Kleine Schriften*. Berlin – Stuttgart 1884, p. 220) on the application of Greek art in modern times, Semper writes: "We must not try and mimic their dead letters. No – one must use up their spirit and re-plant the gentle southern flower of art directly from its place of origin, until it starts flourishing in our uncultivated land [...]".
30 These were showpieces exhibited one year earlier at the World Exhibition in Paris (see: Exhibition of the Prague School of Applied Arts in Paris at the Paris World Exhibition in 1900", *Volné směry* V, 1901, pp. 71–85.) On the Viennese exhibition, see: L. Hevesi, "Österreichisches Museum", in: *Acht Jahre Sezession*. Wien 1906 (reprinted in 1984), pp. 339–340.
31 The design for the whole exhibit was conceived by F. Ohmann, the altar was the work of J. Kastner and his students.

< 86
Victor Horta, Maison Tassel in Brussels, 1892–1893
<< 87
Josef Maria Olbrich, House of the Grand Duke (Ernst Ludwig Haus), workshop of the artists' colony in Darmstadt, 1899–1901
> 88
Füger gold medal, 1896

toilette, the fan and the space. You will do it all with a sharpness of spirit and with humour. In short, you will become a man of ease, no longer the artist".[32]

We could find similar moral judgements in other letters by Plečnik. It is difficult to judge their influence on Kotěra. It is possible that they inspired him to search for a lyrical expression, but Plečnik's deep religiosity never really rooted itself in Kotěra's work. They both turned to local traditions, collected folk embroidery and searched for a Slavic expression. This brought them together but Plečnik, influenced by Semper, was more reserved about transferring folk art directly to architecture, and tried to penetrate its more profound laws. For Kotěra, on the contrary, the wealth of local architecture – both so-called high and folk architecture – provided applicable features for his own work. The early, ideal drawings of both architects – sketches of buildings and monuments which join organically with nature – point to a deeper affinity in their thinking and feeling, and signify a shift away from Wagner's rationalism. Plečnik especially disliked Sucharda's competition model for the monument to Jan Hus in Prague. It seemed to him to maintain too much Secessionist melancholy and was not sufficiently expressive.[33] For that reason, he urged Kotěra to keep the two low columns growing into a flower in his design for the same monument. *"There is something ancient in them. They recall old Slavic tombstones. I am pleased that I did something similar in that garden portal I mentioned [...]"*,[34] he wrote. Kotěra then kept this idea for his Robitschek tombstone in the Jewish cemetery in Strašnice.

Plečnik remained in Vienna, Kotěra took up a professorship in Prague. In time, the two architects went their separate ways. Kotěra slowly distanced himself from Plečnik's moral pleas and the Slovene architect lost his zest for Kotěra's work. However, they remained friends, and it was due to Kotěra that Plečnik later came to Prague. Occasionally, something of Plečnik found its way into Kotěra's work. Kotěra's sketch for the stage design for *Rusalka*[35] in 1901, for example, echoes a façade division which Plečnik created a year earlier for the Viennese Schottenring underground station.[36] In another project which entered the competition for the Austro-Hungarian Bank in Vienna in 1911,[37] he adopted from Plečnik's drawings of the Stollwerk factory façade[38] the transverse windows which became a distinctive mark of Czech Cubism.

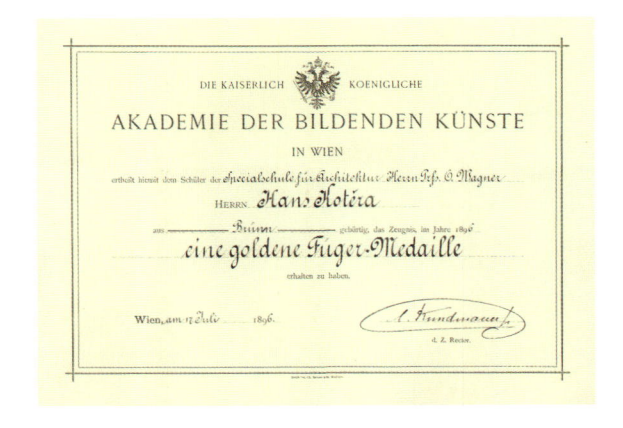

32 Plečnik's letter from May 1901. AA NTM.
33 Plečnik's undated letter from 1901. AA NTM.
34 Plečnik's letter from 22 January 1901. AA NTM. The mention of a portal is related to a work by Plečnik that we know only from drawings and photographs (A. Hrausky – J. Koželj – D. Prelovšek, *Plečnik v tujini./Plečnik abroad./ Vodnik po arhitekturi*. Ljubljana 1998, p. 109).
35 Otakar Novotný (see note 1), plate 132.
36 Plečnik's authorship is confirmed in his letter to Kotěra from August 1901. AA NTM.
37 Otakar Novotný (see note 1), plate 237.
38 Damjan Prelovšek (see note 10), pp. 70–71.

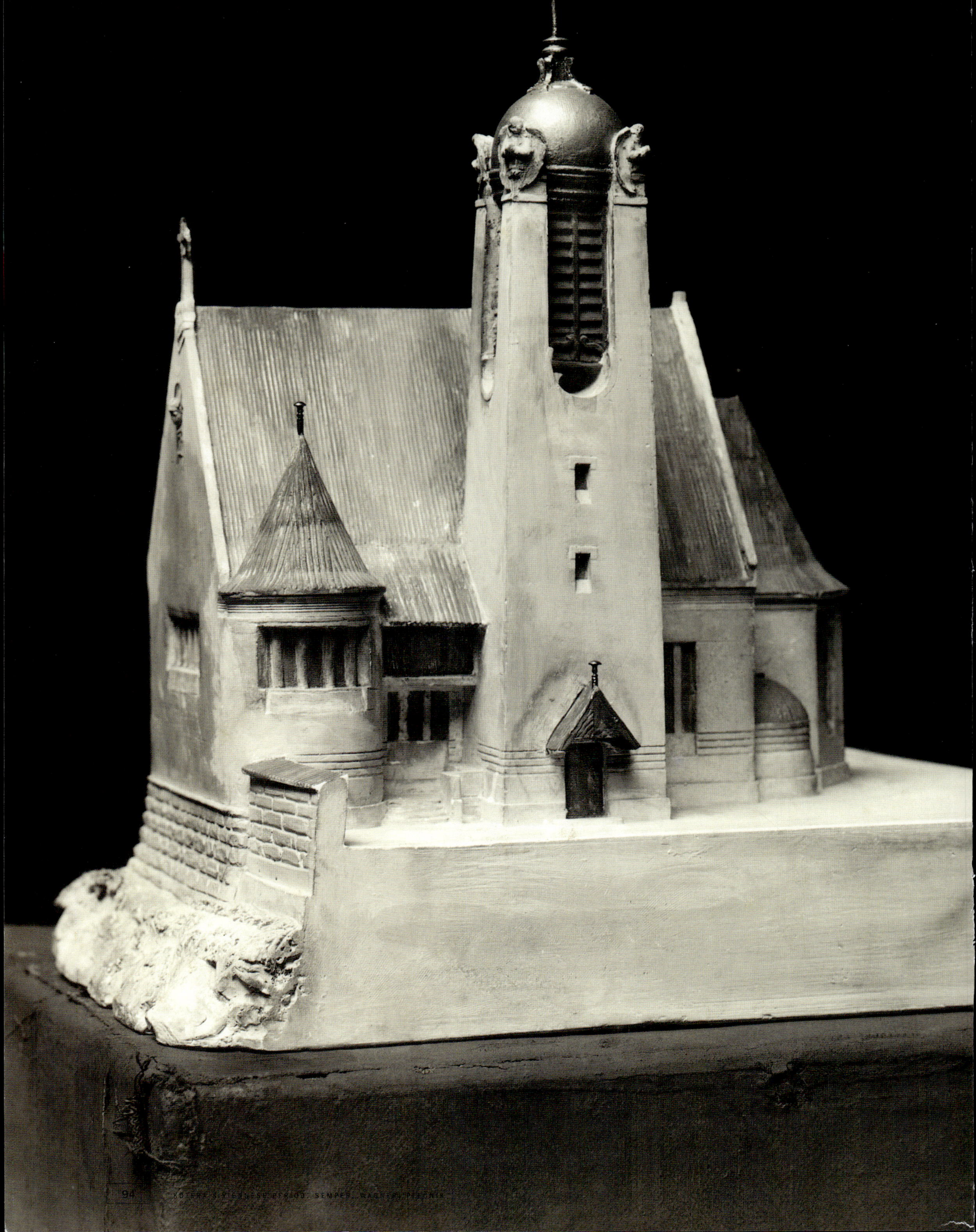

< 89
Design for the reconstruction of the church of St George in Doubravka near Plzeň, model, 1899

The Early Works, 1898–1905

ZDENĚK LUKEŠ

The period prior to Kotěra's arrival in Prague was a time of marked tension between older and new generations of Czech architects. The architectural scene was dominated by historicism and controlled by a group of planners with deeply conservative views. The 1891 Provincial Jubilee Exhibition managed somewhat to generate ripples in what had become stagnant waters: taking its inspiration from Paris, it promoted daring steel construction in the designs for the Palace of Industry, the machine hall, and the lookout tower on Petřín hill. However, this new technology was later used only sporadically, very much in the way concrete construction was still applied only in the buildings' foundations, or to design bridges. The new materials were never seen on façades; if used at all, they would be masked with stucco decoration. During the early 1890s, professor Friedrich Ohmann of the Prague School of Applied Arts began to promote a neo-Baroque style in architecture. However, the local architectural scene generally had not yet accepted the new Viennese Secession. This was not only a matter of architectural conservatism, it was also a matter of politics. For many people, Vienna was not an acceptable partner, even as the home of a new artistic style. The opinion which prevailed in Bohemia was that architecture should be rooted in national traditions.

Nevertheless, the second half of the 1890s saw certain attempts to promote Viennese Seccesion. František Ulrich, the progressive mayor of Hradec Králové, closely followed the Viennese art scene. He invited two students of Otto Wagner – Ottokar Böhm and Hubert Gessner – to design a building for the Business Academy in Hradec Králové (1896–97), located on a prominent site in the town centre. Parallel with this, another Wagnerian working in Vienna, František Krásný – together with Josef Hoffmann, the most prominent representative of the new Secessionist style – developed two projects in the style of advanced Wagnerian Neo-Classicism – one for the competition to design Živnostenská Banka on Na Příkopě street in Prague, the other for the City Theatre in Plzeň. Their theatre design won first prize. However, after strong resistance from conservatives on the town council, the project was instead entrusted to Antonín Balšánek. Despite this turn of events, Krásný created four other works in his native Plzeň which were built in 1897–98; three houses in the city centre, all rendered with a Wagnerian temperance, and Kestřánek's villa on the Karlovy Vary highroad, whose style was much more poetic. Krásný's projects for his Czech clients were exhibited in Prague in 1898. They were a great inspiration for the Mánes Association, which at the time began promoting Secession.

The first Secessionist building in the Czech capital – Ohmann's Corso Palace on Na Příkopě street – was built in 1898. The 1898 Exhibition of Architecture and Engineering, held in Prague-Bubeneč, included other, rather timid manifestations of the new style. These were the pavilion for Marold Panorama (Marold's 360° diorama), designed by Ohmann's student Jiří Justich, and Osvald Polívka's wooden

Uránia theatre. There was even an ironic paraphrase of Viennese fashion built on the premises – an artists' pub named "The Nonsense Inn" designed by Jan Koula, a conservative professor at the Prague Technical College. Yet these were all just sporadic cases. The Czech scene generally kept to the routine of historicism and was dominated by conservative architects of the older generation – Rudolf Kříženecký, Jan Koula, Alois Dlabač, Jan Vejrych, Rudolf Štech, Antonín Wiehl and others. It is not surprising that the members of the Mánes Association were so eager to welcome Viennese Academy graduates from Otto Wagner's special school of architecture. They were aware that this school had become one of the most important centres of Secession and Modernism in architecture. The figure who was to take upon himself the difficult task of pioneering these new ideas in Bohemia was Jan Kotěra.

Jan Kotěra had designed his first projects for the Czech environment while he was still in Vienna. He designed the adaptation of Červený Hrádek castle for his patron Jan Mladota of Solopisky in 1894–96. In 1897 he participated in a competition for Živnostenská Banka in Prague, and another for Kladno Town Hall, and he also sketched a corner apartment house to be built in Plzeň. All these works were created in Wagner's Secessionist Neo-Classicist style. His Plzeň house was most probably a design competing against Krásný (whose plans were later used[1]). Kotěra's Plzeň plan had an exceptional element in it, a corner tower covered by a large helmet. Its other attributes were typical of Wagner's architecture of the period: a bossage plinth, prominent cornice and a decorative attic. Between the windows on the third and fourth floors, the façade was adorned by flat, probably ceramic, vegetative ornamentation. However, the building did not possess the refinement and delicacy of Kotěra's later works.[2]

In 1898, this young, exceptionally talented and no doubt ambitious architect was faced with an extraordinary opportunity: a vacant post for a professor at the Prague School of Applied Arts. Friedrich Ohmann, the former head of the special school of architecture, was called to Vienna to supervise architectural adaptations for the Royal Palace. The Prague school had an excellent reputation at that time. This was perhaps not only due to Ohmann's presence, but also since the school was the centre of Modernist ideas, both in architecture and in the visual arts. Before he left, Ohmann broadened the repertoire of his architectural retro-styles to include new Secession, and several of his students followed in his footsteps.

---

1   On Krásný's early work, see: Zdeněk Lukeš, "František Krásný – vůdčí osobnost nástupu secese v české architektuře 1896–1900 ". *Umění* XXXIV, 1986, p. 536.
2   See: *Volné směry* III, 1899, p. 151. Viennese *Der Architekt* published the project in the same year.

< 90
Peterka's house in Prague, façade – sketch, 1899
> 91
Interior of Jan Kotěra's own apartment in Jenštejnská street in Prague, 1899

An official approval from Vienna was needed in order for the 27-year-old Kotěra to assume the post. He finally succeeded in obtaining it and became Ohmann's successor and head of the special school of architecture at the School of Applied Arts (becoming a professor in 1899).

The question remains whether or not it would have been better for Jan Kotěra to have remained in the Austrian capital for several more years. Vienna was at the time one of the centres of European culture, especially architecture. The most fascinating events on its architectural scene occurred from 1898 to 1907 when Secessionism, with its continuing references to past styles, was quickly replaced by radical, non-decorative Modernism. This move is strikingly clear in Plečnik's designs from the period. It is enough to compare his first solo projects with his plans for Langer's villa, or Zacherl palace. However, Kotěra chose Bohemia and suddenly found himself in a culture which was not prepared for a revolution of this kind. Yet the decision had been made and, as the following years would show, it was the right decision for the development of modern Czech architecture. Nevertheless, the position of the young designer in the somewhat provincial Czech environment was initially very difficult.

The artist who came to Prague in 1898 was not completely anonymous – Kotěra's works were fairly well known, especially within the circle of the Mánes Association. Some of his college studies had been published in the prestigious Viennese *Der Architekt*[3] magazine, which the Czech artistic scene followed closely.

The young architect introduced himself to the Czech capital with an exhibition of fresh sketches from his Italian sojourn. The exhibition was very well received. In the meantime, a series of articles appeared in the press, commenting on the architectural turmoil in Vienna. In a remark about the presentation of František Krásný's designs and the decorations created by Ohmann's student Alois Dryák – included in an article on the Architecture and Engineering Exhibition at Výstaviště (Exhibition Grounds) in Prague in the second volume of the Mánes Association magazine, *Volné směry* – the author concluded: *"Every movement voices a desire to emancipate itself from historical styles [...] Historicism on one side, on the other Modernism, its almost absolute negation [...] Unless we are wrong in our judgement of the*

---

3   Kotěra's work was regularly published in *Der Architekt* from 1895 onwards.

THE EARLY WORKS, 1898–1905   97

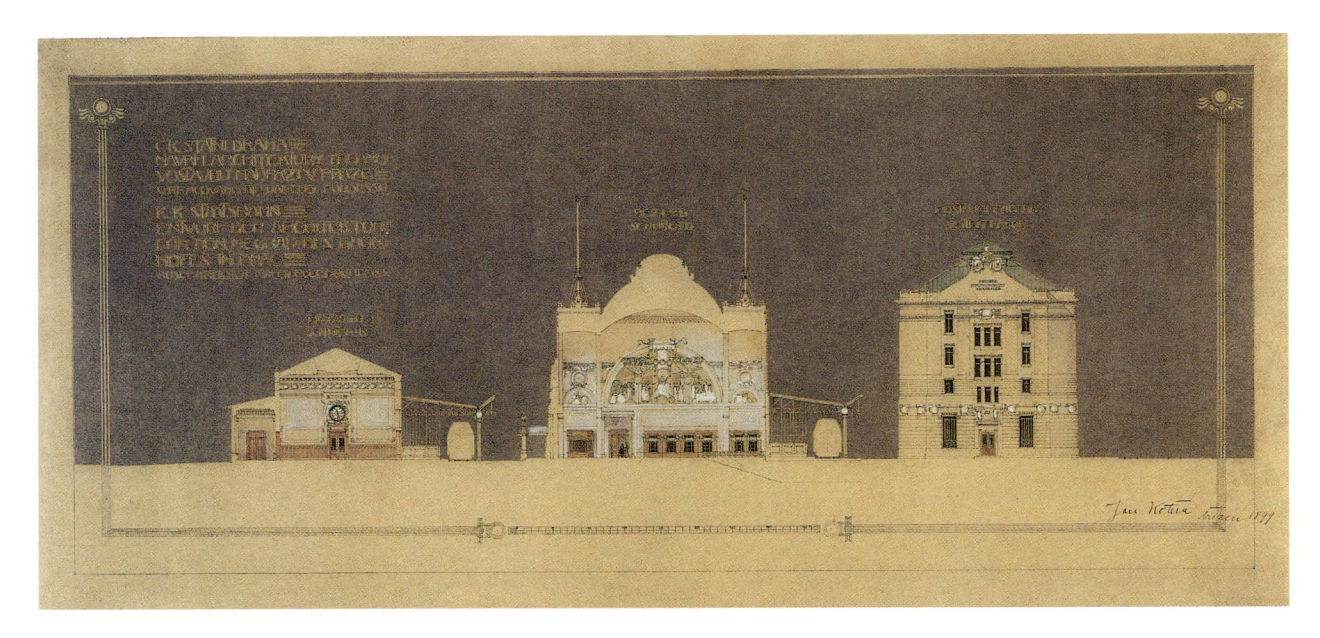

strengths of the emerging young talents, and especially if Jan Kotěra settles in Prague, the present conflicts should escalate into a great struggle and, rest assured, Modernism will win [...]".[4]

The theorist Karel B. Mádl welcomed Kotěra as the 'saviour' of Czech architecture. In his 1898 article "Art of the Future" in *Volné směry*,[5] he wrote: *"He is twenty-seven years old, yet not entirely unknown. Some of his student and professional works were exhibited in Prague and published in local and international magazines. Even before he exhibited studies from his travels, together with new projects at the Mánes exhibition, we knew that in him, a new force was rising in Czech architecture – as necessary as the air we breathe – if it was not to wallow in artistic conservatism long conquered elsewhere. He returns home [...] as an architect who, with the confidence of a man with absolute belief in his salvation, lives and works in modern times"*.

The year 1899 was of crucial importance for Kotěra's early work. In this period, he mainly designed tombstones, furniture and interiors; he also developed detailed plans for a saloon tramcar[6] for the Ringhoffer factory and took part in the competition for the new main railway station in Prague. But most importantly, he won his first prestigious commission to design a building in the very heart of Prague. He was, in fact, asked only to decorate the main façade, vestibule and staircase of a house owned by Lev Peterka (Vilém Thierhier, an experienced engineer and former student of Theofil von Hansen, was entrusted with drawing up the groundplan), a procedure that was rather common at the time.[7] Regardless of the risk, Kotěra seized the opportunity. He composed the façade of the building facing Wenceslas Square in what was an original vision of the Secessionist style. The design was even more radical than the façade of Ohmann's Corso: it had an almost symmetrical façade, vertically divided into three sections. A shallow oriel with large glazed panels formed the central part, whereas the sides were crowned with Secessionist gables. The only element which disturbed the otherwise perfect symmetry was the lively figural decoration above the oriel. The architect abandoned historical morphology altogether, except for the use of a fine bossage plinth. This was unique in Prague

---

4   *Volné směry* II, 1898, p. 521; the author of the text is not known.
5   See note 4, pp. 117–142.

6   The saloon tramcar has survived in good condition, and is now housed in the Transport Museum in Prague.
7   See for example Josef Fanta "Stavby pražské a směry umělecké". *Volné směry* III, 1899, p. 239: *"[...] The poor designer then hands in his detailed and clearly organised drawings to the client, who takes care of the building's completion all by himself. The creator has no say in the matter and, very often, the client will modify the plans to suit his own needs"*.

< 92
Competition entry for Franz Joseph station in Prague, front view, cross-section, 1898
> 93
Mánes pavilion below Kinský gardens in Prague, façades and groundplan study, 1902

at the time. There was no traditional moulding, no decorative jamb framing, nor pediments. Years later, the architect Pavel Janák aptly commented: *"He did away with all moulding as superfluous, something in which the times no longer believed [...]"*.[8] Conservative critics were irritated by the way the smooth surfaces of the façade contrasted with the richly decorated parts (Josef Pekárek, Karel Novák and Stanislav Sucharda were entrusted with the latter). Despite this, it is clear that Kotěra was inspired by two existing architectural works in which the architects had applied a similar scheme – Kestřánek's villa in Plzeň by František Krásný (1897–98)[9] and Osvald Polívka's somewhat spectacular bank in Karlovy Vary (1898–99; demolished in the 1930s).[10]

Kotěra's first important Prague commission is an excellent example of an architecture of refined proportions and subtle poetry. The reactions it provoked reflected accurately the polarity of the artistic scene. The conservatives attacked the building, claiming that it lacked style and was servile to Viennese fashions (in fact, this was the first project in which the architect plainly moved away from Wagner's Neo-Classicism). The Mánes Association artists, however, accepted the young architect into their circle as soon as he arrived in Prague, eulogising over his architectural prowess. Kotěra suffered much in the course of it all, a fact illustrated by this extract from his letter to Richard Gombrich in Vienna: *"Already, with only my first work, they have set their dogs on me. They bark because they are afraid*

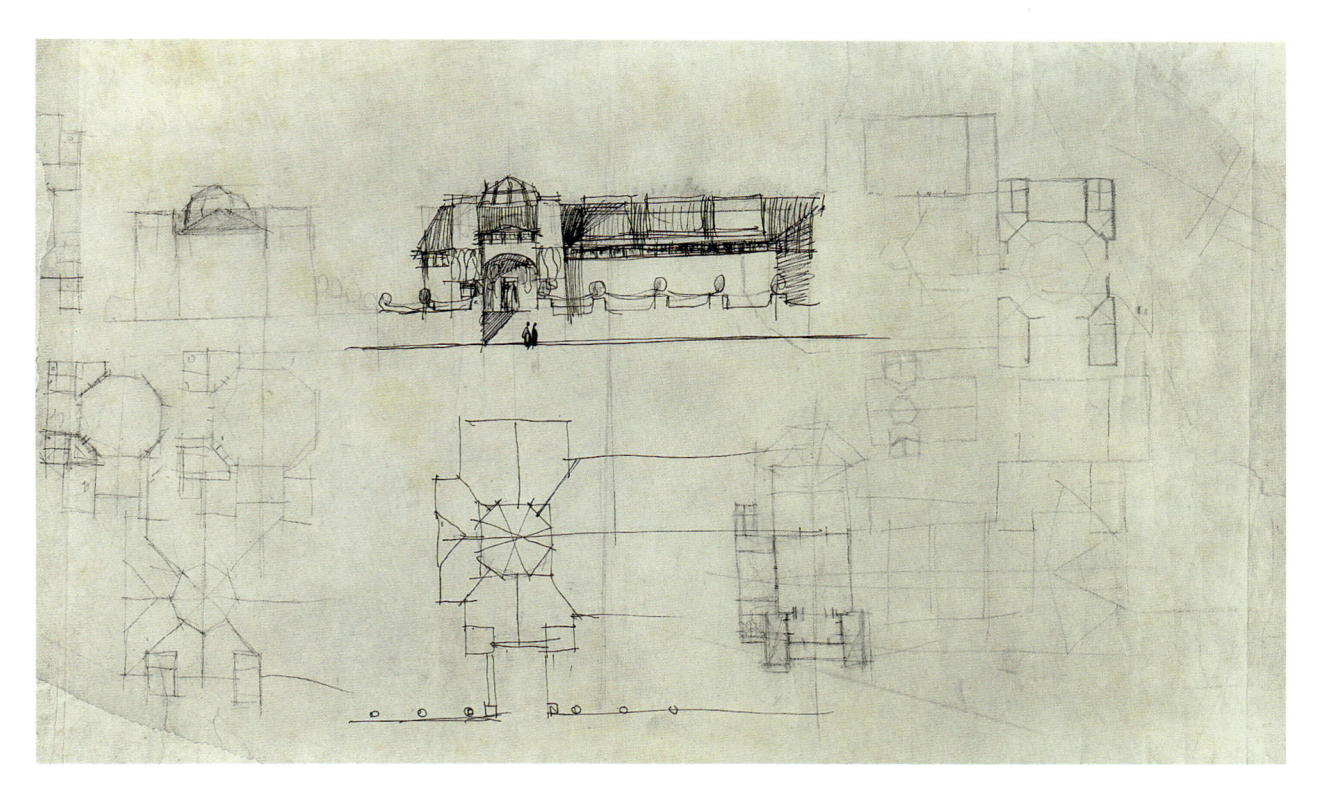

8 Pavel Janák, "K jubileu Jana Kotěry". *Styl* II (VII), p. 87.
9 Zdeněk Lukeš (see note 1).
10 Zdeněk Lukeš, "Podivuhodná Praha Osvalda Polívky". *Technický magazín* XXXIX, 1986, no. 2, p. 38.

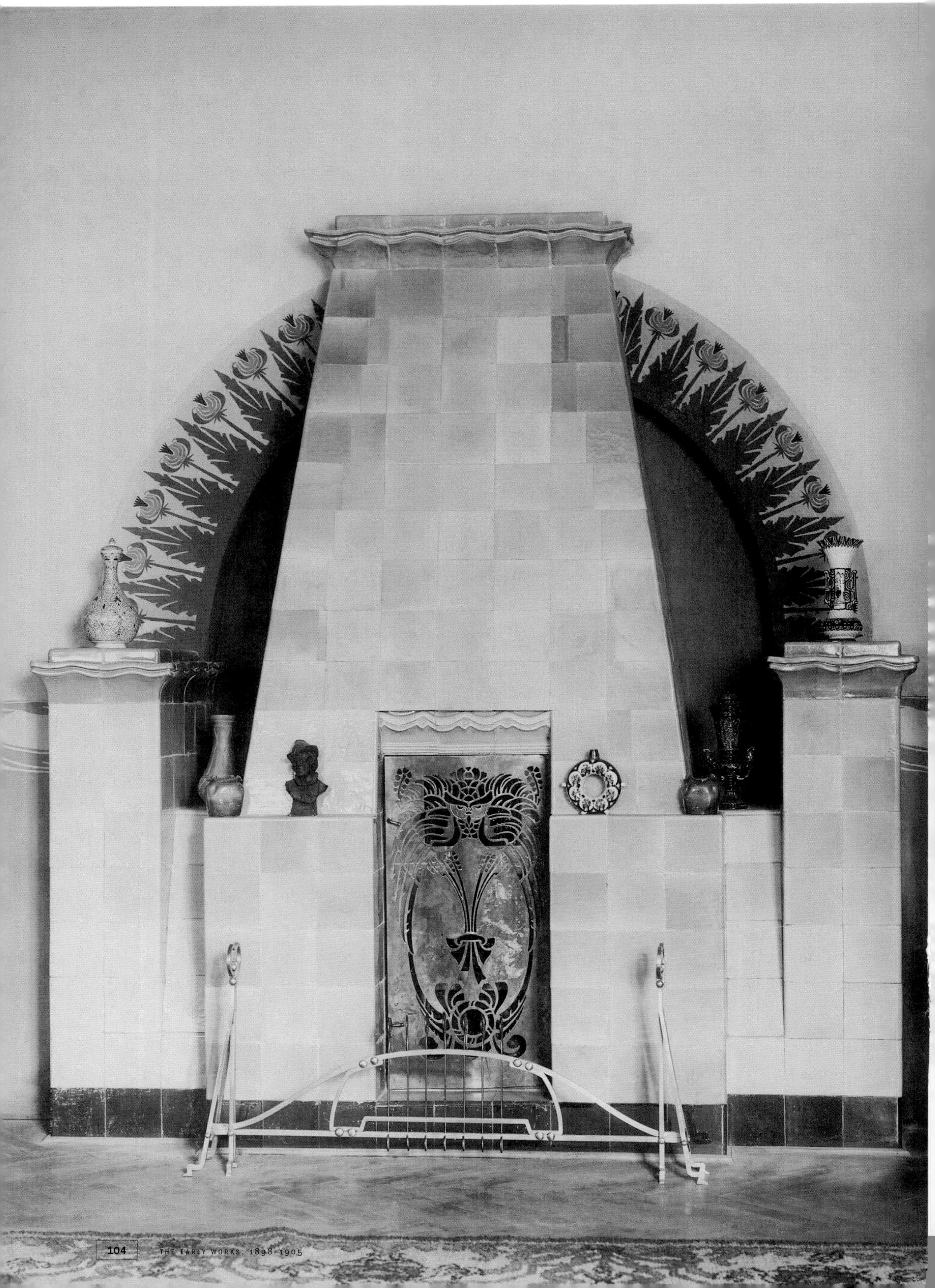

< **98**
Mácha's villa in Bechyně, fireplace, 1902–1903

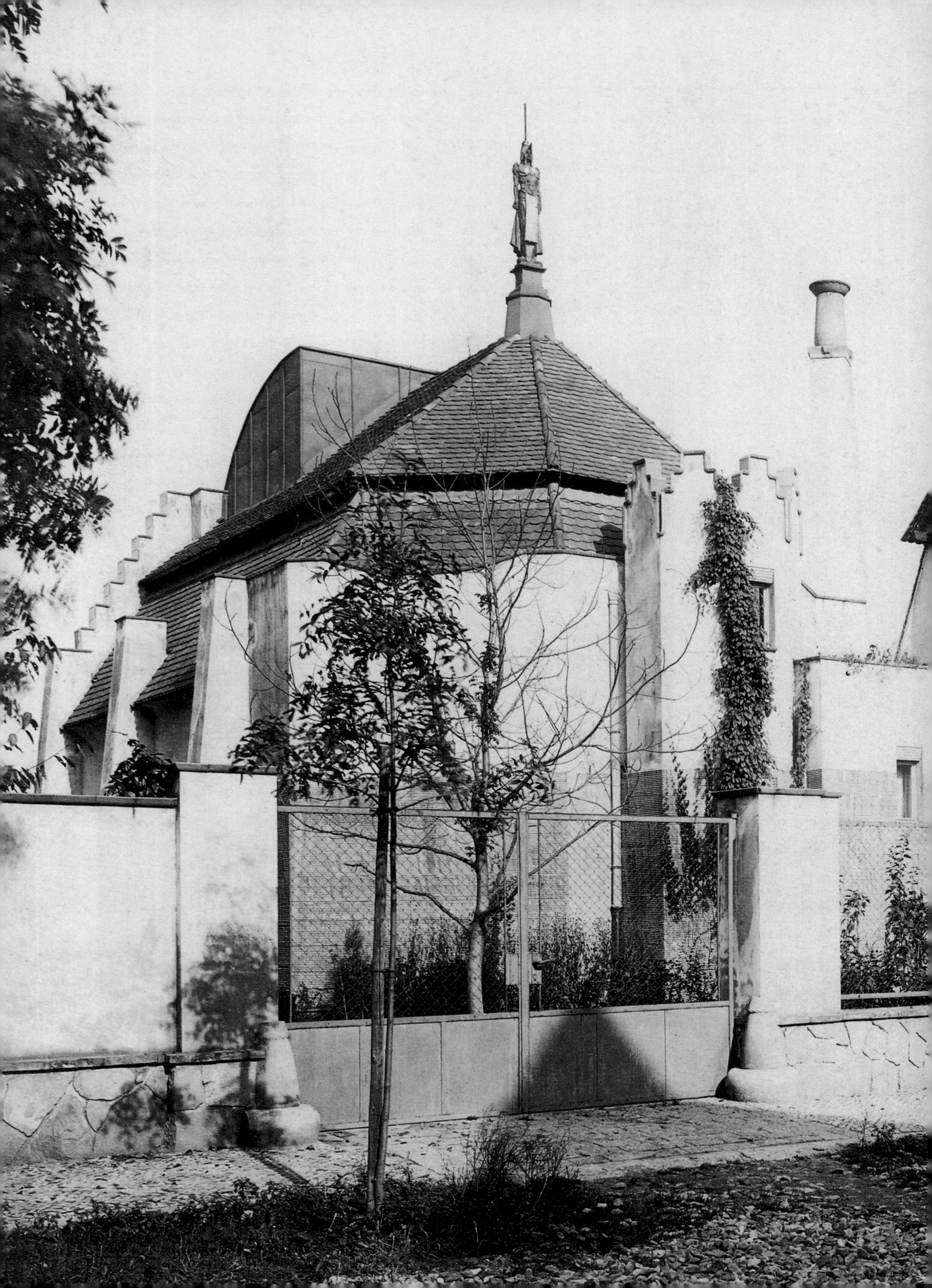

<>101
Stanislav Sucharda's villa and studio in Prague-Bubeneč, 1906–1907

THE EARLY WORKS, 1898-1905

<> 102–105
Stanislav Sucharda's villa and studio in Prague-Bubeneč,
façades – studies, 1904

THE EARLY WORKS, 1898-1905

THE EARLY WORKS, 1898-1905

< **106**
Stanislav Sucharda's villa and studio in Prague-Bubeneč, interior, 1906–1907
> **107**
Stanislav Sucharda's villa and studio in Prague-Bubeneč, interior, 1906–1907

THE EARLY WORKS, 1898-1905

< **108**
National House in Prostějov, 1905–1907

Kotěra won his first truly big commission in early 1903 – the Regional Authorities building in Hradec Králové.[20] It came as a result of Kotěra's friendly relationship with František Ulrich, the mayor of Hradec Králové, initiated during Kotěra's studies in Vienna. Ulrich supported new trends in art and, as previously noted, brought two of Wagner's students – Ottokar Böhm and Hubert Gessner – to Hradec Králové as early as 1896. The Regional Authorities building (1903–04) was to stand on an exposed site, not far from the banks of the Elbe where the old city walls were slowly being replaced by new landmarks (Kotěra's City Museum, his best work, was later included among them). The street façade of the two-storey building was designed in a somewhat non-traditional manner. It is separated into two very different parts: one is fully symmetrical, completed with a protruding cornice, corrugated in the middle section. Underneath it is a rich fresco floral decoration with the municipal coat-of-arms in the centre. The area between the three large windows of the coffee-house and restaurant on the ground floor and the two rows of windows on the two upper floors is left bare. The coffee-house has an apsidal extension at the back, facing the courtyard. On the first floor, facing the street, is an axially symmetrical, finely modelled oriel. The other, narrower part of the façade on the right incorporates the main entrance, framed by pilasters and loggia on the upper floor. Its character is completely different, and creates an extraordinary, unusual tension, a juxtaposition of the symmetrical and the asymmetrical. The interiors of this well-known coffee-house and restaurant had a truly 'grand' appearance. Kotěra designed all the interior furnishing, while his student Otakar Novotný worked on some of the details during Kotěra's travels abroad. (Sadly, this early work of Kotěra was neglected during the 1980s and 1990s, and is now in a pitiable state of repair.)

During the period Kotěra decided to present to the public the results of his teaching activities at the School of Applied Arts,[21] a certain change was occurring on Prague's official architectural scene. In 1903, *Architektonický obzor* published the plans of Secessionist buildings by architects Podhajský and Jurkovič for the first time. Yet, in an article by František X. Harlas, it attacked Ohmann's and Kotěra's graduates from the School of Applied Arts: *"We could almost see it as defiance or intentional contempt for everything that characterises the architect-artist, with the kind of brutality with which they place their copies of Viennese Modernism right next to the most distinguished and most original Prague monuments"*.[22] What the author had in mind was not only Peterka's house but also the two new houses behind Prašná brána (Powder Tower), designed by architects Bedřich Bendelmayer and Emil Weichert. However, only a year later, works by two of Kotěra's followers – František

---

20 *Volné směry* X, 1906, pp. 297–299.

21 Jan Kotěra (see note 18). – The following students were presented: F. Cuc, J. Letzel, K. Šidlík, A. Foehr, J. Šachl, O. Novotný, J. Jiránek, J. Eck, A. Telenský and E. Pelant.
22 *Architektonický obzor* III, 1903, p. 33.

< **109**
National House in Prostějov, interior of the theatre, 1905–1907
<< **110**
National House in Prostějov, façade design, c. 1906
> **111**
F. Tonder's villa in St Gilgen, perspective view from the lake, 1905

Kavalír and Karel Šidlík – won their way onto the pages of *Architektonický obzor* magazine.

For Kotěra, 1903 and 1904 were years of pure diligence. The architect submitted his designs for the façade of the Novák department store on Vodičkova street, rendered in a style similar to the Regional Authorities building in Hradec Králové, however, the prestigious commission was won by Osvald Polívka. Fortunately, another opportunity presented itself: Kotěra was entrusted with the design of the Czech exhibition as part of the Austro-Hungarian pavilion at the World Exhibition in St Louis in 1904. It was an honour that the young architect could not refuse, an opportunity to show the great progress Czech architecture had made since the Paris exhibition in 1900, where it had been represented by works of the older and more conservative architects – Josef Franta, Antonín Wiehl and Jan Koula. Kotěra invited his students and colleagues from the School of Applied Arts to collaborate with him on the St Louis project.

The exhibition featured mainly furniture, decorative objects, paintings and sculptures. Kotěra naturally took advantage of his visit to the United States to study the architecture and urban planning of American cities.

The American sojourn, together with his travels to Western Europe (Paris at the end of the 19th century, Amsterdam in 1905, several trips to Germany and Austria), had a truly formative influence on Kotěra's future work – most of all the work of contemporary Dutch, Belgian and British architects. Around 1905, now that he had already gained a strong position in the Czech architectural sphere, Kotěra was able to start promoting the basic principles of Modernism in architecture. At that time, even the conservative *Architektonický obzor* became resigned and began publishing his students' works (in the end, even its most conservative architects started flirting with Secession!). Influenced by the works of Charles Rennie Mackintosh, Hendrik Petrus Berlage, Jože Plečnik, Josef Maria Olbrich, Leopold Bauer and others, Kotěra slowly began to free his buildings of naturalistic Secessionist decoration, and to replace his lime with coarse plaster.

The transition to Kotěra's greatest creative period was manifested in two buildings. One was of a more intimate character; the other belonged to Kotěra's larger projects: a villa

THE EARLY WORKS, 1898-1905

< 112
Design for Elbogen's villa, 1905

with studio for his friend, sculptor Stanislav Sucharda in Prague-Bubeneč, and National House in Prostějov. Sucharda's villa (1905–07),[23] built in a quiet residential area not far from where the family house originally stood, is another variation on the English cottage, with a staircase-hall and all the other rooms set around it. The dining room, salon and living room were situated, rather unfortunately in view of the Czech climate, to the east and the north. The large studio, a separate building (later ruined by reconstruction work),[24] was placed on the west side. Kotěra designed, in several stages, all the furnishings for this extremely comfortable house. The main façade of the villa was rather ascetic, comprising a minimum of geometric decoration. Stanislav Sucharda's sculptures decorated the interior and the garden.

National House in Prostějov[25] was at the time one of the largest buildings in the country. It was as if this ambitious Moravian city wanted to prove it could afford such a grand edifice. Here, the architect had a difficult task, not unlike the problems facing architects Balšánek and Polívka in their project for Municipal House in Prague. Although he had enough space for the project (since the building was isolated from the surrounding architecture), he still had to incorporate all of the building's various functions: a multipurpose hall, salons, restaurant and coffee-house facilities. To this end, Kotěra created a two-winged L-shaped structure with clearly differentiated functions. The main façade reflected the Darmstadt influence of Olbrich's works, yet it still had far too much ornamentation, if combined with bare coarse plaster. The asymmetrical composition of the material, the mighty towers crowned in stone, and a tall triangular gable echo Kotěra's design for the Mánes pavilion, or even the earlier studies for the decoration of *Rusalka*. The architect took exceptional care in designing the interiors. They were richly decorated in the late Secessionist style and complemented with paintings and sculptures by Jan Preisler, František Kysela, Stanislav Sucharda and others. Kotěra was not fully satisfied with the result – the building's volume was much too dishevelled and restless, far from the ideals of Berlage's or Olbrich's architecture. While the professor had reproached his student Otakar Novotný three years earlier for designing the interior of the Regional Authorities building in Hradec Králové too starkly – now he criticised his student and colleague Richard Novák, who worked on the project during Kotěra's travels abroad, for including too much decoration.

In the three years that had passed, times had simply changed, now ripe for the theses which Kotěra had voiced in his conceptual statement at the turn of the century. Despite all the peripetia involved, we can still see Kotěra's early works in a highly positive light – beginning with his arrival in Prague and ending with the projects created around the year 1905. It was indeed Kotěra who, under very difficult conditions, upheld the principles of Wagnerianism, and laid the foundations for modern Czech architecture. Kotěra's oeuvre was rooted in his teacher's Viennese Neo-Classicism and developed into a personal and poetic Secessionist style. His work from this period had acquired the stamp of ascetic Modernism, the style in which Kotěra excelled, as his next period would clearly show.

---

[23] In 1910 Sucharda's villa was included in the publication *Neue Landhäuser und Villen in Österreich*. Anton Schroll, Wien 1910.
[24] In the 1930s architect Stanislav Sucharda jnr. entirely rebuilt the studio.
[25] See also: Vladimír Šlapeta, *Národní dům v Prostějove*. Praha 1978.

Peterka's House in Prague, 1899–1900

< **113**
Peterka's house in Prague, façade design, 1899
<< **114**
Peterka's house in Prague, 1899–1900

Peterka's house on Wenceslas Square 777, Kotěra's first project realised in Prague, was designed after the young architect returned from Vienna, having completed his studies at Otto Wagner's school of architecture at the Viennese Academy of Fine Arts. The project put him in a truly difficult situation. The allied critics – mainly K. B. Mádl in *Volné směry* – had proclaimed him the saviour of Czech architecture, thus exacting excessive demands on his first professional work. Furthermore, it was among the first buildings in Prague to be rendered in the new Secessionist style (along with Central Hotel in Hybernská street by Friedrich Ohmann – 1899–1901). It was immediately viewed by the older generation and nationalist journalists as an import from Vienna, the resented adversary of the Czechs. What the conservatives found additionally unacceptable about the new style was its sober decoration. As recorded by art historian Zdeněk Wirth, Josef Hlávka, an important representative of historicism in Prague, thus commented on Peterka's house: *"So this is the saviour from Vienna! Looks like it's having a bad hair day!"*. Kotěra complained about this hostility in a letter to his Viennese friend Richard Gombrich: *"Already, with only my first work, they have set their dogs on me"*. What further burdened his first Prague commission was the need to negotiate his ideas to suit the groundplan and construction conceived by Vilém Thierhier, the co-creator of this work. Kotěra's share was limited to the design of the main façade, the decoration of the vestibule and staircase, and the design of the groundplans for the parterre and mezzanine, which he treated as a single, fluid space.

For his client Lev Peterka, banker and Prague town councillor, Kotěra created an architecture in which the basic Wagnerian scheme was complemented with elements of the Western European Art-Nouveau style, particularly that of Victor Horta's Tassel palace in Brussels. The generously open parterre and mezzanine reflected the concept of a busy shopping boulevard, the new image of Wenceslas Square. The soft curves, which accentuated and permeated the entire composition, paid homage to the Baroque. The architect conceived the façade as a single large surface to which he freely inserted naturalistic vegetative ornaments and figural sculptures by Karel Novák, Josef Pekárek and Stanislav Sucharda. R. Š.

Mánes Pavilion in Prague, 1902

< **115**
Mánes Pavilion below Kinský gardens in Prague, 1902
> **116**
Mánes Pavilion below Kinský gardens in Prague,
façades – study, 1902

Thanks to the efforts of Stanislav Sucharda, Jan Preisler, and not least Jan Kotěra, the Mánes Association enjoyed unparalleled prestige during the early 20th century. *Volné směry*, the Association's platform, played a key role in its expansion, as did foresighted exhibition policies, coupled with an insistence on high-quality artworks for its exhibitions. However, the Association lacked gallery space of its own which would enable its members to present the works in an appropriate environment, applying modern principles. The problem was resolved in 1902, when Mánes seized an opportunity to present the work of Auguste Rodin, pioneer of modern sculpture, in what was to be his first large exhibition outside France. To this end, the Association decided to build a provisional pavilion below Kinský gardens in Prague-Smíchov, at the foot of Petřín hill. The simple wooden structure remained in use until the beginning of the First World War. In 1917, the Smíchov district authorities demolished it.

Kotěra not only designed the pavilion, but he also resolved the problem of financing its rapid construction. He conceived it – in the spirit of the 19th century – as a "temple of art", with a characteristic glass dome above the vestibule which the visitors accessed through a triumphal arch positioned between two towering pylons. The critic F. X. Šalda saw it as a "fortress of pride and dreams". The pavilion was different from its main prototype, the stone Whitechapel Gallery in London designed by the Secessionist architect Harrison Townsend, in its use of inexpensive materials, including its folkloric half-timber gable construction. It differed from another classic, the House of the Grand Duke in the artists' colony in Darmstadt designed by Josef Maria Olbrich, in the asymmetrical dynamism of the building's composition.

R. Š.

THE EARLY WORKS, 1898–1905

The First Family Houses: Villas Designed for Mácha, Trmal and Tonder

< 117
Trmal's villa in Prague-Strašnice, 1902–1903
> 118
Trmal's villa in Prague-Strašnice, staircase, longitudinal section, 1902–1903

In his designs for Peterka's house and the Regional Authorities building in Hradec Králové that followed (1901–04), Kotěra attempted to create a modern, urban architecture, whereas in his first family houses, he searched for an architecture able to express the idyll of rural life. He thus joined a pan-European wave of architectural folklorism, especially fervent in Central Europe after the close of the 19th century, where it was represented in works by Stanislaw Witkiewicz, Dušan Jurkovič, Károly Kós and Josef Hoffmann. Kotěra followed the work of British architects Voysey, Baillie Scott and Mackintosh with similar interest. The family houses of the British architects drew their inspiration from similar folkloric and regional sources; however, Central European architects respected above all their unparalleled modernity and high standard of living. In his first villa projects, Kotěra fused the Czech cottage, adapted to serve modern purposes, with the groundplans and spatial features of English family houses.

The series of Kotěra's countryside and suburban villas began with a house designed for the writer Jan Herben in Hostišov near Votice (1901–02). The architect was evidently not pleased with this work, as it was only ever included in the inventories of his works as a design. The architect also never attempted to publish his project for the villa of interior decorator František Fröhlich on Janského street 360 in Černošice near Prague (1902–03). The representative villas from the early years of Kotěra's career included the summer residence of Vendelín Mácha in Bechyně (1902–03), influenced most strongly by English family houses, František Trmal's villa in Vilová street 91 in Prague-Strašnice (1902–03), designed with folkloric motifs, and Ferdinand Tonder's villa in St Gilgen in Austria (1905–06) whose fragile polygonal corpus, covered by an impressive mansard roof the architect placed on the shore of a mountain lake. In all these works, Kotěra placed emphasis on the arrangement of their interior, created in harmony with the prospective owner's specific nature and particular needs. The English one-storey staircase-hall became the leading motif of these interiors. Kotěra elaborated their staircase railings and mezzanine terraces with great care, and adorned them with a variety of ceiling installations. The wide openings that led from the hall through to the adjacent rooms created dynamic movement, further accentuated by apsidal oriels inside the rooms, and by balconies and covered doorways through which the interior blended naturally with the garden.   R. Š.

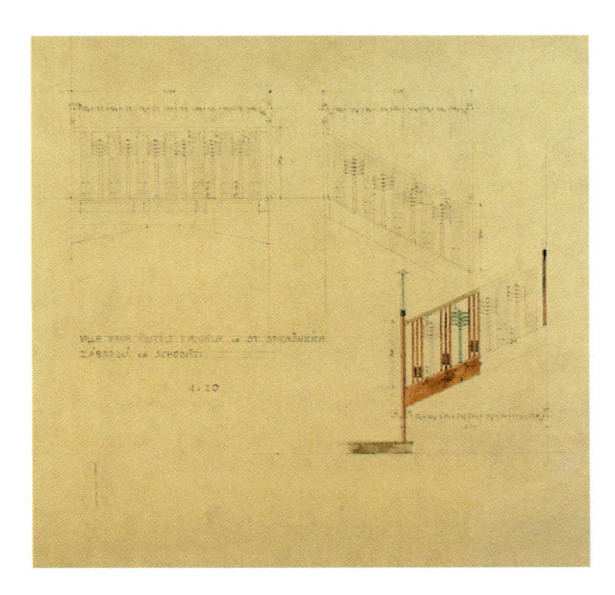

THE EARLY WORKS, 1898–1905 | 125

THE EARLY WORKS, 1898–1905

< **119**
Fröhlich's villa in Černošice, 1902–1903
> **120**
Mácha's villa in Bechyně, 1902–1903
>> **121**
Mácha's villa in Bechyně, staircase-hall, 1902–1903

THE EARLY WORKS, 1898-1905

< **122**
F. Tonder's villa in St Gilgen, 1905
> **123**
F. Tonder's villa in St Gilgen, hall, 1905

Sucharda's Villa and Studio in Prague-Bubeneč, 1904–1907

< **124**
Stanislav Sucharda's villa and studio in Prague-Bubeneč, 1906–1907
> **125**
Stanislav Sucharda's villa and studio in Prague-Bubeneč, stained glass from the staircase-hall, 1906–1907

The collection of family houses from the early period of Kotěra's work culminates in the villa of the sculptor Stanislav Sucharda in Slavíčkova street 248 in Prague-Bubeneč. The architect designed its plans in 1904–05, while the actual building work took another two years to complete. This was one of the last examples of Kotěra's houses whose exterior paid homage to the architecture of English villas. The parallel is obvious in the massive mansard roof, picturesque chimneys, oriels and half-timber gable construction, as well as the asymmetrical layout of its groundplan, including the transverse wing of the sculptor's studio. In comparison with the villas for Herben, Fröhlich, Trmal or Tonder, Sucharda's house displayed almost no elements of folklore, while ornament was applied sparingly.

This was a telling example of how, in projects where he was able to reach an essential agreement with the future owner, Kotěra masterly transformed his villas to fit the client's needs. *"I am really looking forward to this work, for he is a reasonable man"* – the words with which, at the close of 1904, Kotěra announced the beginning of his work on Sucharda's villa to his friend Richard Gombrich. For Sucharda, his colleague from the Mánes Association, Kotěra created a complex spatial organism, accentuating the fact that these were newly formed interiors, and not the remains of the "insides of boxes". They began with a surprisingly monumental, vaulted staircase-hall, which was formerly a gallery for Sucharda's works. The hall expanded into further rooms of varying sizes, whose atmosphere was enhanced by Kotěra's chandeliers and numerous pieces of furniture. The original studio, oriented towards the garden, was unfortunately lost in the Purist reconstruction by Stanislav Sucharda jnr. undertaken during the 1930s.

R. Š.

THE EARLY WORKS, 1898-1905

< **126**
Stanislav Sucharda's villa and studio in Prague-Bubeneč,
hall, 1906–1907
> **127**
Stanislav Sucharda's villa and studio in Prague-Bubeneč,
groundplan, 1904–1905

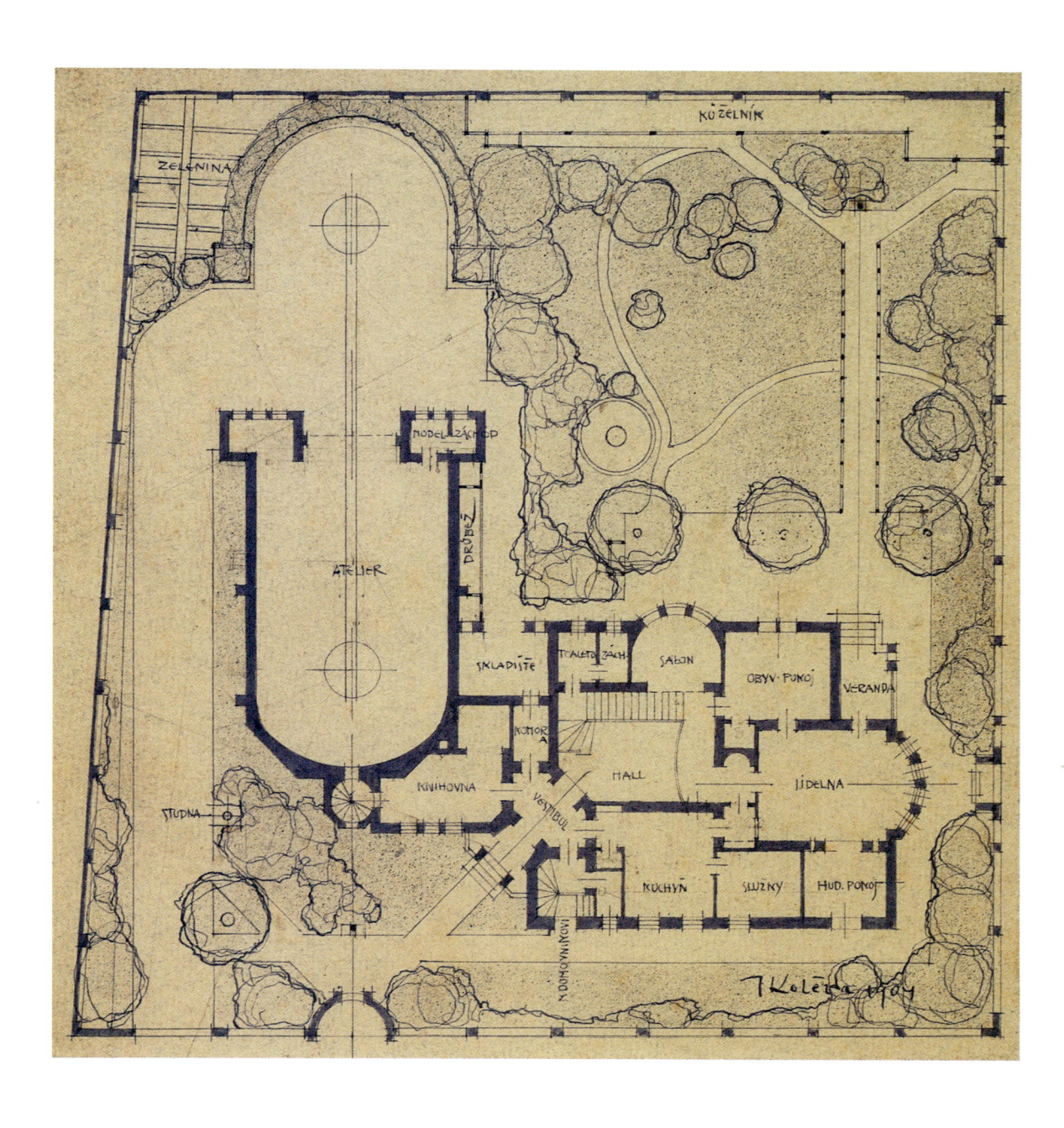

National House in Prostějov, 1905–1907

< **128**
National House in Prostějov, theatre façade, 1905–1907
> **129**
National House in Prostějov, façade design, 1905–1907

National House in Prostějov concludes the first phase of Kotěra's work. In terms of style, this phase could be described as lyrical, youthful, enchanted or soft. It was characterised by the use of vegetative or folk ornamentation, which in Prostějov had already become stylised and geometric, and had moved towards a new stylistic expression.

At the close of the 19th century, Prostějov was cultivating its image as the largest town in Moravia with its own Czech-speaking town council. It invited prominent artists from Prague of modern orientation to design its important public buildings. Thus, it became an enclave of Prague Secession in Moravia. Prostějov was a wealthy town, home of the highly successful machine plants owned by the Wichterle and Kovařík Brothers. Donations from Karel Vojáček, pharmacist and Member of Parliament, and his wife Karla, head of the women's association Vlastimila, enhanced local cultural life. The donors supported the building of a (National) House of Culture which – at the request of Karla Vojáček – was to accommodate a large and small theatre, a modern, "metropolitan" coffee-house, lounge bars and halls for female and male choral societies. The triumphal motifs of Kotěra's design – mainly the arch adorning the façade, framed by two pylons – no doubt aimed to portray the political

THE EARLY WORKS, 1898–1905 | 135

THE EARLY WORKS, 1898–1905

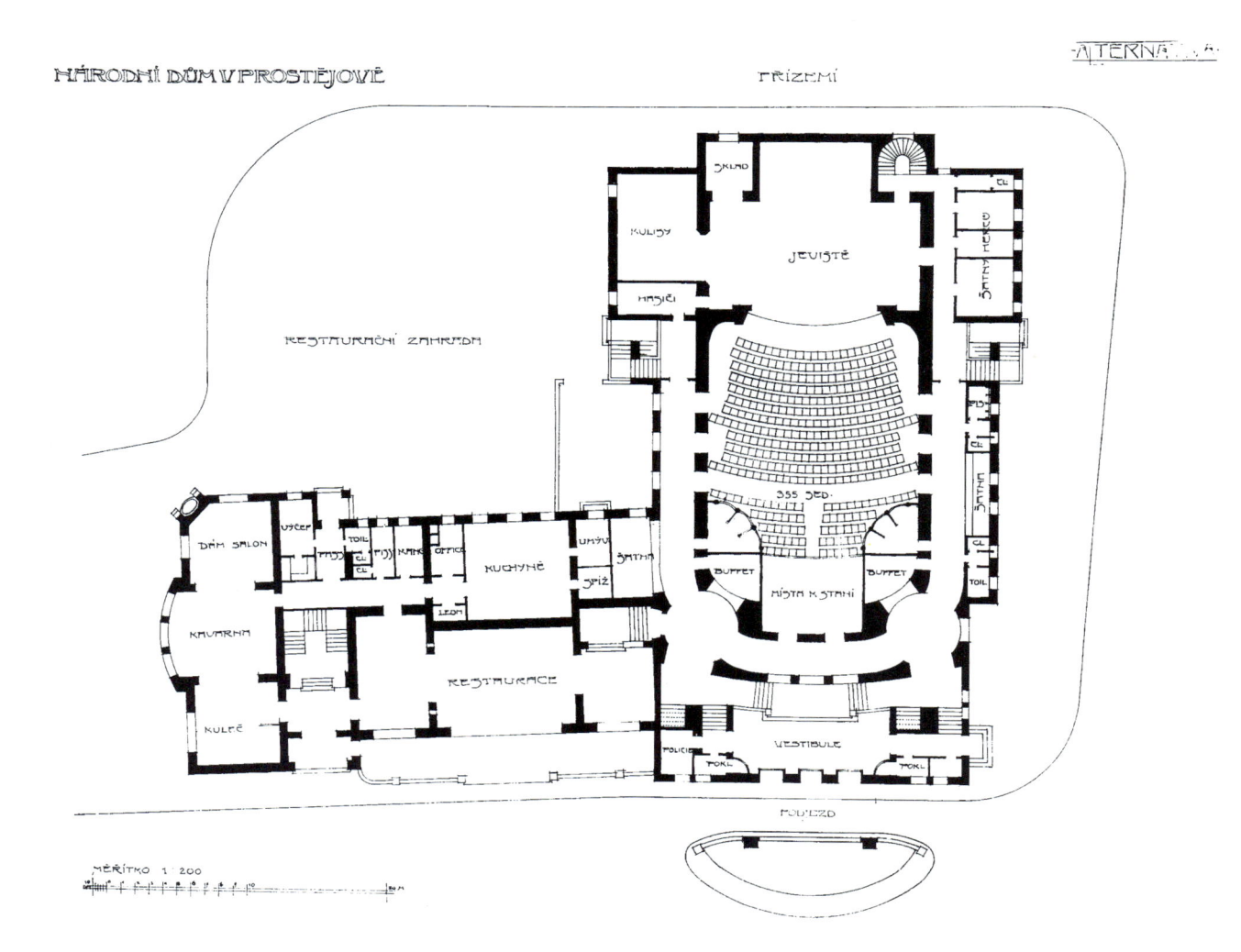

< **130**
National House in Prostějov, small salon, 1905–1907
<< **131**
National House in Prostějov, groundplan, 1905–1907
> **132**
National House in Prostějov, interior of the theatre, 1905–1907

triumph of the Czech nation in Prostějov and the region of Haná, a theme developed in some of the building's decorative artwork. It comes as no surprise to learn that its reconstruction at the time of the Nazi occupation was meant to do away with all patriotic elements; luckily, this was undertaken only partially.

Four different artworks that decorated National House repeated the same motif of a couple, a woman and a man. They included frescos by František Kysela adorning the walls of the theatre lounges, Preisler's paintings *Dream of a Young Woman* and *Dream of a Young Man* which originally decorated the foyer, Sucharda's caryatids of *Hanačka* and *Hanák*, archetypal Czech male and female figures framing the entrance to the theatre building, and the relief portraits of Karel and Karla Vojáček by Bohumil Kafka, decorating Kotěra's monument to the donors which the town erected in front of National House in 1910–11. These works suggest another important theme treated in National House, namely, the equality of the sexes, prompted by the expansion of the women's rights movement in Prostějov in the years preceding the First World War, and reflected in the fact that National House accommodated both female and male cultural societies.

The building's asymmetrical layout – a recurrent theme of Kotěra's monumental works – suggested that the architect had already departed from the principles of Wagner's school. The elevated appearance of its theatre wing façade had its prototypes in the entrance to Kotěra's Mánes pavilion (1902) and the architect's drawing of an ancient church ruin featured on the cover of *A Temple in Ruins*, an anthology of poetry by Jaroslav Kvapil from 1899. Tradition has it that Kotěra reproached Richard Novák, his student and assistant on this project, for using excessive ornamentation on the façades. Due to his continuing conflicts with the town council in Prostějov regarding his fee, Kotěra did not have sufficient control over the practical side of this particular project.

R. Š.

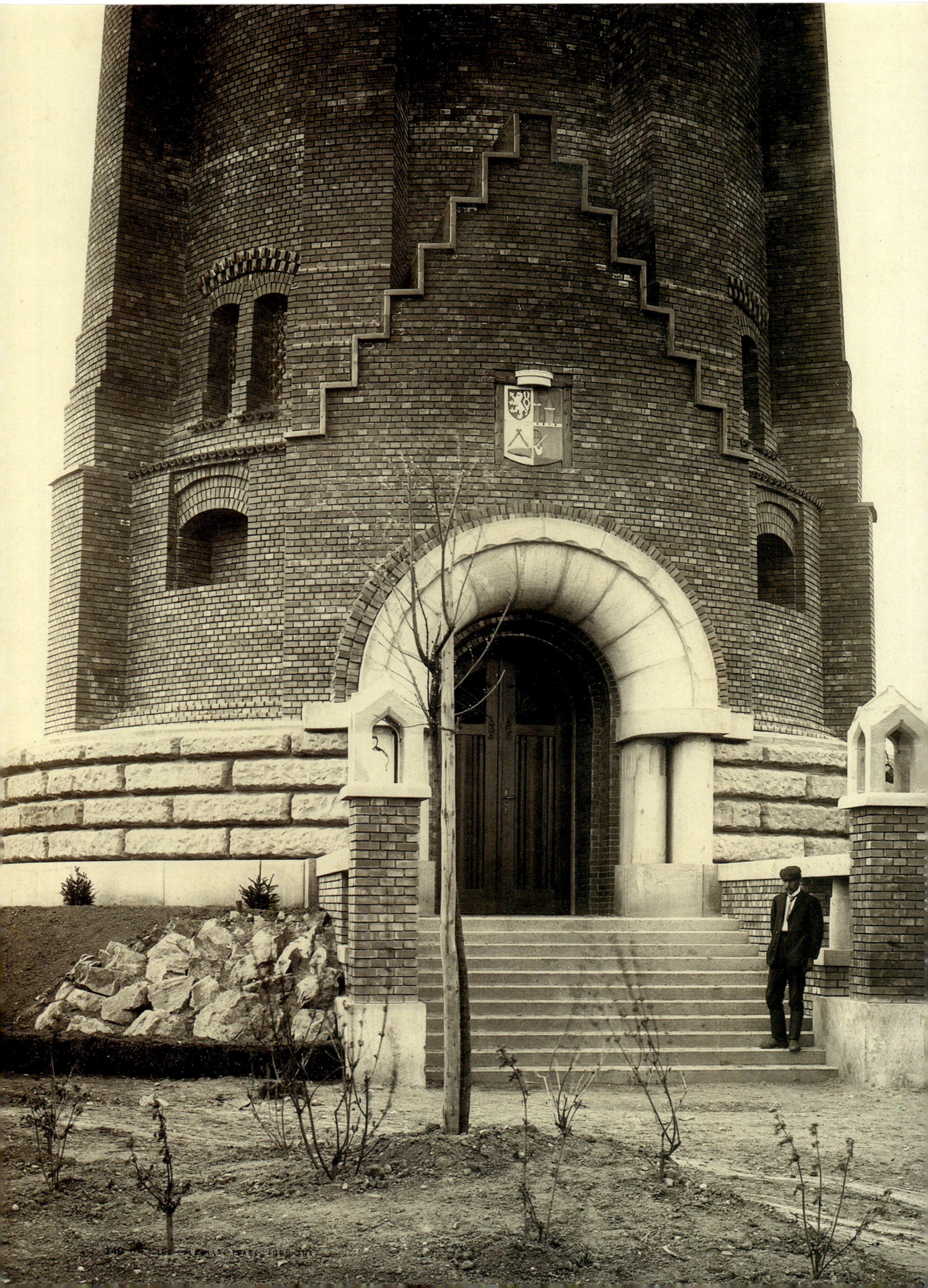

< 135
Vršovice waterworks in Prague-Michle, detail, 1906–1907

The Culminant Years, 1906–1912

ROSTISLAV ŠVÁCHA

In his 1986 ground-breaking interpretation of the work of Ludwig Mies van der Rohe, Fritz Neumeyer distinguished between two fundamentally different positions in European architectural theory promoted around the year 1910. The first was founded on the teaching of the philosopher Friedrich Nietzsche. It utilised his notion of the decisive role human will played in the modern world and could be described as "voluntarism": The architect would cast away all tradition, force his own ideas about form on the environment, and employ these forms in building an entirely new world. Neumeyer declared Peter Behrens, whose style was known among his contemporaries as the *"Zarathustra style"*,[1] as the most prominent representative of this view in German architecture of the early 1900s. Following this, we can easily trace this thinking through the works of the pioneers of Cubism in Czech architecture, especially those of Janák and Chochol.

The second view did not place such importance on the architect's will to create entirely new forms – his *Kunstwollen* – a term used by art historian Alois Riegl. Its advocates believed that the forms for modern architecture could already be seen everywhere: in nature, in the physical laws of gravity, i.e., weight and support, in the rules of construction, even in certain aspects of architectural tradition. Thus the architect's task does not rest in the *invention* of forms but rather in the *search* for them.

If we were to seek prominent architects from the beginning of the 20th century who shared this second view, we would certainly think of Adolf Loos, the enemy of *"pretentiousness of form"*, or indeed any insubstantial change or addition to established form arising *"from a certain need to employ imagination"*.[2] However, Fritz Neumeyer considered Hendrik Petrus Berlage to be the most influential representative of this idea. As early as the turn of the century, this Dutch pioneer of Modernism fought for a form of architecture whose *"clean construction"* would be extracted from natural laws. Even though he rejected historicism, he did not hesitate to cite examples of the constructive arts in the Gothic or even Romanesque styles. These citations are clearly discernible in the details of his Amsterdam stock-exchange building (1898–1903), as well as other works from that period. He was a strong opponent of "voluntarism" when it came to the question of form. *"Because you, as artists, must not only be economical with your motifs; you must also not invent any new ones. The same way as nature reforms its ancient archetypes, you can recreate original artistic forms; you cannot invent any new forms. If you attempt to do so, you will soon discover that your work has no lasting value. You will become unnatural and untrue"*, wrote Berlage in his 1905 book *Gedanken über Stil in der Baukunst*.[3]

This dynamic polarity between Behrens and Berlage set by Neumeyer was, in 1910, much in the thoughts of Czech architects, including those from Jan Kotěra's inner circle. A noteworthy illustration of this are the writings of Otakar Novotný,

---

[1] Fritz Neumeyer, *Mies van der Rohe. Das Kunstlose Wort. Gedanken zur Baukunst*. Seidler, Berlin 1986. – Neumeyer published the revised and enlarged English version of his book under the title *The Artless World. Mies van der Rohe on Building Art*. MIT Press, Cambridge, Mass. 1991. See especially pp. 63–93.

[2] Adolf Loos, *Řeči do prázdna*. Praha 1929, pp. 152–153.

[3] Hendrik Petrus Berlage, *Gedanken über Stil in der Baukunst*. 1905, p. 27.

Kotěra's most steadfast student, especially his article "The Interior, the Architect and the Public", written for the second volume of *Styl* (Style) magazine (1909–10). Novotný was the architect of Štenc House in Prague (1909–11), where his revised use of austere brick forms masterfully reflected the 1906–08 changes in Kotěra's oeuvre. He claimed that contemporary architecture was created from two different approaches. The first was an *"organic"* way, in which the act of creation is opposed to natural laws and arises from the *"imaginary forces"* of the creator's fantasy. This is contrasted with the second, the *"tectonic"* method, entirely respectful of the materials used for architecture and based on the natural laws of weight and support. According to Novotný, the teachings of Gottfried Semper, Otto Wagner and *"the Dutchman Berlage"*[4] defined the way towards the "tectonic" method in architecture.

We are forced to deduce Jan Kotěra's position regarding this polarity from his actions, from the testimonies of his students, and most of all from his completed projects and buildings. During the period in which he created his best works – between the Vršovice waterworks in Michle (1906–07) and the Prague Mozarteum (1911–13) – Jan Kotěra remained almost completely silent as a theorist. His studies with Otto Wagner in Vienna, and the fact that Wagner's 1895 book, *Moderne Architektur*, saw construction as the *"pre-cell"* of architecture,[5] inclined him, however, towards the views of Berlage. Kotěra's conceptual statement "On New Art", from the fourth volume of *Volné směry* magazine (1900), suggests his latent identification with Berlage. Here, the creative work that springs from a pre-given form and does not rest on purpose and construction, is contemptuously labelled as *"utopian"*. According to Kotěra's manifesto, the new forces in architecture lay in the *"constructive creation of space"*, relying on the *"eternal natural issue of weight and support"*. Ornamentation, which Kotěra already saw as something of secondary importance, was not supposed to serve any other purpose but to divide and support the *"mass, clearly expressed in a constructive way"*.[6] The idea of a strict Constructivist style, which Kotěra promoted after 1906, was clearly indicated in his article "On New Art". Yet it was to take almost eight years before Kotěra could find appropriate architectural means to support it.

In 1905, Kotěra travelled to Holland with his students from the School of Applied Arts.[7] There, he saw Berlage's architecture for the first time. His Dutch student Evert Johannes Kuipers, known as *Vyprsk* ("Outburst") among his Czech fellow students,[8] was his guide. According to Bohuslav Fuchs, a graduate of Kotěra who studied at the Prague Academy of Fine Arts in 1916–19, his professor acquired Berlage's book *Grundlagen und Entwicklung der Architektur* (1908) and later used it in his lectures on theory at the Academy.[9] A review of the book, with an extract from it, was published in 1910 and 1911 in *Styl*, Kotěra's home platform.[10] Yet, as Fuchs recollected later, Kotěra the educator was more interested in the Dutch architect's science of building proportions than in the style of his buildings. Another book on proportions Kotěra used as a teaching aid was *Tempelmasse* (1912) by Odilo Wolff, a monk from the Benedictine Emmaus monastery in Prague and a member of the

---

4 Otakar Novotný, "Interiér, architekt a obecenstvo". *Styl* II, 1909–10, pp. 67–70. – On Novotný, see: Vladimír Šlapeta, *Otakar Novotný. Architektonické dílo*. Praha – Olomouc 1980.
5 Otto Wagner, *Moderne Architektur*. Wien 1895. – For the Czech translation see: Otto Wagner, *Moderní architektura*. Jan Laichter, Praha 1910, p. 46.
6 Jan Kotěra, "O novém umění". *Volné směry* IV, 1900, pp. 189–195.
7 Kotěra's school trip to Holland is mentioned in his letter to the Ministry of Culture and Education in Vienna from 22 October 1906, deposited in Karásek's collection at the Museum of Czech Literature in Prague.
8 Cf.: Josef Mayer, "Studijní cesta". *Styl* XIV (XIX), 1934–35, pp. 151–152.
9 Bohuslav Fuchs, *In margine uměleckého odkazu Jana Kotěry*. Dům umění města Brna, 1972.
10 Vilém Dvořák, "H. P. Berlage, Grundlage und Entwicklung der Architektur". *Styl* II, 1909–10, pp. 115–116. – Hendrik Petrus Berlage, "Základy a vývoj moderní architektury". *Styl* III, 1910–11, pp. 62–79.

< **136**
Kratochvíl's villa in Černošice, sketch, 1908
> **137**
Billiard hall in the Arco coffee-house in Prague, 1907

THE CULMINANT YEARS, 1906-1912

< 138
Kotěra's own villa in Prague-Vinohrady, view from the garden, 1908–1909

Beuron art school.[11] In his early conceptual statement "On New Art", Kotěra wrote about the importance of proportions which provide the architect with aesthetic control over the constructive substance of his work. In 1916, Kotěra completed, but unfortunately never published, a book on architectural composition.[12]

Kotěra's Dutch lesson is best revealed in a group of buildings constructed in 1906–07 for the Vršovice waterworks in the Prague suburb of Michle. The group consists of a pumping station on the Vltava river, in Braník, and a water tower, surrounded by three smaller service buildings situated on a small hill opposite Vršovice, on Baarova street in Prague-Michle. For the first and almost last time, Kotěra was presented with the task of designing an industrial structure, a concept held in low esteem in the hierarchy of architectural tasks throughout the 19th century. Nevertheless, this architectural genre succeeded in imposing its own specific language and metaphor on architects. In Michle, Kotěra dealt with the usual image of industrial architecture by using elements whose character felt both "industrial" and Berlagean in spirit. This is most true of the exposed bricks and highlighted tectonics. The gate leading to the water tower could be seen as a citation from Berlage's Amsterdam buildings or a fine variation on some of their elements.[13] The same could be said of the coulisse behind the gate in the form of a tiered pyramid, and the manner in which the bottom of the water reservoir "sits" on the tower's supporting pilasters. The metal ornaments on the reservoir tank and the protruding cornice of its semi-circular helmet, are much more Viennese and Wagnerian in character.

Two of Kotěra's villas, designed only one year after the Vršovice waterworks, Kraus' villa in Bubeneč (1907) and Marek's villa in Holoubkov near Rokycany (1907–09), suggest that the development of Kotěra's work after 1906 is a more complex synthesis and cannot be understood merely as an appropriation of Berlage's brick vernacular and tectonics. They are joined – as are several of his interiors and unrealised projects – by Götz's villa in Chrustenice near Beroun (1908), which Otakar Novotný saw as *"the most faithful Czech translation of the English cottage"*.[14] However, the Kraus and Marek villas point to something different from the *English cottage*. They show a tendency for austerity and a reduction of decorativeness. In this, they reflect the strong trend of the Wagner school from the beginning of the 20th century, most obvious in the works of Max Fabiani, Hubert Gessner, Josef Hoffmann, as well as Wagner himself. Of all the Viennese works of this period, apparently aiming to achieve the same goals as Berlage, if via a different path, Kotěra was most impressed by the Hochstätter family house designed by Hoffmann (1906).[15] Both Kraus' and Marek's villas draw abundantly from it: especially the latter in its spatial composition and volume, in the form of its roof and in the division of the façades with alternating sections of brick and coarse plaster.

In light of his work from 1906–1913, the right entrance façade of the Trade and Industry Pavilion at the Chamber of Trade and Commerce Jubilee exhibition (1907–08), completed with Jan Štursa's impressive figural sculptures in archaic Greek style, represents a somewhat Expressionist detour

---

11 Odilo Wolff, *Tempelmasse*. Anton Schroll, Wien 1912.
12 Fragments of the missing text in this work were published by Kotěra's student František Lydie Gahura in his book *Estetika architektury* in 1945.
13 Compare in particular Berlage's Algemeen Nederlandschen Diamantbewerksbond in Amsterdam from 1899. – Jan Gratama, *Dr. H. P. Berlage Bouwmeester*. Rotterdam 1925, plate 56.
14 Otakar Novotný, *Jan Kotěra a jeho doba*. SNKLHU, Praha 1958, p. 40.
15 *Josef Hoffmann zum sechzigsten Geburstage 15. Dezember 1930*. Wien 1931, no page-numbering.

for Kotěra. It is a turn which further complicates the image of the architect's work after 1906.[16] The expressive, or even Expressionist impact of this part of the pavilion is achieved mainly by a certain tension between the obtuse angle of the gable and the acute angle of the window, shaped as a tiered pyramid. The left-side entrance, with its narrow windows inside the lisene belts, brings to mind Frank Lloyd Wright's Willits house (1902). However, similar forms occur in the works of other European architects. The unusual, segmented groundplan of the pavilion was inspired by Classical architecture, or the Baroque Classicism of Gianlorenzo Bernini.[17] After an early drawing of a *Temple to Eros and Psyche* (1898), similar forms appeared in the architect's sketches for monuments in 1907–08, which are today part of the Collection of Prints and Drawings at the National Gallery in Prague. Two employees of Kotěra's studio, Pavel Janák and Josef Gočár, certainly had a strong impact on the final appearance of this pavilion.

Kotěra's early works around 1898–1902 could be understood as a gathering of elements from progressive European architecture – by Wagner, Olbrich, Horta, Townsend and Mackintosh. In Kotěra's hands, these elements were slowly transformed into a very individual style which culminated in National House in Prostějov in 1905–07. Kotěra's work of 1906–08 underwent an analogous development. Clear citations of Berlage or Hoffmann receded in 1908, and gave way to Kotěra's own special idiom.

---

16 See: Rostislav Švácha, "Expresionismus v české architektuře", in: Alena Pomajzlová (ed.), *Expresionismus a české umění, 1905–1927*. Národní galerie, Praha 1994, pp. 205–226.

17 Jan Kotěra's letters from Italy in 1898 and fragments of Kotěra's texts about architectural composition published in 1945 by František Lydie Gahura (see note 12), include an interpretation of Bernini's piazza in front of St Peter's church in the Vatican.

< **139**
City Museum in Hradec Králové, north wing façade – detail, 1909–1913
> **140**
Laichter's house in Prague-Vinohrady, façade – detail, 1908–1909

Kratochvíl's villa in Černošice (1908–09) probably comes closest to the contemporary Viennese works. Its Viennese quality rests above all on the basic theme, a type of small Neo-Classicist or Biedermeier rural castle with a rather impressive roof whose layout is reminiscent of Josef Hoffmann's Hochstätter house. Similar to Kotěra's older villas, including Marek's villa, its interior develops around a large staircase-hall linked to a mezzanine terrace. The area in which Kotěra departed from the Viennese reductionism of the period lies in the exceptional rawness of the brick facing on all the façades. In the hands of Viennese architects, such as Leopold Bauer and his Hecht's villa in Brno-Pisárky (1909–11), this brick facing had a decorative role. In Kotěra's interpretation, this decorativeness is entirely missing.

Kotěra's own villa in Hradešínská street in Prague-Vinohrady represents an even more obvious shift from decorativeness towards *"truth"* – the most important theme of Kotěra's architecture. Yet the architect did not break all links with Josef Hoffmann's Hochstätter house. In comparison to it, however, the forms of Kotěra's villa seem simpler and more geometrical, more so because of a very low roof supported by a rounded gable. The façades are more telling of the inner spatial divisions, and the garden side displays an almost Loos-like irregular distribution of window openings. All this is heightened by the material quality of the coarse plaster, brick facing and window lintels made of concrete. Inside, surprisingly, was a large living room with a glass ceiling – a "type" of space whose attractive quality Kotěra admired in his 1898 letters from Italy.[18] He later utilised this particular element in the pavilion for the World Exhibition in St Louis (1904), in the foyer of National House in Prostějov (1905–07), and in the Arco coffee-house in Prague (1907).

Kotěra's inclination towards Berlage's view that construction lay at the heart of architectural creation did not yet make Kotěra a constructional innovator. He was actually a rather conservative architect in matters of construction, since he began to use reinforced ceilings only sometime after 1908. However, his projects for the Koruna insurance company building (1911) and the lower part of the Mozarteum (1911–13) were designed with a reinforced skeleton in mind.[19] The notion that the role of the architect consists in the creation and construction of space did not imply either that the actual physical construction of Kotěra's buildings would be really reflected in their tectonic "looks". It seems that Kotěra was more interested in creating buildings whose external appearance would correspond with the functional organisation of their interior,[20] while at the same time expressing basic tectonic principles, i.e. that weight should be perpendicular to its support. In this respect, he

---

18   Cf.: Josef Šusta (ed.), "Z italských dopisů Jana Kotěry". *Umění* IV, 1931, pp. 113–128, 269–275, 313–316, 356–359, especially pp. 274, 316. – For Kotěra's spatial "typology", see: Rostislav Švácha, *Od moderny k funkcionalismu*. Praha 1985. – Rostislav Švácha, *The Architecture of New Prague*. MIT Press, Cambridge, Mass. 1995. – Rostislav Švácha, "Jan Kotěra et ses élèves", in: *Prague Art Nouveau*. Snoeck-Ducaju & Zoon, Bruxelles 1998, pp. 173–176.

19   Bohuslav Fuchs is the only author who engaged in more detail in the constructive aspect of Kotěra's buildings, *In margine* (see note 9), no page-numbering, chapter: "Technika Kotěrových staveb".

20   See the interpretation of Ákos Moravánszky, *Competing Visions. Aesthetic Invention and Social Imagination in Central European Architecture*. MIT Press, Cambridge, Mass. 1998, pp. 200–206.

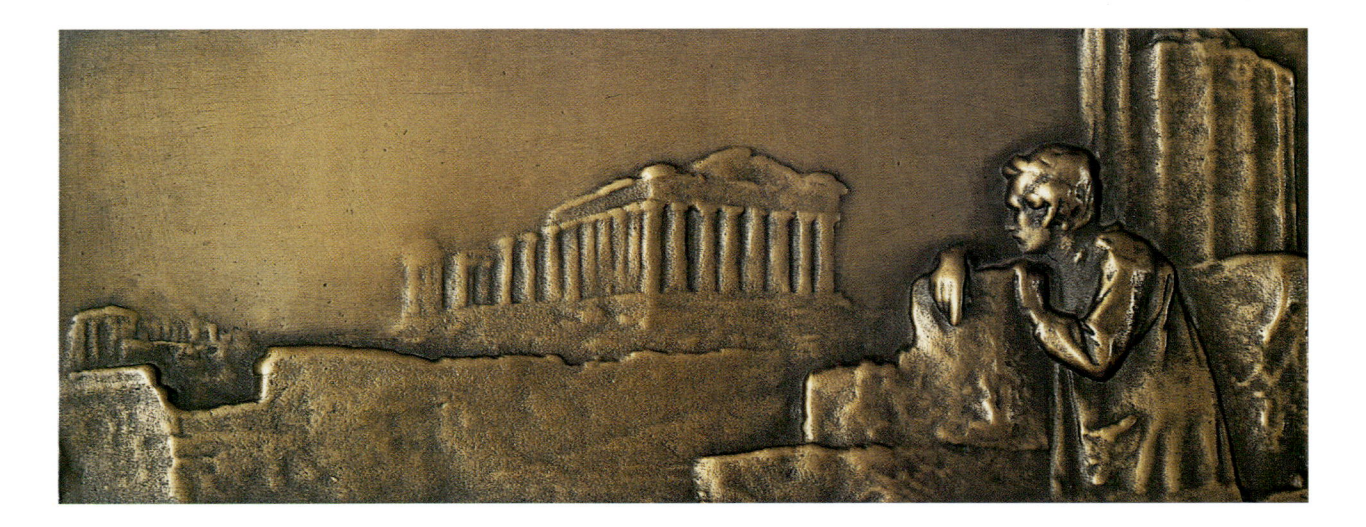

was perhaps closer to Semper and other 19th century rationalists than to Berlage, whose tectonics are much more literal in comparison with Kotěra's. The aspect in which Kotěra's work at a certain moment went beyond both his predecessors and contemporaries, was that of *"economy"* – to use Berlage's term. This economy lies in the degree of abstraction and asceticism in the tectonic images of Kotěra's interiors and façades. Kotěra's Laichter house (1908–09) in Chopinova street in Prague-Vinohrady, was a move away from traditional tectonics to a consistently geometric relief of exposed bricks, coarse plaster and glass.

This project was commissioned by Jan Laichter, a close friend of the philosopher Tomáš Garrigue Masaryk and the publisher of Masaryk's most important writings.[21] There could hardly have been an architecture more appropriate to Masaryk's insistence on self-control and moral values as the only elements that can bring together different classes of society, than Kotěra's ascetic style.[22] Kotěra came into contact with Masaryk's inner circle on many occasions. In 1901, in Hostišov near Tábor, he built a villa for Jan Herben, Editor-in-Chief of *Čas* (Time), the daily affiliated to Masaryk's Progressive party. In 1910, speaking in the Viennese Parliament, Masaryk personally ensured support for Kotěra's School of Architecture at the Academy of Fine Arts in Prague,[23] and in 1911 he resided on Mickiewicz street in Hradčany, in Groh house, designed by Kotěra. In 1920, he entrusted Kotěra with the initial project for his presidential quarters at Prague Castle. However, Laichter's house remains Kotěra's most intimate link with Masaryk's intellectual world. From a typological point of view, Laichter's house is a hybrid. The owner's publishing house was located on the ground floor, linked with his apartment on the first floor via a hall with a staircase. The next two floors were set aside as rented apartments. Kotěra succeeded in giving the whole project an austere form which Laichter's (and Masaryk's) journal *Naše doba* (Our Era) later described as *"unquestionably beautiful"*.[24]

The severe style of Kotěra's buildings from 1908–09 led to the monumentality reflected in his design for the City Museum in Hradec Králové (1909–13).[25]

The project was commissioned by the Museum's Board of Trustees, headed by František Ulrich, the Mayor of Hradec Králové.[26] A great patron of modern Czech architecture, he employed Kotěra at the beginning of the 20th century to design the Regional Authorities building and the first large coffee-house in Hradec Králové. In the following

---

21 Jan Laichter, "Jak se prof. T. G. Masaryk stal redaktorem Naší doby". *Naše doba* XXXII, 1924–25, pp. 348–355.
22 Cf.: Rostislav Švácha, "Czech Architecture in Plečnik's Time and the Ideal of Democracy", in: *Josip Plečnik. An Architect of Prague Castle*. Prague 1997, pp. 27–39.
23 Jan Kotěra, "Redakci Socialistických listů!", *Socialistické listy* II, no. 3, 19 January, 1919, p. 6.
24 Ž (=František Žákavec), "Architekt Jan Kotěra zemřel", in: *Naše doba* XXX, 1923, pp. 447–448.
25 Rostislav Švácha, "Poznámky ke Kotěrovu muzeu". *Umění* XXXIV, 1986, pp. 171–179.
26 Ludvík Domečka, *Třicet let veřejné činnosti JUDr. F. Ulricha*. Hradec Králové 1925.

< 141
Stanislav Sucharda, *Architect* – plaque for Jan Kotěra, from the cycle for the decoration of Peterka's house in Prague, c. 1899
> 142
Bedřich Feuerstein-Alois Wachsman, cover for *The Temple of Work*, a book by Jindřich Fleischner, 1916
>> 143
Antonín Slavíček, *Ironworks in Kladno II*, 1908

years, Ulrich remained Kotěra's and Gočár's most important client.

Kotěra began to work on the museum project in 1905 or 1906. He conceived it as structures that were freely evolving in the space available, in harmony with their functions. This approach ignored Wagner's rule that a public edifice should have a symmetrical groundplan. Evidently, at that time the museum, from the outside, would not have differed much from National House in Prostějov, but its groundplan would have been similar to the "small water mills" incorporated into the groundplans of Frank Lloyd Wright's family houses. While the work of the American Modernist became generally known in Europe only in 1910, Kotěra would certainly have been familiar with it ten years earlier.[27] Vladimír Šlapeta stressed the fact that Kotěra had introduced Wright's work to Europe.[28] Karel Herain, the architectural historian, wrote about the museum's first completed variant in 1907, noting that it had not yet extricated itself from the *"decorative inclinations"* fragmenting the whole into a *"confusion of decorative details"*.[29]

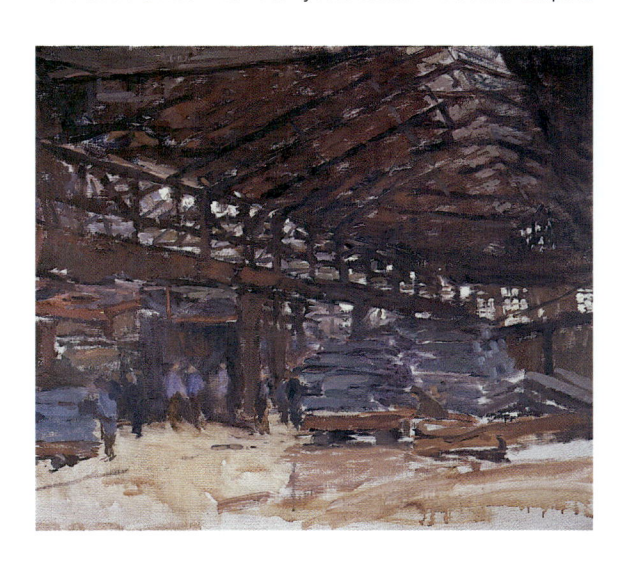

However, the Board of Trustees felt that they could not finance such a demanding and extravagant project. They negotiated with Kotěra for several months to reduce the scale of his project. *"I will have to reduce the ornamentation of the façade"*, stated Kotěra, writing to the Board in 1908 of his new intentions. *"There is not much I can do to change the mass and form, but we could use inexpensive materials. In that sense, I am restricting the use of stone to a minimum*

---

[27] "Architektura v Americe". *Volné směry* IV, 1900, pp. 177–180.

[28] Vladimír Šlapeta, Czech Inter-War Architecture from the Point of View of International Relations. Unpublished thesis for the School of Architecture, Czech Technical College, Prague 1979. – Vladimír Šlapeta, "Česká meziválečná architektura z hlediska mezinárodních vztachů". in: *Umění* XXXIX, 1981, p. 309. – Vladimír Šlapeta, in: Jiří Kotalík (ed.), *Tschechische Kunst 1878–1914*. Darmstadt 1984, p. 146. – Vladimír Šlapeta, "Frank Lloyd Wright a česká architektura", *Frank Lloyd Wright a česká architektura*. Obecní dům, Praha 2001, pp. 38–55.

[29] Karel Herain, "Ulrichův Hradec Králové", in: *Umění* III, 1930, p. 331.

THE CULMINANT YEARS, 1906-1912

< 144
City Museum in Hradec Králové, entrance, 1909–1913
> 145
City Museum in Hradec Králové, model, 1909–1913

and working on the façade, using concrete for the building's plinth. [...] I would use brick for the ground floor and the main tectonic division of other parts of the building. All the remaining surfaces would then be faced only with coarse plaster."[30] In October 1908, Kotěra's studio completed a new version of the project – already very close to the ascetic character of Laichter's house – under the supervision of Josef Gočár.[31] However, the work began only in spring 1909, using a design in which Gočár did not participate. The museum halls and the reading room were opened to the public in October 1913, *"without much ceremony"*, and *"with really simple means"*.[32]

The Enlightenment bestowed upon the museum the role of a sanctuary, a temple of a modern secularised society.[33] The dignity and grandeur required of the temple's appearance forced 19th century architects to use reliable, effective metaphors of monumentality. They adorned museum buildings with noble domes, they used sculptures, colonnades and porticoes to decorate their façades and interiors.[34] It was all intended to signify a "temple of science" – a highly symptomatic notion of the 19th century. It was also meant to reflect the true temple-like status of the museum in the period's strictly hierarchical architectural set of values. However, in the early 20th century, concern was growing that the splendour and monumentality of museum buildings stood in the way of their educational and scientific functions. One cannot disregard the fact that *"because of the splendour and the sheen of their surroundings"*, the museum collections *"cannot attain their full effect"*, as archaeologist Hynek

---

30   Letter from Jan Kotěra to the Museum's Board of Trustees from 11 June 1908. It is now kept in the archive of the Museum of East Bohemia in Hradec Králové.
31   See: (***), "Pieta k autorovu dílu". *Naše doba* XXXII, 1924–1925, pp. 246–248. – (***), "Kotěrovo dílo". *Naše doba* XXXII, 1924–1925, pp. 436–438.
32   "Muzejní čítárna". *Ratibor* XXX, no. 40, 4 October 1913, p. 4. – Karel Wellner, "K Hudečkově výstavě". *Ratibor* XXX, no. 43, 25 October 1913, pp. 3, 5. – The most detailed information about Kotěra's work on the museum was presented in the article "Stavba musea", in: *Orlické proudy* III, no. 43, 10 September 1910, pp. 3–5.
33   Milena Sršňová – Rostislav Švácha, "Muzea a galerie". *Stavba* VI, 1999, no. 2, pp. 30–39.
34   Rostislav Švácha, "Teigova kritika důstojnosti". *Architektura* XLIX, 1990, nos. 5–6, pp. 12–13.

152 THE CULMINANT YEARS, 1906-1912

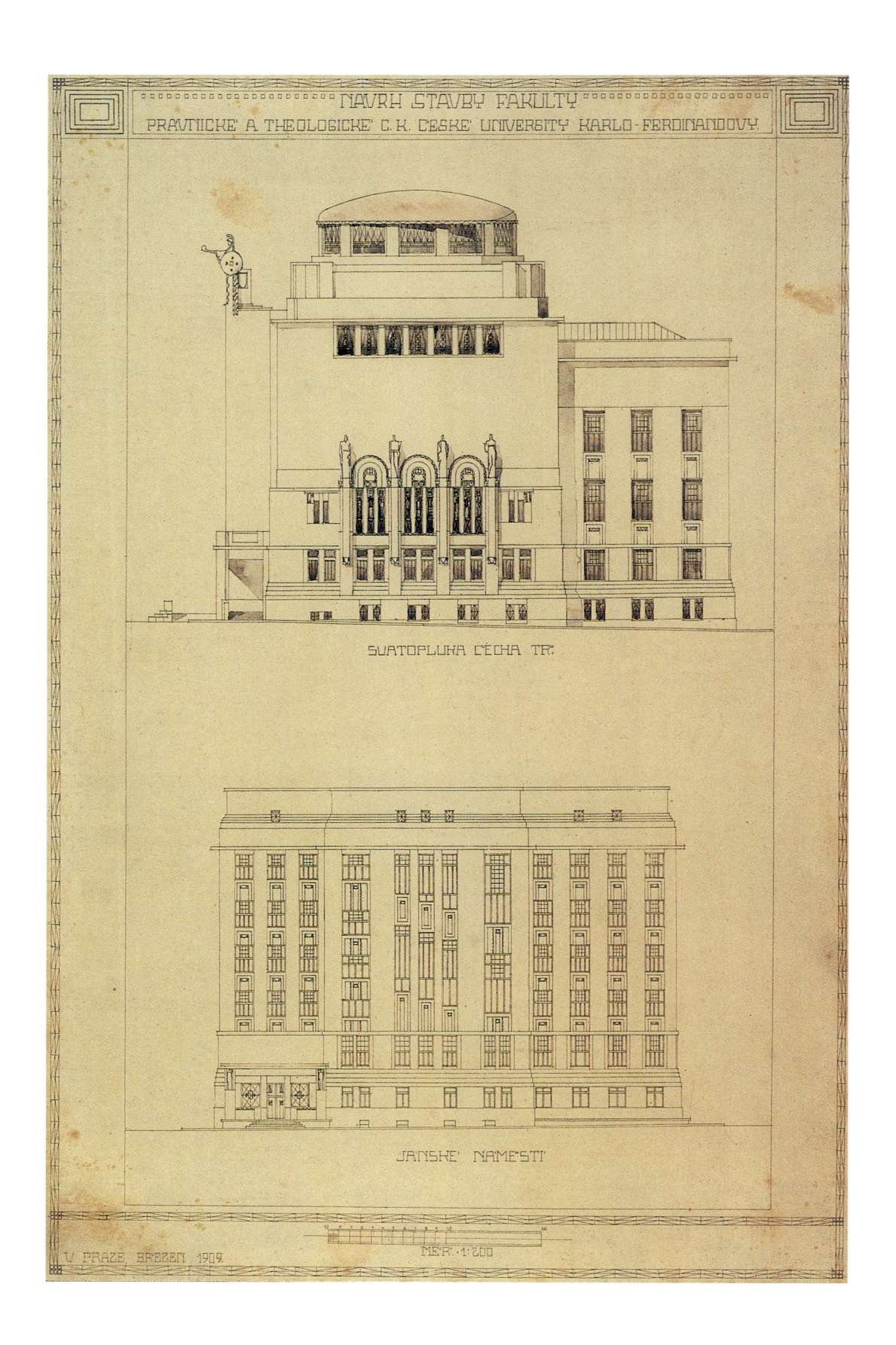

< 146
Law and Theology Faculty building, Czech University of Charles-Ferdinand in Prague, second project, façade plans, 1909

Vysoký wrote in 1901.[35] This is how the museum prepared the ground for an architectural interpretation that was both civil and modern in character. Kotěra did not fully depart from the hierarchies of 19th century architecture, in which the temple embodied the highest conceivable value. On the plaque *Architect*, which sculptor Stanislav Sucharda[36] created for Kotěra, this theme is represented by a Greek temple. *"Isn't every building a temple?"* Kotěra is said to have asked in a debate with the critic František Xaver Šalda.[37] Kotěra's design for the City Museum in Hradec Králové contains a similar vision of the museum as a sanctuary of science. The groundplan, Wrightean as it is, lacks neither transept nor presbytery, while the dome looms above the entrance, guarded by two of Sucharda's goddesses. The outer frame of the entrance below the dome is strikingly similar to that of the Romanesque receding portal, without the arch.[38]

However, the idiom with which Kotěra presents this more or less traditional idea of a temple of science in Hradec Králové, is truly revolutionary. We are not speaking here only of the moral austerity of the museum, with its references to Laichter's house or even Berlage, but of the fundamental industrial tone of the whole concept. The halls on the upper floors are illuminated by factory clerestories, its dome more reminiscent of a lighthouse or water reservoir, while the brick façades oscillate between Berlage and popular factory buildings of the period. It seems as if the architect wanted to emphasise the fact that this Hradec temple of science was essentially a work place. He designed it – according to a later text by Otakar Novotný – as a *"work place and not a place for garish representation"*.[39] Kotěra created, in a single building, the synthesis of temple and factory – bringing together two opposed metaphors in the period's hierarchy of architectural values.

In 1908–09, Kotěra transformed the idea of a temple of science by infusing it with an industrial character. Providing a certain parallel, the architect's friend from the Mánes Association, Impressionist painter Antonín Slavíček, treated the same subject. He was painting that masterpiece of Gothic architecture, St Vitus' Cathedral at Prague Castle. However, in the course of this work, he "discovered" the ironworks in Kladno, near Prague, and this ostensibly "lower" subject matter, *"a rather terrible thing"*, increasingly drew his attention. *"I relinquished glorious Gothic art and instead I travel to the Kladno ironworks [...] these ironworks are truly spectacular"*, Slavíček admitted in a letter to a friend.[40]

The works of both Kotěra and Slavíček already show recognition of the beauty of the themes and reality which surrounded them but had not been considered worthy by the previous era. In his famous essay "The New Beauty: Its Genesis and Character" (1903),[41] the main spokesman of Slavíček's and Kotěra's generation, František Xaver Šalda, appealed to the artist to observe the world with unprejudiced eyes. Kotěra's and Slavíček's approach at the end of the first decade mirrors the period transition of architectural values, an exchange of "high" for "low". According to literary historian Růžena Grebeníčková, the process was set in motion before 1900 by the decadent movement,[42] and had far-reaching

---

35 Vý (=Hynek Vysoký), "Muzeum". *Ottův slovník naučný* XVII, Praha 1901, pp. 890–892.
36 The *Architect* plaque remains in private ownership in Prague.
37 František Xaver Šalda, "Příklad". *Tvorba* 1926, pp. 137–138.
38 I am grateful to my colleague Rudolf Chadraba for this insight. – I tried to use Chadraba's iconological theory of "imitative antithesis" which, in my opinion, could serve to clarify the striking analogies between the museum in Hradec Králové and the Municipal House of the City of Prague by architects Balšánek and Polívka (1905–11), in the introductory article "Poznámky ke Kotěrovu muzeu" (see note 25) and more recently in the article "Politika Obecního domu". *Architekt* XLIII, 1997, nos. 14–15, pp. 72–74.
39 Otakar Novotný, *Jan Kotěra a jeho doba* (see note 14), p. 36.
40 Cf.: Karel Srp, "Indexy lomu", in: Petr Wittlich (ed.), *Důvěrný prostor, nová dálka*. Obecní dům, Praha 1997, pp. 169–199.
41 František Xaver Šalda, "Nová krása: její geneze a charakter". *Volné směry* VII, 1903, pp. 169–181.
42 Růžena Grebeníčková, *Tělo a tělesnost v novověkém myšlení*. Prostor, Praha 1997, pp. 84, 91.

consequences in avant-garde art.[43] The way in which the two artists ascribe the same importance to the sacred and the work space, the temple and the factory, anticipated the development towards technical civilism and industrial art beginning around 1910, the provocative gestures of Italian Futurists, or the beauty of machines, telegraph wires, factories and power stations which Czech poet Stanislav Kostka Neumann praised in his *New Songs* (1911–14).

The powerful changes in modern European society provided the backdrop for this trend towards industrial subjects. The most important change was the rise of the factory workers, and their successful political parties. The period ushered in the view that manual work represented a true source of values, and there was even something sacred about it – *"the prayer of the hands"*, in the words of poet Antonín Sova.[44] In his books *The Social Question* (1898) and *Ideals of Humanity* (1901), Tomáš Garrigue Masaryk proposed a highly original approach to social issues. It was a process which, to different degrees, engaged many of the pioneers of Modernism in art and architecture, including Hendrik Petrus Berlage, who was a staunch socialist, deeply convinced the ideals of social and economic equality.[45] In this same period, Viennese and Darmstadt Modernists began creating an image of the *"house of work"*, a work-dwelling for artists and craftsmen set in the middle of a park or the centre of a whole new city, towering *"like a temple"*,[46] a temple in which *"work would represent a divine service"*.[47] This was the dream of Kotěra's friend from his Viennese period, Josef Maria Olbrich. We can trace the changes and diverse forms this idea took, from Olbrich's Darmstadt House of the Grand Duke (1901), and Kotěra's City Museum in Hradec Králové (1909–13) or Behrens' AEG turbine hall in Berlin (1909),[48] to the 1916 book *The Temple of Work* by the Czech philosopher and Social Democrat Jindřich Fleischner, and even the vision of a *"cathedral of Socialism"*, which formed the base for Walter Gropius' programme for the Weimar Bauhaus in 1919.

Kotěra's political views were not as left-oriented as Berlage's. Nevertheless, he did feel a need to react to the *social question*. In a similar manner, the spatial design and the accompanying artistic features of National House in Prostějov (1905–07) most likely reflected another great theme of Kotěra's times, the call for the equality of the sexes.[49] In his early text "On New Art" (1900), Kotěra already considered the *"chair for our modern worker"*[50] as an important subject for architecture. Furthermore, in a letter to his Viennese friend Richard Gombrich, he wrote about his project for the workers' housing colony for railway employees in Louny from 1909. This project, which was the beginning of a whole series of Kotěra's designs for working-class settlements, he described as his *"dearest thought"*.[51] Nevertheless, it was Kotěra's "temple of work" in Hradec Králové, with its strict industrial forms, that remained the architect's strongest comment on the social environment of his era.

The austere style of the museum in Hradec Králové was reflected in several of Kotěra's projects for monumental buildings from 1909–12. The first was his design for the university buildings of the Law and Theology Faculty in Prague. This was a project in which Kotěra was engaged from 1907 until the end of his life. It caused him all kinds of problems and Kotěra was never in a position to control its final outcome. Its first design in 1907 had a more sobre, more tectonic character than National House in Prostějov, designed a short time before. The 1909 variation was a twin of the City Museum in Hradec Králové, with a single difference – the Faculty dome had an oval groundplan, and its sturdy base was moved to the outside corners of the building.

In the project for the Peppina Villa hotel in Opatija, Croatia, designed in 1910, the dome was transformed into a one-storey

---

43 Cf.: Rostislav Švácha, "Josef Chochol: pokus o intimnější portrét". *Umění* XLII, 1994, pp. 21–49. – Rostislav Švácha, "Architektura dvacátých let v Čechách", in: *Dějiny českého výtvarného umění* IV, II. Academia, Praha 1998, pp. 10–35.

44 For the politics of working-class parties in Bohemia, cf.: Otto Urban, *Česká společnost 1848–1918*. Svoboda, Praha 1981.

45 Hendrik Petrus Berlage, "Základy a vývoj moderní architektury". See note 10.

46 Josef Maria Olbrich, in: Hermann Bahr (ed.), *Ein Dokument Deutscher Kunst*. Leipzig 1901, p. 6. – Cf.: the unpublished thesis by Blanka Rambousková, *Umělecká kolonie v Darmstadtu*. FF UP Olomouc, 2000.

47 Josef Maria Olbrich, "Unsere nächste Arbeit". *Deutsche Kunst und Dekoration* VI, 1900, pp. 366–369.

48 Cf.: Francesco Dal Co, *Figures of Architecture and Thought. German Architectural Culture 1880–1920*. Rizzoli, New York 1990, pp. 235–237.

> **147**
> Project for the Peppina Villa hotel in Opatija, Croatia, 1910

49 Edith Jeřábková, "K ideovým aspektům Národního domu v Prostějově". *Umění* XLIV, 1996, pp. 411–424.
50 Jan Kotěra, "O novém umění" (see note 6).
51 "Z dopisů Jana Kotěry svému příteli R. G. ve Vídni". *Stavitel* V, 1924, pp. 61–65. – Rostislav Švácha, "The Lemberger-Gombrich Villa in Vienna by Jan Kotěra". *Umění* XLII, 1994, pp. 388–392.

coffee-house pavilion, placed adjacent to the square block of the hotel building. The art historian Václav Vilém Štech perhaps best expressed the problematic side of Kotěra's liberal treatment of the dome. He noted that this motif is *"always introduced externally – it does not grow"*.[52] The hotel's façade, composed entirely of loggias in front of the hotel rooms, acquired a skeletal, almost pre-Constructivist expression. The sides were crowned by two gloriettes with flagpoles above its prominent cornice. They lent Peppina Villa an appearance which closely resembles Adolf Loos' Villa Karma at Lake Leman (1904).

In 1911, after designing the "temple of knowledge" – the university buildings on the monumental bank of the Vltava – and the hotel on the Adriatic coast, Kotěra entered a competition to design the the Koruna (Crown) insurance company building, to be erected at the busiest location in Prague, at the bottom of Wenceslas Square. Kotěra's concept for the building was to express the hubbub of the modern metropolis. This was a new quality which he admired and described in his letters from Rome in 1898.[53] To achieve the desired effect, Kotěra had to enter again into the world of early Expressionism and Constructivism. The dynamic tiered and rounded forms of Kotěra's Koruna project had a sense of the streamlined architecture of Erich Mendelsohn, created after the First World War. In the interior of the building, the two-storey shopping "ship", with a glass hull and a rounded stern and bow, confidently "sailed" into the lofty space of both the passageway and hall. This metaphor was the most striking element of Kotěra's project – unfortunately never realised.

The façades of the Urban Hotel in Hradec Králové (1911) and Slavia Bank in Sarajevo, Bosnia (1911), receded further into the building with each floor. This feature reinforced the plasticity of their construction, resting either on supporting pillars or on a system of lisenes. Kotěra used the same

---

52 Cf.: Štech's review of Kotěra's posthumous exhibition from 1926, kept in the Archives of the National Gallery in Prague, AA 2777. – A shorter version of Štech's text was published in *České slovo* on 16 April 1933.

53 Josef Šusta (ed.), "Z italských dopisů" (see note 18), pp. 120, 126, 272.

< 148
Competition entry for the multi-purpose building for the *Koruna* insurance company in Prague, model, 1911

idea in his most important building from the beginning of the second decade, the department store designed for the music publisher Mojmír Urbánek on Jungmannova street in Prague. Kotěra designed the project for Urbánek's House, known as the Mozarteum, in 1911–12. It was opened in October 1913, together with a concert hall in its rear wing, which backed onto Františkánská zahrada (Franciscan gardens). Everything which the daily press wrote about the concert hall – *"with its tasteful simplicity, everything in it lends itself to the concentration of minds* [...] *however, its treatment is perhaps too ascetic"*[54] – could have been said about the Mozarteum's entire architecture.

Kotěra enclosed the building which, at the time of its completion, stood much higher than the surrounding houses, in a mighty reinforced concrete frame. He used large windows, on both ground and first floors, to open its interior onto the street. Finally, he crowned the entire building with a metal-plated triangular gable. The brick façade of the second to fifth floors gradually retreated into the background. The effect was intensified by clusters of concrete lisenes which – together with the window-sill moulding – created the tectonic spine of the Mozarteum's façade. The skeletal construction of the ground and first floors introduced a whole new element into Kotěra's architecture, what was later coined as a "showcase type" – a space that opened up the whole side of the building onto the street. The impression of an almost fluid space, freely passing from one room to the next, was further enhanced by the wide openings which linked the rooms of Urbánek's own flat on the second floor. The triangular forms, echoed in the brick patterns of the window sills, the metal-plated gable and the joints of the lisene frames, could be interpreted as a homage to the system of proportions and composition suggested by Berlage in his book *Grundlagen und Entwicklung der Architektur* in 1908.

The younger generation of Prague architects – Janák, Gočár, Chochol and Hofman – accepted the idea of architectural "voluntarism" after 1910. According to this idea, what was decisive for the architectural form was the creative force of the imagination; the *"spirit"* of the architect-artist, and not the *"materiality"* of physical laws. In 1910 Pavel Janák, Kotěra's former colleague and the main spokesman of this group, declared Wagner's work, and with it also Kotěra's, too materialistic, too subordinate to tectonic rules, too servile to architectural function and social altruism.[55] A year later, Janák worked his way through to his first Cubist experiments. Not long after, the architects from the Amsterdam school, led by Michel de Klerk, reproached Berlage with the same arguments, while in Germany, the Expressionist ideas of Hans Poelzig and Bruno Taut began to find their established platform.

During this period, the renewal of Classicism represented the "third way" of European architecture. It differed from the Cubist-Expressionist stream, as well as the Berlagean-Wagnerian insistence on tectonics and construction. This renewal constituted a wide, almost pan-European movement. In Berlin, it was related to the austere legacy of Schinkel, in Vienna mainly to the Biedermeier idyll. Josef Hoffmann became the main Viennese architect during this period. His

[54] K., "Otevření Mozartea". *Právo lidu* XXII, no. 272, 4 October 1913, p. 9.

[55] Pavel Janák, "Od moderní architektury – k architektuře". *Styl* II, 1909–10, Kronika, pp. 105–109.

most important works were his Skywa-Primavesi villa and the Austrian pavilion at the 1914 German Werkbund Exhibition in Cologne.

Jan Kotěra's work had Neo-Classicist elements from its beginnings, even in the architect's most ascetic, most rational buildings created after 1908 – Laichter's house, the City Museum in Hradec Králové and the Mozarteum. This element of Kotěra's architecture began to intensify sometime after 1908, becoming a line developing in parallel with the austere style of the Museum in Hradec Králové or the Mozarteum. It included works such as the Vojáček monument in Prostějov (1910), the Prague bridge kiosks in Hradec Králové (1910–11), Charvát's villa in Vysoké Mýto (1911), the adaptations for Baťa's villa in Zlín (1911) and the building of the General Pension Institute on Rašínovo embankment in Prague, created somewhat later (1912–14). The Neo-Classicist tendency in these works pervades Kotěra's tectonics to such an extent that we cannot be certain if, in their character, they are more related to Laichter's house, the City Museum in Hradec Králové and the Mozarteum, or to the emerging Neo-Classicist series. The sporadic use of anthropomorphous Cubist detail increased the complexity of this synthesis in Kotěra's oeuvre from the second decade onwards.

< **149**
Slavia Bank in Sarajevo, Bosnia and Herzegovina, sketch, 1911
> **150**
Urbánek's house – Mozarteum in Prague, 1911–1913

Despite this complexity, one thing is certain. In these works, Kotěra moved away from the industrial vernacular of his masterpieces dating from his culminant years – 1906–12. He returned to the traditional hierarchy of architectural values, in which the factory finds itself somewhere low down, with the palaces and temples towering high above.

The Vršovice Waterworks, 1906–1907

160 THE CULMINANT YEARS, 1906–1912

< **151**
Vršovice waterworks in Prague-Michle, perspective view, 1907
> **152**
Vršovice waterworks in Prague-Michle, 1906–1907

The Vršovice waterworks complex marked a turning point in the work of Jan Kotěra. Contrary to his softly modelled buildings from the period between 1899 and 1905, it was characterised by austere, tectonic forms, drawing their inspiration from the work of Hendrik Petrus Berlage. Kotěra saw Berlage's architecture for the first time in 1905 when he travelled to Holland with his students from the School of Applied Arts.

The Prague suburb of Vršovice, which had acquired the status of a town in 1902, commissioned the new waterworks. The district was home to rather luxurious apartments, usually equipped with flushing toilets and bathrooms, which Kotěra's new building was to supply with water. The water for its reservoirs was drained from the Vltava, at Braník. From the Braník pumping station, designed by Kotěra in the same year (1906), a pipeline led to a small hill opposite Vršovice, to the grounds situated on what is today Baarova street 1121 in Prague-Michle. The plans included two service buildings for the waterworks complex, elaborate entrance portals for the ground-level water reservoir and, most importantly, the main water tower, whose chalice-like contours have remained a defining landmark of the area to this day.

Kotěra produced a masterly sketch of his waterworks complex in Michle in watercolour. Its soft, colourful forms lent the composition of the Michle complex a unified expression, while still conveying the architect's former inclination towards Impressionism, also reflected in the subtle decoration of the water tower drum. The emphasis on the forms which reveal both the construction and function of the individual buildings – with unplastered brickwork and concrete – already introduces the idiom of Kotěra's 1908–1912 projects, created at the height of his architectural career.

R. Š.

THE CULMINANT YEARS, 1906–1912 161

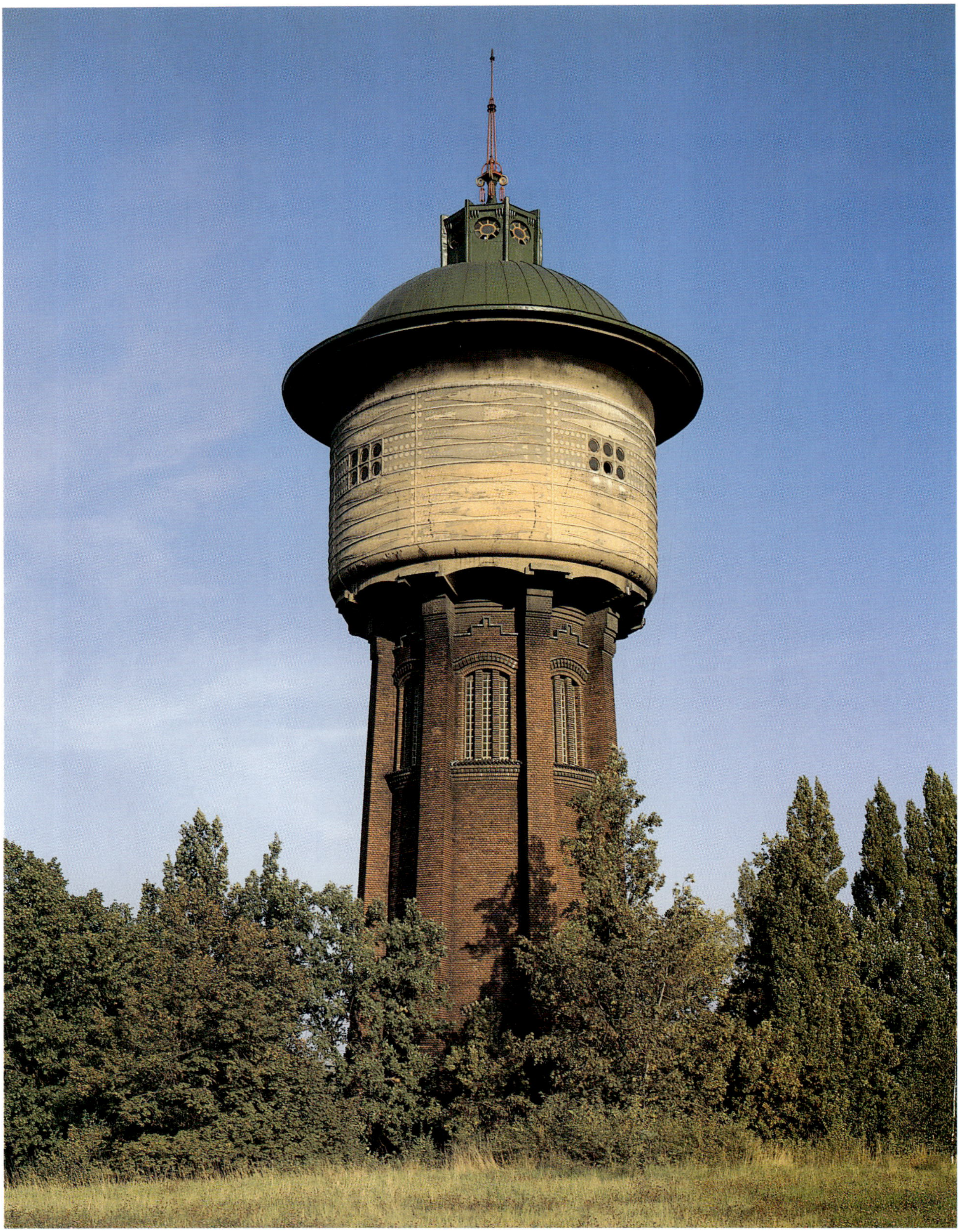

< **153**
Vršovice waterworks in Prague-Michle, 1906–1907
> **154**
Vršovice waterworks in Prague-Michle, windows – detail, 1906–1907
>> **155**
Vršovice waterworks in Prague-Michle, water-tower entrance – detail, 1906–1907

THE CULMINANT YEARS, 1906–1912 | 163

1907-1910 – The Villas Designed for Götz, Marek, Kraus and Kratochvíl

< 156
Götz's villa in Chrustenice, 1907–1908
> 157
Kraus' villa in Prague-Bubeneč, 1907

The development towards a severe pre-Constructivist style, introduced in Kotěra's works in 1908–1909, can be traced almost step by step in the four suburban or rural houses that began with Götz's villa in Chrustenice. In them, Kotěra did not abandon the principle of richly partitioned interiors, employed in his first villas. This was a tendency which often led him to create elaborate asymmetrical groundplans. The motif of a two-storeyed staircase-hall, with a terrace on its upper floor, remained their focal point. The living quarters were enhanced by intimate corners and secluded alcoves projected from the central hall through a variety of doorways. Most of the interior spaces were linked together via fine views through from one room to the next.

The 1907 villa designed for engineer Götz, a Rudná-Dušníky-Nučice district mining official, on the border between Chrustenice and Loděnice, most closely resembled Kotěra's early works influenced by the architecture of English villas. The architect gave it a rather steep roof, a half-timber gable construction and oriels resting on corbels.

The villa designed in Holoubkov near Rokycany (1907–10) for engineer Karel Marek, an Austrian Railway Ministry official (and minister for a short period), and the less renowned Kraus villa on Sibiřské náměstí 280 in Prague-Bubeneč (1907), whose façade was decorated with a relief by Stanislav Sucharda, were inspired by the contemporary work of Viennese architect Josef Hoffmann, particularly his Hochstätter house (1906). Kotěra designed Marek's villa with a small rural Biedermeier castle in mind, as witnessed by the motif of a small metal pinnacle marking the building's imaginary centre. It was most probably through Marek's influence that Kotěra later won his large-scale projects for railway-workers' housing colonies in Louny and Záběhlice near Prague.

The same rural villa, however, dressed in an austere Berlagean brick cloak, is the idea behind Kotěra's 1908–10 project for the house commissioned by Emil Kratochvíl, director of the Králův Dvůr ironworks – built on Karlštejnská street 282 and 283 on the edge of the Černošice villa district near Prague. This was the same client for whom Kotěra's friend Jože Plečnik would later design a tomb in Křivoklát prior to the outbreak of the First World War. Kotěra also designed a school (1908) and a workers' housing colony (1920) for the Králův Dvůr ironworks. After 1918, he was voted chairman of the company's Board of Directors. R. Š.

THE CULMINANT YEARS, 1906–1912

166 THE CULMINANT YEARS, 1906–1912

< **158**
Kratochvíl's villa in Černošice, 1908–1910
<< **159**
Marek's villa in Holoubkov, south façade – detail, 1907–1910
> **160**
Marek's villa in Holoubkov, staircase-hall, living quarters, 1907–1910

THE CULMINANT YEARS, 1906–1912 | 167

Jan Kotěra's Own Villa in Prague-Vinohrady, 1908–1909

< 163
Kotěra's own villa in Prague-Vinohrady, street view, 1908–1909
> 164
Kotěra's own villa in Prague-Vinohrady, living quarters, 1908–1909

The architect's own family house, built in 1908–1909 on Hradešínská street 1542, on the border between the Prague suburbs of Vinohrady and Vršovice, was not confined by the influence of English villa architecture and Viennese neo-Biedermeier, so easily traced in Götz's, Marek's and Kratochvíl's villas from 1907–1909. Besides Kotěra's family, the villa housed his entire architectural studio, and for a time also his special school of architecture founded in 1910 as part of the Prague Academy of Fine Arts. To comply with this variety of functions, the architect conceived the building as a complex system of interiors focused around his apartment's living quarters. The glass roof which covered this large living room offered ideal lighting for the suite of heavy furniture designed by Kotěra, a figural composition painted by Jan Preisler and an Impressionist landscape by Kotěra himself.

In its exterior, the building appeared as an asymmetrical composition of simple, austere geometric sections. A low pavilion roof supported by a cornice with supple, rounded corners covered its central part. The asymmetrical window openings with exposed concrete lintels were cut into the façades, whose only other decoration was the exposed brick of its lower, and the coarse plaster of its upper parts. The parterre extended into a landscaped garden, captured in Kotěra's exquisite drawings. The style of Kotěra's residence was repeated, only in a simpler, purer form, in his designs for the workers' housing colonies in Louny (1909) and Zlín (1915). The colonies became an inspiration for the pioneers of Purism in Czech architecture, as testified in the reproductions of Kotěra's own villa in the anthology *Život* (Life) II, published in 1923 by Jaromír Krejcar and Karel Teige, leaders of the Prague architectural avant-garde.   R. Š.

172 THE CULMINANT YEARS, 1906–1912

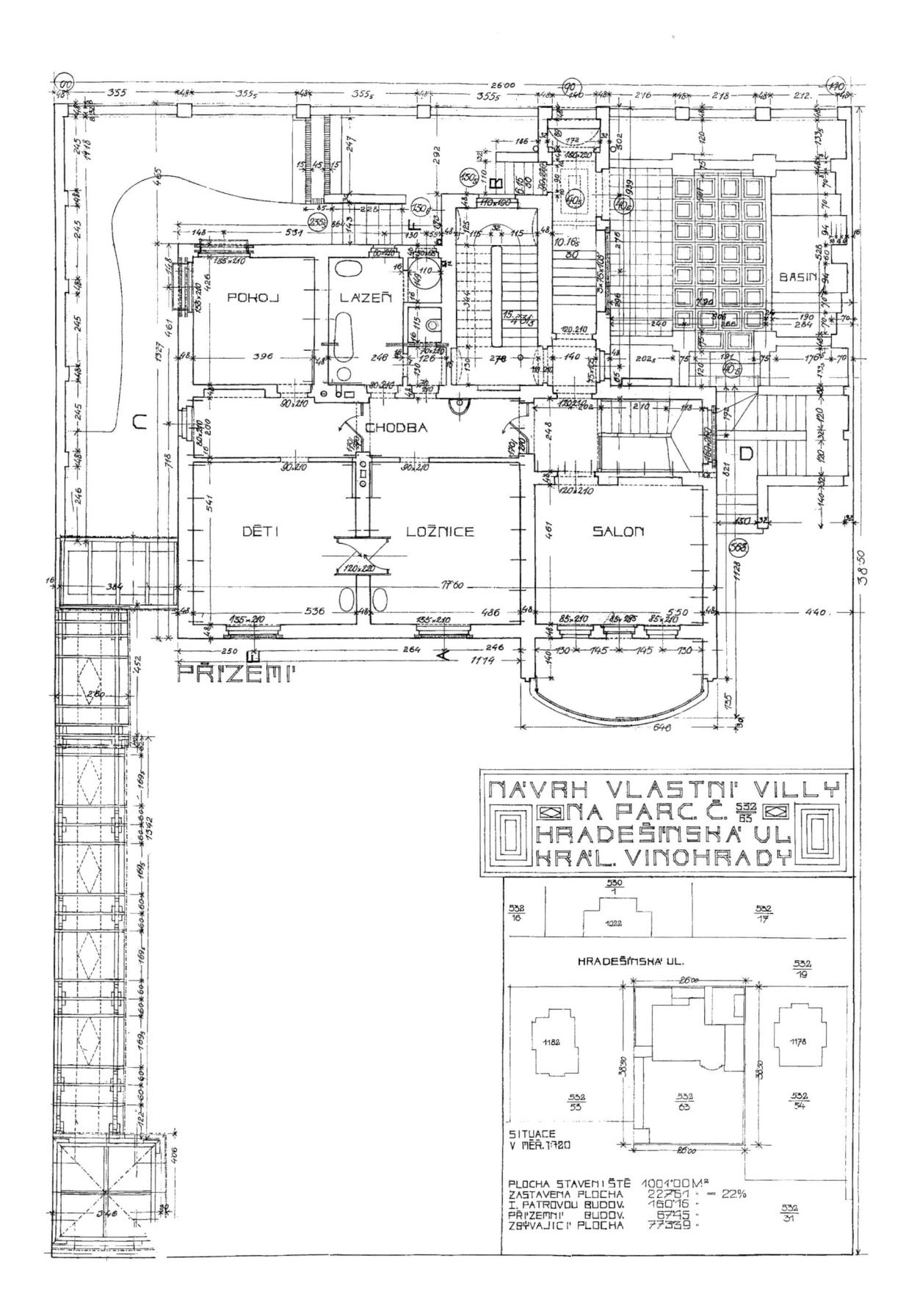

< **165**
Kotěra's own villa in Prague-Vinohrady, ground floor – groundplan, 1908–1909

> **166**
Kotěra's own villa in Prague-Vinohrady, perspective view of the villa and garden, 1909

Laichter's House in Prague-Vinohrady, 1908–1909

< 167
Laichter's house in Prague-Vinohrady, photograph with drawn figural sculptures, 1908–1909
> 168
Laichter's house in Prague-Vinohrady, façade – pastel sketch, 1908
>> 169
Laichter's house in Prague-Vinohrady, façade – model, 1908

Two buildings crown Kotěra's work created in 1908, a crucial year for the development of his architecture: his own villa in Hradešínská street in Prague, and the house for the publisher Jan Laichter in Chopinova street 1543, set within a continuous row of apartment houses opposite Rieger park. The building was the seat of Laichter's publishing house, which specialised in philosophy, sociology, arts and sciences. In the Fine and Applied Arts edition which, at the time of the building's completion, was managed by art historian Zdeněk Wirth, Laichter published books by the following authors: Otto Wagner (*Modern Architecture*, 1910), M. H. Baillie Scott (*House and Garden*, 1910) and Heinrich Wölfflin (*Classical Art*, 1912). The repertoire of Laichter's publishing house included yet another prominent author, the future president of the Czechoslovak Republic, Tomáš Garrigue Masaryk. The staircase-hall which linked the ground with the first floors was decorated with ornamental paintings by František Kysela and led into Jan Laichter's

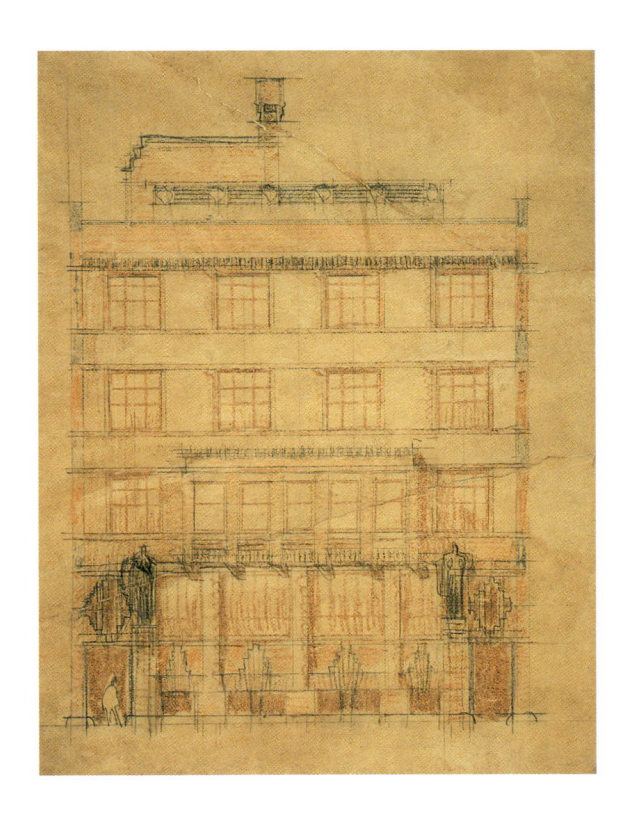

THE CULMINANT YEARS, 1906–1912 | 175

176 THE CULMINANT YEARS, 1906–1912

< **170**
Laichter's house in Prague-Vinohrady, façade – pen-and-ink drawing, 1908
> **171**
Laichter's house in Prague-Vinohrady, 1908–1909

own apartment. The next two floors were set aside as rented apartments, each accessed by a separate entrance and staircase.

Kotěra developed the shape of this building through soft crayon drawings and a clay model cast in plaster, whose form retained the same soft quality employed in the drawings. He contemplated the use of figural sculpture to decorate the façade. In the execution phase, however, the house stiffened into a strict, geometric composition whose ascetic character was well suited to the ethically and socially critical policies of Laichter's publishing house. There was no building in Central Europe at the time which was characterised by such a severe and tectonic form as Laichter's house. The works that did acquire this form after Kotěra include Béla Lajta in Budapest, as well as works by some of Wagner's students in Vienna, including Jože Plečnik with his Church of the Holy Spirit in Vienna-Ottakring, made of reinforced concrete.   R. Š.

THE CULMINANT YEARS, 1906-1912

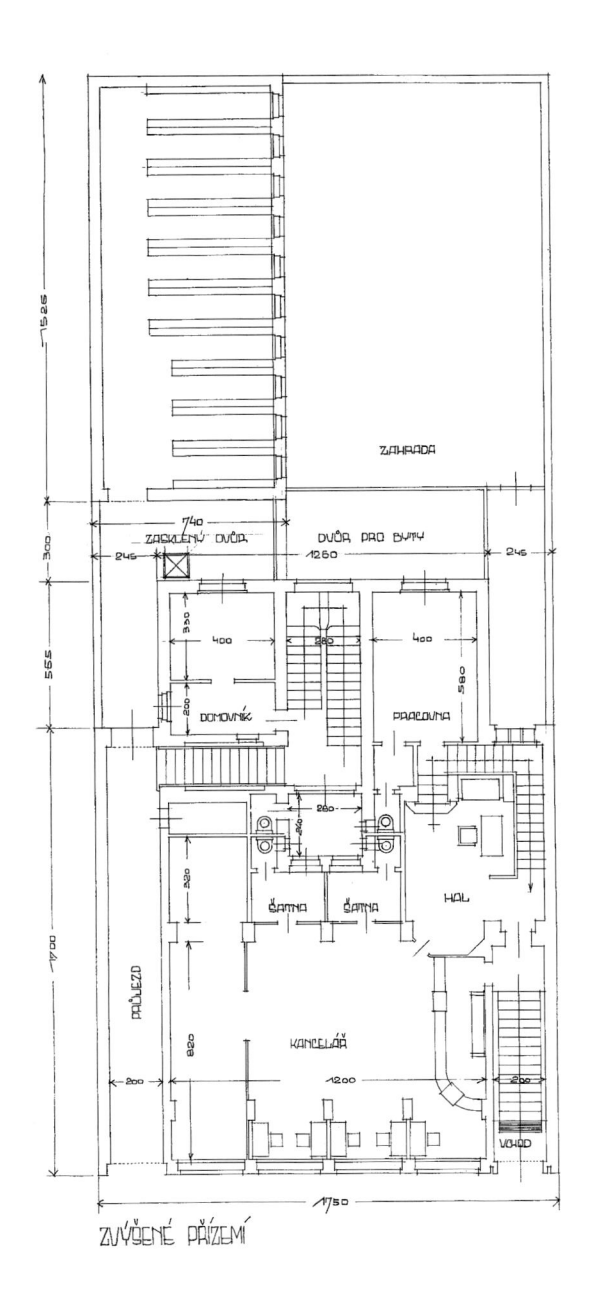

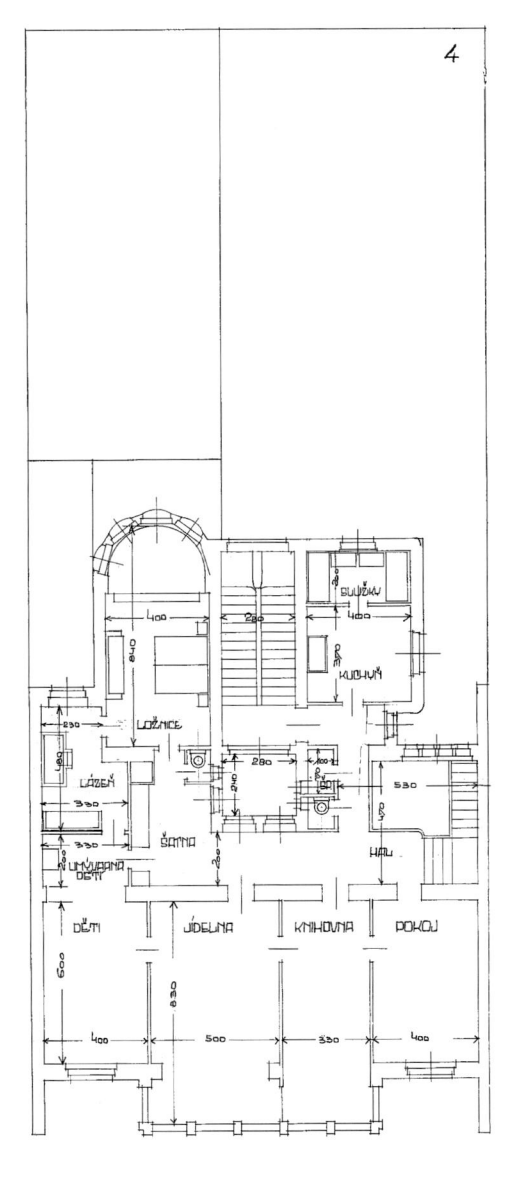

< **172**
Laichter's house in Prague-Vinohrady,
groundplans of the raised ground floor and first floor, 1908–1909
> **173**
Laichter's house in Prague-Vinohrady, staircase-hall, 1908–1909

The City Museum in Hradec Králové, 1906–1913

180 THE CULMINANT YEARS, 1906–1912

< **174**
City Museum in Hradec Králové,
perspective view of the first final version, 1907
<< **175**
City Museum in Hradec Králové, detailed sketch of the first final version, 1907
> **176**
City Museum in Hradec Králové, first sketch, c. 1905

Although the architect had certainly wished to leave behind numerous important public buildings, particularly in Prague, what remained a somewhat early climax of his career was the city museum of history and decorative arts in Hradec Králové (1909–1913). This sophisticated museum architecture for the liveliest city in Eastern Bohemia is a testament to the swift cultural growth of the Czech rural environment. From the end of the 19th century onwards, these towns viewed the cosmopolitan and extravagant Prague with resentment, intent on competing with the Czech capital in the fields of art and culture. Kotěra's modern vision of the museum in Hradec Králové surpassed the antiquated, pompous style of Prague's Municipal House by architects Antonín Balšánek and Osvald Polívka (1905–12), the most glamorous building of that period in Prague. It was telling proof that, with Kotěra's help, the countryside certainly provided a setting equal to the task.

The Board of Trustees of the Hradec Museum commissioned Kotěra to create a project for the new museum building, since the museum at the time was housed in cramped conditions in the city's historical centre. However, it was Dr František Ulrich (1859–1939), the extraordinary mayor of Hradec Králové, who was Kotěra's true patron and client. He negotiated the necessary financial means for the new museum in the Czech regional assembly and assumed responsibility for the work during its construction from Hradec Králové city council. Two of Sucharda's goddesses guarding the entrance to the museum celebrated Ulrich's role as the creator of the new Hradec Králové, a modern Pericles. The sculpture on the right-hand side mimicked the gesture of Athena Parthenos by Phidias. Together with Stanislav Sucharda, sculptor Jaroslav Horejc and painter Jan Preisler aided in the decoration of the museum.

The city designated the space for its new museum on the Eliščino embankment by the Elbe, below the city's elevated historical centre. Kotěra's first sketches for it date from around 1905 and, in 1907, he sent the Board his first – he probably hoped definitive – plans for the museum. In 1908–09, after long and arduous negotiations with the Board and with mayor Ulrich, Kotěra designed a second version. Throughout Kotěra's work on the project, the rooms set aside for the day-to-day running of the museum – exhibition halls, conference hall, library, offices for the curators – remained unchanged. The museum also maintained its dynamic, asymmetrical ground-plan, resembling Wright's prairie houses, together with its typical

THE CULMINANT YEARS, 1906–1912 | 181

THE CULMINANT YEARS, 1906-1912

< **177**
City Museum in Hradec Králové, entrance, 1909–1913
> **178**
City Museum in Hradec Králové, sketch of the second final version, 1908

attributes of a "temple of science", mainly its impressive dome. The museum façade, which in the first versions recalled National House in Prostějov (1905–07), grew simpler with time. Kotěra slowly relieved it of ornamentation, until finally reaching a phase in which the ascetic styles of his own villa and Laichter's house (1908–09) were transformed into a building of truly monumental proportions. Around 1910, there were no public buildings in Central Europe which could compare to its austere appearance, except perhaps Plečnik's church of the Holy Spirit in Vienna-Ottakring. We might interpret it as a reaction to the excessive splendour of new museums built during the period – Prague's National Museum or the Museum of Decorative Arts, for example – a quality of architecture which, in the early 20th century, met with strong social opposition. Kotěra's museum in Hradec Králové did not aspire to the status of an ostentatious symbol, but instead was conceived as a place of work. This explains the architect's unusual style, alternating between the monumental attributes of a temple and the forms typical of industrial architecture of the period.

R. Š.

THE CULMINANT YEARS, 1906-1912

< **179**
City Museum in Hradec Králové, fountain at the foot of the staircase, 1909–1913
> **180**
City Museum in Hradec Králové,
History – figural sculpture by Stanislav Sucharda, 1909–1913
>> **181**
City Museum in Hradec Králové, ground floor lecture hall, 1909–1913
>>> **182**
City Museum in Hradec Králové, first floor exhibition hall, exhibition of art and industrial advertising, 1914

THE CULMINANT YEARS, 1906–1912 185

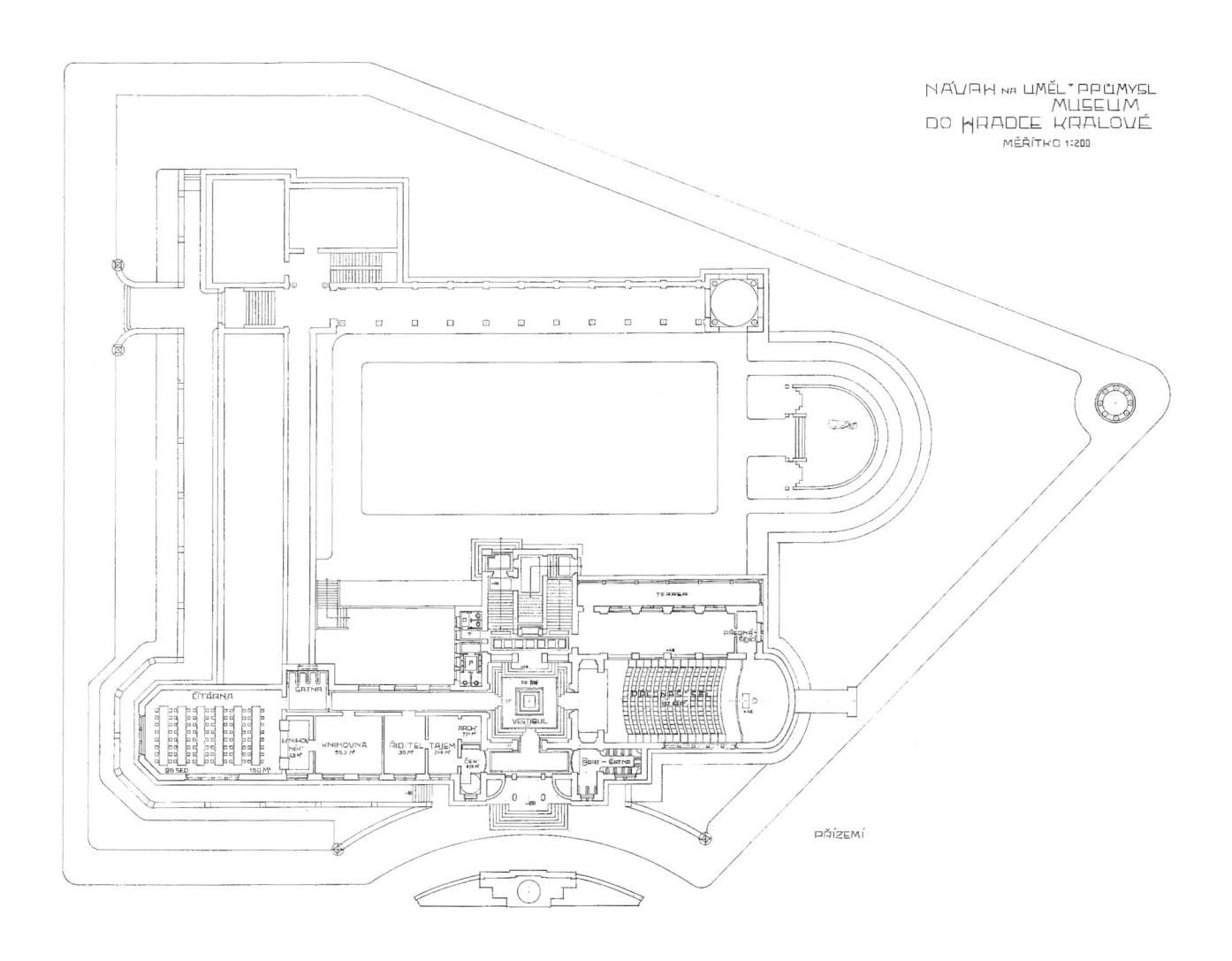

< **183**
City Museum in Hradec Králové,
ground floor plan with sketch of the extension,
drawing by Josef Gočár, 1908
> **184**
City Museum in Hradec Králové, rear view, 1909–1913

Project for the Multi-Purpose Building for the *Koruna* Insurance Company in Prague, 1911

< 185
Competition entry for the multi-purpose building for the *Koruna* insurance company in Prague, façade facing Wenceslas Square, 1911
> 186
Competition entry for the multi-purpose building for the *Koruna* insurance company in Prague, groundplan of the parterre, 1911
>> 187
Competition entry for the multi-purpose building for the *Koruna* insurance company in Prague, perspective view, 1911

Wenceslas Square in Prague, an elongated marketplace founded in 1348 by Emperor Charles IV, was gradually being transformed at the close of the 19th century into a modern boulevard surrounded by tall buildings of department stores, hotels and banks. As architectural Modernism grew stronger, the metamorphosis that it generated in architecture began to manifest itself in an important location at the bottom of Wenceslas Square, where the square joins Na příkopě street. In 1911, the First Czech Joint-Stock Insurance Company announced a select tender for this location, for a polyfunctional palace that would house a large department store and a number of offices, joined by a spa complex and cinema. Kotěra participated in this competition with an exceptionally progressive design, a hybrid of Modernist elements, early Constructivism, and aerodynamic Expressionism anticipating the Berlin works of Erich Mendelsohn. The precondition for this modern concept was the reinforced concrete frame, which the architect used here for the first time. Kotěra's project for the Koruna Palace, especially its two-storey department store set inside an open parterre with a large passageway and a richly glazed and streamlined interior, anticipated the metropolitan architecture of the 1920s. Though Kotěra's project did not win the competition – his student Antonín Pfeiffer's design was finally used – it was, nevertheless, to become an example for the first generation of Purist and Constructivist architects in Prague. The project for a hotel on the bank of the Vltava by Jaromír Krejcar, a graduate of Kotěra's school at the Academy of Fine Arts, published in 1923 in the avant-garde anthology *Život (Life)* II, drew abundantly from Kotěra's project.

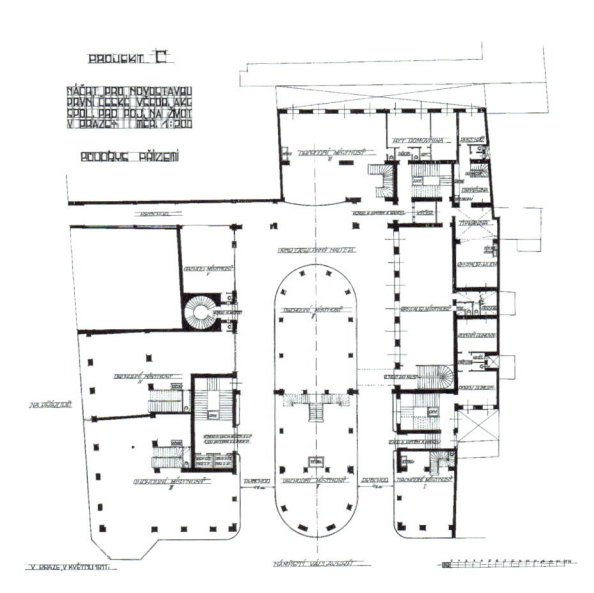

R. Š.

THE CULMINANT YEARS, 1906–1912 189

Urban Hotel in Hradec Králové,
1910–1911
Slavia Bank in Sarajevo,
1911–1913

< **188**
Urban Hotel in Hradec Králové, 1910–1911
> **189**
Urban Hotel in Hradec Králové, interior of the main hall, known as the Palm Garden, 1910–1911

The austere and impassioned style of the museum in Hradec Králové (1909–13) was echoed in only a few of Kotěra's projects drafted around the year 1910, all of them unrealised. The architect's projects built during this period were more classical in style, much more tranquil than that of the museum. Here, the architect analysed in detail the problems of the tectonic and stereometric division of the façade, and the artistic issues underlying receding and layered façades. It seemed as if he were preparing for his concept of the Mozarteum in Prague (1911–13), the final work of his most creative period. The Slavia Bank in Sarajevo (1911–13) and the new wing of the Urban Hotel in Hradec Králové (erected in 1910–1911 on what is today Československé armády street) – together with the reconstruction of Prague bridge in Hradec Králové (1910–11) – are considered Kotěra's most remarkable projects from the period between his two major works, the Museum in Hradec Králové and the Mozarteum. The extension of the Urban Hotel, now unfortunately devalued by the inappropriate adaptation of the adjacent houses, included a hotel and coffee-house near the Regional Authorities building (1901–04), whose rear wing was linked to the Urban Hotel.   R. Š.

Urbánek's House – Mozarteum
in Prague, 1911–1913

< 192
Urbánek's house – Mozarteum in Prague, façade – model, 1911
> 193
Urbánek's house – Mozarteum in Prague,
façade – pastel drawing, 1911

The department store for the music publisher Mojmír Urbánek on Jungmannova street 748 in Prague, whose project the architect developed in two variants (1911 and 1912) and realised in 1913, ends the culminant phase of Kotěra's work. Once again, the architect worked his way through to the final version by executing softly drawn fine sketches and another of his free models of the façade. Armed with the possibilities of the building's reinforced concrete and its tectonic frames, Kotěra here developed his principle of receding surfaces and the simultaneous layering of tectonic features, already tested in projects for the Urban Hotel and Slavia Bank (both from 1911). It was completed with an open parterre with Štursa's female half-length figures. With its exposed brick composition and pronounced reinforced concrete construction, the façade of Urbánek's house, known as the Mozarteum, fully expressed the architect's sense for tectonic poetry: a theme introduced into European architecture before Kotěra mainly by Hendrik Petrus Berlage and Auguste Perret.

Mozarteum, in its typology and functional composition linked with Laichter's house, consisted of two parallel wings linked by a narrow staircase-hallway. The back wing extended into a lower concert hall facing the Franciscan garden. Urbánek's bookstore and publishing house were located on the bottom two floors of the building, while his large apartment took up the third floor. It was to have had the additional luxury of a garden on the flat roof of the concert hall. Kotěra treated the interiors of Urbánek's apartment, and the rented apartments on the upper floors, as a continuous, fluid space, spreading along the enfilade parallel to Jungmannova street. The opera singer Růžena Maturová often performed in the Mozarteum's concert hall. In 1916, Kotěra designed a villa for her in Trója in Prague but it was never built. During the 1930s, Emil František Burian, theatre director and composer, adapted the hall to suit his avant-garde D theatre. When, in December 1913, the Italian Futurists – Russolo, Severini, Carrà and Boccioni – finally presented their work in Prague, the exhibition was organised in Urbánek's house, in what was known as Havel's Gallery.

R. Š.

PLÁN PRO NOVOSTAVBU OBCHOD. DOMU
NAKLADATELSTVÍ P. MOJMÍRA URBÁNKA
V PRAZE II. Č.P. 748.
MAJIT. PANÍ KRISTINA URBÁNKOVÁ.

HLAVNÍ PRŮČELÍ.

MĚŘÍTKO 1:100.

V PRAZE, V BŘEZNU 1912.

< **194**
Urbánek's house – Mozarteum in Prague,
façade – pen-and-ink drawing, 1912
> **195**
Urbánek's house – Mozarteum in Prague,
façade – pencil drawing, 1911

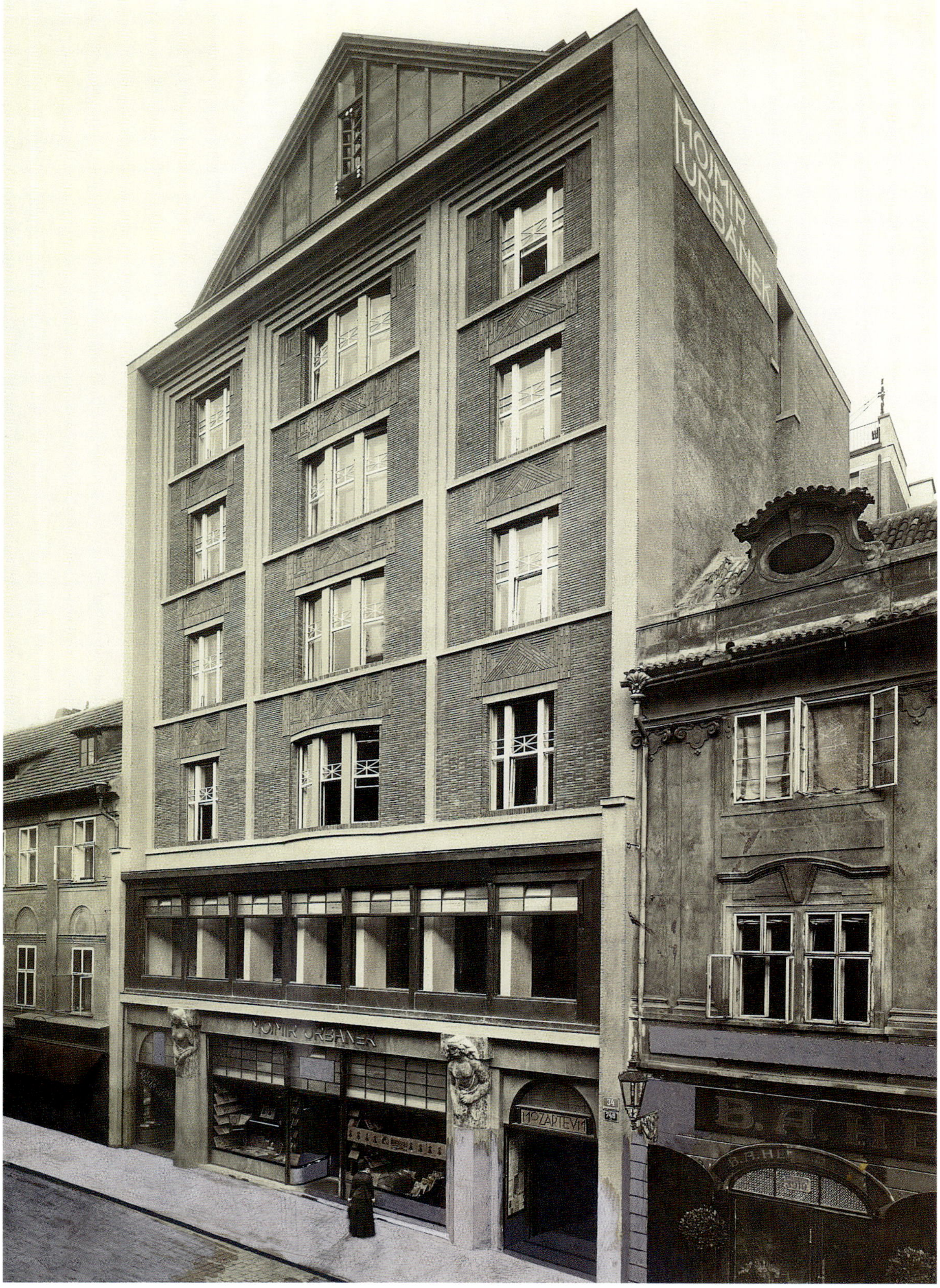
MOJMIR URBANEK
MOJMIR URBANEK
MOZARTEVM

< **196**
Urbánek's house – Mozarteum in Prague, 1911–1913
> **197**
Urbánek's house – Mozarteum in Prague,
cross-section and groundplans, 1911–1913
>> **198**
Urbánek's house – Mozarteum in Prague,
drawing of the concert hall, 1912
>>> **199**
Urbánek's house – Mozarteum in Prague,
concert hall (adapted for the Švestka gallery), 1911–1913

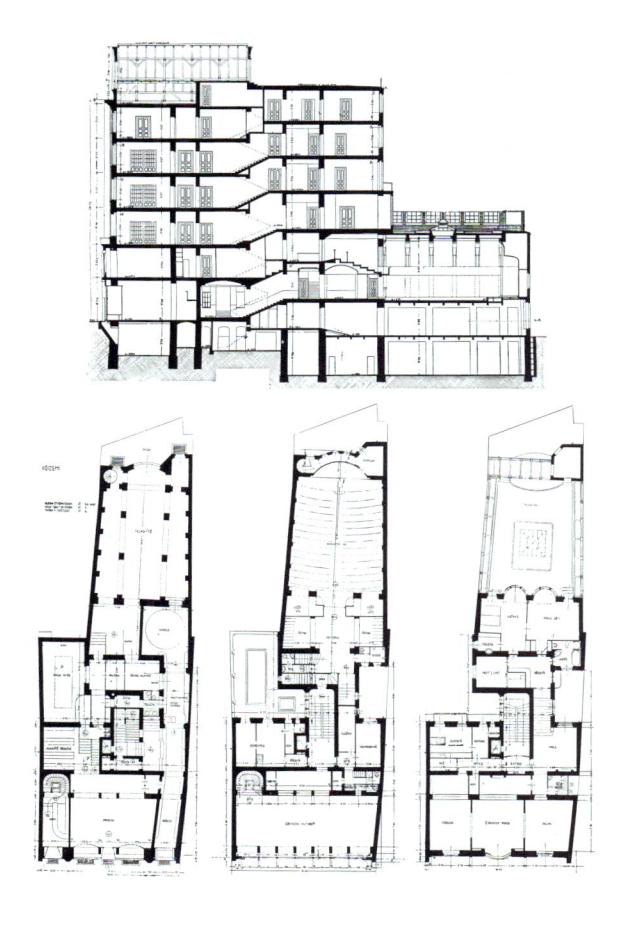

THE CULMINANT YEARS, 1906–1912

THE CLOSING PHASE OF KOTĚRA'S WORK, 1913–1923

< 200
General Pension Institute in Prague, entrance section, 1912–1914

The Closing Phase of Kotěra's Work, 1913–1923

PETR KRAJČI

With the passing of time, trees yield under the weight of age, walls crumble away and people grow old. The final phase of Kotěra's work belonged to a less fortunate period, quite accurately defined by the years preceding the outbreak of the First World War and the architect's death in 1923. His work of this period was marked by the architect's deteriorating health, but also by the devastating effects of a war which caused the building industry to come to a halt, and brought radical changes to the political climate. Kotěra possessed an indefatigable energy. It underlined everything he did, from the manner in which he professed his beliefs, to the way he coped with numerous complex problems – which were not always of a professional nature. Nevertheless, it was this admirable quality of his character, coupled with his implacable attitude towards mediocrity (which mediocre people never forgive), which finally drained away his mental and physical resources.

After he moved to the Academy of Fine Arts in Prague from the School of Applied Arts where, through Kotěra's generosity, Jože Plečnik[1] was able to assume his professorial chair, far greater possibilities in education opened up for Kotěra. The calibre of his students at the Academy generally surpassed that of his students at the School of Applied Arts.[2] However, the strong impact he was to have on the future elite of Czech architects was possible only under certain favourable conditions. In 1911, Kotěra completed his own villa in Prague-Vinohrady, designing an architectural studio for his work on its second floor. He employed his most talented students – above all Josef Gočár – in this private studio, and during the War gradually moved all of his work, including his School of Architecture, to these premises.

While the School of Applied Arts prepared its students for team work and collaboration, the Academy was an exclusive art school which focused on developing the individuality of its students. The creative turmoil which began in 1910, the nervous whirling anticipation of the forthcoming War, together with the great changes that followed, placed Kotěra in an unprecedented position. The Academy graduates[3] became his competitors, and he was suddenly forced to come to terms with new artistic challenges, presented by people half a generation younger.

During this period, the Neo-Classicist tendency grew stronger in Kotěra's work, the result of his desire to achieve a timeless quality in his architecture. Rather than creating a sharp division in his work, this trend was suggested in subtle details. Thus, it would be quite difficult to set a clear boundary between Kotěra's most productive years and the final period of his work. However, the General Pension Institute on the Podskalí embankment in Prague and the castle area in Ratboř near Kolín could be considered as such. In 1912–14, Kotěra was entrusted with designing the Institute building's façade, while his colleague, Josef Zasche, was in charge of the interior layout. The building's exterior formed a substantial part of the newly erected Podskalí block and,

---

1   The friendship between Plečnik and Kotěra was enduring and well documented. Plečnik took on a number of Kotěra's students at the School of Applied Arts. See: *Josip Plečnik - architekt Pražského hradu*. Exhibition catalogue, Praha 1997, p. 659 (index).

2   For a list of Kotěra's students at the School of Applied Arts, see: Pavel Janák, "Tři školy architektury" in: *Sborník UPŠ*, 1932. - Otakar Novotný, *Jan Kotěra a jeho doba*. Praha 1958, p. 141. - Sources: Archiv hlavního města Prahy, fond Vysoké školy uměleckoprůmyslové.

3   For a list of Jan Kotěra's students at the Academy of Fine Arts, see: *Almanach AVU*. Praha 1976, p. 112. - Otakar Novotný (see note 2), p. 141. - Source: Archiv AVU.

202 THE CLOSING PHASE OF KOTĚRA'S WORK, 1913–1923

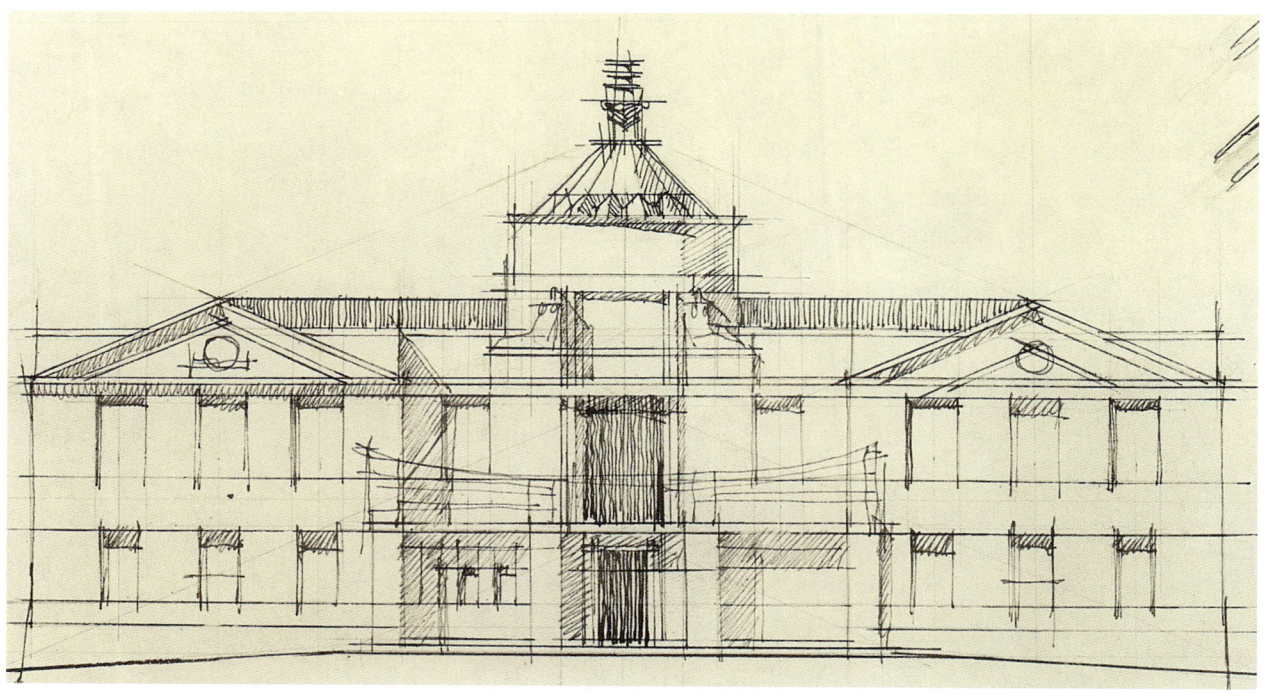

< 201
New castle in Ratboř, façade design, 1911
<< 202
New castle in Ratboř, façade design, 1911
> 203
New castle in Ratboř, entrance – detail, 1911–1913

despite its plasticity, was characterised by the somewhat orderly and consistent use of an orthogonal line, in comparison with the buildings of the previous Modernist period. The lines were enhanced by details of geometrical wrought iron motifs and stained glass decorating the main riverside entrance. The fine lace grilles of the ground-floor windows and railings above the main entrance and on the building's corners, the projecting Chicago windows[4] with their additional partitioned panes, the opaque stained glass ornamentation around the entrance – all these elements were composed of strictly orthogonal and diagonal lines. Only the stained glass adorning the entrance, and the brackets symbolically supporting the entrance and corner projections, employed spherical motifs. The imposing main entrance facing the embankment was carefully balanced with the reduction of the building's mass on its corners. Kotěra treated this building, with its set groundplan and function, somewhat unschematically, although it does betray a certain pathos. In this context, it is worth noting Jaroslav Rössler's Workers' Accident Insurance building on Bubenské embankment, constructed ten years later and resolving a similar problem.

The adaptation of the old castle owned by the Mandelík family in Ratboř (1912–15) and, more importantly, the building of the new castle[5] west of the old building in 1911–13, fully indicate the line of Kotěra's work moving towards eternal forms, Neo-Classicist trends and the desire to use contemporary means to express an architectural ideal. The perfect axial symmetry of the new castle's façade, one of the last examples of this typology in Bohemia, is echoed in the groundplans. The concept of the interior contrasts with the monumental façade, accentuated by Štursa's sculptures personifying *Spirit* and *Matter*. There are no ceremonial halls and no monumental central hall spread over two floors. An earlier work from Kotěra's best creative period, Bianca villa in Prague-Bubeneč, designed for the Petschků family in 1910–13, anticipates the castle in Ratboř in certain aspects: the strict axial symmetry of the main façade, the cylindrical side oriels on the ground floors, two sculptures by the same artist,[6] and a wharf-like motif extending from the top of the roof's ridge (or dome in the case of the castle).

---

4   In Czech architecture, also employed by Hypšman, Kotěra's fellow student at Wagner's school, for example in his office building on Národní třída.
5   The Mandelíks were a Jewish farming family from the Kolín region. They earned their noble title in the second half of the 19th century. Also well known cultivators.

6   In his late period, Kotěra collaborated mainly with Jan Štursa, professor and colleague from the Academy of Fine Arts.

THE CLOSING PHASE OF KOTĚRA'S WORK, 1913–1923

The first designs for the new castle in Ratboř are far more striking than the resultant work. The material and formal aspects of the entrance portico, with the radically abstracted fluting of the prismatic columns and bevelled surfaces enveloping the main door, resemble Janák's Cubist kiosks at the north end of Hlávka bridge in Holešovice. The façade is sparingly constructed, enhanced with segmented windows of fine geometrical form, and decorative railings on the central and side balconies. The vernacular features of the west façade, recalling the organic walls of Italian country houses, are visible only from a distance, from the opposite hillside.

Kotěra's design for the new Royal Palace in Sofia[7] for a competition announced in 1912, is another monumental task from the pre-War period. The extensive project included both the palace and its grounds and required Kotěra to produce an organic and functional design which would alter the city's urban structure. This he combined with an effort to create an adequate representation of the monarchical seat. The available plans deal mainly with the overall concept and remain within the scope of traditional typology. They use an austere architectonic language, accentuate the monumental elements and, in certain details, call to mind the work of Schinkel or Semper. Kotěra would later use some of these motifs again.

The series of works completed before the First World War ends with a newly erected building for the Lemberger Palace in Vienna (1913–15). In certain respects, this work crowned Kotěra's endeavours of the second decade. The extensive complex in the villa district on the north-west outskirts of Vienna, famous for its vineyards, is situated on the corner of a large site. Designed as a new home for two families of Kotěra's friends, the building had a rather complex groundplan, hidden behind a façade that was already Neo-Classicist. It displays a hint of Kotěra's former style in the raw masonry surrounding the windows on the first floor. The geometrical fluting on the west façade perhaps represents a reconciliation with Cubism, yet its basic austere physiognomy and compact volume associate it with Kotěra's new Neo-Classicist tendency.

Kotěra never really accepted Cubism, not in the sense of a new philosophical artistic foundation, as Pavel Janák and other theorists of the movement defined it. Nor could he ever identify with it on a personal level, even if he did earnestly engage in solving some of its issues. He was, after all, a student of Wagner and the mysticism of the new style was alien to him. As time would later show, Cubism certainly did not prove to be the definitive artistic world view. Remaining true to his generosity, Kotěra never restricted his students in their own quests, yet he never really felt the need himself to adopt their extreme positions, as he still had his own accounts to settle with the ruling environment. It is also questionable to what extent Kotěra considered the Cubist movement to truly differ from Modernism and late geometric Secession. His longing for truth as the fundamental artistic criterion did not comply with the visionary arguments in favour of the new style, proclaimed in writing by Pavel Janák. Rather than forcing himself to adopt the zeal that emanated from sketches by Janák and Hofman, or from Chochol's and Gočár's buildings, in some of his new de-

---

[7] Otakar Novotný also participated in the competition with a purely Cubist project resembling a crystalline druse.

< 204
Competition entry for the monument to Jan Žižka on Vítkov hill in Prague, 1913
> 205
Competition entry for the Austro-Hungarian Bank in Vienna, 1911

signs Kotěra reworked the forms and shapes of geometric groundplans developed in his Modernist works.[8]

Nevertheless, by quietly entering a competition for the memorial to Jan Žižka on Vítkov hill in Prague in 1913, Kotěra once again proved his qualities as an architect. Among a colourful group of revolutionary Cubist designs from the young generation of architects and sculptors, his design, created in cooperation with Jan Štursa, ranks among the best. He produced a striking drawing, radiating an energy focused into a cluster of sharp edges, a work suggesting the discipline and discretion necessary to restrain the form so as to intensify the effect of the dynamic sculpture. Simplicity and elegance – these are the qualities which show that Kotěra had what it took to come to terms with the new trends. However, he chose to remain loyal to the eternal and essential theme of truth in artistic creation.

Summing up Kotěra's works from the years prior to the First World War, several characteristics are immediately clear. His work shows a clear inclination towards monumentality and simplicity – both in the building as a whole and in the architectural details. The architect seeks and finds the

[8] The role of geometric forms in Kotěra's work is yet to receive full acknowledgement. However, we cannot overlook the rationality of the geometric constructions in some of his projects, mostly tombstones and monuments (the War memorial in Příbram, Hácha family tombstone).

THE CLOSING PHASE OF KOTĚRA'S WORK, 1913-1923

architectonic archetypes, he renders the tectonics and construction clearly visible, and achieves a striking conciseness and austerity – almost aridity – of style. If the historical forms are visible at all, they are transformed or appear as direct citations, unlike those of his contemporaries who avoided mediation in their work. We should also add that, at this time, many of Kotěra's buildings and projects from the earlier period were still not completed. With the architect's illustrious, uncompromising attitude, they consumed a significant amount of his creative force and human strength. For this reason, it would be impossible to clearly define the end of the so called "peak" of Kotěra's work, especially considering the way in which certain strategies, forms, spatial solutions and details of his architecture slowly matured and developed – sometimes without any visible change – through the different periods.

The Czech architectural scene could not avoid the irreversible transformations that occurred in the country with the outbreak of the First World War in 1914. A rapid transition to a war economy immediately halted the building industry. The departure of men to the battlefields not only restricted artistic life but many important figures never returned. The restrictions on political life included censorship, diminishing the number of public debates and artistic freedom. Jan Kotěra was closely linked to existing government circles which – despite the great autonomy of culture and language in Bohemia – were still seen as representatives of monarchical rule. Although he held a strong position in the Czech community, due to his artistic battles of the past, his loyalty to the Monarchy put him in a truly difficult and contradictory position.

Above all, he considered it essential to continue his teaching. In 1910, when he moved to the Academy of Fine Arts in Prague, he systematically worked on creating the conditions for a professional architecture course. The studio space in his villa in Vinohrady, which he used for his own work, was made available for Academy lectures during the last years of the War. Kotěra's assistants, whom he chose from among his students, created many of his project designs. This was part of the natural development of the relationship between the master and his student, beneficial for both sides. The influence of Gočár's and Janák's Cubist

< 206
Lemberger-Gombrich villa in Vienna, façade, 1913
> 207
Design for a monument, 1915

views in some of the works dating from the War period well illustrates this point.

The war drastically diminished the number of construction projects. Kotěra's growing fondness for monumentality and eternal themes, realised in the previous periods through a series of designs for tombstones and monuments, met the sad demand of the times – war memorials. Although none of these memorials was ever realised, Kotěra used their designs to test the solidity of crystalline forms, as if he were following an arch back to his Cubist experiences of 1913. In its final form, the 1917 war memorial for Jihlava was the most monumental of all. The drawing of the tumulus, culminating in the figure of a naked grieving warrior with a tilted sword, a work by Jan Štursa, truly expresses the tragedy of the period, with its unexpected and terrifying deaths. The protruding points of a star half-buried in the ground from one of the two variants of the war memorial for Příbram bring a sense of alienation. The column decorated with war symbols planned for Nové Hrady, or a similar design for Slaný, both from 1916, evoke this same emotion. Several other designs for family tombstones for Olšany

208 THE CLOSING PHASE OF KOTĚRA'S WORK, 1913–1923

< 208
Design for the war memorial for Příbram, 1917
> 209
Design for the military cemetery in Slaný, 1916

cemetery in Prague – the Janoušek, Nosek and Hácha tombstones – provide another example of works in which Kotěra, in his own way and with the necessary distance, responded to the Cubist call. His preoccupation with Cubism manifested itself in several sketches for a mausoleum at an unspecified location and in the design of the façade of a farm warehouse in Telč in 1917.

Parallel to these themes of eternity, throughout the war Kotěra maintained his interest in one of the fundamental themes of architecture – the human dwelling – via a broad range of architectonic works: urban planning, the newly designed settlement of workers' houses in Prague-Záběhlice, the first plan for Baťa's colony in Zlín, or the individual commissions for family homes. While, for his "eternal" tasks, Kotěra stepped up his research on the relationship between artistic and spatial design, mindful of the building's function and the borders of form expressivity, all involving masterly use of the materials, for his housing commissions, however, he kept to his well-established principles and techniques. These urban conceptions were sensitive to the slope of the terrain, and they made good use of restricted sites. They could function autonomously as a whole – either as an open public or entirely private space which was structured naturally. The architectural expression of the various dwellings was austere, influenced by past experiences with the Louny housing colony. It grew even simpler, while maintaining a sense of the expressiveness of architectonic detail. In the projects for communal dwellings, Kotěra cultivated types of family houses he had already created in Louny, however, in the individual commissions for villas (such as the house for Ms Maturová in Prague-Trója in 1916, or for Mr Rýdl in Dobruška in 1917–18), he began to simplify the building's external capacity and reduce the diversity of building materials. He moved from finely structured exposed brickwork and combed stucco to large smooth surfaces with large doors and windows. Essentially, his work developed in harmony with the period trend, characterised by an increase in scale, simplified volume and greater expressivity. Janák's sketches from the war period display these same features, in which he transformed the pointed motifs of the pioneering period of Cubism into cylindrical and circular structures.

The demise of the monarchy and the birth of the Republic in the autumn of 1918 brought radical political change which directly affected cultural and artistic issues.[9] Kotěra was respected for his role in the struggle for a new understanding of architecture, but not by everyone. In the new period

9   On the situation after the First World War, see: Otakar Novotný (ibid.), p. 86 ff.

of Czech national euphoria, Kotěra's healthy relationship with the enlightened members of the Austrian establishment, which earlier supported him in realising his visions, was viewed rather negatively. Nevertheless, he continued his teaching without any difficulties. Not long after the War ended, a separate building for a special school of architecture was constructed, east of the main Academy building, designed by Kotěra and later completed by Josef Gočár, Kotěra's successor at the school.

In the post-War period, Kotěra devoted much energy to the completion of the Prague University buildings, an extensive project which dragged on for years. From the first sketches in 1907, the project underwent substantial revision. Following the post-War rejection of the idea to carve a tunnel through Letná hill in the direction of Dejvice, the urban context of the project was significantly transformed. The political changes also redefined the future users themselves. Dozens of competing projects, based upon the idea of a road or tunnel to be carved through Letná along the axis of Svatopluk Čech bridge, were no longer valid, including a large-scale project for Pařížská avenue. The decision of the State Urban Planning Commission to divert all transport to the two embankments did not really affect the design aspect of Kotěra's buildings, symmetrically positioned on both sides of the bridge. It did, however, fundamentally change the orientation of the entrances, as well as his design for the adjacent public spaces. The Law Faculty, completed only after Kotěra's death by architect Ladislav Machoň, was the only part of the planned complex that was finally built, based on Kotěra's third and fourth versions of the university buildings. The design incorporates a striking motif of a decorated triangular gable, evocative of the large gables on Kotěra's Chamber of Trade and Commerce pavilion or the Mozarteum.

The university buildings – which in time proved to be truly burdensome for Kotěra – were part of the second stage of the regulation of the Prague embankments which began at the start of the 20th century. The ingenious urban configuration of the Old and New Towns and Malá Strana, intersecting at the Vltava river, began in the latter half of the 19th century to spread out in a linear fashion with a line of public buildings designed for the newly erected Vltava embankment. Another proportionally conceived district was developed in stages from Charles Bridge northbound along the right bank of Vltava. Kotěra's urban plan, which included

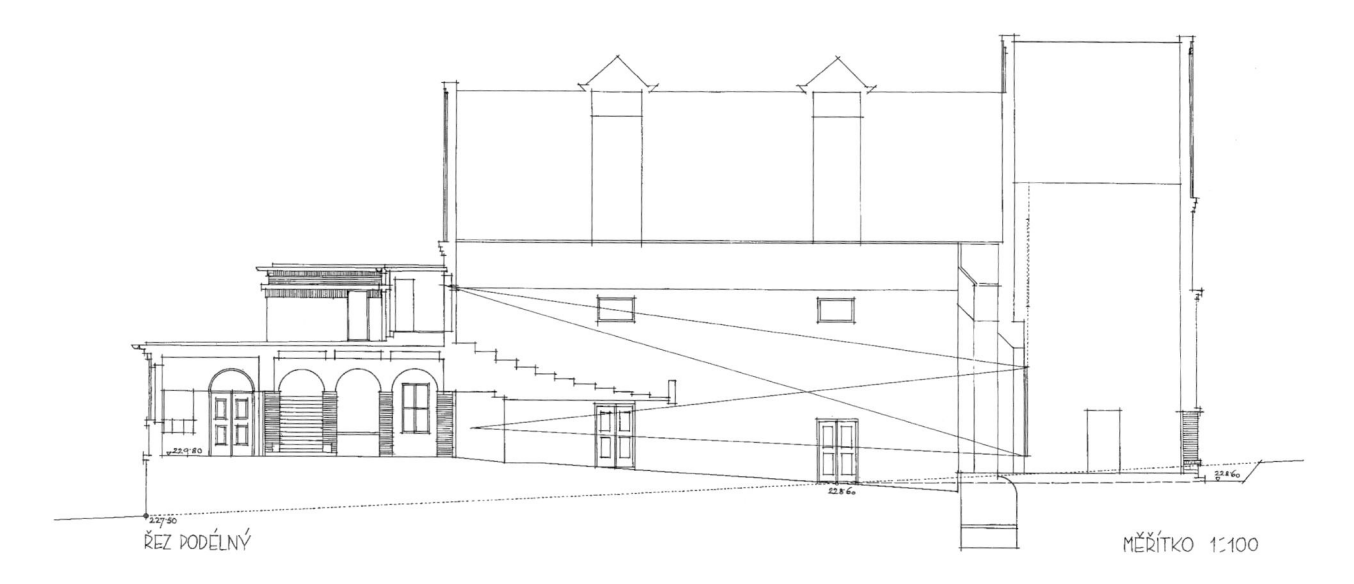

< **210**
Design for the cinema in Zlín, longitudinal section, 1916
> **211**
School of Architecture at the Academy of Fine Arts in Prague-Letná, completed by J. Gočár, 1919–1920, 1923–1924

Kvasnička's finely modelled new Na Františku hospital, concluded the first stage of the regulation work. The post-War period radically changed the scale of the as yet unregulated embankments, whether this involved the complex of ministerial buildings in the Petrská district between the convent of St Agnes and Těšnov, Hypšman's plan of a similar disposition in Podskalí below Emmaus monastery or the Workers' Accident Insurance building on the Bubenská approach road by Hlávka bridge.

At first, Kotěra designed the university buildings as oblong blocks, symmetrically enclosing both sides of Svatopluk Čech bridge. However, after the first sketches in 1907, their architectural style underwent radical change, both in the overall concept and in the details. This was a project where one could precisely follow the universal constants of Kotěra's work through a gradual change in the modelling of the external mass. In the first two variants, the building was crowned with a dome that resembled the sublime form of the Hradec Králové museum. Later, it was radically simplified, becoming an almost archetypal longitudinal edifice with a saddle roof and high gable. The interplay of the protruding gables was meant to emphasise the public nature of the two buildings and complete Pařížská avenue, both from an urbanist and semiotic point of view. Due to a series of adverse circumstances, the second building was never erected. Furthermore, the large gable of the former building of the Society of Architects and Engineers, which made perfect spatial sense as a counterpoint to the gable of the Law Faculty, has been irretrievably lost in a recent reconstruction.

Kotěra's architectural language grew simpler with time. His works designed just before the War acquired the purest forms of architectonic abstraction. The designs and details of the post-War period display a definite inclination towards academic trends.

Kotěra was involved in urban planning projects several times during this period – the designs of workers' housing colonies, competitions for centrally located banks in Prague, and those for the seats of large corporations. They include his project for the Prague Credit Bank on Wenceslas Square (1920), the Industrial Bank on Na Příkopě street and the Prague Credit Bank at Na Můstku (both 1921). None of these projects was ever realised. The corner buildings that he designed, however, were linked by an austere Neo-Classicist morphology, reminiscent of the General Pension Institute from Kotěra's pre-War period.

The project for the administrative building owned by the Vítkovice-Ringhoffer-Kopřivnice company in Smíchov in 1920 differed from the standard architectural designs of the period in several respects typical of Kotěra, including a lavish corner entrance with Štursa's sculptural decoration. This was also never built. The main building of the Vítkovice mining company in Prague, on the corner of Olivová and Politických vězňů streets, remained Kotěra's only completed building of this kind. Its expressive façade complies with period trends. The use of the articulated exposed joint brickwork for the upper section above the moulding is evocative of the Lemberger house in Vienna, while the expressive window framing, set within sunken vertical fields, resembles some of Plečnik's sketches. The cultivated details and the

< **212**
Competition entry for the building of the Prague Credit Bank in Prague, 1921
> **213**
Administrative building of the Vítkovice mining and metallurgical company in Prague, façade design, 1921

overall composition rank this building among the consistent standard works designed by Kotěra.

Only the reconstruction of Rýdl House in Dobruška, undertaken during the First World War (1917–18), brought out once more the qualities that we commonly find in Kotěra's work. Horizontal forms, strict, fine composition, and cultivated detail – these are the characteristics we will see in the last of Kotěra's buildings of this type – the Štenc villa in Všenory (1921), located on beautiful hilly terrain above the Berounka river. It seems as if, in this work, the architect synthesised his notions of a cultivated and pleasant dwelling place. A sense of serenity and acceptance of destiny emanates from its simply conceived exterior, as it does from the interior furnishings, also designed by Kotěra.

The last work Jan Kotěra created, quite symbolically, was a family house – the kind of architecture to whose cultivation he greatly contributed, in every sense, architectural, artistic and spatial. The house in question was the unfinished Laichter villa in Dobruška (1923). Ever since Kotěra completed his own villa in Vinohrady, his designs for residential architecture began to manifest an increasing simplicity, more conventional features and a growing expressivity in the spatial design and details. For his Charvát villa in Vysoké Mýto (1909–10), Kotěra was already using materials and details that were unknown in his work at the time. Its spatial composition was also not typical for Kotěra during that period, unlike the Lemberger villa in Vienna completed at a later date. The unrealised projects for the villa for Ms Maturová in Prague-Troja (1916) and Pulchart's

STAVBU PROVÁDÍ
PRAŽSKÁ SPOLEČNOST PRO STAVBY
BETONOVÉ a ŽELEZOBETONOVÉ

< **214**
Administrative building of the Vítkovice mining and metallurgical company in Prague, 1921
> **215**
Administrative building for the Ringhoffer factory in Prague-Smíchov, entrance – sketch, 1922

house in Solnice do not differ much from standard architectural production at the time.

Kotěra's anticipated yet sudden death at the beginning of 1923 was felt as an irredeemable loss by the entire architectural, artistic and cultural community. Štursa's funeral oration reflected his appreciation for this architect, who was not afraid of new trends, who became an example to many, and who finally opened the *"windows onto Europe"* for his generation. His extensive contacts, both in Bohemia and abroad, generated a huge response to this sad event. Kotěra's activities – as an educator, organiser, member of Mánes and other associations, were suddenly seen on a grand scale. Even though the new post-War generation accepted his works with some reserve, he definitively influenced the development of modern Czech architecture. He directed Czech architecture and art to a place of continuous self-reflection, he cultivated an ability to analyse artistic stimuli, a longing to be true and ethical in one's work, and the belief that the lack of these qualities cannot fail to influence the results. His continual effort to reach a true expression, the austerity of his work and the concern he had for public matters remain – despite all the transformations in artistic styles and trends – a lasting value which Kotěra fulfilled, both through his life and his architectural work.

NÁVRH STAVBY FAKULTY
PRÁVNICKÉ A THEOLOGICKÉ
C.K. ČESKÉ UNIVERSITY KARLO-FERDINANDOVY

PRŮČELÍ DO MIKULÁŠSKÉ TŘÍDY.

PRŮČELÍ DO JÁNSKÉHO NÁMĚSTÍ.

PROJEKT A.
V PRAZE V DUBNU 1913.

MĚŘ. 1:200.

< **216**
Law and Theology Faculty building, façade design, 1913
> **217**
Law and Theology Faculty building, detail, 1913

THE CLOSING PHASE OF KOTĚRA'S WORK, 1913–1923

The New Castle in Ratboř,
1911–1913

< **218**
New castle in Ratboř, 1911–1913
> **219**
New castle in Ratboř, 1911–1913

The austere rationalist and tectonic style promoted in the early 20th century works of many European architects – led by Berlage, Wagner and Perret – reached a crisis around the year 1910. It anticipated the exhaustion, at least temporarily, of its creative potential. Several solutions were offered. One aspired to subjectivism and creativity, and its implications can be traced back to Czech Cubist architecture, German Expressionism and the Amsterdam school in Holland. Another stream which proved just as strong was the revival of the Neo-Classicist tradition, whose followers did not adopt such a radical stance towards rationalism as did Cubist or Expressionist architects, but they instead developed certain latent possibilities of rationalist expression. The revival of Neo-Classicism in Central Europe had an additional side to it since it represented the quest for local architectural identity. Many of its architects and art historians became interested in the local tradition of the Empire style and the Biedermeier. It was at this time that the first monographs on the history of architecture around the year 1800 were published in Germany, reflected in Czech culture through the studies of a friend of Jan Kotěra's, the art historian Zdeněk Wirth.

Kotěra's new castle in Ratboř near Kolín, erected in 1911–13 for the Mandelík family, owners of a local sugar refinery, responded to the initiatives of Josef Hoffmann, who was becoming the most prominent representative of the new Empire and Biedermeier styles in Austria. In his projects for Ratboř, which also included the completion of the old Renaissance castle (1912–15), apparently also some adaptations of the Mandelíks' sugar refinery, Kotěra meticulously examined Hoffmann's work, which he knew and closely followed from the time he returned to Prague. The generous symmetry of the castle's exterior, crowned with a dome and accentuated by Štursa's figures *Matter* and *Spirit* in poses reminiscent of Michelangelo's sculptures, was not reflected in its interior layout. The interior was instead divided into two spacious apartments, and the dome was not part of its design. Only the mould of the iron railings, together with a handful of other features, could be said to reveal Kotěra's reserved interest in Cubism.

R. Š.

THE CLOSING PHASE OF KOTĚRA'S WORK, 1913-1923

< **220**
New castle in Ratboř, staircase-hall, 1911–1913
> **221**
New castle in Ratboř, fountain at the end of the hallway, 1911–1913

The Late Villas: Baťa, Bianca, Charvát, Rýdl, Štenc, 1909–1922

< **222**
Charvát's villa in Vysoké Mýto, 1909–1911
> **223**
Baťa's villa in Zlín, staircase-hall, 1910–1912

Kotěra's exquisite works from 1908–11 – Laichter's house, the museum in Hradec Králové, the Koruna project and the Mozarteum – appeared to have drained Kotěra's energy. The architect abandoned the ascetic and visionary line of his architecture, continued by the young generation of the 1920s, in order to move towards the more tranquil, cosy safehold of Neo-Classicism. Kotěra's Neo-Classicist side-step produced one work of exceptional harmony which no longer had the rawness that characterised the new Ratboř castle; it was decorated with sculptures by Jan Štursa. This work was the Bianca villa in Prague-Bubeneč, on Na seníku street 48, built in 1910–11 for the Bondy family of *rentiers* and entrepreneurs from Prague. The 1920s reconstruction removed the typical features of Kotěra's style, which the new adaptation in 2000–2001 has attempted to recreate.

For the rural entrepreneurs Charvát and Baťa, Kotěra designed a new villa or, to be more specific, an adaptation of an existing one, in Vysoké Mýto (1909–11) and Zlín (1910–12). They both testified to the fact that Neo-Classicism did not appear in Kotěra's work suddenly. It was suggested in the rationalist style of many of the architect's supreme works, filtering through a variety of finely graded syntheses. The villa in Vysoké Mýto in Rokycanova street incorporates an impressive roof, stone facing of the plinth and Neo-Classicist garden loggias into a groundplan which echoed the scheme of Kotěra's own villa. Kotěra's reconstruction of Rýdl's house in Dobruška of 1917–18 was another rustic and folkloric variation on Neo-Classicism in his oeuvre. This work could easily have entered the debate on the advent of the Rondo-Cubist *National style* which Pavel Janák and Josef Gočár began after 1918. Finally, the villa for the art book publisher Jan Štenc, built on the border between Všenory and Dobřichovice, which Kotěra designed just a year before his death in 1922, could be considered a revival of the austere style of his works after 1908.

R. Š.

224 THE CLOSING PHASE OF KOTĚRA'S WORK, 1913-1923

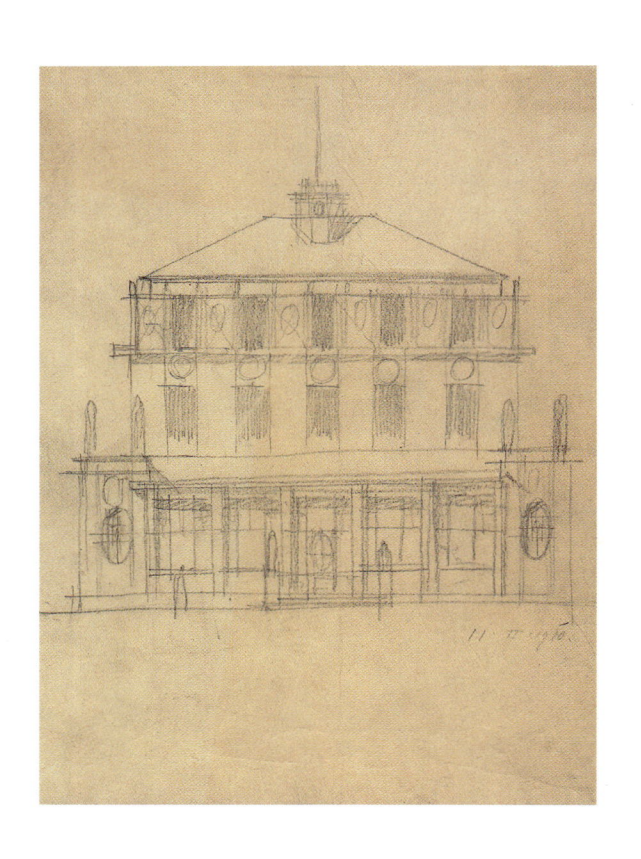

< 224
Reconstruction of the Bianca villa in Prague-Bubeneč,
sketch of the façade, 1910
<< 225
Reconstruction of the Bianca villa in Prague-Bubeneč,
detail of the façade with Štursa's sculpture *Day*, 1910–1913
> 226
Reconstruction of Rýdl's house in Dobruška, 1917–1918

1. PATRO

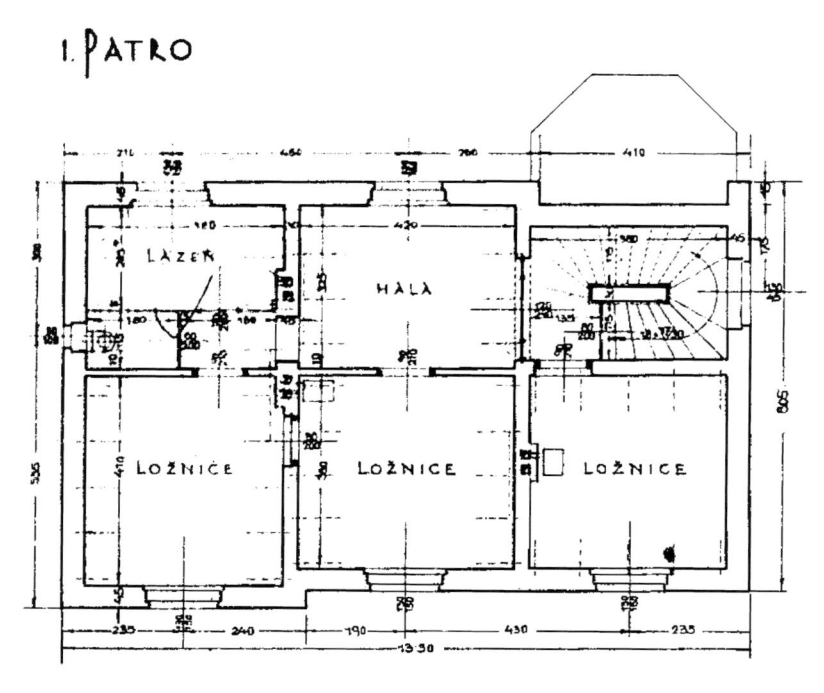

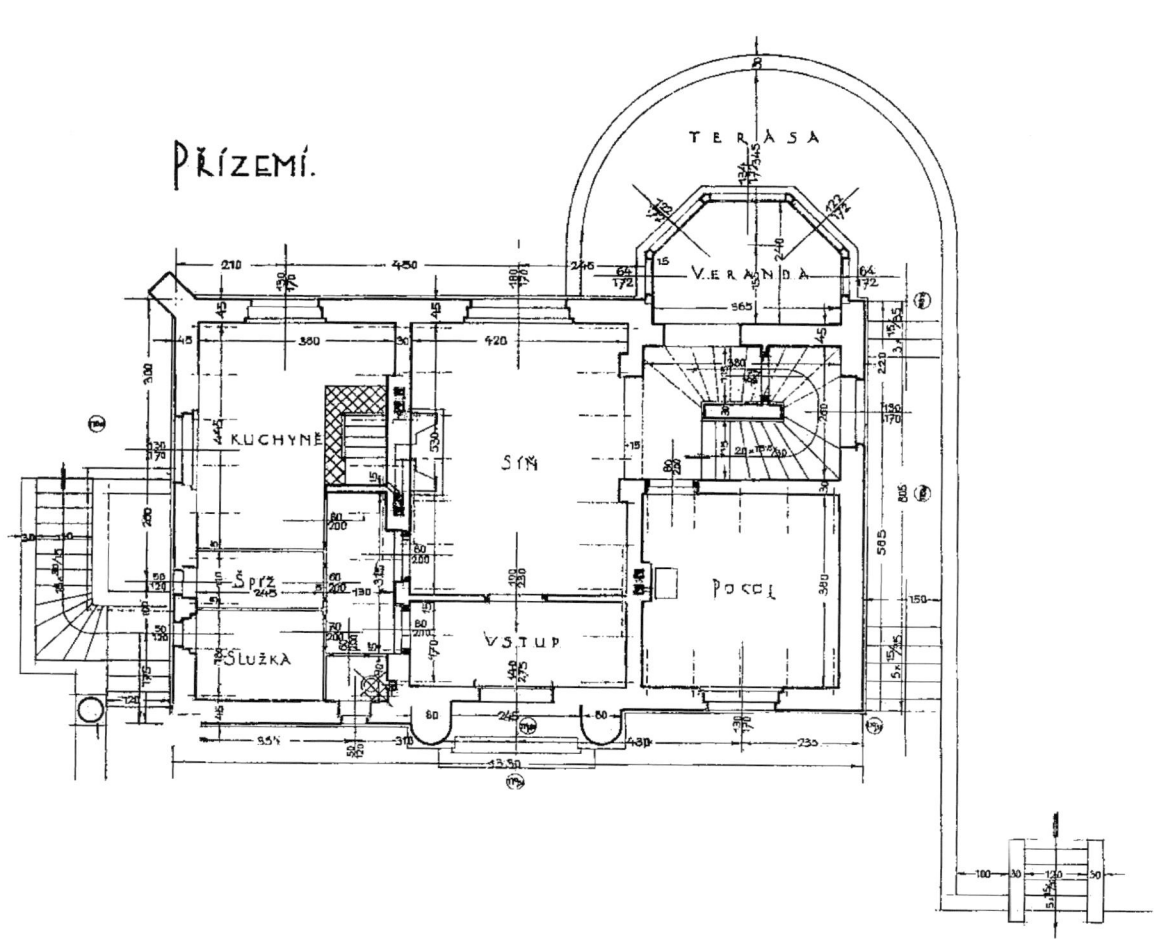

PŘÍZEMÍ.

< **227**
Štenc's villa in Všenory, groundplans, 1921–1922
> **228**
Štenc's villa in Všenory, 1921–1922

General Pension Institute in Prague, 1912–1914

< **229**
General Pension Institute in Prague, 1912–1914
> **230**
General Pension Institute in Prague, entrance, 1912–1914

The office building of the General Pension Institute, located on Rašínovo embankment 390 and built between 1912 and 1914, is a prominent example of projects which consistently developed the main themes of Kotěra's most important works. Kotěra's role in the project was somewhat limited by his collaboration with Josef Zasche, the most skilled German architect active in Prague, whom the bi-lingual pension insurance company entrusted with the construction and groundplan design for its new building, in an effort to balance the commissions between Czech and German architects. The progressive construction of the building, whose ceilings and parts of supporting pillars were made of reinforced concrete, encouraged Kotěra to reveal the modern tectonics on the building's façades. This blending brought unusual unity to both the interior and the exterior. Kotěra treated the main façade as a grid-like relief, shallow at the top and deep at the bottom and in the central projection. He then inserted polygonal bay windows into the central section of this façade and bevelled the sides of its vertical pillars. The Cubist balcony railings accentuate the fine dynamic interplay between the bevelled and polygonal features introduced by the architect, a variation on the same motifs employed in the new Ratboř castle. The building tends to be neglected by art historians, which is all the more surprising when we recall Karel Teige's commendatory words published in his book *Modern Architecture in Czechoslovakia* from 1930.

R. Š.

236 THE CLOSING PHASE OF KOTĚRA'S WORK, 1913-1923

< 239
Law and Theology Faculty building,
sketch of the second version, c. 1909
> 240
Law and Theology Faculty building,
perspective view and profile of the hall, 1913

The triangular, hexagonal and other compositional schemes which both Berlage and Wolff studied intently, created a basis for some of Kotěra's drawings, anticipating a Cubist form of detail. Bohumil Kubišta's Cubist paintings could provide a distant parallel to this search for numerical and proportional relationships, essential for sound design work. After 1913, the triangular, hexagonal and oblique-angled forms were typical throughout Kotěra's work, including his designs for tombstones and monuments. Kotěra's most steadfast student Otakar Novotný, the author of the only monograph on Kotěra from 1958, saw this as a symptomatic loss of the artist's sense of security, which was gradually replaced by compositional and proportional speculation. *"Kotěra abandoned his intuition and instead began, more than ever, to include rational considerations in his architecture."* Kotěra's lecture on composition from the end of the First World War, which survived in fragments in *The Aesthetics of Architecture*, a book written in 1945 by his student František Gahura, seems to suggest a rather different approach – more attentive to the emotive content of the form and much more reliant on visual experience.

Kotěra's Law Faculty still remains one of the most imposing buildings in Prague from the 1920s, particularly its impressive gallery hall. A more thorough assessment of its art-historical value awaits us in the future.

R. Š.

240 KOTĚRA THE ORGANISER

< 246
Installation of the 16th members' exhibition of the Mánes Association, 1905
> 247
Installation of the third members' exhibition of the Mánes Association in the New Town halls (U Štajgrů) in *U Nováků* palace in Prague, 1900

Kotěra the Organiser

RADMILA KREUZZIEGEROVÁ

"Kotěra was not only an architect, he was an overwheming force which permeated all spheres of our life. He created, introduced changes, influenced and organised the most diverse spheres of our society. He was indeed the driving force behind the substantial changes in our artistic life which was neighbourly and provincial before his arrival from Vienna. He transformed it into a self-confident European environment, from which it was possible to work both in touch and in harmony with the world. He systematically introduced new people and new trends to this country and brought our art to the world: Venice, Rome, Munich and America. He realigned the social position of Czech artists, led them out of the darkness of smoke-filled pubs and extracted fees for them worthy of their work and importance. He looked for work and commissions for the artists from his own generation [...] yet he was also able to work with the young and discover their abilities [...] and he propagated modern art in circles where the only thing that could prevail was the personal charisma and discreet elegance of this man of the world."

The emotional charge of these words cannot be explained merely by the period's typical pathos. This previously unpublished review by Václav Vilém Štech, written just after he had visited Kotěra's posthumous exhibition in 1926,[1] reveals profound personal involvement. A series of other reviews, as well as obituaries published three years earlier, positively assessed Kotěra's role in the social and artistic life of Prague at the beginning of the 20th century. Let us try to re-evaluate this role from our present position. We will focus primarily on his membership of the Mánes Association of Fine Artists, especially his role in organising exhibitions.

The Mánes Association of Fine Artists

At the time of Kotěra's arrival in Prague in 1898, the Mánes Association of Fine Artists had just begun the most significant period in its history.[2] After ten years of existence, the Association had published its second volume of *Volné směry*, a journal that was still searching for a profile and audience of its own.

Immediately after Kotěra's appointment to the School of Applied Arts, his colleague Stanislav Sucharda introduced him to the Mánes Association. Thanks to the journals *Der Architekt* and *Ver Sacrum*,[3] as well as the spring exhibition

---

1 The text of V. V. Štech's review is deposited in the National Gallery Archive, collection 51, V. V. Štech, AA 2777.
2 The situation within Mánes and its general activities are best described and analysed in "SVU Mánes v letech 1897–1907", an unpublished dissertation by Lenka Bydžovská, ÚTDU ČSAV Praha 1989. The article includes further reading on the Mánes Association.

In her book *Volné směry, časopis secese a moderny*. Praha 1993, written together with Roman Prahle, she develops the same thesis.
3 "Concurenz um den Fügerpresis: Fürstliches Schwimmbad". *Der Architekt* II, 1896, p. 47, plate 86. – "Der Architekt, Supplementheft: Aus der Wagnerschule". *Ver Sacrum* I, 1898, p. 25. – News about Jan Kotěra winning the Prix de Rome appeared in *Volné směry* I, 1896–97, p. 482.

KOTĚRA THE ORGANISER 241

of Krasoumná jednota (Unity of Fine Arts),[4] Kotěra's early works from Wagner's studio were already well known in Prague. In his article in Čas (Time) journal, Jan Herben used direct quotations from Adolf Loos' original review in Neue Freie Presse. The positive commentary on the work of Wagner's school and especially Jan Kotěra (together with Jože Plečnik and Hubert Gessner), included the following extract about the Temple to Eros and Psyche: *"Once again, this architect has silenced an entire series of heatedly gesticulating ornamentalists with his simple, great, Classical pose – a recurring phenomenon in the history of architecture, revealing the dominance of Classical culture which permeates our entire being"*.[5] Loos' prophetic words expressed the latent quality that was to permeate Kotěra's future work.

On the occasion of the Architecture and Engineering Exhibition in 1898, Volné směry devoted considerable space to architecture. A discussion – "Modernism versus the National Style"[6] – flared up after the publication of a short article commenting on a supplement in Der Architekt dedicated to Wagner's school. The 1899 January issue of the journal included reproductions of Jan Kotěra's drawings and sketches from his Italian journey of 1898. More importantly, it featured K. B. Mádl's article "Art of the Future",[7] which analysed the difficult situation in contemporary Czech architecture. According to K. B. Mádl, the change in Prague architecture that had occured with the impact of Fridrich Ohmann's activity at the Prague School of Applied Arts, would finally be completed by his successor, Jan Kotěra.

Kotěra soon became engaged in the activities of the Association. After the departure of editors Karel Kusáček[8] and Karel V. Mašek, Kotěra, together with Stanislav Sucharda, Jan Preisler and Josef Schusser, made great changes to the journal's conception, beginning with the fourth volume. Thanks to Kotěra's collaboration with K. B. Mádl, the journal devoted much more space to the latest architectural news, including both local and international events, and also to the applied arts.

A special issue of Volné směry devoted exclusively to architecture (IV, nos. 8–10), featured Kotěra's symbolic drawing of architecture on its cover. It included his famous conceptual statement "On New Art",[9] as well as extracts from both his own and his students' work.[10] The extracts of modern architecture which Kotěra chose to accompany the important article by K. B. Mádl "Style of Our Time" reflected Kotěra's orientation in contemporary architecture. Using photographs, they introduced to Europe the work of Frank Lloyd Wright.

Kotěra was Editor-in-Chief for several later volumes (V–VII), and influenced the journal's graphic design with his vignettes and headings.

During the same period, Kotěra befriended a number of members of the Mánes Association – Stanislav Sucharda, Jan Preisler, Jan Štenc and others. In the first decade of the 20th century, this group became the driving force for a great variety of the Association's activities. Kotěra's relationships with several other members of Mánes, art historian K. B. Mádl, Dr Klika and Dr Heveroch, were equally important. For them, he later designed villas, interiors, tombs and individual pieces of furniture.

Owing to his distinctive personality, an unquestionable organisational talent, necessary contacts and his direct, friendly

---

4   Politik, 1. 1. 1899.
5   Čas XII, 1898, p. 501.
6   Volné směry II, 1897–98, p. 281.
7   Karel B. Mádl, "Příchozí umění". Volné směry III, 1898–99, pp. 117–142.
8   Karel Klusáček was dismissed from his post with Josef Franta, among other things also for his unscrupulous attacks against Jan Kotěra. Lenka Bydžovská (see note 1), pp. 118–119.
9   Jan Kotěra, "O novém umění". Volné směry IV, 1899–1900, pp. 189–195.
10 Kotěra continued to provide space for the reproductions of his students' work on the pages of Volné směry.

< **248**
Installation of the exhibition of works by Auguste Rodin in the Mánes pavilion, central octagonal hall with views through to the exhibition halls, 1902
> **249**
Meeting with Auguste Rodin,
from the left – seated: A. Rodin, J. V. Novák,
from the left – standing: F. Herčík, A. Mucha, R. Klenka of Vlastimil, J. Mařatka, J. Kotěra, E. Čenkov, A. Hofbauer, R. Vácha, M. Jiránek, 1902

11 In his letter of 28 April 1908, Max Švabinský mentioned that he promised to invite important guests to the opening – the mayor, the governor, the archduke. However, he believed it would be better if Kotěra was to invite them: "[...] *if you invite them, then they will certainly come to this opening*". AA NTM, Jan Kotěra's correspondence, no. 102.

< 250
Rodin's letter of thanks to J. Kotěra for his exhibition design, 1902

manner, as well as the nature of his work, Jan Kotěra soon held a leading position in Mánes. Kotěra placed great importance on solving architectural tasks in their entirety, including works of art in the building's interior and the composition of the façades. In commissioning sculptures, paintings, furniture and applied-art works, Kotěra gave priority to his friends from Mánes. His social contacts were as important,[11] although he never used them to his own advantage. This is clear from the small number of commissions that Kotěra won for public buildings. As the leading representative of the Association and its chairman for many years, Kotěra represented Mánes at numerous meetings and was a member of various committees and juries.

Of great importance was Kotěra's role as the representative of Mánes on the Board of Trustees of the newly established Modern Gallery. We could speculate that it was thanks to Kotěra's influence that this conservative institution purchased paintings by artists such as Antonín Slavíček, Antonín Hudeček or Max Švabinský. In 1905, Kotěra designed the first exhibition of the Modern Gallery collections at the Wiehl pavilion at Výstaviště (Exhibition Grounds) in Stromovka park. Its installation was to remain more or less unchanged until the beginning of the Second World War.[12] The majority of representatives of other Czech associations supported the idea of the Modern Gallery as an institution oriented towards promotion of Czech art. However, Kotěra and his colleagues from Mánes attempted, if to no effect, to ensure that it had an international character.

Kotěra often participated as a juror in various competitions,[13] be it as a representative of the Mánes Association or the Association of Architects. The latter was founded in 1908 as a division of Mánes; its members were mostly Kotěra's students and assistants. These architects, who published their work in the newly founded *Styl* journal, later voted Kotěra their first chairman. One of the major aims in the Association's programme was a repeated request to introduce architectural design competitions for public building commissions. On Kotěra's 50th birthday in March, 1922, the Architects' Society, which had taken over the activities of the Association after the First World War, made him an honorary member.[14]

The role that Jan Kotěra later played in the founding of the Czech Union of Applied Artists was especially important. In 1913, after the creation of the Austrian Werkbund, its president, Baron Bachofen, asked Kotěra to initiate a similar Czech institution in cooperation with the Prague Chamber of Trade and Commerce. Kotěra was fully aware of the significance of such an institution, especially in the organisation of international exhibitions. He gladly accepted the offer and took on the task of establishing the Czech Union. In his letter of invitation to the members of the preparatory committee, he stressed the reasons for the founding of the Austrian Union: *"As we are already well aware, this Union, identical to its German counterpart, was created to organise the best work within the applied arts, to negotiate and promote the work of artists and craftsmen, and finally to negotiate its export abroad through international exhibitions"*.[15] Kotěra made the same demands on the Czech filial institution, stressing the urgency of its founding. The new Czech Union

---

12 He also designed the adaptation of the pavilion in 1909. According to his own testimony, Jan Kotěra was a member of the board of trustees of the Modern Gallery for 19 years. Source: Archív ÚDU AV ČR, Wirth collection, Jan Kotěra's letter to Z. Wirth from 20 December 1921. The letter confirms that Kotěra's resignation from this post was a result of his dissatisfaction with the conception of the Modern Gallery. He was deeply convinced that the Gallery had to be run by someone who would be both qualified and responsible.

13 The most important competitions in 1908 included the one for the Old Town hall and for the Letná tunnel. J. Kotěra was also invited to participate in the preparatory committee for the garden towns and the juries for the Prague city cemetery.

14 Letter from 7 March 1922. AA NTM, Kotěra's correspondence.

15 Jan Kotěra's letter of invitation for Union membership from 23 June 1913. ÚDU AV ČR, Kotěra's correspondence.

political elite to the opening. The larger space also contributed in showing the works at their best. Jan Štenc, in a letter to Stanislav Sucharda, at the time chairman of the Association, described the preparations: *"Kotěra was great, he personally went to the bigwigs from all the Ministries, and to those outside the service. They will all be there tomorrow [...] I invited a hundred people, all Germans, bank managers and other scoundrels of their kind [...] They are really fussing over us in the Künstlerhaus as well. They keep coming, bringing people in and having conferences in front of our paintings [...]".* [27]

During that period, the Mánes Association artists became aware of the need for their own exhibition hall or pavilion. The request – raised by the Association's chairman Stanislav Sucharda at the opening of the first exhibition[28] – was granted in 1902. In that year, the Association organised an exhibition in Prague of Auguste Rodin – the first exhibit of the artist's works outside France. The Palace of Industry, which the Prague municipal council promised Rodin for the exhibition, was not free at the time and Rodin refused to use the adapted church of St Wenceslas. Mánes offered to build a provisional pavilion, which Kotěra designed in three days and which was built in less than a month. It was entirely financed by members of Mánes, especially its chairman Stanislav Sucharda. Another chapter in this book focuses on the building of the pavilion, analyses the different interpretations of its asymmetrical ground plan, as well as the treatment of the main façade. Rostislav Švácha[29]

---

27 AMP, Mánes collection, file 35, 6.1.7.

28 First exhibition of the Mánes Association, Stanislav Sucharda's address, in: *Volné směry* II, 1897–98, pp. 231–232.
29 Rostislav Švácha, "Poznámky ke Kotěrovu muzeu". *Umění* XXXIV, 1986, pp. 171–179.

< 253
Installation of the Czech Art exhibition,
7th Mánes Association exhibition, 1903
> 254
Installation of the Czech Art exhibition,
7th Mánes Association exhibition, 1903

discussed the pavilion's links with the museum in Hradec Králové, as well as the wider European context of both buildings.

I would therefore like to emphasise the functional logic of the pavilion, which enabled it to remain operative for some ten years, despite its initial purpose to house a single exhibition.[30] The "triumphal arch" of its entrance led to a passage with the box office and another small office located at the sides. The passage then led into a central octagonal hall with a glass dome, which housed the dominant works in the exhibition (Rodin's *The Kiss*, Bílek's *Moses*, etc.). The remaining section of the transverse wing served to house the drawings and prints, providing them with a more intimate space. The large hall, situated in the longitudinal wing, had overhead illumination and its space was divided by partitions of varying sizes. During the Rodin exhibition the hall was used as a whole and its ceiling was covered with a transparent fabric (like the New Town exhibition halls). To provide a neutral background for Rodin's sculptures, Kotěra left the walls painted grey, adding only the greenery. In later exhibitions, the walls blazed with colour, adorned with only a simple decorative frieze. The overall decoration had a lot in common with Kotěra's interior designs of the period. The change to an ascetic style, free of decoration, which dominated Kotěra's architecture in 1905–1910, manifested itself in his exhibition designs. This is especially true of the 16th members' exhibition in the spring of 1905. The space, rearranged by partition walls, was painted in neutral tones of white, grey and black. However, the octagonal hall at the entrance was bright orange, and the corridor was painted yellow. The walls were covered with Secessionist stylised ornaments. Nevertheless, the passageways, which at the Association's 7th exhibition were decorated with folk ornaments, now created a tectonic framework. This interior was listed as the first exhibit in the catalogue, also designed by Kotěra. The architect's exhibition designs created an effective environment, supporting the motto of the Association to present the best of Czech and international modern art.

Kotěra continued to be offered organisation and design work for exhibitions abroad – both for the Mánes Association and Czech art in general. This was probably the result of the success of his design for the Rodin exhibition (Rodin personally wrote to Kotěra praising both the pavilion and the exhibition design).[31] Sometime in 1906, Kotěra began entrusting the exhibition designs to Otakar Novotný, his closest assistant, himself also a member of the Mánes Association, or to his other colleagues.

30 During the First World War, the pavilion provided shelter to war refugees. It was demolished in 1917.

31 Undated letter. Private property.

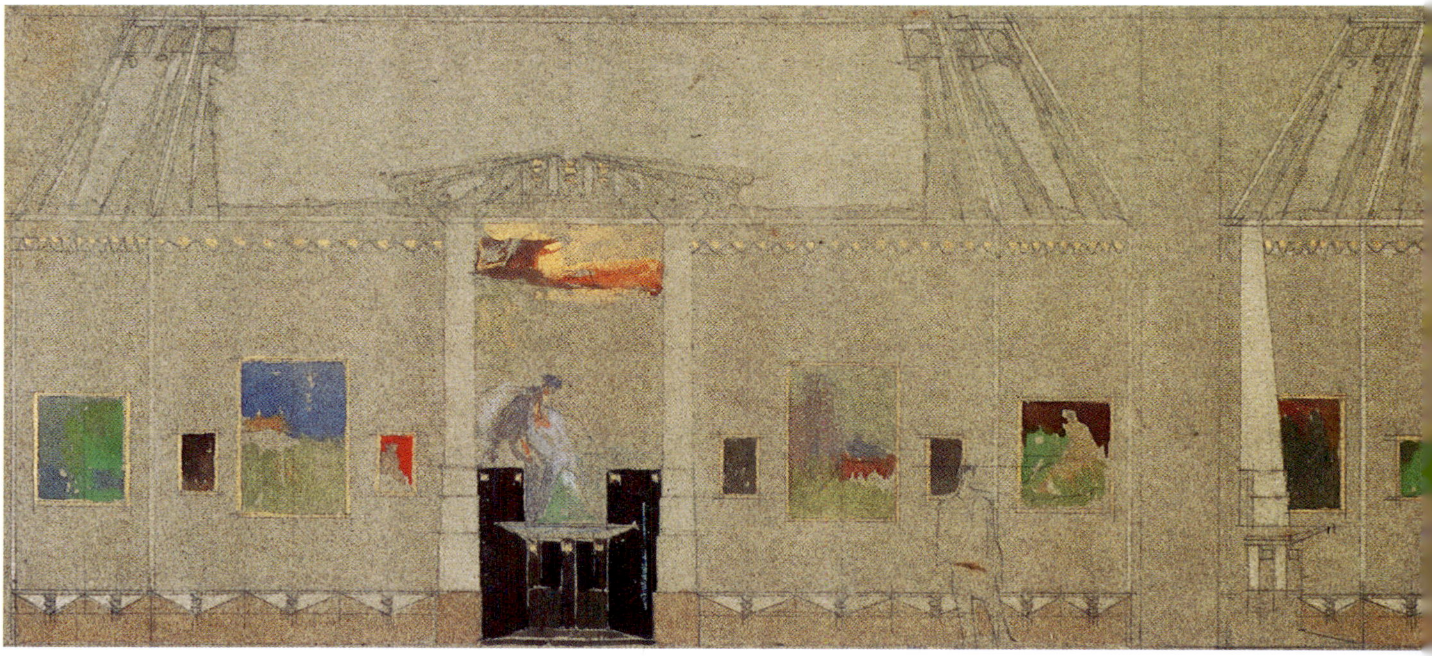

<> **255**
Installation of the Czech section at the World Exhibition in St Louis, plan for the arrangement of the exhibits, 1903

The International Exhibitions

Kotěra's work on the exhibition design for the School of Applied Arts at the Paris World Exhibition in 1900 was his first experience with international events. In this task he succeeded Friedrich Ohmann; both architects won a silver medal for their work.[32] The organising and creative work for the next exhibition in St Louis (1904) was more complex and demanding. As the chairman of the committee for the Czech section of the Austrian pavilion, Kotěra was entrusted by the government to organise an exhibition of Czech art (it was originally meant to include Polish art as well), to design it and be financially responsible for it.[33] For this first large independent international presentation of Czech art, Kotěra's design emphasised the folk idiom which was particularly effective in its combination of wood and textiles used in the interior. Once again, Kotěra used overhead lighting. The success of this exhibition brought Kotěra a rare sense of satisfaction: *"I really worked hard for this exhibition, but it was worth it. I am so proud of the quality of our young generation. They make the Secessionist Viennese seem small and affected"*.[34] Volné směry published a long review with many photographs,[35] and the exhibition was mentioned in other journals. The journey to St Louis itself was important for Kotěra where he was able to study and photograph local family houses.[36]

Kotěra made great efforts to promote Czech art in the period before the First World War. This is illustrated in his letter to Josef Franta, written in an attempt to describe the circumstances in which the exhibition on Christian art in Vienna in 1912 was being organised (Kotěra took part in it as a representative of Mánes): *"In the very first years after my return to Prague, I knew that there was no reason for our art not to be a part of international competitions [...] I wanted to be helpful, to assist in achieving our recognition, and I directed my efforts toward this goal. It was – and still is – my dream to see us, Czech artists, gain an independent reputation [...] I succeeded in securing the first independent Czech section at an international exhibition. It was in St Louis. It will be followed by an exhibition in London, two exhibitions in Munich, two in Venice and, finally, participation in the exhibition in Rome [...] As you can see from this short recapitulation, maybe the final score is not ideal, yet my conscience is clear. I believe I managed to achieve at least what the circumstances allowed. I do not have to mention that I sacrificed a lot of my time, energy and, indeed, money, to fulfil these efforts"*.[37]

It was most probably due to Kotěra's efforts and contacts that Mánes and Czech art in general were represented at

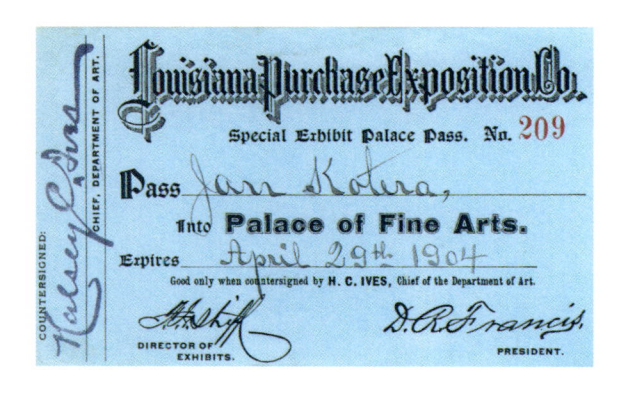

---

[32] Letter from 26 August 1900. LA PNP, Čapek-Chod correspondence.
[33] Letter from the governor's office to S. Sucharda from 25 October and 17 November 1903. AMP, Mánes collection. File 37, 6.1.22.
[34] J. Kotěra's letter to his friend R. G.(ombrich) in Vienna, in: *Stavitel* V, 1924, p. 61.
[35] "Interieur c. k. umělecko-průmislové školy v Praze pro výstavu v St. Louis 1904". *Volné směry*, 1904, p. 119.
[36] The photograph album from the journey to St Louis is today part of a private collection.
[37] Letter to J. F. from 8 March 1912. AA NTM, estate of Josef Fanta.
[38] The history of this "emancipation" of Czech art at international exhibitions was first mentioned during the preparations for the Czech section of the international exhibition in Paris. The majority of Czech artists agreed on their shared roles. They included

< 256
Installation of the Czech section at the World Exhibition in St Louis, 1904
<< 257
Pass for the World Exhibition in St Louis, 1904
> 258
Catalogue cover for the 16th exhibition of the Mánes Association, 1905

international exhibitions, in their own independent sections, and by works chosen by their own juries.[38]

Kotěra's exhibition designs also stood the test on an international scale. For his design of the first independent Czech section at the international exhibition in Munich in 1905, Bavarian Prince Ludwig awarded Kotěra the Order of St Michael, Third Degree.

The lists of Kotěra's exhibitions do not include the preparations for the exhibition on Christian art in Düsseldorf in 1910,[39] the participation of Mánes in the Hagen Jubilee Exhibition in Vienna in 1908[40] and, most importantly, the successful exhibition organised in Munich in 1913. For this, Bavarian Prince Ludwig awarded Kotěra another Order of St Michael, on this occasion Second Degree. In 1914, as a representative of the Czech Union of Applied Artists, Kotěra was appointed commissioner of the Czech section at the World Exhibition in San Francisco.[41]

After the First World War, the Ministry of School and Adult Education followed suit by organising similar commissions for international exhibitions. After a request from the Ministry of Foreign Affairs, this Ministry planned to organise an exhibition of Czech art in Paris in 1919. Together with Max Švabinský and Antonín Matějček, Jan Kotěra was entrusted with both the design and the practical preparations for this important exhibition.[42]

Apart from art exhibits, Kotěra was involved in designing exhibitions, sometimes entire pavilions, for big factories and companies. The pavilion of the Lichtenstein ceramics factory in Poštorná for the Milan exhibition in 1905 is a noteworthy example. The architect used the entire range of the factory's tile products to cover the ground, walls and ceiling of the pavilion, rendering the entire space a showcase for their products. In 1906, Kotěra designed the Ringhoffer factory pavilion, again for an exhibition in Milan. In 1910, he continued with the forestry exhibition in Vienna and in 1920, the Kopřivnice rail cars in Milan. The architecture of these pavilions reflected the style of Kotěra's buildings from the relevant period. The Lichtenstein pavilion was created at a time when Kotěra favoured Secessionist decorativeness and folk art motifs. The design for the Ringhoffer

---

a separate section as part of the central art commission, its own jury, an independent stand, and a rather large financial donation. Although the petition was not submitted in the end due to lack of interest on the part of professors at the Academy of Fine Arts, at least the requests for participation in the work for the commission, and for the separate stand for the School of Applied Arts and the Chamber of Trade and Commerce, had been met. In: *Volné směry* I, 1896–97, pp. 527–528; *Volné směry* III, 1898–99, pp. 114–115. When Mánes did not succeed in gaining a similar status, it resigned from its participation in the Munich exhibition (1901).

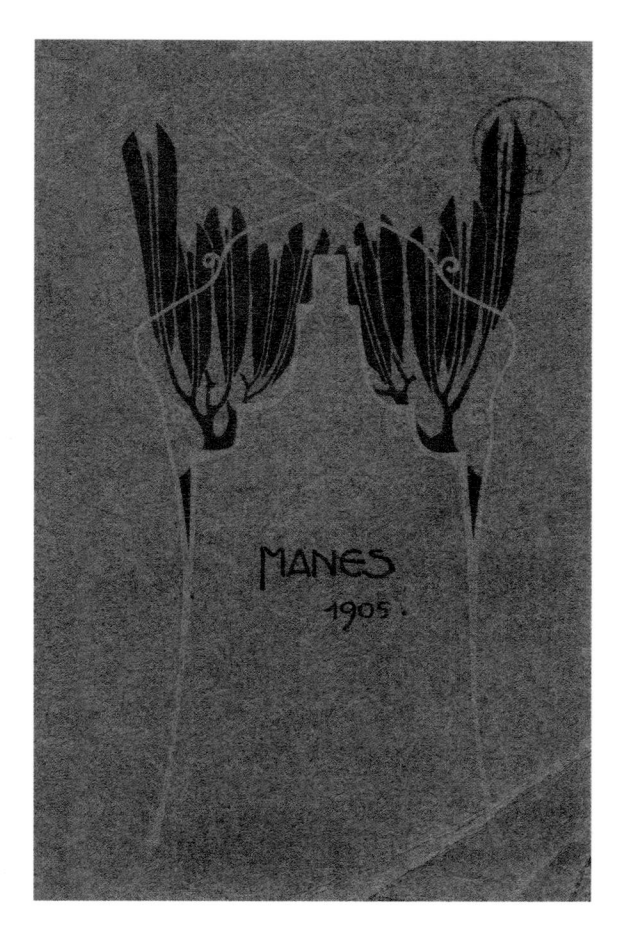

39 AMP, Mánes collection, file 42, entry 1912.
40 AMP, Mánes collection, file 38, entry 1908. Jubilee Exhibition in Vienna.
41 Letter from 1 July 1914. LA PNP.
42 Kotěra went to Paris at the beginning of 1919, and again in May the same year. – E. Beneš, letter of recommendation for J. Kotěra and H. Jelínek to Lafferr, the Minister of Art and Education, from 29 January 1919. AA NTM, Jan Kotěra's correspondence, no. 320.

pavilion was simpler from the point of view of function and material used, but the décor, lightly Wagnerian in style, also contained folk elements. The overall impression was Neo-Classicist, both in structure and detail. The pavilion for the Kopřivnice rail cars corresponded to the increasingly Neo-Classicist traits in Kotěra's late works.

Kotěra did not often exhibit his own work, except at the very beginning of his career. This makes the success of his posthumous participation in an exhibition of decorative art in Paris in 1925 – where Bedřich Feuerstein[43] *"won"* the Grand Prix for him[44] – even more significant.

In 1926, the Mánes Association presented Kotěra's work at a large retrospective held at Obecní dům (Municipal House). In its scope, this exhibition remains unparalleled to this day. It provided an opportunity to recapitulate not only Kotěra's own work, but also the effects of modern Czech architecture in general. It also testified to the number of Czech architects who felt their work was part of Kotěra's legacy. After Kotěra's family bequeathed his estate to the National Technical Museum during the exhibition, the Mánes Association of Fine Artists requested from other owners of Kotěra's works that they follow their example.[45] So it was in part thanks to Mánes that Kotěra's estate has remained intact, deposited in the Architecture Archive at the National Technical Museum in Prague. The Mánes Architects' exhibition in 1930, organised once again in Obecní dům, was later referred to in reviews as the exhibition of Jan Kotěra and his school, since many of his works were shown there, along with those of his students and colleagues.

We often read in Kotěra's obituaries that he built very little, and wasted his talent organising other events, a fact which is simply not true. Kotěra's contemporaries highly appreciated both his teaching and his role as an organiser. His belief that painting, sculpture, and other fine-art disciplines should be completely integrated with the applied arts and architecture – very much in the sense of the notion of *Gesamtkunstwerk* – was reflected in his art exhibition designs. Conceived as residential interiors of a truly unique style, they left a strong impression on both viewers and future presentations of Czech fine art.

---

[43] Bedřich Feuerstein, *Z dopisů*. Praha 2000, pp. 106–107.
[44] Letter from 1 October 1925, in which the Club *"would like to announce that it has joined the Mánes Association so that Kotěra's interior design is acquired for the collection of the Museum of Decorative Arts"*. Even if the exhibition in question was not specified, we may surmise that it was the exhibition of decorative arts in Paris in 1925. Kotěra's participation is mentioned in the exhibition catalogue. AMP, Mánes collection, entry with the Architects' Club correspondence.
[45] AMP, Mánes collection, 1926. Jan Kotěra's exhibition.

< **259**
Installation of the Modern Gallery permanent exhibition, 1905
< **260**
Installation of the Mánes Association section at the Exhibition of Austrian Art in London, 1906
> **261**
Installation of the Austrian section at the World Exhibition in Munich, Štursa's hall, 1913

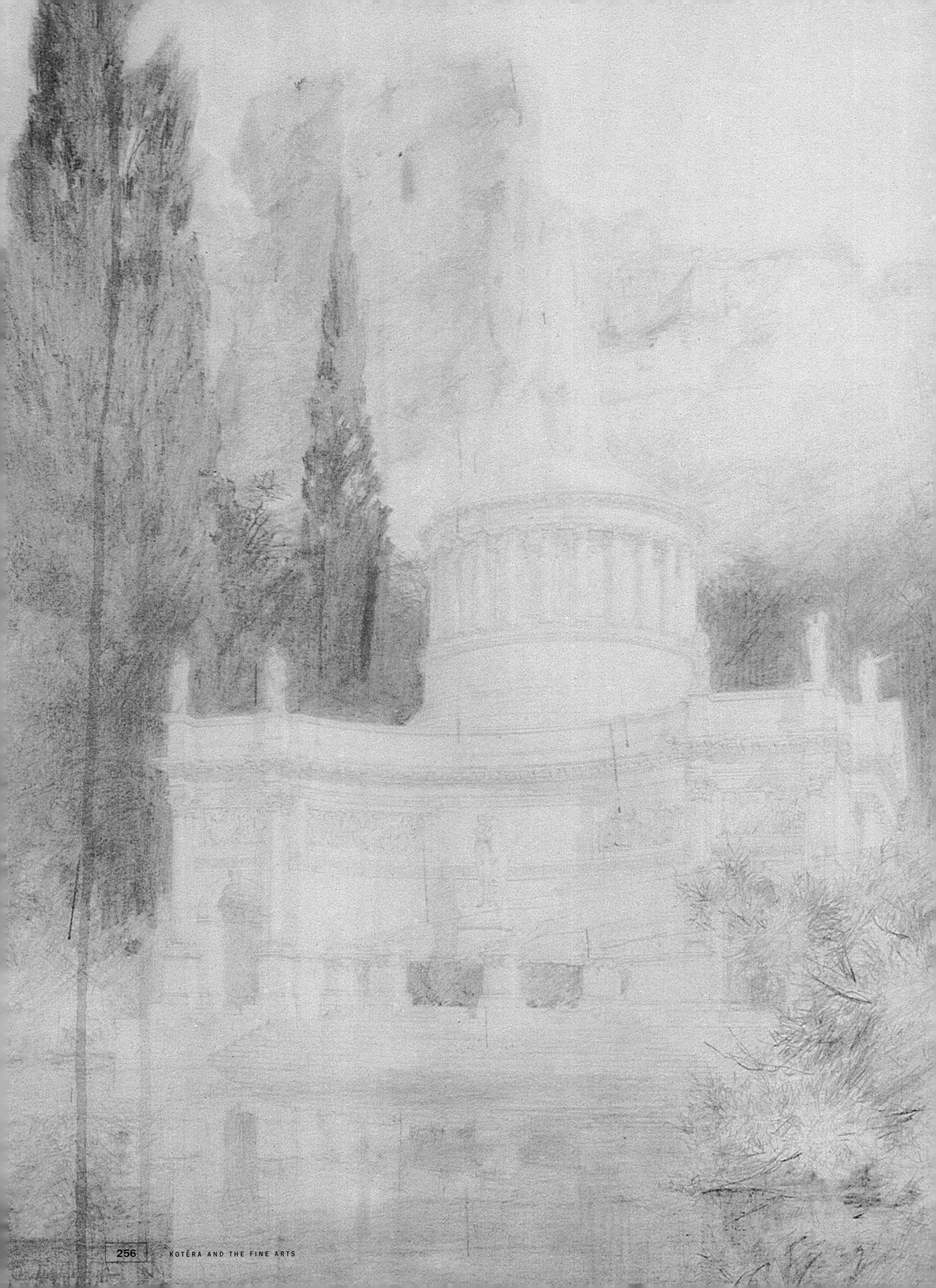

< 262
Temple to Eros and Psyche – The Roman Fantasy, 1898
> 263
From Venice, 1901

Kotěra and the Fine Arts

ALENA POMAJZLOVÁ

Jan Kotěra presented his work to the Czech public in 1898, after completing his studies with Otto Wagner in Vienna and undertaking a journey to Italy. The Topič salon exhibition, featuring Kotěra's latest drawings and studies from that period, seemed more like the presentation of an artist than an architect.[1] The event also appeared to augur Kotěra's definitive return to Bohemia. In the autumn of that year, he began teaching at the School of Applied Arts in Prague as the successor to Friedrich Ohmann. Arriving in Prague at the turn of the century, Kotěra presented himself as a figure of truly wide perspective with an immediate knowledge of the international trends in architecture and the arts. He had progressive views and, more importantly, great self-confidence and a desire to create new art. In Prague, he found himself at the beginning of an era in which issues of artistic creation were being reformulated. The organisation of artistic life was also undergoing transformation and Kotěra was to take an active part in these changes.

The new artistic views were propagated mainly by the Mánes Association, initially an insignificant student association which in the 1890s suddenly became a major organiser of artistic events. In February 1898, the first exhibition of its members in the Topič salon launched a decade of its most important activities.[2] Following the suggestion of Stanislav Sucharda, Kotěra joined the Association, and immediately became fully engaged in its organisation and creative endeavours. He joined the editorial staff of *Volné směry* journal,[3] where he introduced himself in one of the few articles he ever published, the conceptual statement entitled "On New Art".[4] In it, he declared himself a follower of recent artistic trends which searched for new forms of expression, the only forms – according to Kotěra – able to survive in modern times. With this in mind, he opened *Volné směry* to new ideas in architecture and art.

First and foremost, Kotěra was an architect working in the spirit of these new trends. His early sketches from Italy already display this shift from the historicism which burdened his student projects, towards a new understanding of art. Even when they depicted historical buildings or their parts, these sketches had nothing in common with the refuted concept of historicism. They used natural scenery to frame the depicted building, together with figural staffage which gave the drawings a civil tone, bringing them closer to the progressive contemporary views on architecture. As K. B. Mádl noted in his article "Art of the Future", these drawings should be seen more as *"studies of a landscape*

---

[1] Some of these drawings were reproduced and published together with K. B. Mádl's article "Příchozí umění", which put great faith in Kotěra's return, hoping it would prompt a revival in Czech art. See: *Volné směry* III, 1899, pp. 119–142.

[2] Together with Antonín Slavíček's landscapes, especially *Birch Mood* with a style highly illustrative of the period, the exhibition featured the works of Jan Preisler (a collection of drawings) and Stanislav Sucharda – *Willow* and *Treasure*. These two artists left their mark on Prague's artistic life at the turn of the century. Kotěra would continue to meet them in the circle of the Mánes Association and to collaborate with them on his projects.

[3] Kotěra edited the volumes IV–VII (1900–1903). In 1901, he became Editor-in-Chief.

[4] Jan Kotěra, "O novém umění". *Volné směry* IV, 1899–1900, pp. 189–195.

painter enamoured of the picturesque views of architecture, than the drawings of an architect who, in the classical realm of his art, should, after all, walk armed with a ruler, compass and measuring rod".[5] Kotěra did not strive to reconstruct or document the buildings so that he could later use them in his architectural work. Instead, he created drawings of what would best be described as landscape "moods" or "fantasies". *"I am looking above all at the overall character, mood, impression"*, Kotěra wrote from Italy. The emphasis on mood was certainly influenced by the period fondness for landscape "moods" which at the turn of the 20th century dominated the landscape genre. Their emphasis on personal experience inaugurated a whole new wave of individualism in the arts. This also applied to architectural drawing, which achieved a far greater freedom and began to express the individual styles of the architects. Even Kotěra's compulsory compositional study from Italy – *Temple to Eros and Psyche – The Roman Fantasy* (1898) could be described as an independent drawing. It is comparable to the idealism which characterised the early works of Max Švabinský or Ferdinand Engelmüller who, at the time, set their visions in idealised southern landscapes. The same type of imaginary architecture appeared in Kotěra's stage design for Dvořak's *Rusalka* (1901), and his illustration for the *Tale of the Red Knight* (1902). The latter was developed into a symbolic *"fortress of new endeavours"* in the Mánes

---

5 K. B. Mádl, "Příchozí umění". *Volné směry* III, 1898–99, p. 134. – For the traditional manner of the architectural drawing of *"ruled Gothic churches"*, see Miloš Marten's essay "Štěstí rezonance". *Volné směry* VII, 1902–03.

< **264**
Musical Impressions, c. 1901
> **265**
Rialto, 1908

pavilion. Here, it was conceived as modern Secessionist architecture.

Kotěra's personality radiated much more vividly from his small architectural sketches, particularly his primary specifications of mass and form. We should also note his 1901 designs inspired by music entitled *Musical Impressions*, as well as his designs for tombstones. This line of expression culminated in his drawings for the monument to Jan Žižka in Prague (1913).[6] It is not a coincidence that the same abbreviated form was used in Kotěra's caricatures. Created as marginal, "trivial" drawings outside his major works, they used highly modern means – an emphasis on the main characteristics of the subject, with economy and conciseness of expression – which reaffirm their role in the formulation of modern art. In a very similar manner, Kotěra's drawing of a Cubist house was also created as a marginal sketch, produced just for fun, but its exaggeration perfectly captured the logic of Cubist architecture. We could say that, in his caricatures, like his Italian sketches, Kotěra strove to acquire a truly unified expression. This aspiration accompanied him throughout his career, and strongly influenced his choice of artists with whom he collaborated.

It was probably in this idea of unity that Kotěra frequently worked through his designs to the last detail (including the furniture, lights, mounts, decorative ornaments on the walls and floors, etc.). In his large-scale works, however, Kotěra collaborated with others, mainly his colleagues from the School of Applied Arts and the Mánes Association. He had a fine sense for acquiring the services of not only those who understood his architecture, but who were also excellent artists in their own right. This often gave rise to outstanding works of art which brought together progressive forms of architecture, sculpture and painting.

There were four main areas of Kotěra's architecture in which he collaborated with artists from other fields. He commissioned sculptors (chiefly in the early Secessionist period) to work on both the interior and the façade, however, in time they began to focus mainly on the portal as the most prominent element of the façade. The new conception of the city monument was another area in which the architect worked in close collaboration with sculptors. The third area involved the painted decoration of interiors, and the fourth – involving all the different disciplines of the visual arts – were Kotěra's exhibition designs.

It was the Mánes Association which created the opportunity for Kotěra to work on exhibition installations. In 1900, as a member of the Mánes exhibition committee, he was the

---

6 Zdeněk Wirth, who researched this part of Kotěra's work, used the term "Malerarchitekt" (Architect-Painter) to describe the style of architectural drawing which evoked the architectonic line, form and mass through ingenious and expressive abbreviation. See: Zdeněk Wirth, "Ke Kotěrově výstavě". *Volné směry* XXIV, 1926, pp. 97–99. Also: Zdeněk Wirth, "Jan Kotěra kreslíř". *Umění* (Štenc) XV, 1943–44, pp. 253–270.

official architect of the 3rd exhibition of its members organised for the New Town Halls in Vodičkova street in Prague.[7] Kotěra made an effort to introduce new types of exhibitions than were customary until then. More responsive to the artworks they presented, they reflected a new attitude towards artistic individuality, and expressed and reinforced the very status of art.[8] The first Mánes exhibition attempted a new approach and somewhat reduced the numbers of exhibits, placing them with greater care with regard to their context.[9] Yet truly substantial change came only with Kotěra's arrival. His designs did away with overcrowded exhibitions and left enough space for visitors to appreciate each of the works, allowing each artist to excel. The installations were simple and easy to view. The works of art no longer "filled" the exhibition, they gave meaning to it. The exhibition of Auguste Rodin's works (1902), for which Kotěra also designed the new exhibition pavilion in Kinský gardens below Petřín hill, was a true achievement in this field.[10]

This event, whose results were only short-term and whose outcome is known only from period photographs, was, however, extremely important for the period understanding of art. The new type of presentation not only pointed to the public's approach to art, but it also helped to establish the artist and his work in modern society.

After his experience with the designs for the Mánes pavilion, Jan Kotěra was entrusted with the reconstruction of the interior and the new display of the collections of the Mod-

---

7   The exhibition included paintings, sculptures, drawings, prints, as well as works of applied arts – ceramic crockery, jewellery, etc. It featured an extensive collection of works by František Bílek.
8   The traditional manner of organising exhibitions – the so-called salons – was already considered passé. The salons displayed current artwork, both in fine and applied arts, with no aesthetic or qualitative criteria. The works were installed alongside one another in rows, and complemented with decorative works. (At the time, salons were usually held at the Rudolfinum Gallery in Prague).
9   See: Karel Mašek, *Tři léta s Mánesem*, undated. It states, among other things, that the opening of this exhibition was the first private view ever organised in Bohemia. It "*brought together an educated, pleasing group of people, truly interested in art*". In his opening speech, Stanislav Sucharda noted that the Rudolfinum had never seen such a joint presentation of Czech artists in a single exhibition hall; pp. 75–79.
10 For Kotěra's exhibition designs, see the chapter by R. Kreuzziegerová in this publication.

< 266
Jan Kotěra at the lido, 1915
> 267
Cubist house for Mrs K. Heveroch, c. 1915

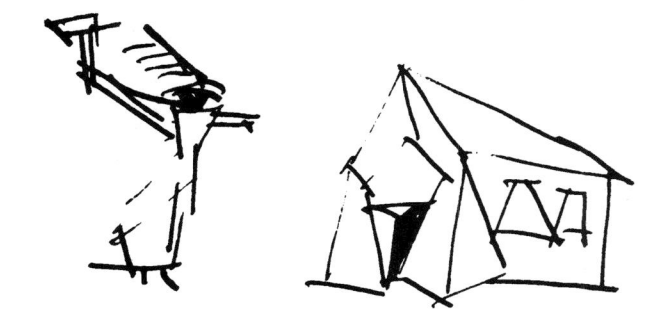

ern Gallery in Wiehl's pavilion at Výstaviště (Exhibition Grounds) – 1905, reopened in 1911. Later, Kotěra became involved in acquiring a new location for the gallery, while the first plans for the State Gallery on Kampa Island designed by Ladislav Machoň used Kotěra's initial material and spatial divisions. Kotěra also participated in the design and organisation for exhibitions of Czech art abroad. His presentation of the School of Applied Arts at the 1904 World Exhibition in St Louis was a specific commission he undertook. It incorporated works of fine art as equals alongside the applied-art designs – Schikaneder's decorative panels above the seats, Sucharda's large-scale relief *Prague and the Vltava* above a fireplace, and other sculptural works from Sucharda's school.

In the first phase of Kotěra's work, Stanislav Sucharda – his colleague from the School of Applied Arts and the Mánes Association – was his chief sculptor.[11] In December 1899, they entered a competition together to design the monument to Jan Hus – one of the most extensive and demanding of contemporary projects, designated for a location in the very heart of Prague. Kotěra entered the competition with two different works, first as architect to Stanislav Sucharda with a design for a work entitled *You Sprang up above the Mire*, the second time as the main author (with Sucharda as his colleague) of *You Vanished in Purity and Left a Furrow*. According to an article later published in *Volné směry*,[12] Kotěra's notions of the contemporary monument were strongly marked by Jože Plečnik's design for the monument to Guttenberg in Vienna (1898), created in collaboration with O. Schimkowitz. The article emphasised the architect's role in the monument's overall concept, especially in the cohesiveness, unity and monumentality of the work. Kotěra and Sucharda had a similar aim in mind and agreed to represent Jan Hus as a symbolic, monumental figure, without the allegorical and historical associations which were common at the time and evident in Šaloun's winning design in which he placed the dying Hus on the pyre, surrounded by a lively figural staffage. On the contrary, Sucharda's concept was based on a very modern approach to individuality.[13] It accentuated openness, ambiguity, and invited the observer's fantasy.[14] It seems that Sucharda learnt a lesson from the problems he encountered in his previous monument to Palacký where the symbolic and historicist sculpture was of secondary importance to the established architectural form. Inspired mainly by Rodin, Sucharda's vision of the monument to Jan Hus was focused on the central symbolic sculpture, while the architecture was reduced to a low decorative plinth and the rounded boundary stones that surrounded it. Here, the emphasis lay in ensuring that the monument fitted well into the given

11 Sucharda also collaborated with Kotěra's predecessor, Friedrich Ohmann, creating the sculptures *Danger* and *Protection* for the Assicurazioni Generali building in Prague. His relief *Peasants Returning from the Fields* was part of the decoration for Ohmann's interior for the 1900 World Exhibition in Paris, completed by Kotěra.
12 Jan Kotěra, "Jože Plečnik". *Volné směry* IV, 1901, p. 68.

13 Sucharda's own words are most illustrative of this point: *"Jan Hus alone creates a monument unto himself. No other historical figure except him. He is the dominant to which one must subordinate all the rest, every form and every detail"*. Quoted according to K. B. Mádl, "Husův pomník". *Volné směry* V, 1901, p. 68.
14 According to Jan Kotěra: *"I believe that a work of art should not hide or simply contain the artist's intention. I believe it should provoke a harmonious response in each observer. To achieve this goal, it has to provide the greatest possible freedom so that this harmonious echo may be continually shaped in the observer's fantasy"*. See note 13.

environment of the Old Town Square. We should add that Kotěra and Sucharda were the only artists who truly respected the prerequisite of this competition regarding the location of the monument. Although the design was not accepted, it certainly influenced – like the symbolic image of Hus created by František Bílek – the definitive appearance of Šaloun's monument. This competition was a telling example of the difference between the representatives of historicism and the followers of a more symbolic, sculptural approach to monument design. Another important competition in which Kotěra participated, in collaboration with Jan Štursa, was the monument to Jan Žižka on Vítkov hill in Prague (1913), a competition which already showed the influence of the youngest generation of Cubist artists and architects. The architect's role in this competition was greater for it required elaborate landscaping and sufficient access to the monument from the foot of Vítkov hill. Many of the designs treated the monument in an abstract, architectonic, rather than sculptural manner (especially Janák and Gutfreund, partly also Machoň with Horejc, Hofman, etc.).[15]

They incorporated pointed forms and acute angles, at least in the morphology of the base and surrounding site. Štursa's and Kotěra's design was an equestrian monument made from a single block of stone, with schematised warriors with shields lining both sides of the equestrian statue. The stylised appearance of this sculptural group, with its regular arrangement of warriors, left an impression of an abstract, rhythmical architectural structure. Its "synthetically robust" form, suppressing all detail, utilised the scheme of Kotěra's first sketch for the monument with its fundamental division of mass. The soft morphology of Secessionist symbolism was replaced by an expressiveness so striking that the monument was criticised as "too German". Neither of the avant-garde monuments was accepted in the end. Once again, this competition proved that it was difficult to articulate modern art forms to suit a traditional task, expressing the crisis in monument design itself.

Štursa and Kotěra created another monument in a similar spirit, however, in a more classical tone. Their war memorial for Jihlava (1917) shows the figure of a grieving soldier leaning against his sword, placed on a pyramid-shaped tumulus. Along with other monuments – the Vojáček monument in Prostějov (1910) produced in collaboration with the sculptor Bohumil Kafka, or the design for the war memorial in Příbram (1917), etc. – Kotěra collaborated with sculptors on smaller tasks – commissions for tombs and tombstones. Although relatively small in size, the drawings of these tombstones reveal that Kotěra conceived them as monumental forms, more akin to his buildings than to memorials.

Stanislav Sucharda and Jan Štursa, Kotěra's main sculptors, created works illustrative of two different styles in Kotěra's architecture – the first still linked with Secessionist Symbolism, the second with the rational constructive order of Modernism.

---

[15] See the reproductions supplementing the article by Otakar Novotný, "Architektura symbolická, Pomník a Žižkův pomník". *Volné směry* XVIII, 1915, pp. 78–89. – Rostislav Švácha, "Citadela-mohyla", in: Czech Cubism Exhibition Catalogue, 1909–1925. Hatje, Stuttgart 1991.

< 268
Stanislav Sucharda, Jan Kotěra, *You Vanished in Purity and Left a Furrow*, competition entry for the monument to Jan Hus, 1900
> 269
You Sprang up above the Mire,
competition entry for the monument to Jan Hus, 1900

Kotěra invited Sucharda to collaborate with him on the sculptural decoration of National House in Prostějov (1905–06). Sucharda concentrated mainly on the sculptures adorning the portal on the eastern façade. He created stylised figures of the archetypal Czech male and female, *Hanák* and *Hanačka* on the pylons of the portico, carved in relief, using strongly geometric, simple forms. In this work, Sucharda suppressed his soft pictorial style used to treat the transition between light and shadow familiar from his reliefs and posters, in favour of a more condensed form, fully subordinate to the architecture.[16] Another of Sucharda's commissions was the earthenware figural decoration for the fountain on the south-western part of National House's façade. Although stylised geometrically, the treatment of its surface and its colour lend it a softer expression. Once again, Sucharda used materials more common for the applied arts than sculpture for the figures framing the portal of Kotěra's City Museum in Hradec Králové (1906–13). The seated female figures personify *History* and *Industry*. These figures symbolise the fact that, despite its use of unplastered brickwork and its architecture being more reminiscent of a factory, this building is chiefly a "temple of spirit". In these allegories, Sucharda parts with Secessionist linearity and moves towards a solid plastic form inspired by Classical art. Their thrones, clad with bricks, repeat on a smaller scale

16 Sucharda's figures complementing Gočár's designs for a tumulus at Bílá Hora (1908) employ the same kind of geometrical stylisation. Sucharda used a similarly flat figural sculpture to decorate the column on another of Kotěra's designs – the interior of the Old Town Hall mayor's office (1907–08), where the material (wood) allowed him a more lavish, naturalistic and decorative form.

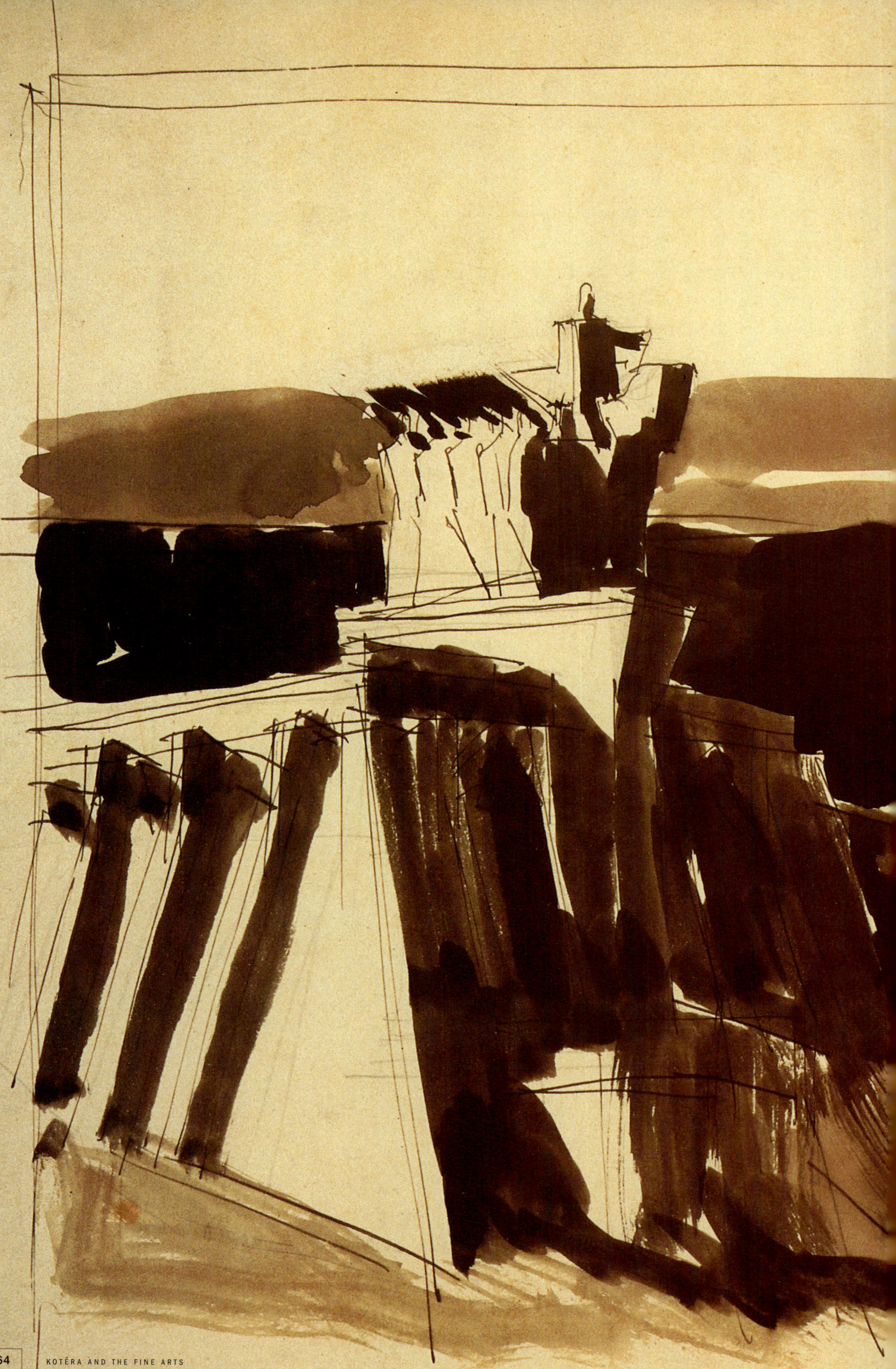

<> 270
Study for the monument to Jan Žižka, 1913

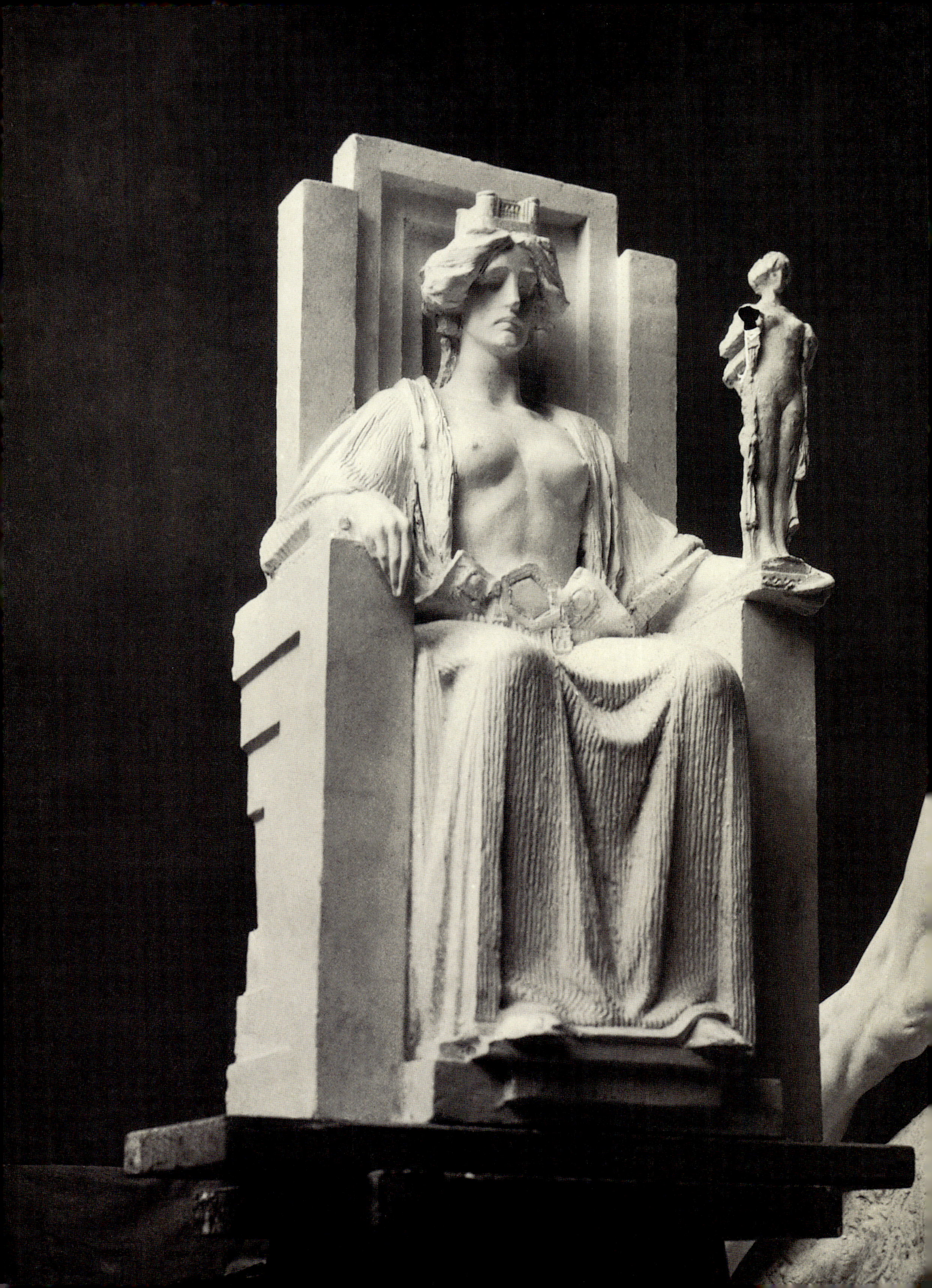

< 271
Stanislav Sucharda, *History*, model for the figural decoration of the museum façade, 1908–1912

the concave design of the entrance of the museum's main façade. Their liberated Classical form and hieratic austerity correspond with Kotěra's efforts to remove superfluous elements from his buildings and create an architecture that was simple, well built and with no exterior decoration.

Kotěra's effort to achieve a constructive, orderly and artistically "pure" work was manifested in the requirements he placed on his artists. He wanted artists whose expression would correspond with his architecture. With a façade that excluded all other decoration, the portal was the key location for the sculpture. It was a place where the sculpture could function as an architectural feature, and at the same time fulfil its own aesthetic function, intensifying the overall expression of the building. In Prostějov, the decorative work was governed by an ethnographic, regional tone,[17] in Hradec Králové, it evolved around the main allegory reflecting the orientation of the museum – the chief non-artistic links between the two buildings.

Jan Štursa, another sculptor whose work reflected Kotěra's architectural views, was able to sense Kotěra's inclination towards monumentality and the solid classical form, an affinity evidently strengthened by his journey to Italy in 1907. It was expressed by a suppression of Rodin-inspired Symbolism and a shift towards Bourdellean Neo-Classicism. Štursa conceived the sculptural frame of the Trade Pavilion portal at the 1908 Jubilee Exhibition of the Chamber of Trade and Commerce in Prague in a similar style. He envisaged two ascending rows of Classical female figures with garlands, rising symmetrically from each side of the portal. In so doing, he both preserved and intensified the rhythm of the architectonic forms of Kotěra's design. Moreover, he reinforced the simplicity of the façade and its triangular composition. The sculptures do not constitute part of the façade, they are placed before it. Their monumental size and relatively independent position create an artistic idiom parallel to Kotěra's architecture. They complied with the requirements of Štursa's mentor Émile A. Bourdelle, expressed in his Prague lecture in 1909. According to Bourdelle, the sculptor was to try and suppress the symbolic content of his work. He also had to strive for the sculpture's relative independence from the architecture. This search for a parallel which was visual and not semantic nor literary, remained at the core of Štursa's art in his sculptural decoration for Kotěra's architecture.

The other façade of the Trade pavilion was decorated with Štursa's relief depicting *Industry* and *Trade*. Its civilian elements indicated a new thematic and stylistic direction in his sculpture.[18] Štursa's caryatids, decorating Kotěra's Urbánek house – Mozarteum (1912–13) already had a stylised, classical form. They did not frame the asymmetrical entrance but were placed axially on the edges of the central window. Their stylisation conformed to the simple architectural divisions of the building.

Štursa's sculptural decoration of imposing residential buildings was somewhat different, almost Baroque in character. This is well illustrated in the sculptural work adorning the façades of Bianca villa in Prague-Bubeneč (1910–13). For this commission, the first of its kind, Štursa created a traditional pair of figures – *Night* and *Day*, conceived as a male

---

17 Stylised folk ornaments, designed by František Kysela, also appear in the sgraffito decoration of the façade.

18 Period photographs and preparatory models are the only available sources on Štursa's sculptural decoration for the Jubilee Exhibition. One of these models is featured on a photograph depicting Kotěra's studio. Kotěra's private collection included other works by Štursa – a sketch for *Diana*, 1914, sketch for the *Burial in the Carpathian Mountains*, 1915, sketch for *The Gift of Heaven and Earth*, 1917–18, *Greek Sailors* oil painting, and a number of drawings.

and female nude with draperies. He placed the statues as free-standing sculptures on the sides of the building, on the level of the first floor.[19] In his allegorical works *Spirit* and *Matter*, created for Mandelík's castle in Ratboř (1911/12–1915), Štursa returned once again to classical sculpture. Placed on the building's cornice, these figures framed the central dome from both sides. As in the works for the Bianca villa, Štursa once more adopted the full, sculptural form of the female and male nude. In their classical monumentality, the artist found the artistic expression appropriate for this new task while, at the same time, creating independent sculptural works.

After the First World War, Štursa designed the sculptural decoration for Ringhoffer's factory in Smíchov although it remained only on paper. He was also to have created the sculptural decoration for the portal of the university's Law and Theology Faculty (1918). The stylised tympanum crowning the entrance to the main building of the Vítkovice mining company in Prague, designed in his Civilist phase by Otto Gutfreund, an artist from the new generation, could be considered one of the last sculptural decorations to appear on Kotěra's façade.

Kotěra also managed to attract the leading artists of his time to decorate the interiors of his buildings. Jaroslav Horejc, a student of Sucharda, designed most of Kotěra's interiors, both with sculptures and works of applied art. Horejc suited Kotěra for his synthetic approach to art, uniting plasticity with decorativeness, and for his fondness for the classical form, inspired chiefly by Classical Greek sculpture. Like Štursa, Horejc was profoundly influenced by E. A. Bourdelle, whom he met on the occasion of Bourdelle's visit to Prague in 1909. Horejc mainly worked as an applied artist, however, he was also a prominent sculptor. For Kotěra he designed the sculpture *Ploughman* in 1911 for the castle in Ratboř, along with a stylised figure inspired by Bourdelle for the fountain in the main foyer of the Grand Hotel in Hradec Králové. The figural composition for the fireguards in Baťa's villa in Zlín (1918) was another of his designs. The two artists also collaborated on works of a smaller scale. One of them was Kotěra's design for a wooden casket for a private altar containing Horejc's ceramic relief *Virgin Mary with St Cecilia*. Horejc's work was also represented in Kotěra's private art collection.[20]

Paintings formed an important part of the interior decoration of Kotěra's architecture. He pioneered a new concept of decorative painting, emphasising the autonomous, artistic character of the work and introducing a new understanding of decorative values. These bore no literary or mythological associations of the kind seen in the decoration for the National Theatre, the most extensive and most representative work in Czech art up until that time. This requirement for new decorativeness was best fulfilled by František Kysela, who designed wall paintings and stained glass for Kotěra (the windows of the Hradec Králové museum, 1911). His largest wall paintings decorated the interior of the Arco coffee-house (1907) and the small salons of National House in Prostějov (1908), while ornamental decoration covered the walls of the Grand Hotel in Hradec Králové (1911). In his commission for Prostějov (where we can compare the original drawings with the final design), Kysela

---

19 The original sculptures are today located at the entrance to the castle in Zbraslav, part of the National Gallery in Prague.

20 See: Jana Horneková, "České art deco 1918–1938". *Umění a řemesla*, 1998, pp. 18–28.

< **272**
Stanislav Sucharda, *Prague and the Vltava*, relief, 1902
> **273**
Jaroslav Horejc, sculpture for the fountain in the Palm garden of the Grand Hotel in Hradec Králové, 1911

brought figurative painting and stylised decoration together into a single composition, defined by ornamental frames. The consistent two-dimensional conception and the combination of harmonious colours transform the mural into a unified belt running the entire length of the interior, without interfering with the original function of the walls.

Jan Preisler, however, was Kotěra's chief painter. Kotěra was already planning to install a painting by Preisler in Peterka's house on Wenceslas Square while it was still being constructed. Preisler's triptych *Spring*, first featured at the 3rd exhibition of the Mánes artists, as well as being Preisler's groundbreaking work, became a symbol of new painting. It expressed Preisler's struggle to achieve the synthesis of all the diverse styles in the visual arts, and to unite them in a modern painting that would be both symbolic and decorative. This, together with an effort to bring out the painting's inner logic of composition, fully corresponded with Kotěra's own ideals, where construction and the arrangement of space were seen as fundamental in his own work. Preisler also strove to capture the inherent laws of the painting. According to him, the painting should be a precise, organically composed integral work, where everything is placed with a clear purpose in mind, whether instinctive or logical,[21] a reference to Munch on the one hand and Cézanne on the other. These parallels between Kotěra's and Preisler's views were not simply a matter of coincidental agreement between two artists belonging to the same period. They expressed more profound period trends that were focused on an attempt to unite different artistic genres and reach a modern style based on new principles that followed the inner laws of the artwork. Preisler's first substantial work, *Painting from a Larger Cycle*, took pride of place in one of the halls of Kotěra's own villa in Hradešínská street, manifesting the strong links that existed between the two artists.[22]

The monumental compositions which decorated the restaurant in the Regional Authorities building in Hradec Králové, the vestibule of National House in Prostějov and the dome of the museum in Hradec Králové, remain the most important works created by Preisler for Kotěra's interiors.

Preisler's painting for the interior of the Regional Authorities building in Hradec Králové (1903–04) was his first decorative work for a building designed by Kotěra. Preisler chose to give it the form of an easel painting, employing all of his typical figural elements. During the preparatory work, he suppressed his early Symbolist and Secessionist motifs (visions of a seductive naked female figure, the female profile resembling elements from *Painting from a Larger Cycle* and *Spring*), and created a stylistically and thematically unified painting, symbolically blending reality with vision. The figures of the man and woman were both repeated, their poses resembling (in the case of the man, almost mirroring) each other, the only difference being that the background figures were rendered in contrasting colours. The work may be understood as a single scene, and at the same time as a pictorial blend of reality and imagination. The same kind of "synthesis" characterises its artistic execution.[23] Kotěra later achieved a similar ambiguity in his architecture, especially in the museum in Hradec Králové, where he united the theme of the temple with industrial architecture, creating a synthesis of the two main streams of development in Modernist architecture.[24]

For the sopraportas of the vestibule of National House in Prostějov, whose painting decoration was created as an addition to the original design, Preisler painted two monumental works in oil (1906–07). For the first, Preisler chose the central theme of *Temptation*, already developed in his earlier sketches. Its central figure was a dreamy young man, surrounded by three female figures. Other figures

---

21 In a letter to Stanislav Sucharda from c. 1912; printed in a catalogue for Preisler's exhibition from 1919.
22 According to the catalogue for Preisler's exhibition in 1928, the following works by Preisler were also part of Kotěra's private art collection: *Death of Icarus*, 1898, *Black Lake*, 1904 – now kept in the National Gallery, *Riders*, *Young Man with Two Girls*, *Three Young Women Dressed in White on a Hillside* – now in the National Gallery, *Female Nude on Yellow Drapery by the Water's Edge*.

23 See: Petr Wittlich, "Preislerovo Jaro. Slohová syntéza a vývojové tendence českeho umění kolem 1900" *Umění* XXVIII, 1980, pp. 401–421. – Petr Wittlich, *Česká secese*. Praha 1982.
24 Rostislav Švácha, "Teigova kritika důstojnosti". *Architektura* XLIX, 1990, nos. 5–6, pp. 12–13.

> **274**
Jan Štursa, figures decorating the entrance to the Chamber of Trade and Commerce pavilion, Chamber of Trade and Commerce Jubilee exhibition, 1908

274 | KOTĚRA AND THE FINE ARTS

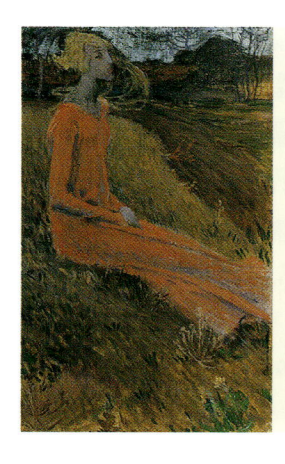

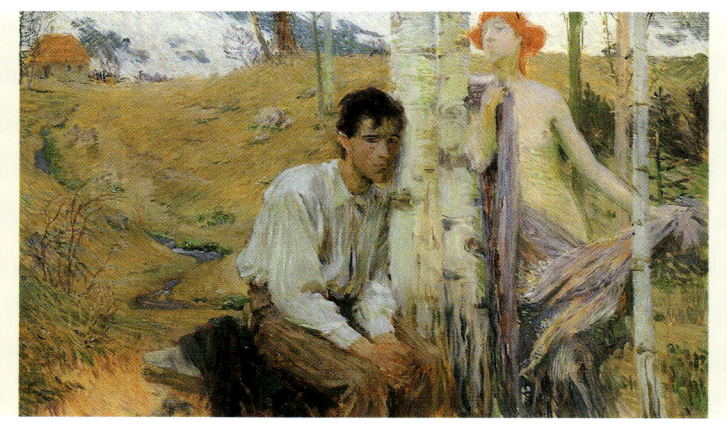

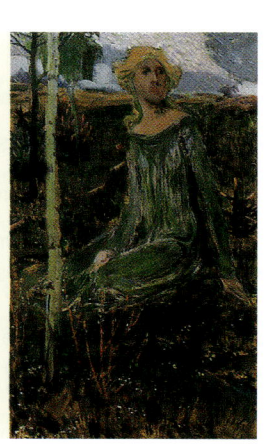

< 277
Jan Preisler, *Spring*, study for the painting for Peterka's house in Prague, oil on canvas, 1900
> 278
Interior of the restaurant in the Regional Authorities building in Hradec Králové, painting by Jan Preisler on the front wall, 1903

276 KOTĚRA AND THE FINE ARTS

< **279**
Vestibule of National House in Prostějov, painting by Jan Preisler on the front wall, 1905–1907
> **280**
Jan Preisler, study for the mosaic decoration of the museum in Hradec Králové, c. 1910

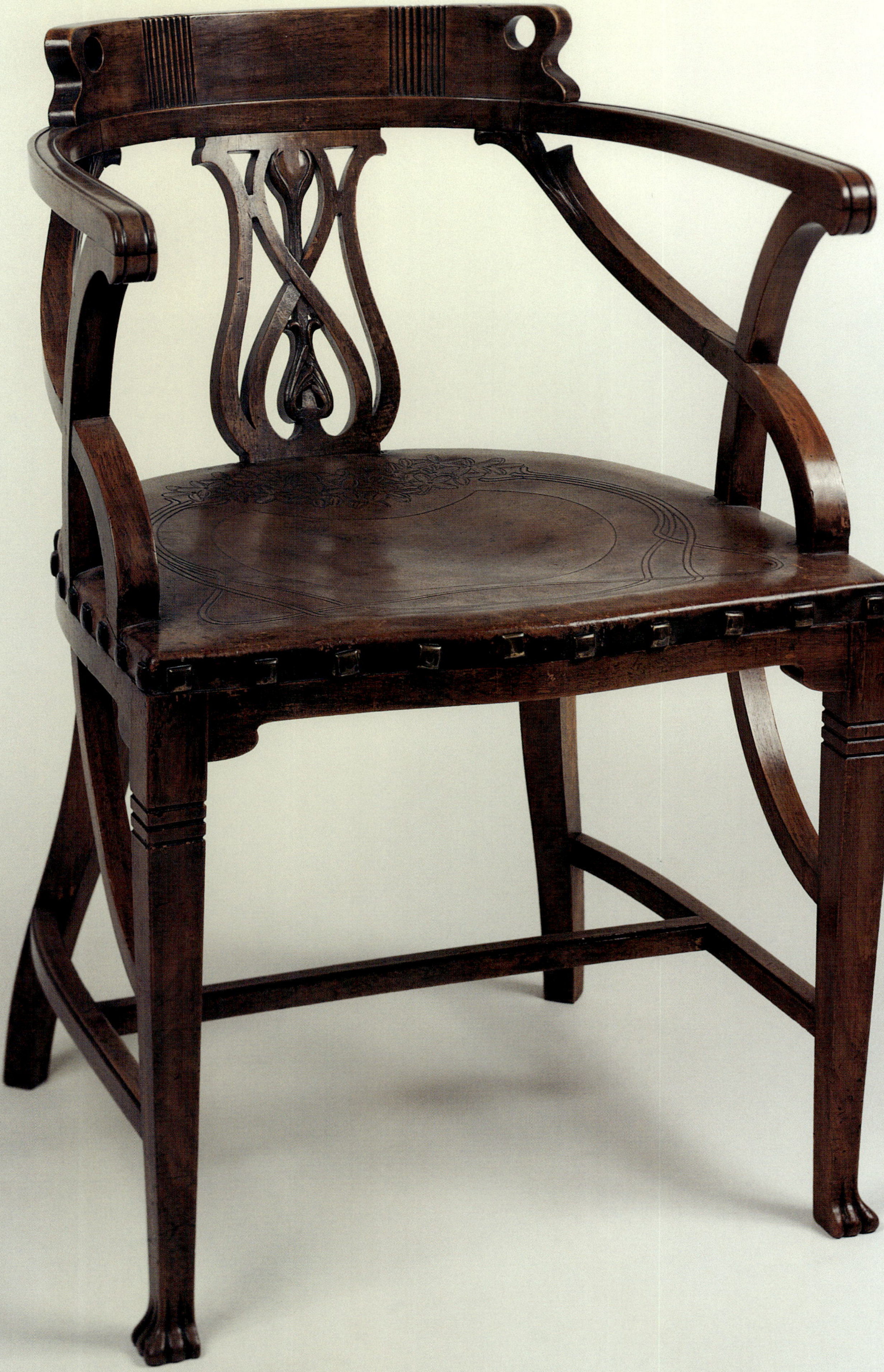

< 281
Armchair for the National Theatre in Prague, 1902

Interior and Furniture Design

DANIELA KARASOVÁ

Were changes of style visible in Kotěra's works? What role did style play in his oeuvre? We can look for answers to these questions in the monograph written by Kotěra's student Otakar Novotný.[1] We can also view the extensive collection of furniture in the Museum of Decorative Arts, which covers the entire creative span of this prominent figure of Czech and world architecture. It presents a worthy challenge to evaluate Kotěra's interior design from these specific points of observation. The collections and single pieces of furniture, some of which were part of Kotěra's prominent buildings, illustrate the different periods of the architect's work, as well as the influences to which he was perceptive and open but which he managed to absorb and transform into an original style.

Kotěra's Viennese studies had a deep and lasting influence on his views on architecture, interior and furniture design. He based his concept of architecture on Wagner's insistence on the priority of construction and creating a space from which beauty would arise naturally – *"that which is impractical and lacks purpose cannot be beautiful"*.[2] Kotěra argued for a balance between construction, function and form in architecture. In 1900 he published his views on architecture, fine and applied arts in *Volné směry*,[3] illustrated by works of specific architects holding similar views.

As a residential architect, Kotěra was inspired by the examples of English single-family houses. His villas on the outskirts of Prague, Hradec Králové and in south, west and north-eastern Bohemia developed the principles of the English cottage, modified to suit Czech needs. Their main qualities included a functional space, good ventilation, natural and artificial light and modern hygiene facilities. In them, Kotěra developed the local country house conceived as an enclosed Scandinavian type, and enhanced it with elements of southern architecture – terraces, balconies, loggias, protruding oriels and oriel windows opening the house out onto nature. He considered this union between the house and nature as one of the main conditions for quality living. His workers' housing colonies were a foreshadowing of the 20th century garden towns and the strong social dimension of Czech architecture from the inter-War period.

The family villas, interiors, furniture, and household accessories had a prominent place in Kotěra's work and, in their scope and importance, form a principal part of his oeuvre.

On one hand, this focus on interior decoration and furniture, including household artefacts, became an expression of Kotěra's profound interest in the culture of living and the breadth and depth of its *Gesamtkunstwerk*. On the other hand, it was something of a "virtue born of necessity". It resulted from the professional rivalry between two generations of Czech architects. The older generation was focused around the Prague Technical College, while the younger, more modern, generation was oriented towards the School of Applied Arts and Academy of Fine Arts in Prague. The latter group looked up to Kotěra who, from the very beginning of his Prague residence, struggled against the Czech

---

1 Otakar Novotný, *Jan Kotěra a jeho doba*. Praha 1958, p. 56.
2 Otto Wagner, *Moderní architektura*. Praha 1910, p. 30.
3 Jan Kotěra, "O novém umění". *Volné směry* IV, 1900, pp. 189–195. – Jan Kotěra, "Jože Plečnik". *Volné směry* VI, 1902, pp. 91–98. – Jan Kotěra, "Luhačovice". *Volné směry* VIII, 1904, pp. 59–60.

reactionary spirit, patrioteering, xenophobia and "home-bird" attitude. This rivalry caused Kotěra to miss out on large commissions in Prague. He compensated for this by accepting both public and private commissions, including numerous family villas and houses in other, smaller towns in Bohemia.
The 1900 Paris World Exhibition brought to light the differences in Czech architects' understanding of interior decoration. The two typical interiors of the period – the Prague Chamber of Trade and Commerce and the School of Applied Arts – made these differences strikingly clear. Josef Fanta's interior for the Prague Chamber of Trade and Commerce – a Czech intellectual's study with a private chapel containing an altar and period furniture by Jan Koula – despite its Secessionist details is historicist in its typology and construction (ornamental furniture, metal mounts, textile upholstery, carved details, juvenile mascarons). The interior of the Prague School of Applied Arts, whose concept and execution Kotěra inherited from the architect Ohmann, was conceived in a truly Secessionist spirit, free of historicist tendencies. Kotěra's colleagues and students from the School of Applied Arts also participated in its execution. The space designated for the School's exhibition inside the Austrian pavilion (Hungary, Bosnia and Herzegovina had separate pavilions), was dominated by Kotěra's oval divan, whose wooden frame was upholstered in fabric, with appliqué in the form of stylised pomegranates in grey-violet – a melodious interpretation of floral Secession that was so typical of Kotěra's early work.

Peterka's house (1899–1900) on Wenceslas Square, housing a bank and several apartments, was Kotěra's first large commission in Prague. A collection of furniture Kotěra designed for one of its apartments has survived to this day. It includes kitchen and bedroom furnishings, both rendered in the Secessionist style, with certain folkloric traits. In this,

< 282
Divan, from the interior of the Prague School of Applied Arts at the World Exhibition in Paris, 1900
> 283
Kitchen dresser from Peterka's house in Prague, 1899

it echoes the Ethnographic exhibition and confirms Kotěra's fondness for folk art, which continued to provide inspiration for his work. The kitchen dresser made of dark wood with two light-coloured maple-root panels, with a red marble slab from Slivenec near Prague, and a top cupboard whose doors are adorned with a geometric mosaic made of faceted glass, is a prototype of Kotěra's floral Secession with rustic features. Underneath its cornice is a discreet strip of relief decoration with vegetative and figural ornaments (a female and male profile).

Kotěra succeeded in attracting the best artists to collaborate with him on his projects (besides being an excellent professor, he was also good at organising people).[4] They included the sculptors Stanislav Sucharda, Ladislav Šaloun, Jan Štursa and Jaroslav Horejc, the painters Jan Preisler and František Kysela, and the wood-carver Jan Kastner. Almost all of them were of Kotěra's own generation. Preisler's celebrated triptych Spring was designated for the interior of Peterka's house.[5] Preisler created artworks for a number of publicly and privately owned buildings which Kotěra designed, as did Štursa. This blend of art and architecture is described in more detail in another chapter of this book.

In 1905–06, Kotěra designed a villa for Dr Ferdinand Tonder (1852–1916) in St Gilgen, Austria, on a lakefront in the Alps. He also furnished a Secessionist salon (c. 1902) for this art-lover, amateur musician and lawyer from Prague.[6] Max Švabinský's painting Destitute Landscape, for which Kotěra designed a frame in the style of Tonder's other furnishings, formed an integral part of this design.[7] The prism-shaped small maple and rosewood cabinet and two hexagonal tables of different sizes, which have all survived, suggest a shift from Kotěra's lyrical vegetative (although always constructively conceived) Secession, to a geometric, classical form which would become even more evident in his later works. The work also showed the influence of the architect Jože Plečnik, Kotěra's fellow student, friend and successor at the School of Applied Arts after Kotěra moved to the Academy of Fine Arts in 1911.

Kotěra's 1902 furnishings for a study for Karl Hoffmeister, pianist and professor at the Prague Academy of Music, were a synthesis of Secessionist lyricism and a Constructivist approach. They recalled some of the later works of Frank Lloyd Wright: compare Kotěra's armchair and Wright's small horseshoe-shaped Barrel armchair. The corner cabinet with its mirror, open chests made of dark-stained oak, lamps

4 Otakar Novotný, (see note 1), p. 112.
5 Jiří Kotalík, Jan Preisler. NG exhibition catalogue. Praha 1964, p. 12.
6 Ottův slovník naučný, part 25. Praha 1909, p. 557.
7 Volné směry VII, 1903, p. 123.

INTERIOR AND FURNITURE DESIGN

< **284**
Groundplan of a room incorporating the carpet design and disposition of the furniture, c. 1900
> **285**
Small table, from the salon of F. Tonder in Prague, 1902

and blue-green textile finishes with appliqué in different shades of the same tone, were complemented by a settee with armchairs inspired by traditional, luxuriantly upholstered English easy chairs and sofas. The elegant Secessionist brass and copper mounts completed the well balanced lines and forms of this large collection. The folding screen in three parts, geometrically divided with its upper section stylised into a chessboard made of coloured glass, and its lower part covered with textile, evoked the geometric interpretation of Secession, analogous to the designs of Scottish architect Charles Rennie Mackintosh.

The priority given to the utility, function, and type of interior for which the object was designed, instead of an insistence on style and "artistic impression", became especially evident in Kotěra's simply conceived armchairs of light-coloured beech with cane weave, created for the interior of the Modern Gallery.[8]

The 1903 furniture collection, designed in light-coloured wood, which the Prague Museum of Decorative Arts acquired from the family of art historian Antonín Matějček, is similar to Kotěra's Ferdinand Tonder collection in its transformation of elements of Classical architecture. It used small decorative columns, ending in carved capitals and supporting a wide cornice, and a strip of ornaments carved in relief, which accentuated the elegant line of the construction. The furniture acquired a certain tension through the contrast of its vegetative ornamentation – distinctly coloured, finely carved – and the geometrically designed veneer. The Museum collection is completed with an upholstered kitchen chair made from light-coloured maple wood, with barrel-shaped extensions on the lower end of its legs over a continuous stretcher, the kind that would often appear in Kotěra's later furniture designs. It is a fine example of functional and aesthetic detail.[9]

Kotěra's goal to create a modern comfortable interior is well illustrated in his efforts to design elegant and functional modern chairs and armchairs for special purposes – working, dining or resting. For his public interiors (coffee-houses, restaurants, public halls and theatres), he chose his chairs mostly from Thonet Brothers Co. Nevertheless, some of them he designed himself – chairs for the Arco coffee-house

---

8 Český svět I, 1904–05, no. 14, p. 26.

9 Olga Herbenová, *90 a jedna židle*. UPM exhibition catalogue, Praha 1972, cat. no. 69.

in Prague, for National House in Prostějov, and for the lecture hall of the museum in Hradec Králové.

In 1904, Kotěra designed the exhibition of Czech fine arts at the World Exhibition in St Louis. Its central theme was a stylised national Secessionist ornament, comparable with the Rondo-Cubism of Gočár or Janák from the Paris Exhibition in 1925. (Many other works by Kotěra from this period have the same characteristic nationalist features – the patterned decoration of the Grand Hotel restaurant, the Regional Authorities building in Hradec Králové, the furnishings for the Regional committee conference hall in Jindřichův Hradec, which includes the design for an armchair resembling a throne or seat from a Gothic cathedral,[10] the interior and furniture of Sucharda's villa in Prague, and finally the completion of National House in Prostějov). The St Louis Exhibition design was a joint project of the teachers and students from the School of Applied Arts. Its team was similar to that which created the 1900 design for Paris (Jan Kastner, Celda Klouček, Anonín Hellméssen and others). The joinery, carving and inlay work was executed by the Prague-based Strnad & Vaníček company, the stonemason's work by the Šalda company, and the locksmith's work by Nejedlý. The maiolica dishes were produced by a specialised school of ceramics in Bechyně, the gussets from carved maiolica by Kasalický & Somerschuh in Rakovník, the bronze casting was executed by Bendelmayer & Červenka, and the binding work by Spott in Prague.[11]

For the exhibition in St Louis, Kotěra also designed a cut-glass bowl set in Czech crystal made by the Harrachov glassworks. He created it in a traditional, spherical form, as a vessel with a lid on a central shaft with solid polygonal small glasses and a deep, smooth cut. The design had two different variants, the first of which, incorporating a decorative band adorned with vine leaves and grapes, has not survived.

We may characterise Kotěra's work from this period as an *"inclination towards a greater tranquility and simplicity of form, when the decoration of his objects was restricted to the absolute minimum and his fondness for colour increased [...]"*.[12] The furnishing of Laichter's house[13] from the period 1908–09 is marked by economic rationality which to a certain extent replaced his Secessionist lyricism. The furniture decoration disappeared almost completely, or was reduced to inconspicuous details. The colours were replaced by a temperate harmony of dark-stained or natural oak, brass cuffs on the legs of the furniture, and smooth leather. The Laichter house dining room is comparable in type with that of Sucharda's villa. It consists of an oblong table and horseshoe-shaped armchairs, a dresser with open shelves, and a display case with a built-in clock. The furniture for Sucharda's villa was designed in soft wood, decorated with a narrow vertical painted strip inspired by folk art. The Laichter house dining room furniture was made of stained oak, ascetic and stark, sometimes lit by a discreet decorative detail (such as Secessionist inlays depicting a romantic landscape on the inner sides of the drinks cabinet door). The furniture was of a solid construction and clearly subordinate to its function. The dresser was lined with mother-of-pearl, the display case had a built-in clock, completed with a hammered relief dial designed by Ladislav Šaloun.[14] There was a clock similar to this one, with a design by Stanislav Sucharda, decorating the dresser in Sucharda's dining room.

The museum in Hradec Králové is an excellent example of the peak of Kotěra's architecture, design and decorative work. The same is true of its decoration, including the head-office, library and reading room, lecture hall and original display-cases. Almost all have survived, including their detailed documentation. Their quality deserves a whole separate chapter, however, I will restrict this commentary to the inventory

---

10 Český svět I, 1904–05, no. 11, p. 343.
11 Volné směry VIII, 1904, p. 120.
12 Otakar Novotný (see note 1), p. 34.
13 Josef Šusta, "Z italských listů Jana Kotěry". Umění IV, 1931, p. 113.
14 Prague 1891–1941. Exhibition catalogue. NG, UPM, NTM. Edinburgh 1994, cat. no. 15.

> **286**
Interior designed for K. Hoffmeister, 1902

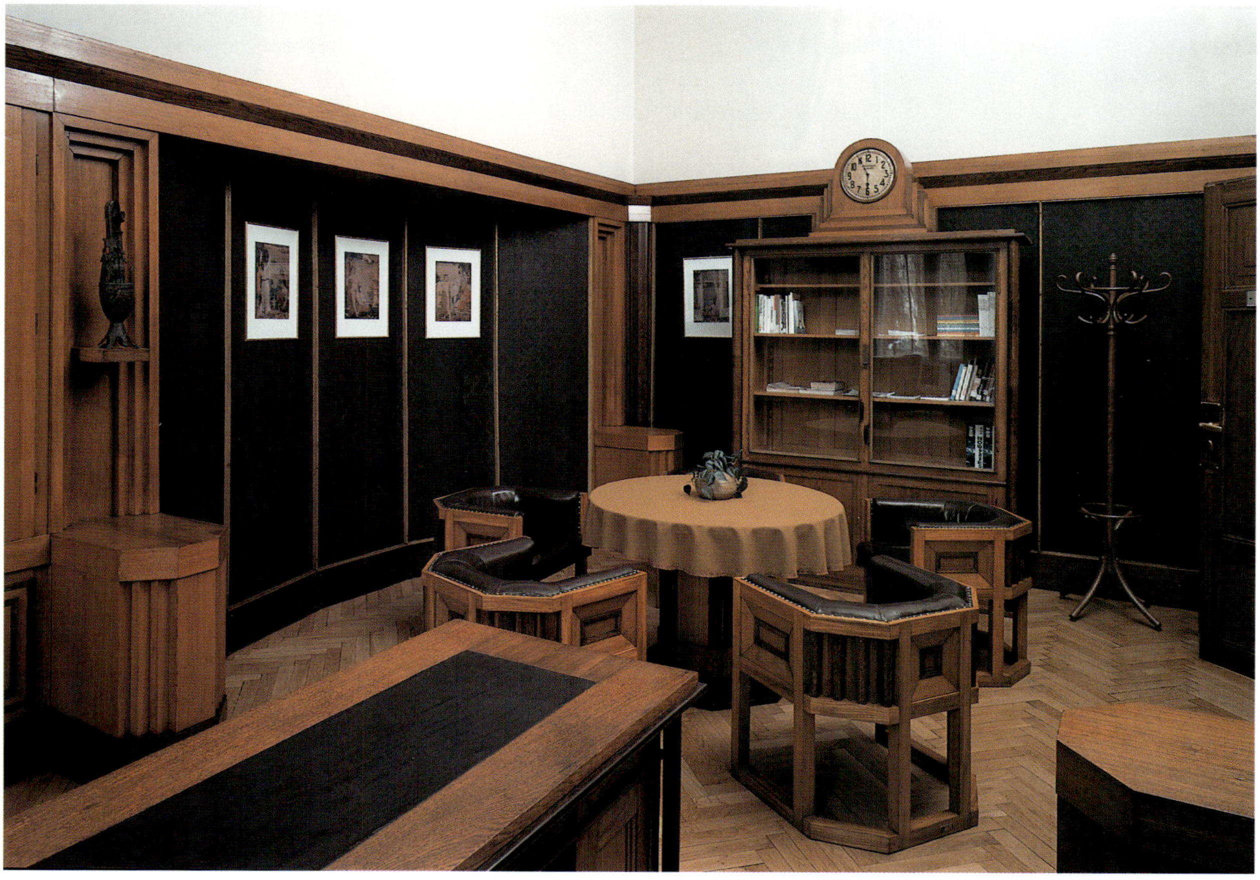

< **289**
General manager's office, Museum in Hradec Králové, after 1913
> **290**
Decanter and glasses, 1910 version

INTERIOR AND FURNITURE DESIGN 289

brown leather. The wainscoting adorning the walls and the gallery railing, with the inlaid coat-of-arms of the city of Hradec Králové, was made of light-coloured oak and rosewood. The adjoining room for the lecturer originally had somewhat different furniture made of soft wood with a white varnish finish, and decorated with small columns, smooth or undulated. The furnishings for the head-office, secretary's office and the archive were made of lightly polished elm wood and stained oak, produced by the cabinet-makers' society in Hradec Králové in 1914. They comprised two writing desks for the general manager and secretary, a round table with five horseshoe-shaped armchairs upholstered in leather, bookcases for files, flower stands, umbrella stands, and other objects. The interior was completed with chandeliers and adjustable wall and table lamps made of brass and glass. Other ceiling and wall lamps made of brass and opal glass, or bronze and faceted glass, have survived in various parts of the museum. The State Industrial Metalworking School in Hradec Králové produced these in 1924. The museum display-cases in black-stained oak were made at the beginning of the 1920s by the cabinet-makers Josef Sháněl, Josef Michálek and František Košťál. The style of the museum's hanging metal lamps anticipates the Functionalist period, while still preserving the poetry of the golden era of design at the very beginning of technological expansion.

Lamps and chandeliers almost always formed part of the *Gesamtkunstwerk* of Kotěra's interiors, with their designs developing in parallel with these interiors. Their form corresponded with the technological innovations of forged grilles, railings and other metal components of architecture. They were mostly wrought objects made of copper and brass,

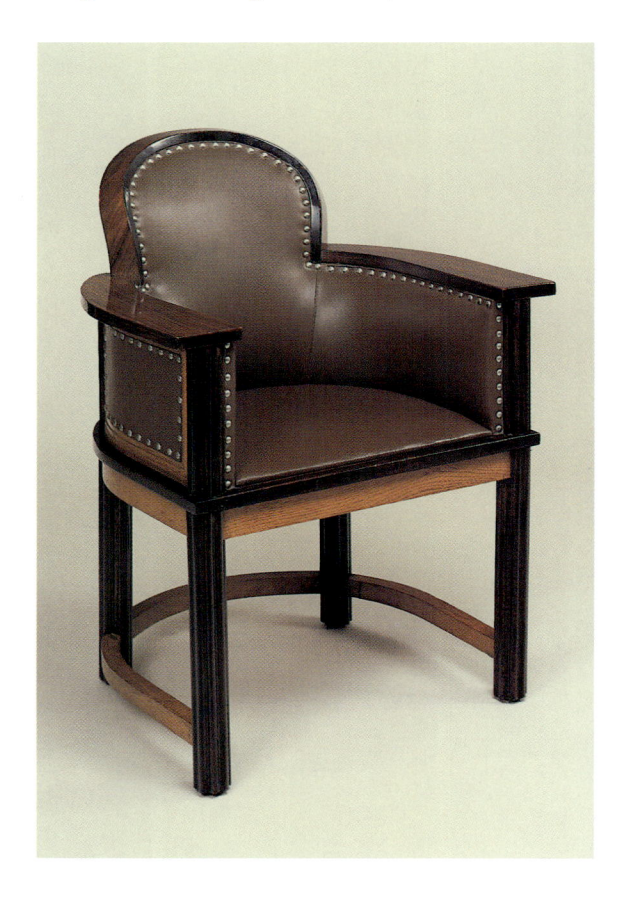

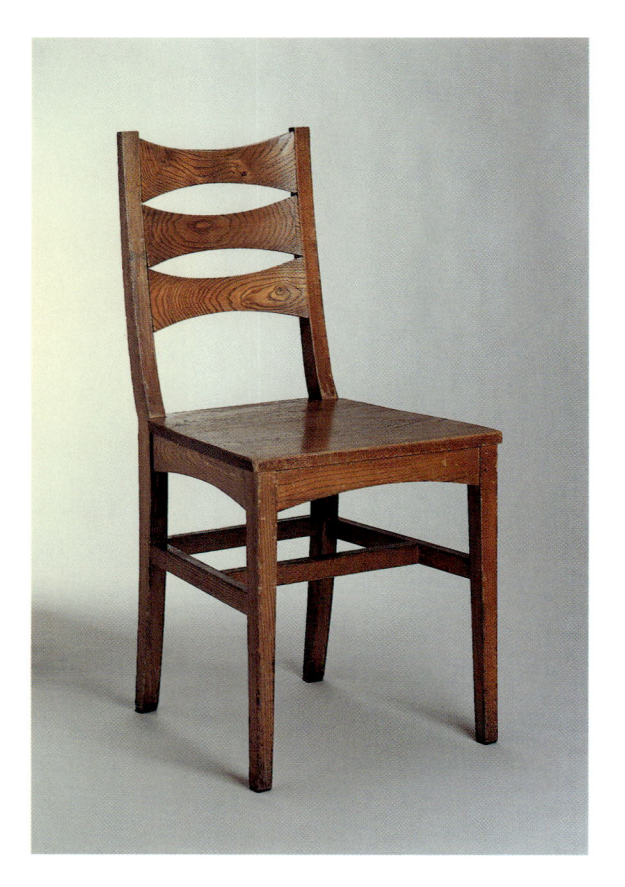

< **291**
Armchair for the lecturer from the museum lecture hall
in Hradec Králové, after 1913
<< **292**
Chair from the reading room of the museum in Hradec Králové,
after 1913
> **293**
Three-legged chair from the museum in Hradec Králové, after 1913

finished with spherical or elongated glass bulbs or faceted rods, and shades made of textile or paper. In his early Secessionist phase, the chandeliers, table and wall lamps and girandoles were welcome opportunities for Kotěra to indulge his fantasy. The publication *My Work and That of My Students* contains a series of original designs for chandeliers which decorated the halls and rooms of Peterka's house. The stylised vegetative and floral motifs, wrought and chiselled, were alternated with volutes of wire, decorative metal-sheet friezes, faceted glass rods and small chains. The sliding system for the adjustable chandeliers was designed in a variety of forms, like the ceiling rosettes. The bulbs were made of colourless, milk or painted glass, some of them decorated with stained and painted glass. The lamps sometimes formed part of the wainscoting or mirror (as in Hoffmeister's interior). The lighting Kotěra designed for his saloon tramcar was equally imaginative. The architect set the frosted glass ceiling bulbs into profiled brass crowns, matching the design of both ceiling and interior.

Kotěra's designs from this period onwards, increasingly guided by function and utility while still restricting the decorative aspects, display stylised floral and geometric motifs. They are generally spatial compositions attractive in their own right and providing the finishing touch to the interior. For public areas (the hall of the Jindřichův Hradec town hall building, the reading room in the City Museum in Hradec Králové), Kotěra employed a series of identical lights, linked in one single composition, decorative to varying degrees, or ceremonial where the occasion required. By 1910, these works had evolved into simpler, more solid and robust designs – the wall girandoles in Mandelík's villa, the lamp from the hall of Marek's villa in Holoubkov – finally acquiring the decorative and Rondo-Cubist forms of the chandeliers in Štenc's villa in Všenory. Conversely, the lavish crown chandelier from the Heveroch interior combines wrought floral motifs with small cut square openings and faceted glass rods. Kotěra designed the majority of his chandeliers for gas lighting. They were later adapted to be powered by electricity.

It would not be an overstatement to describe Kotěra as the first Czech industrial designer. He designed mass-produced objects: textile designs (carpets, curtains, tablecloths), wall

INTERIOR AND FURNITURE DESIGN

decorations and designs for linoleum, cutlery, crockery, handbags, fans and period jewellery; he designed interiors and exteriors of saloon tramcars – including lamps, seating and tables.

The furniture collection designed for Karel B. Mádl, Kotěra's colleague from the School of Applied Arts, professor of art history, librarian, art critic and writer, originates from approximately 1910. In this collection, Kotěra moved away from natural wood complemented with carved details and decorative mounts, replacing them with white or light-coloured coats of paint. The bedroom and dining room furniture was painted white, its legs covered with metal or stained black. The contrast between the angular mass of the cabinets and furniture and the undulating columns which reduced their volume to give an effect of lightness, was typical of this large collection. The light-coloured furniture, brightening the interior, is evocative of Charles Rennie Mackintosh's "Hill House" in Helensburgh near Glasgow. In comparison with the decorative, brightly coloured furniture by Mackintosh, however, the smooth, minimally segmented surfaces of Kotěra's designs are more austere, more functional in their essence.

Kotěra's Cubist "episode" – as Otakar Novotný aptly defined it in Kotěra's monograph,[16] originates from the same period (c. 1910). Kotěra personally was never a follower of Cubism, despite the fact that some of his students and colleagues were among its most prominent advocates in Bohemia. Cubism as an artistic movement succeeded Secessionist lyricism, particularly its "moodiness",[17] unacceptable in modern times, and brought a new sense of sobriety, defying the accepted architectonic and constructive criteria of the time. Kotěra never put limitations on his students in their search for new trends, including their interest in Cubism. Personally, however, he approached it with caution, aware of the problems and restrictions it imposed on the practical side of architecture and interior design. He treated Cubism more as a form of geometric Secession, which indeed is what this style partly was, despite its followers' and theorists' complex philosophical rationales.

Cubist tendencies appear sporadically in Kotěra's furniture and interior design even before 1910 (geometrically inlaid veneers for his furniture collection for the Matějček family in 1903). Traces of Cubism can be observed in his architecture and furniture for the City Museum in Hradec Králové, the new Ratboř castle for the Mandelík family in 1911–13 (in the details of the façade treatment, the entrance, the terrace railings and the interior – corridor walls and lamps) and in the reconstruction of the Mandelík's original manor in Ratboř in 1912–15 (doors, covers for the heating system). His designs for memorials and tombstones from the First World War also have strong Cubist features. Kotěra designed small decorative objects for Kamila Heveroch in the late stage of his career – jewellery and fans, as well as carpets and textiles. Some of these decorative objects, especially the jewellery, also had Cubist traits. These variations in furniture design, carpets, curtains, fans, cutlery and jewellery, ex-libris bookplates and other small objects designed for Kamila Heveroch,[18] testify to Kotěra's wider interests and talents, and demonstrate the masterly painting technique and draughtsmanship which characterised his entire oeuvre.

Kotěra's design of the dining room and study for the distinguished Czech doctor, Antonín Heveroch,[19] marks the closing phase in the development of Kotěra's interior and furniture design, as represented in the collection at the Museum of Decorative Arts in Prague. It was created in 1919, and photographic reproductions were published in

---

16 Otakar Novotný (see note 1), pp. 56–62.
17 Pavel Janák, "Proti náladě v architektuře". *Umělecký měsíčník* I, 1911–12, pp. 78–107.
18 Jan Kotěra's designs from the archive of prints and drawings at the Museum of Decorative Arts in Prague.
19 Antonín Heveroch (1869–1927), Czech doctor, neurologist, psychiatrist. One of the founders of Czech psychiatry.

> **294**
> Silver cabinet from Laichter's house in Prague, 1907–1908

Styl magazine,[20] as well as in a separate illustrated publication.[21] Heveroch's house was located in Prague 2, on U Karlova street 15, inside the garden of the District Asylum for the Mentally Disabled where Dr Heveroch was director (1919–27). The treatment of this interior is well illustrated in the dining room – designed for Mrs Kamila Heveroch and bearing her monogram (KH) on the console below the portico clock. It testifies to Kotěra's return to a certain decorativeness, characteristic of most Czech and European architects in the turbulent period at the end of the First World War (followed by the fall of the Austro-Hungarian empire and the rise of the independent Czechoslovak Republic). The Rondo-Cubism of Gočár and Janák, Plečnik's very personal form of historicism or the new wave of Art Deco – all were aiming towards a similar goal.

One of the last of Kotěra's works – the villa and interior furnishings designed for the house of the publisher Jan Štenc in Všenory near Prague in 1921–23 – creates a strong analogy to this collection of furniture. Pavel Janák, Kotěra's student and assistant, chose it to illustrate his 1925 article "A Teacher of Living Standards", published in *Výtvarná práce* journal. *"When we speak of the importance of Jan Kotěra in the founding, development and prosperity of our modern architecture, we think not only about his monumental work but also, to the same degree, about his art of the living space [...] there could be no more appropriate place for the saying 'flinging windows open to let fresh air in' as in this case. Together with modern architecture, a new culture entered the dwelling place of modern man. Even more importantly, with it came blazing sunlight and fresh, healthy air. It was Jan Kotěra who entered this old household of Czech architecture carrying new principles with him. It was he who, with his architecture, won the trust of his contemporaries for a completely new lifestyle. He not only brought new ideas for the exterior and interior of residential buildings, but he also turned the interior towards the new order and designed it to suit the needs of modern, natural life [...]."*[22]

---

20 *Styl* I (VI), 1920–21, plates 70–72.
21 Photo-documentation of the house and interiors for A. Heveroch, U Karlova 15. Library of the Museum of Decorative Arts in Prague.
22 Pavel Janák, "Učitel bydlení". *Výtvarná práce* III, 1925, pp. 169–182.

294 INTERIOR AND FURNITURE DESIGN

< **295**
Tablecloth from Laichter's house in Prague, 1907–1908
> **296**
Curtain from Laichter's house in Prague – detail, 1907–1908

FAMILIE
ADOLF
LANDSBERGER

< 306
Landsberger tomb in the Jewish cemetery in Frýdek, unused version, 1904
> 307
Vault of Mladota of Solopisky at Kosova Hora near Sedlčany, 1898

Sepulchral Architecture

VANDA SKÁLOVÁ

Kotěra's series of more than thirty designs for tombs and tombstones was created in a period when questions of sepulchral architecture, sculpture and the character of the modern urban cemetery in general met with a far greater response in society than it does today. This is especially true of the second half of the 19th and the beginning of the 20th centuries. The discussion of the modern and, most importantly, the urban cemetery, was certainly provoked by many factors - the secularisation of society, the creation of inter-confessional cemeteries (cemeteries in which the deceased were buried regardless of their religious creed), the movement for cremation and the scattering of ashes of the deceased on consecrated ground, the clearance of city centres which resulted in the demolition of small cemeteries adjacent to the churches and the founding of large central cemeteries on the city outskirts. Each of these subjects is in itself an interesting problem, both from the general social point of view and because of the consequences it had on the architecture and urban planning of the period.

In the context of such changes in society's attitude towards death and the life to come, the voices concerned with the aesthetics of modern cemeteries began to grow louder. There were societies for the "elevation" of cemetery art being formed around the globe,[1] exhibitions of this specific artistic discipline,[2] special periodicals and manuals, "recipe books" with detailed instructions on what a modern gravestone or an ideal cemetery should look like. There were also albums featuring reproductions of sepulchral architecture, including both the final form of these works and their designs. Some of these were purely commercial initiatives, while others testified to the manner in which so-called cemetery art participated in the modern development of architecture and urban planning.

Two such manuals could prove interesting for our research. They both comprise several volumes and were published in Vienna by Anton Schroll – publisher of anthologies on the Wagner school and the book in which Jan Kotěra presented his special school of architecture at the School of Applied Arts in Prague in 1902.[3] The first, *Künstlerische Grabdenkmale. Moderne Architektur & Plastik von Friedhöfen und Kirchen in Oesterreich-Ungarn*, was published in 1905. Its seven volumes, comprising large photographic plates, presented – among others – tombstones designed by Jan Kotěra and several other Czech architects and sculptors. Much like the first manual, the second one – by the same

---

[1] Such as the Society for Tombstone Art, founded at the turn of the 20th century in Wiesbaden.

[2] Such as the travelling exhibition for the "elevation" of cemetery and tombstone art in 1905 (Berlin, Munich, Essen, Darmstadt, Cologne...), as well as the Ideal Cemetery exhibition organised in the Czechoslovak Republic in 1921–22. The 'Cemeteries' section in the Czech magazine *Kámen*, for example, published articles about similar activities at home and abroad.

[3] Jan Kotěra, *Práce mé a mých žáků*. A. Schroll, Wien 1902 (both the Czech and German versions were published).

publisher and with an even more elaborate title[4] – included high-quality photographs of the finished works, as well as designs of sepulchral architecture. In it, we will find the groundplan and design, whose originals are believed missing, of the interior for Kotěra's first work of sepulchral architecture, a vault for the noble family of Mladota of Solopisky. Another specialised series by the same publisher[5] features reproductions of the wrought-iron work for Kotěra's tombs. These publications included most of Kotěra's tombstones designed prior to 1905, while details of his Janoušek tomb were published separately in 1921 in the English magazine *The Studio*, where this work met with high acclaim.[6]

The inclusion of Kotěra in these publications testifies that his work in this field was highly valued within a wider, European context. Furthermore, the quality period reproductions are today a rare source of information about the original look of these tombs and the (often missing) works of decorative art that adorned them.

Kotěra's works were also well received in Bohemia. His first ever realised project – a vault for Baron Jan Mladota of Solopisky – was reviewed with great enthusiasm in the pages of *Moravská revue*. The journalist's praise, delighting in Kotěra's vault and comparing it to a hymn, ended with the following words: *"Baron Mladota of Solopisky has reason to be proud of this work of art, a vault in the true sense. No tomb has appeared with such force and magnificence in thousands of years, since the forgotten Egyptian mastabas."* The reproductions of Kotěra's works were not only featured in specialised publications, but also in the popular weekly magazines such as *Český svět* (The Czech World).[7] In 1911, *Styl* magazine[8] devoted a special section to the theme of cemeteries, publishing the translation of Scheffler's article "Tombstone Monuments", as well as "The Park and the Cemetery" – a lecture by professor Högg. The articles were supplemented with reproductions of Czech tombstones, and both featured works by Jan Kotěra. The only separate review featuring Kotěra's work in sepulchral architecture was published in *Kámen* magazine – a short article by Emil Edgar.[9] The author acknowledged Kotěra's *"extensive and important […] work in this field of modern architecture"* and recommended that master stonemasons visit the architect's tombstones in their free time. He even included a partial list of tombstones in the article. Kotěra's gravestones and tombs were considered the most progres-

---

4 *Grabkapellen, Grüfte, Crematorien, Leichenhallen, Friedhofkapellen, Mausoleen & Grabdenkmale aller Art*. A. Schroll, Wien, c. 1904–05.
5 *Uměleco-zámečnické práce provedené ve Vídni a v jiných městech rakousko-uherských ve slohu moderním. Práce české*. Part 4, A. Schroll, Wien c. 1905 (Part 3 was also devoted to Czech works).
6 *The Studio* LXXXII, 1921, pp. 236–237.
7 "Nové náhrobky na Olšanech" – photographs of the Mráz vault in Olšany. *Český svět* III, 1907, no. 24.
8 *Styl* III, 1911, pp. 125–148.
9 Emil Edgar, "Hrobky a náhrobky Kotěrovy". *Kámen* III, 1922, volume 3, p. 5. – Emil Edgar, architect and the editor of *Stavitelské listy* and *Kámen* magazines, devoted special attention to sepulchral architecture. He was the author of brochures such as *Hřbitov* (1922), *Kolumbaria a popelnicové háje* (1923) or *Před založením hřbitova* (1937).

< 308
Elbogen tomb in the Jewish cemetery in Prague-Strašnice, clay models – variants, 1901
<< 309
Robitschek tomb in the Jewish cemetery in Prague-Strašnice, clay model, 1902
> 310
Design for a tomb, 1900–1902

sive works to be seen in Czech cemeteries. They were usually presented together with the works of Josef Zasche, Antonín Engel, Otakar Novotný or Jan Štursa.

Kotěra's tomb designs – including plans and photographs – were featured in articles and exhibitions of his work. However, there was never any attempt to evaluate them for their own merit, and both Zdeněk Wirth and Otakar Novotný only did as much as to include them in general summaries of Kotěra's works – and even then not in their full number. The latest research on the sepulchral architecture of Jan Kotěra was undertaken in the 1990s by Vlaďka Valchářová.[10]

Considering the rather large number of tombstones which Kotěra designed in the course of his long career, we should ask ourselves what these commissions meant to him. There is very little – in terms of written material and correspondence – that we could closely link to specific designs. There is nothing in Kotěra's own writing about the nature of these works or the methods involved in their creation. We must therefore turn to plans, sketches and the numerous completed works in order to try and understand them. We could suppose that small projects in general – in view of the demanding nature of short-term commissions – allowed the architect to remain financially secure when no other work was available.[11] This certainly does not suggest that Kotěra considered these works uninteresting or routine. He took every architectural task as a challenge, an impulse to find a new form and – especially in the beginning – an opportunity to experiment. However, in the chronology of Kotěra's sepulchral works, one could trace certain principles in dealing with volume and construction which are characteristic for the relevant periods of his architecture in general.

Kotěra's first work in the field of sepulchral architecture, the above-mentioned vault for the Mladota family of Solopisky in Kosova Hora, holds a unique position among these works. Its perspective drawing, reproduced on many occasions, displays Kotěra's monumental vision of the building, resting on an exceptionally high plinth made of stone bossage, crowned with a segmented gable whose surface was meant as a base for a symbolic figural scene. The perspective sketches included figural staffage, which became an indispensable part of a number of Kotěra's other designs. In this particular drawing, the minute human figure intensifies the impression of the massive vault. The final work is somewhat surprising, smaller in size and not fully decorated. Of the original decoration, only the double-winged entrance door with a decorative grille remained.

During the early period of this work (1901–04), Kotěra designed several tombstones for the Jewish cemetery in Prague-Strašnice, each of similar mass. The basic motif was a stele resting between two obelisks by the head of

---

10 Vlaďka Valchářová made a list of the architect's tombstones as part of her work on a catalogue of Jan Kotěra's works, supported by a grant from the Ministry of Culture of the Czech Republic. See also note 15.
11 In a letter to Richard Gombrich from 21 September 1904, Kotěra writes: *"I have no news about any possibilities of work. The small Jewish tombstone (they have already become my daily bread) and then the station in Plzeň, I suppose […]"*.

the grave, and they all incorporated the use of wrought and chiselled details – grilles, lamps and metalwork. Kotěra's basic scheme for these pieces, as well as his concept of the relationship between space and volume, can be traced on a number of sketches and designs, as well as some fascinating photographs of now lost tombstone models (most probably made of terracotta) which were published in *My Work and That of My Students*. These sketches relate mostly to two of his works from this period, the Elbogen (1901) and Robitschek (1902) tombs for the Jewish cemetery in Strašnice. The two works, created almost in parallel, differ greatly in their final composition, in the materials used and in their treatment of the decorative elements. They document the manner in which Kotěra was able almost simultaneously to use completely opposite approaches. The Elbogen tomb combines black marble with light-coloured granite and a minimum of decorative elements adorning the slab and columns – the flat profiling of two layers of granite and the gilded inscription. The wrought-iron grille at its entrance, bearing an elaborate composition of motifs of vine leaves and tendrils "pouring down" in dynamic spirals onto the steps of light-coloured granite, is an exquisite piece. It is also a masterly example of craftsmanship from the Prague locksmith Emil Klingenstein,[12] as was the entrance grille with floral motifs derived from folk art used for the adjoining, smaller Robitschek tomb. It employed a type of stele with two obelisks on the sides, however, modified in proportion; the central slab was crowned with a column. The motif of the column was repeated again at the foot of the tombstone. Its small side columns[13] served to support the entrance grille. The entire tombstone, made of light-coloured sandstone, was crowned with capitals decorated with vegetative ornaments resembling other works by Kotěra from the same period (such as the 1900 competition design for the monument to Jan Hus).

In 1904, Kotěra created two more designs which could be linked with the above-mentioned tombs. One was the tomb for the industrialist Adolf Landsberger in Frýdek – Kotěra's only tomb design in Moravia; the other a tomb in Strašnice, made for the trainee solicitor Max Perutz. Some watercolour designs of the former – unique and original feats of draughtsmanship – have been preserved in the collection of Kotěra's work. The tomb had a truly unique design – a tree rising up from the centre of an octagonal tombstone, on which stood a metal grille decorated with vegetative ornaments and sculptures of four grieving figures.[14] However-

---

12 For wrought ironwork on Kotěra's buildings, see: Jan Mohr "Umělecké kovářství a zámečnictví v Čechách na přelomu 19. a 20. stoleti". *Sborník Hefaistonu* (as *Zpravodaj památkové péče a ochrany přírody*), Přerov 1985.

13 The Jewish cemetery in Strašnice featured an identical small column, used as a separate smaller Perutz gravestone unlisted in either Wirth's or Novotný's inventories of Kotěra's works. Although its origin is not substantiated with plans or other documents, its connection with the Robitschek tombstone is unquestioned.

14 One of Kotera's designs for the memorial to the Vojáčeks in Prostějov (1910) bears some resemblance to this idea

< 311
Design for a tomb, 1900-1902
< 312
Design for a tomb, 1900-1902
> 313
Design for a tomb, 1900-1902

er, the final tombstone was simpler, with an "obelisk-stele-obelisk" scheme of black polished granite bearing a typical gilded inscription. The slab – bearing an inscription in German quatrain (depicted in Kotěra's watercolour design) and the names of the family members – was framed with small mosaic stones made of glass covered in gold leaf. The stone structure was enhanced with tall lanterns resting on columns by the foot of the grave, and a metal grille adorning the small gate – all of which Kotěra designed. Unfortunately, both features are now missing. The small Perutz tombstone in Strašnice employed a variant of the same basic scheme developed in Kotěra's previous works, including the hammered bronze grille with vegetative motifs (now missing). Identical to the Landsberger tombstone, created in the same year, it featured a mosaic of coloured glass, both on its stele and on the obelisks.

Together with these designs for the Jewish cemeteries in Strašnice and Frýdek, Kotěra designed a number of other tombstones, especially for Prague cemeteries. They included works of much smaller proportions and simpler decoration, as well as featuring complex designs, often commissioned by distinguished society figures. Outside both these groups stands the unusually high sandstone cross bearing the head of Christ, designed by Kotěra for the parents of the writer Alois Jirásek in Hronov (1902). This traditional type, complemented with a hammered grille, stems from *"inspiration from folk stone crosses"*.[15]

In sector ten of the sixth cemetery in Olšany, three of Kotěra's tombstones created in 1903–06[16] stand in close proximity to one another. The often reproduced tombstone of actor Vojta Slukov, created in collaboration with sculptor Stanislav Sucharda, was the first to be built. For this work, Kotěra combined two types of stone. The granite slab of the tombstone, light-coloured to contrast with the dark polished cross, was complemented with a sandstone sculpture depicting a broken oak tree. The original lantern, placed on a column to the right of the tombstone, as well as the wrought ironwork (all from the workshop of Franta Anýž), have not survived.

The second in the series was the tombstone for the actor Eduard Vojan, simply decorated with two columns crowned with a gable, and geometric relief work. Between the columns stood a slab of dark granite on which, in the niche below the gable, Kotěra had placed Sucharda's bronze sculpture of a grieving boy seated under a weeping willow. Kotěra provided an impressive architectural frame for the sculpture while the simplicity of his design was highly effective. The impression of calmness, achieved by focusing all attention onto a single point, is especially significant in comparison with Slukov's tombstone, based on the marked tension between the vertical, static slab corpus and the dynamic

---

15 Vlaďka Valchářová – M. Kaňka, Jan Kotěra – Funeral Architecture. A grant project. AA NTM, unpublished.
16 All three sculptures were executed by master stone-carver Václav Žďarský.

SEPULCHRAL ARCHITECTURE

< **314**
Design for a tomb, 1900–1902
> **315**
Elbogen tomb in the Jewish cemetery in Prague-Strašnice, 1901

KAROLINE ELBOGEN GEB. MATZKA
GEB. AM 16. NOVEMBER 1810. GEST. AM 22. SEPTEMBER 1900

פה בשדה אחוזה משאה מנוחתה והשובה והצנועה
מרת שעינא ע"ה בת המנוח ה"ה ליב כ"ץ מאטצקא ז"ל
אשת המרומם ה' זעליקי עלבאגען נ"י
הל' בש"ק כ"ח אלול תר"ס לפ"ק

<> 316
Elbogen tomb in the Jewish cemetery in Prague-Strašnice, detail of the grille, 1901

SEPULCHRAL ARCHITECTURE

< **317**
Robitschek tomb in the Jewish cemetery in Prague-Strašnice, 1902
<< **318**
Design of the wrought-iron grille for Perutz's tomb
in the Jewish cemetery in Prague-Strašnice, 1904
> **319**
Perutz's tomb in the Jewish cemetery in Prague-Strašnice,
design, 1904

line of the dead tree, broken and "caressing" the tombstone.[17] Moreover, Vojan's tombstone was the first of a series of monuments designed as architectural niches with an inserted sculptural work (others include Groh's, Janoušek's and Laichter's tombs).

The last of the three works was the Štěpánek family tomb of 1906. Its massive tiered torso was made of light-coloured granite (resembling a stone sarcophagus), dominated by a subtle bronze sculpture of an angel, decorated with oblong tendril-like wrought-iron frames on both its sides.[18] The theme of a figure framed within a decorative wrought-iron grille, together with Kotěra's choice of materials and a certain tendency towards geometric forms (most visible in the angel's figure), recall the watercolour sketch for the unrealised project for the Landsberger tomb in Frýdek.

In the same period (1903), Kotěra completed the much simpler Kožíšek tombstone, one more in line with his standard sepulchral work. The work was completed with a child's bust by Stanislav Sucharda. With minimal changes, Kotěra repeated the same scheme much later (1921) for his Navrátil family tombstone in the Vinohrady cemetery.[19] In 1904 Kotěra designed his largest work for Olšany cemetery – a tomb for the Czech surgeon and university professor Karel Maydl. In collaboration with the sculptor Bohumil Kafka, he created a tomb with a high smooth stele made of black marble, adorned with three floral wreaths in bronze, interlaced with ribbons. This naturalistic sculptural decoration was completed with a bronze lamp (now lost) bearing stylised folk ornaments which stood on a low column placed in front of the stele. The dominant gilded inscript on "MAYDL" was an integral part of the gravestone. Without a title or first name, it has remained the only inscription on the stele to this day.

Kotěra created the Mráz family tomb in 1906. The tomb, published on many occasions, was destroyed in the 1930s.[20]

---

17 Petr Wittlich, "Preislerovo Jaro. Slohová syntéza a vývojové tendence českého umění kolem 1900". Umění XXVIII, 1980, pp. 401–422. Petr Wittlich uses Kotěra's tombstone to support his thesis about the basic dualism of the Secessionist style and the polarity between its abstract-geometric and sensual-organic elements. Here, their relationship "[...] displays a very basic counterpoint to the Secessionist style syntax, undistorted by the usual overwhelming surface decoration [...]".

18 Jan Kotěra has been credited with this sculpture. Václav Mašek, metal founder from Karlín, was mentioned as the person who executed it.

19 Kotěra's designs present a number of different solutions for the Navrátil tombstone. The fact that an established (15 years old) scheme was employed after Kotěra had already found various new ideas for his tombstone designs, raises the question whether this tombstone was Kotěra's work at all. The bust of a boy was signed by the sculptor A. Houdek.

20 According to information from the Olšany cemetery administration, the tombstone (like Rubeš's later on) was still not paid for in the 1930s. Its lot was sold and the new owner built a different tombstone in its place.

< **320**
Vojan tomb in Olšany cemetery in Prague, 1904
<< **321**
Slukov tomb in Olšany cemetery in Prague, 1903
> **322**
Maydl tomb in Olšany cemetery in Prague, 1904
>> **323**
Mráz tomb in Olšany cemetery in Prague, 1906

Its concept was rather unusual. Conceived as a pergola, it combined the supporting elements of stone with wooden truss beams, carved (probably also painted) with a vegetative design inspired by folk ornaments – such as we often see in Kotěra's works from this period (the exhibition pavilion in St Louis, the Marek and Trmal villas). Over the central part of the grave, a lamp was suspended from one of the beams, positioned so as to suggest an "eternal light". In his design, the architect counted on the effect of climbing plants trailing over the pergola's stone posts, creating an intimate enclosed space. The "interior" of this effectively austere and elegant structure evokes the image of a private temple and is without doubt one of Kotěra's most original contributions to the design of the modern tombstone.

Rubeš's tomb (1908) met the same fate as the Mráz family tomb and was replaced at the end of the 1930s. Since we have no photographs of it, we can only suppose – judging by the surviving plans – that it was a simple, vertical structure with a dominant pylon and lantern. The austerity of its decorative elements – the pylon's profile and the overall monumental appearance – links Rubeš's tomb with an important work by Kotěra from the period – the City Museum in Hradec Králové.

By 1906, Kotěra had already produced fifteen tombstones. In these he employed numerous different designs, characterised by a variety of forms, often suggesting contradictory decorative trends, and a wealth of Secessionist ideas. In the following period, fewer of his sepulchral works were built and part of his designs remained only on paper, analysed and reworked to the smallest detail. Reflecting the change in his other works, Kotěra simplified his tombstone designs, most of all reducing their decoration. He began to work more with the mass, and less with the surface details. He began to use an abundance of classical architectural features – columns, cornices and gables. In several of these commissions, he restricted his role to designing a sort of coulisse, a background for the sculpture or an architectonic frame which did not influence the design in any substantial way.[21]

Kotěra's family tomb in Vinohrady cemetery (1909) employed elements typical of this change in style. It was one of his simplest sepulchral works. A profiled entablature crowned two oval granite columns, fluted at the top. Between them stood a smooth black marble slab. The simplicity of this work provided a parallel with the architect's own villa, designed and built in the same period.

Between 1909 and 1915 Kotěra received no significant commissions for tombs or tombstones, although later he did create several more sepulchral works. They were illustrative of the change in Kotěra's style, and of his acceptance and original treatment of Cubist influences which he had previously rejected. This change was visible in his simplification of the architectonic elements, in the geometric tendency of his entire formal repertoire, as well as in certain details – such as the original design for the grille on the Nosek tomb (1916), or the lettering design for Janoušek's tomb (1915). In his later works, Kotěra enclosed the entire contour of the tomb into simple forms, decorating them with different variants of aedicules and niches, their elements modified to acquire both a classical and simple look. The beginning of the 1920s marked a new conceptual phase in Kotěra's drawings and plans. The architect began to conceive his works on the basis of a geometric grid. He used circles, triangles, hexagrams, and other geometric figures as bases for his compositions, into which he would then "impress" his designs. This change in his artistic approach testifies to Kotěra's increased interest in the theory of architectonic proportions, their scale and different approaches to composition. In this search, Kotěra was guided by the work of the Dutch architect Hendrik Petrus Berlage, and the Benedictine monk Odilo Wolff.[22]

Kotěra worked on urban designs for military cemeteries on two occasions during this period, in Slaný and Olšany (Prague). If we disregard the differences in the specified locations, we could say that Kotěra adopted a similar approach for both. He conceived both cemeteries as central spaces decorated with monumental Cubist influenced statues placed at their

---

21 These were: the early Milde family tomb in the arcades of Vyšehrad cemetery (1900, together with S. Sucharda), the Tichý family tomb in the same cemetery (1912, decorated with the *Pastoral Madonna* by B. Kafka), and finally in the design for the Waldes family tomb in the Jewish cemetery in Prague-Strašnice (1917–18, together with J. V. Myslbek).

22 Hendrik Petrus Berlage, *Grundlagen und Entwicklung der Architektur*, Berlin 1908, Odilo Wolff, *Tempelmasse*, Wien 1912. I wish to thank R. Švácha for pointing out this fact.

< **324**
Kotěra family tomb in Vinohrady cemetery in Prague, 1909
> **325**
Rubeš tomb, design, 1908

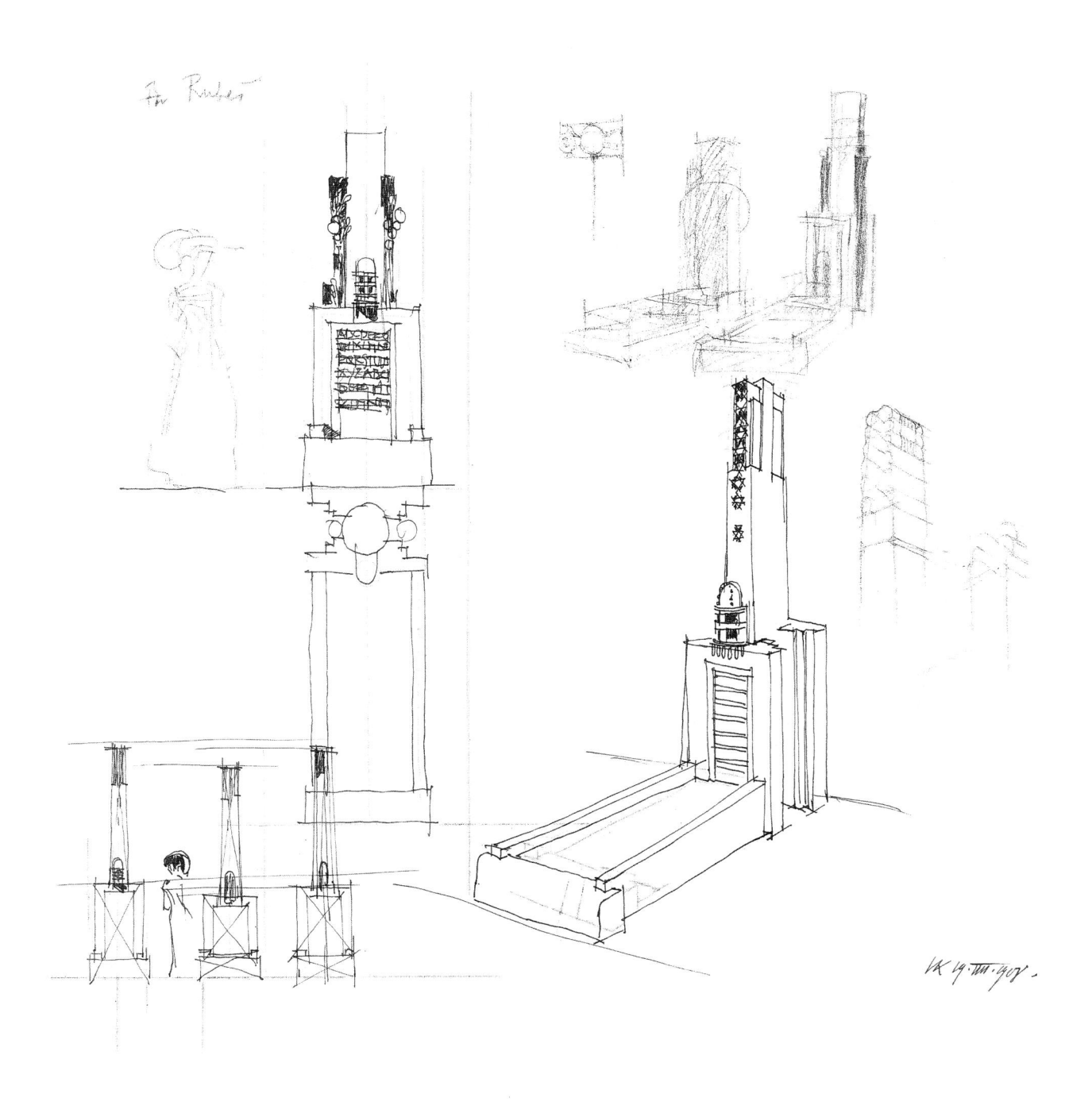

centre. Apart from the general concept, he designed a detailed network of pathways for both cemeteries, as well as the surrounding plant beds. However, neither of the projects was ever realised.

In 1915–16, Kotěra designed two highly effective works – the Janoušek and Nosek family tombs, located in close proximity to each other in the seventh cemetery in Olšany. The architect's drawings from his sketchbook, kept in the Architecture Archive at the National Technical Museum in Prague, demonstrate the procedure he adopted for the former (reproduced in 1921 in the English *Studio* magazine). Kotěra started from an initial idea of a tomb in the form of a small canopy,[23] creating a structure resembling a small temple. However, with time, the idea was revised and the tomb acquired the form of a deeper niche, and finally became a stylised sandstone portal, its arch crowned with a tympanum decorated with the stone sculpture of the *Crucifixion* by Jan Štursa. In decorating his sepulchral works, Kotěra commonly used allegories, symbols or simple ornaments. This tomb was Kotěra's only work treating a traditional sacral theme.[24]

The Nosek tomb (1916) was conceived entirely by Kotěra. The impressive design and precise stonework make it one of the most fascinating pieces from the architect's late period. The two slabs of polished black granite are "fastened" together by a cross, whose background is formed by a symmetrical tendril composition made of light-coloured sandstone. In his first sketches, Kotěra designed a variant with a cornice at the top of the stone structure, however, he finally decided instead to use the more effective open form of tombstone. Along the entire edge of the grave, the architect created space for greenery between the stone curbs he designed.

During this period, Kotěra created another tomb outside Prague for Arnošt Mandelík[25] in the Jewish cemetery in Kolín. In front of the slab, finished with a simply profiled cornice supported by a bracket, stood a prismatic pedestal with a sculpture by Jan Štursa. It differs from the standard Jewish gravestone, especially in that it has a figural sculpture, which was unusual for the period, as it is now.

In the same year (1915) Kotěra produced designs for Dr Emil Hácha's tomb in Vinohrady cemetery. Kotěra conceived it as a low wide niche made of granite, bordered on each side by a column crowned with a shell limestone sphere. The columns' capitals and shafts were to be decorated with stylised vegetative ornaments.

---

23 Kotěra tested the same idea with his design for the Waldes tomb. However, he never managed to complete a tomb based on this scheme.
24 The other exception was Kafka's *Pastoral Madonna*, decorating the Tichý family tombstone in the arcades of Vyšehrad cemetery.

25 Kotěra adapted the old castle in Ratboř for the Mandelík family, and built a new castle in 1911–13. Arnošt was one of the four sons of the entrepreneur Bernard Mandelík (the others being Robert, Erwin and Otto). I wish to thank Ms Dagmar Mandelíková for this information on her family.

<>326-329
Designs for the Janoušek tomb in Olšany cemetery in Prague, 1915

Jan Kotěra designed the tombstone for Alois Kotěra in 1916. We have at our disposal detailed plans of this work and drawings supplemented with precise coordinates of the specific site – Olšany cemetery – but the work did not survive, nor did any photographs. The plans show a simple small tombstone, with a Cubist influenced slab which fans out into three points. Kotěra added a lantern designed in a similar Cubist style.

In 1918, Kotěra designed a large tomb for the Greif family in Hostomice. The spacious tomb was once again designed as a niche, formed by a wall with slightly curved wings on both sides; Kotěra designed several variations on this tomb. They evolved around the same basic concept but with a modified cornice. In one of the designs, Kotěra worked with sharp geometric details, in an alternative he used only rounded forms. However, this tomb was never built according to Kotěra's plans.

In the same year, Kotěra designed a tomb for the psychiatrist and neurologist Antonín Heveroch, whose family were among Kotěra's close friends. The architect created two different designs for this tomb. The drawings for the first developed around the theme of a column, which was either positioned as a dominant gravestone slab or otherwise rested on a high plinth, reminiscent of an altar stone. There were two variants of the column in the first design. One had a shaft decorated with a figural relief and crowned with a fine, geometric capital. The other reduced the column's decoration to an elaborate voluted capital. The second design used Jan Štursa's sculpture *The Wounded*. It was this design which was finally built, only the sculpture came from the workshop of Jaroslav Horejc.

In May 1920, Kotěra designed a family tomb for another client, the publisher Jan Laichter. The tomb was created for Laichter's home town of Dobruška. It developed around a basic theme of a wall with recesses or niches, with a central

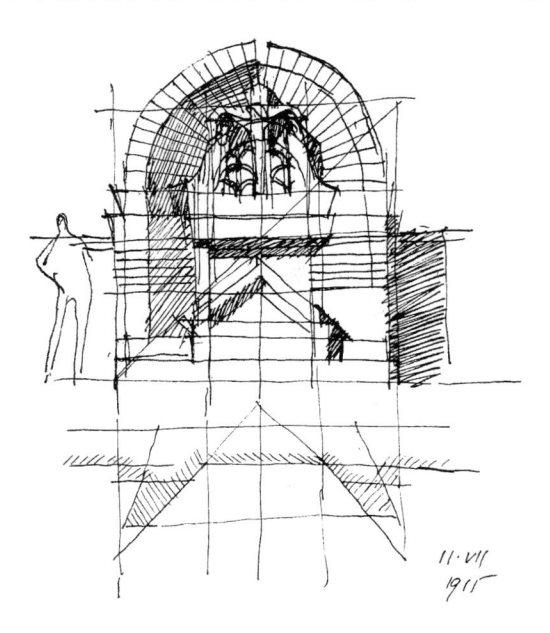

SEPULCHRAL ARCHITECTURE

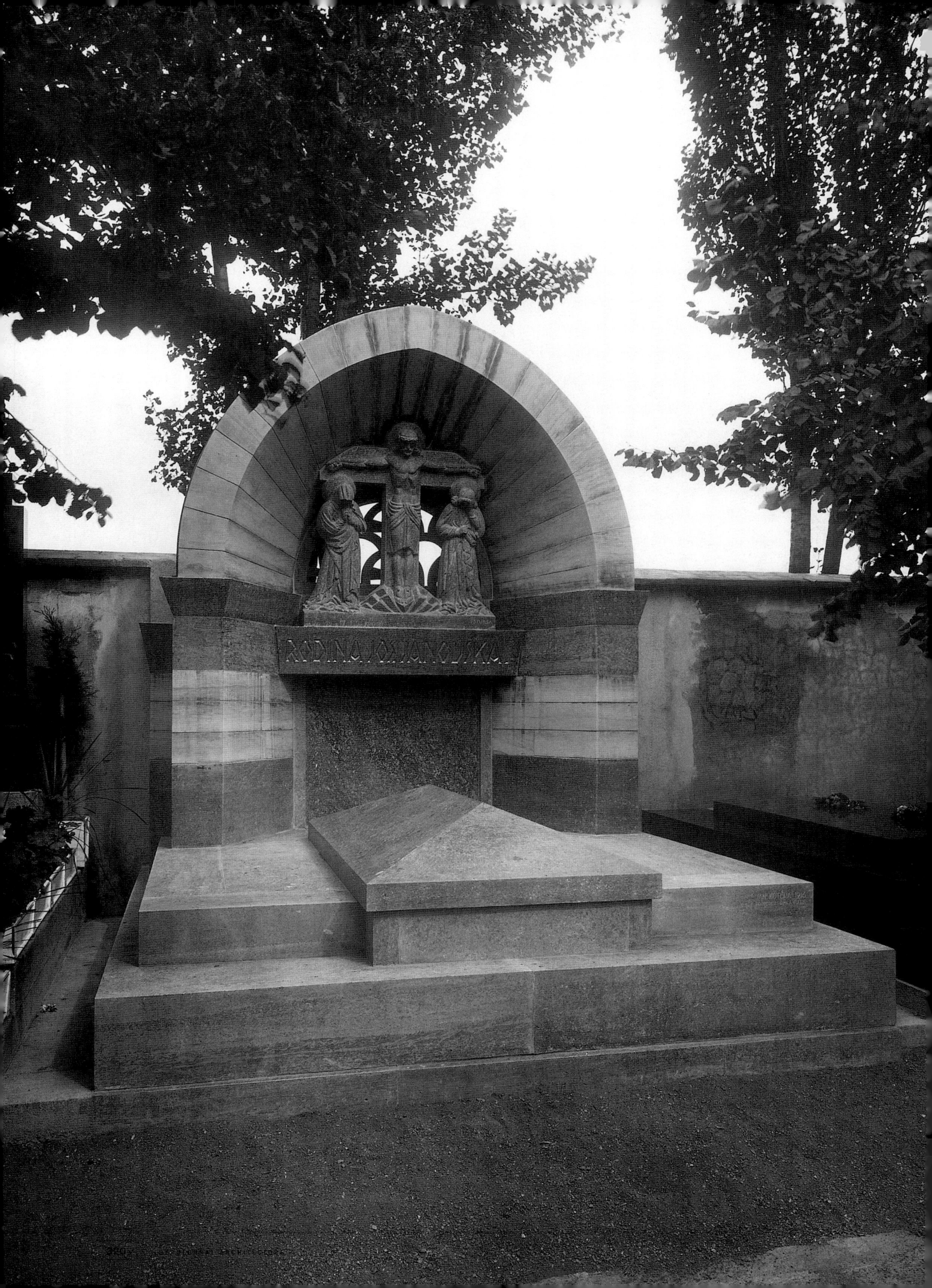

< 330
Janoušek tomb in Olšany cemetery in Prague, 1915

bronze relief entitled *The Pilgrim and Death*, created by the sculptor Antonín Kalvoda. For his design, Kotěra envisaged an elaborate hedge to be planted around the tomb, as well as a small gate with a wrought-iron grille and a lamp made of glass and beaten copper. However, none of the latter details were used.

In 1921, Kotěra designed the tombstone for the entrepreneur Zikmund Feldman for the Jewish cemetery in Kolín. The three variants of the design once again developed around the idea of an aedicule or portal, making full use of the graded cornice decorated with geometric ornamentation. The tombstone itself was far simpler and smaller than the original design. It consisted of a slab crowned with a simple triangular gable made of black polished granite, with no additional decorative details.

Kotěra's last sepulchral work was the large tomb for Dr Antonín Schauer for Olšany cemetery. The tombstone, for which Kotěra designed a specific site, was situated on an atypical diamond-shaped plot. Kotěra built a low back wall before which he placed the gravestone slab in a shallow niche. The tomb was dominated by a column made of red granite which in the original design had an elaborate decorative capital, completed with a cross and a crown of thorns. However, in the execution phase, the column bore the sculpture *Dove* by Otakar Španiel.[26]

If we consider the works which Jan Kotěra left behind in the "field of cemetery art", at least one third of them were both successful and inventive works, especially in the context of the period quest for the ideal form of the modern tombstone. The architect's work on his sepulchral projects included landscaping and carefully placed greenery decorating his tombstones and cemeteries. Whereas in some of these commissions Kotěra designed the entire concept – from the architectural form and stone-carving to the decorative details – in others he welcomed the designs of other fine and applied artists. He was able to incorporate them in his work, using them to achieve a particularly strong and unified effect. The placement of the inscription, as well as the lettering itself, played an important role in his tombstone designs. On several occasions, the architect designed the lettering especially for the commission in question. All of these works, especially the applied-art details, show the influence of folk art and ornamentation.

In the entire history of modern Czech architecture, we could hardly find a figure of Kotěra's stature in this field, both for the well-balanced quality of his works and for the number and variety of his designs. In conclusion, mindful of the proverbial "death and the life to come", we can only add that Jan Kotěra died unexpectedly at the age of fifty-one. Many of his customers outlived him, and the sad irony – documented in the period press cuttings, obituaries and photographs from the funeral service – was that many of the people for whom he designed not only homes or interiors, but also their "final dwellings", met to pay their respects at the architect's grave.

[26] The correspondence between Dr Schauer and Jan Kotěra documents the fact that Schauer approached not only Otakar Španiel but also Karel Dvořák with the same request to create a sculpture for the tombstone.

SEPULCHRAL ARCHITECTURE

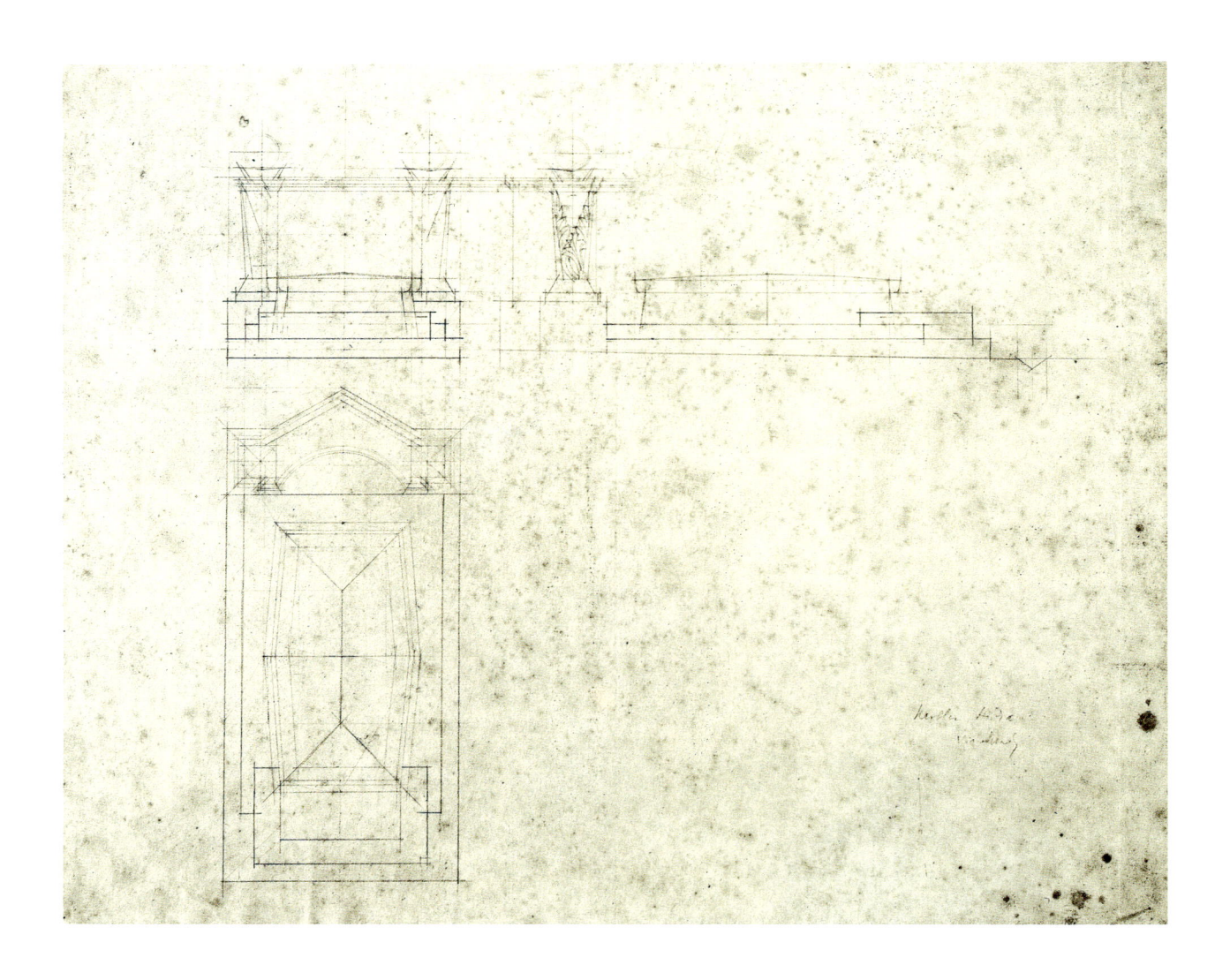

< **334**
Hácha tomb, design, 1915
<< **335**
Tomb for Alois Kotěra, sketch, 1916
>> **336**
Schauer tomb in Olšany cemetery in Prague, 1922

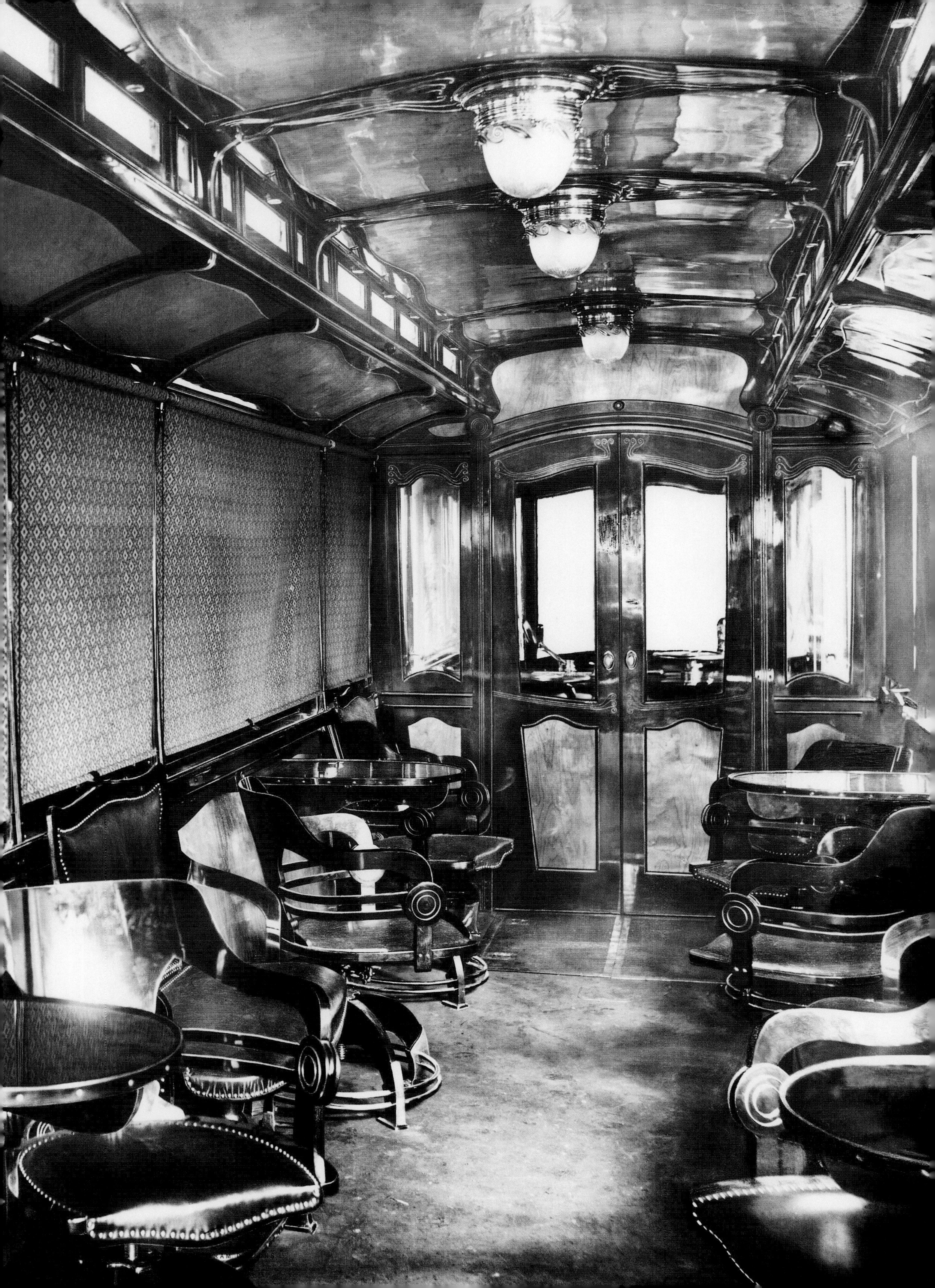

> < 337
> Luxury four-axle tramway motorcar for the Prague Transport Company (saloon car no. 200), interior, 1899

Rail and Tram Designs

LUDVÍK LOSOS

Kotěra arrived in Prague at a time when the conditions were already ripe for his participation in the design of rail and tram vehicles. In 1884, the School of Applied Arts began to cooperate with the construction department of the Ringhoffer Rail Car Works in Smíchov. This cooperation evolved around the figure of professor Stribral who, as the Ringhoffer family architect and director of the School from 1897, took care of organising the commissions and included his colleagues and talented students in the design work. On the 1st of September that same year, the newly established Public Transport Company of the Royal City of Prague began operating the city tramlines,[1] entrusting the Křižík Company with the construction of the first tracks and the commission of the engines. However, the Transport Company management was still searching for a unified type of a tramcar. Unable to reach an agreement, they purchased both four-axle and small two-axle vehicles, designated for the less frequented lines. After purchasing its first series of vehicles, the management placed an order with the Ringhoffer factory for a representative saloon car to be used for official journeys and for the Prague Lord Mayor.[2]

As a student of Otto Wagner and on Stibral's personal recommendation, Kotěra was assigned the unusual task of designing this saloon tramcar which the factory management decided to include among its prestigious exhibits for the 1900 Paris World Exhibition. Originally planning to supply it at the price of a serial tramcar, after its Paris success the factory donated the car to the city of Prague free of charge.[3]

This prestigious commission already revealed the chief quality of Kotěra's design work, an indivisibility of form and function. Contrary to tradition, whereby the architect – designer designed only the interior and furnishings for the tramcars, Kotěra also designed the car's exterior, intervening in the construction of its body, defining the rhythm of the windows, as well as the shape of the frames and doors. His interior design for this saloon car – conceived as a conference room – was restrained, relieved of historicism and decorative and non-functional ornamentation. He furnished it with mahogany swivel armchairs, combined with brass and upholstered in dark leather, and proceeded by arranging chairs in pairs around small tables fixed beneath the larger windows, and placing upholstered benches for two persons beneath the smaller ones. What was exceptional about this saloon car was the high quality of its materials: walls covered with light-coloured maple panelling in mahogany frames, and doors and partitions made of cut glass. The external decoration was focused on the wavy mahogany window frames as a contrast to the static lines of the vehicle's body, complemented with a simple, polished, cream-coloured finish in a light green shade. At the bottom of the sideboard, it bore an inscription made in bronze lettering with a cast bronze coat-of-arms of the city of Prague, enveloped in a stylised garland of linden sprigs made of wrought tombac.[4]

The design was unparalleled in its simplicity, as were the changes Kotěra introduced in the customary construction

---

1 Pavel Fojtík – Stanislav Linert – František Prošek, *Historie městské hromadné dopravy v Praze*. Praha 1995, 2000, p. 57 ff.
2 The Ringhoffer order book. Year 1899, order no. 320, serial no. 62663.
3 Stanislav Linert, *Vozidla pražské tramvajové dopravy*. Nadatur Praha 1996, p. 42.
4 The inventory of the original furnishings has survived in the Ringhoffer company catalogue for the Paris World Exhibition.

of tramcars. They would have inspired his colleague Justich, a student of Friedrich Ohmann, to design another of the exhibits for the Paris World Exhibition – the so-called saloon coach for short leisure journeys. Although his design employed the entire spectrum of styles common to the high Secession, Justich broke away from decorativeness. He intervened in the design of the car's body, changed the shape of its sides and even created an untraditional bogie for it.[5]

Kotěra's design for the Lord Mayor's saloon tramcar did not comply with the period requirements and the fashion of manufacturing saloon cars with pompous interiors. There is no doubt that this austerity provoked a conflict with Stibral, who was highly influential at the Ringhoffer factory in the acquisition of commissions for the school staff.[6] Nevertheless, the factory recognised Kotěra's interest in creating a functional serial production vehicle, as well as the high quality of the details in his designs. It continued to entrust him with the design of its "exhibits", which demanded a flawless execution, as well as its tramcars, which did not require an elaborate interior but instead a practical and modern approach.

In 1904, Kotěra was assigned with his next commission, a 1st- and 2nd-class car for the Bukovina Regional Railway, combining the possibility of use for individual passengers, as well as groups or families. The car obviously represented an attempt on behalf of the Railway to offer higher standards for passengers who could not afford the luxury of a separate saloon car.[7] Kotěra's design for the interior respected the usual furnishing scheme. He kept to the customary partitioning of the car's interior, adding a sightseeing veranda on one end, framed by large rectangular windows and a glazed

---

5   Ludvík Losos – Ivo Mahel, *Salonní vozy Ringhoffer*. Nadatur, VÚVK, Praha 1999, pp. 182–184.
6   Collected authors, *VŠUP sto let prace*. Vysoka škola uměleckoprůmyslová, Praha 1985.
7   Sketches of one version of this car have survived in the Archive of Design Sketches of the Ringhoffer Company. Sign. Group I, 1A:2. Dated 6 December 1904.

< 338
Luxury four-axle tramway motorcar for the Prague Transport Company (saloon car no. 200), 1899
> 339
Luxury four-axle tramway motorcar for the Prague Transport Company (saloon car no. 200), detail of entry steps, 1899

front. The Prague State Railways directorate ordered two similar cars in 1906. Like the previous car, Kotěra kept the original scheme of the interior partitions, including the customary compartments, however, he designed the middle of the 1st-class section as a single large space which occupied the entire width of the car's body but could still be divided into two halves by a curtain, and furnished it with additional stools and a small table. The compartment, which opened out to the side corridor to create more space, could also be divided with a curtain. Kotěra reserved one end of the car for a veranda with a glazed panel at the front, a fixed wall-buffet and a small lavatory, and designed white wickerwork furniture for it. He also transformed the exterior of the car. Already in this work, he applied what was now a typical feature, providing a certain "rhythm" to the side walls – two- or three-part windows, whose narrow pane was fixed while the wider window slid open. The train had impressive large triple leaf springs, ensuring greater comfort during travel.[8]

Unfortunately, no documentation survived of Kotěra's next commission, the saloon car for the Southern Railway. The only available material includes drawings of details such as the hinges for folding beds, or his design for luggage nets or etched glass door panels.[9] These details were very characteristic of Kotěra, he always prepared their technical drawings very carefully, and personally monitored the quality and precision of their execution. The architect's complex understanding of design, which combined form and function, meant that it was necessary for him to penetrate the very principles of construction. He contemplated the functional side of the vehicle, the need for a solid car body, in contrast with the requirement for large windows. He studied the practical implications of the proportions of the car entrances, the lighting and a number of other technical parameters which improved the utility of the car and reduced the production costs. The car bodies were still wooden at that time, and their construction required complex joining work. This was especially true of the connections on which the stability of the car body, strained by jolting during travel, was largely dependent. Kotěra took great interest in these issues and made an effort to comprehend the construction principles and their practical execution.

The factory's construction department soon grew to appreciate the architect's role in the manufacture of their vehicles, most of all the high standard of his work. From the end of the 19th century, the Ringhoffers produced luxury sleeping and dining cars for the CIWL (Compagnie Internationale de Wagon Lits) which commonly provided its own documentation and employed its own architects for these commissions.

---

8   Ludvik Losos – Ivo Mahel (see note 5), p. 209. – Car no. 745 was also exhibited at the World Exhibition in Milan.
9   Design sketches have survived in AA NTM, Kotěra collection.

The factory was therefore fully aware of the international development in the sphere of the production and design of rail vehicles and could appreciate the modernity of Kotěra's design.

In 1904, the factory received an order for a large series of motorised tramcars for the Prague Transport Company and Kotěra was finally offered an attractive commission – to design a serially produced tramcar. Kotěra eliminated the heavy bogies of the traditional cars, placing the car frame onto two single axles, whose unusually large base (3.6 m) was designed to secure smooth running. He widened the entrances, enlarged the platforms and lightened the car body by placing four large windows on each of its side walls. His tramcar, produced in the following year,[10] especially its wide rounded front, spacious platform and large windows on the sides, was to determine the design of Prague tramcars for many years to come. The architect was still not satisfied with the results, however, and seized an opportunity which presented itself the following year: the Ringhoffer exhibit for the World Exhibition in Milan included a tramcar. No longer bound by the client's financial limitations, Kotěra designed a car that fully accommodated his ideas for a modern public transport vehicle. He used his previous serial model design, yet chose a different arrangement and interior furnishings for it. He combined seating positioned lengthwise on one side of the car with horizontal seats on the opposite side. The lightly upholstered seats were given textile covers. The car was equipped with a clock suspended from the ceiling in its

[10] Order book of the Ringhoffer company, year 1904, order no. 755, serial no. 67419–433.

< **340**
Two-axle motorcar for the Prague Transport Company, 1904–1905
> **341**
Two-axle motorcar for the Prague Transport Company no. 193, 1906

centre and placed inside an elaborate frame with a small ceiling light underneath. He used three-part windows with specially designed frames on the sides of the car's body (no doubt also designed to strengthen the car's structure). The upper third of the narrow side windows was separated by a crossbar and this space was used to display colour slides of Prague's important landmarks. The panels on the tramcar's exterior were framed with yellow ornamented lines, with a large bronze coat-of-arms in the centre, enveloped in a garland of linden sprigs made of wrought tombac. Kotěra designed one-axle bogies to ensure smooth running, better suspension and to remove the characteristic "shriek" of Prague tramcars when they took a sharp bend. After the Milan exhibition, the City of Prague purchased the car, however it was classified as saloon car number 193 and used only for sightseeing tours.[11]

We can trace Kotěra's influence in the production of 14 large motorcars and 12 four-axle trailers for the Vienna–Baden Intercity Railway, produced as a subcontract for the Siemens

---

11 Ibid., order no. 804, serial no. 67761. – On the future destiny of this car, see: Stanislav Linert (see note 3), pp. 46 and 47.

Company in 1906. The car bodies were equipped with striking elongated ventilation roof extensions placed at their head and again utilised two-wing doors with narrow panes inside specially designed frames (which the architect had already used for his Prague saloon tramcar). Its interior was extremely simple and functional, consisting of three rows of Kotěra's favourite swivel chairs, this time constructed by the Thonet Brothers. These cars still had the usual, identical windows on their side walls. Only his second delivery of 15 trailer cars for Baden in 1908 included alternating narrow and wide windows, enhancing the side walls. Light-coloured and painted in soft dove-grey, the sideboards were once more decorated with centrally placed emblems made of wrought tombac – the joint initials of the rail company set inside a large frame of stylised chestnut leaves, typical of the Baden spa promenades.[12]

That same year, Kotěra had another opportunity to design a railway car, this time for the Swiss M. O. B. (Montreux-Oberland Bernois) Railway, which commissioned a dining car from the Ringhoffer Company. The M. O. B. was already a renowned tourist route and, despite being a narrow-gauge railway, offered luxury services. Although limited by the size of the car, Kotěra designed a spacious, light interior, with wide windows and comfortable folding seats upholstered in leather. He wainscoted the interior walls using simple geometric patterns and decorated the edges of the individual panels of the smooth cylindrical ceilings with ornamental strips. The same strips were used to decorate the lighting

---

[12] Hans Sternhart – Hans Pötschner, *Hundert Jahre Badner Bahn*. J. O. Slezak, Wien 1973.

< 342
Two-axle motorcar for the Prague Transport Company, interior, 1906
> 343
Four-axle dining car for the Swiss Montreux-Oberland Bernois Railway, interior, 1911

fixtures. The well-balanced and discreetly designed interior proved very popular, and was ordered twice more in the same design. This car was also used to represent the Ringhoffer Company at the World Exhibition in Milan.[13] Again, Kotěra designed the cars using a light cream-coloured finish, intended to emphasise the cleanliness of electric transportation, which was much publicised at the time. These cars were withdrawn from circulation only after the end of the Second World War, when they were converted into standard passenger cars.

Kotěra continued in his efforts to influence urban design. For the exhibition of the Chamber of Trade and Commerce which was being organised in Prague in 1908, he designed another truly revolutionary tramcar prototype. The car had an unusual concept – a wide, central entry platform and two separate passenger compartments with transversally positioned seats, both ending in separate small compartments for the drivers. The architect designed a long ventilation clerestory which stretched to, and incorporated, both

[13] Ringhoffer company catalogue for the World Exhibition in Milan.

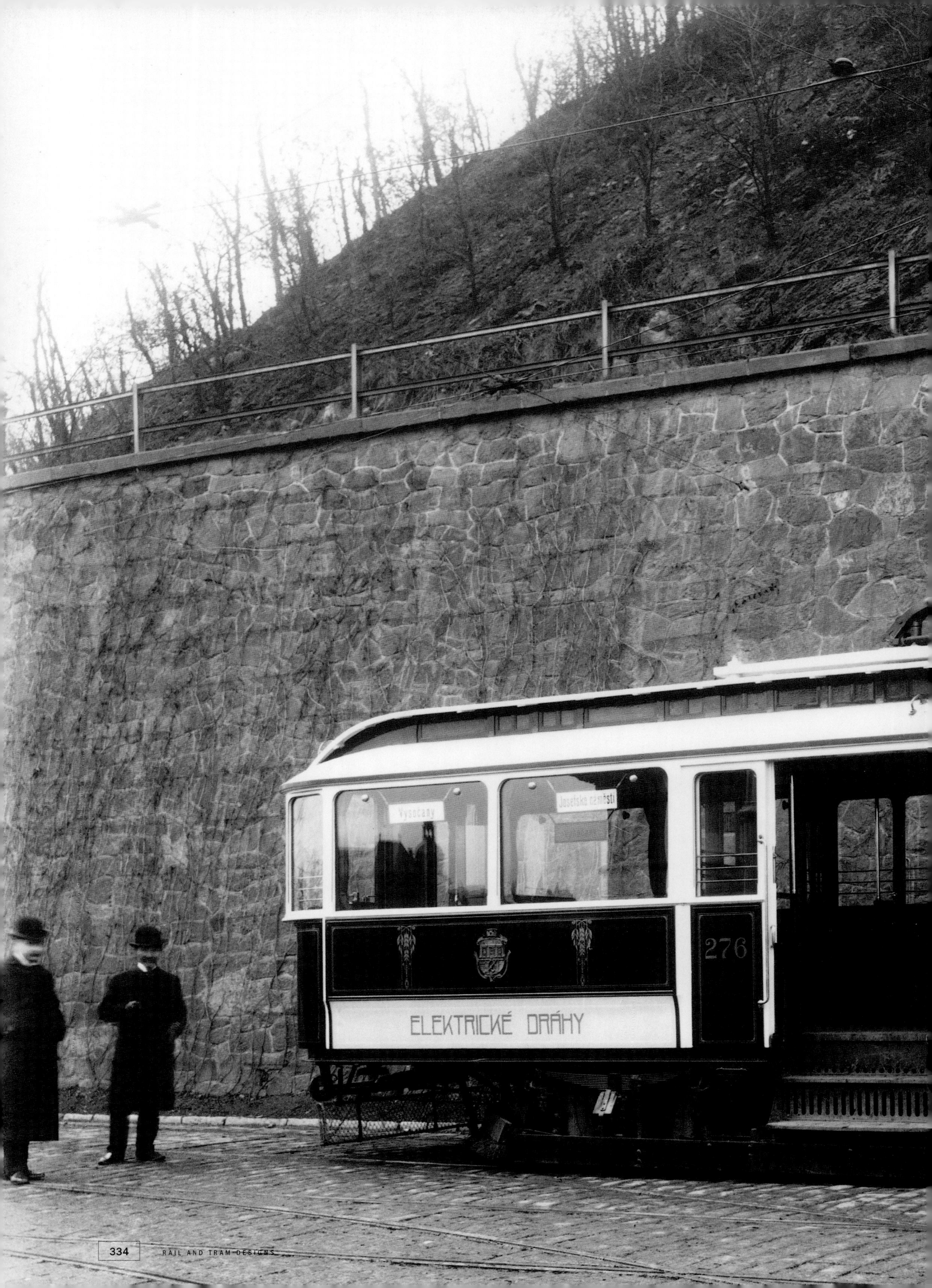
Vysočany
Josefské náměstí
276
ELEKTRICKÉ DRÁHY

<> 344
Two-axle motorcar for the Prague Transport Company with central entrance, 1908

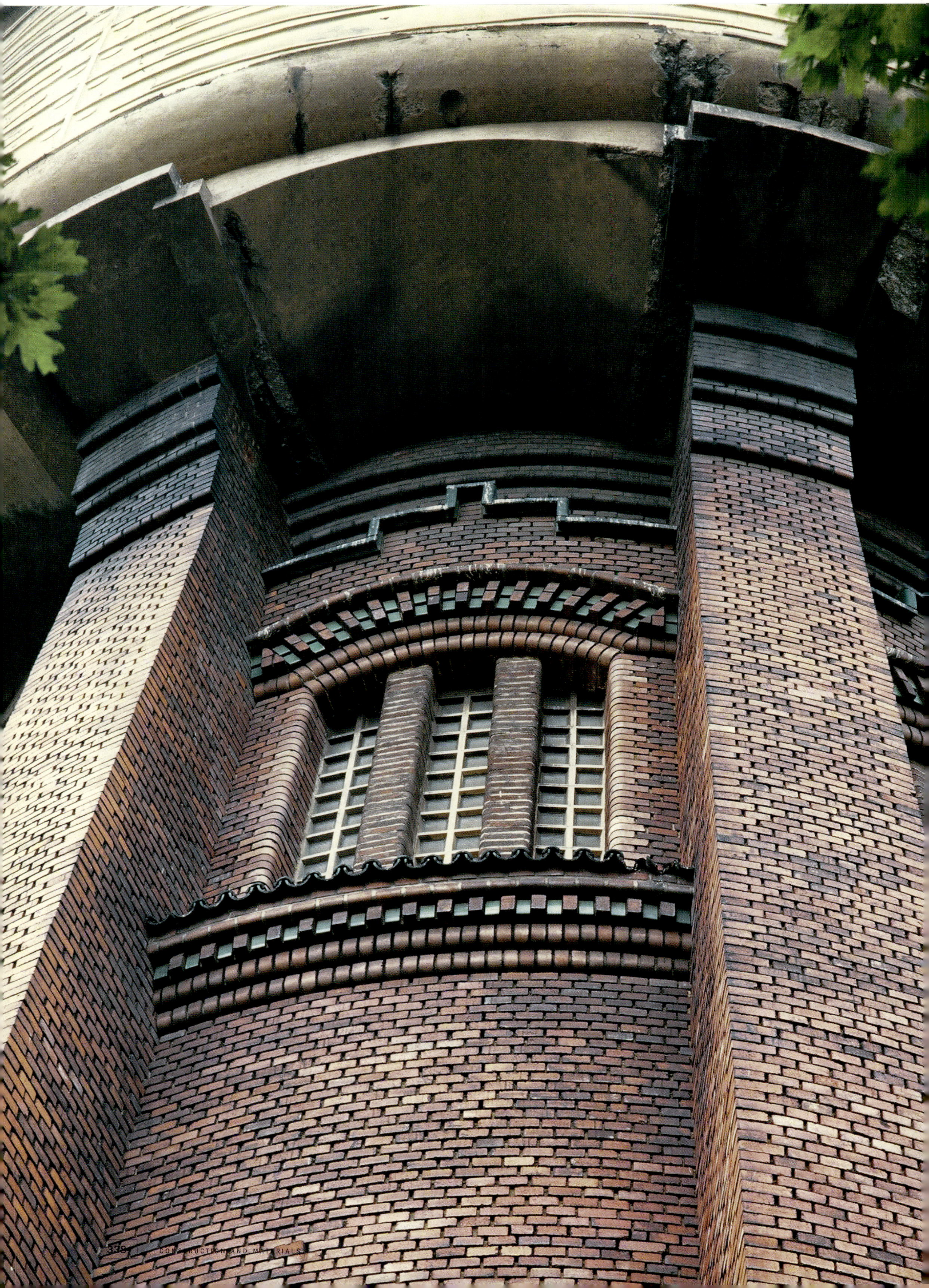

< 348
Vršovice waterworks in Prague-Michle, detail, 1906–1907

Construction and Materials

VLAĎKA VALCHÁŘOVÁ

Jan Kotěra is considered the father of modern architecture in this country. Yet how did his pioneering practice relate to the choice of building materials and construction technologies used in his architecture? Kotěra became known for his purity of bare construction which was, however, achieved using building methods that were customary for his time. The composition of exposed bricks combined with ceramics and coarse plaster, characteristic of his best works, was clearly inspired by industrial architecture. However, the successful completion of the building works was often strongly influenced by the personal qualities of the architect, the personality of the particular client and cooperation with the companies which executed the work. Taking the example of some of Kotěra's projects completed between 1900 and 1920, we will see what made his buildings exceptional in these terms. *"Kotěra – initiator and organiser"*, this was how Jaromír Krejcar referred to his teacher in his obituary from 1923, recalling, in particular, Kotěra's educational and social activities. Kotěra's organising and diplomatic abilities were as accurately illustrated during the building (and maintenance) of the Mánes Association exhibition pavilion. When, at the beginning of 1900, the city council earmarked part of the former fortification plot at the foot of Petřín hill for the provisional pavilion of the Mánes Association, Kotěra invited the Mánes members to join him in creating an album with reproductions of their unpublished works to acquire financial means for this construction. Thanks to Kotěra's personal contacts, the building plot was placed under the authority of Smíchov town hall which granted it free-of-charge to the Mánes Association in March 1902, under a single condition – that it would be returned by the end of August in its original state. Kotěra designed the pavilion in the course of three days, while František Hubáček, a carpenter from Malá Strana, built it during a single month. The exhibition of Auguste Rodin, for which the pavilion was constructed, was opened on 10th of May 1902. Kotěra designed the pavilion using simple means: he used a classical wooden framework, sheeted on both sides and plastered. The only complicated part of the construction was the arched portal at the entrance, crowned with a glass dome and incorporating two towers on its sides. The architect stretched a decorative canvas underneath the wooden rooftruss, while the roof was made in part of bitumene covering, and part glass. The floor was laid with fired clay tiles in selected areas. After the Rodin exhibition had finished, it seemed a pity to demolish the beautiful Secessionist pavilion, thus the Mánes members appealed for it to be preserved in the following explanatory note: "[...] *the location at the foot of Kinský gardens has already been consecrated since it is now credited with promoting the glory of the Czech name beyond our borders* [...] *it is necessary to work consciously and continually to attract foreign visitors to Prague, to lure them and organise events on a European scale for that purpose* [...]".[1] They were granted an extension until the end of 1902, which was followed by regular

1   AMP, SVU Mánes fund, file 113, sign. 8.1.

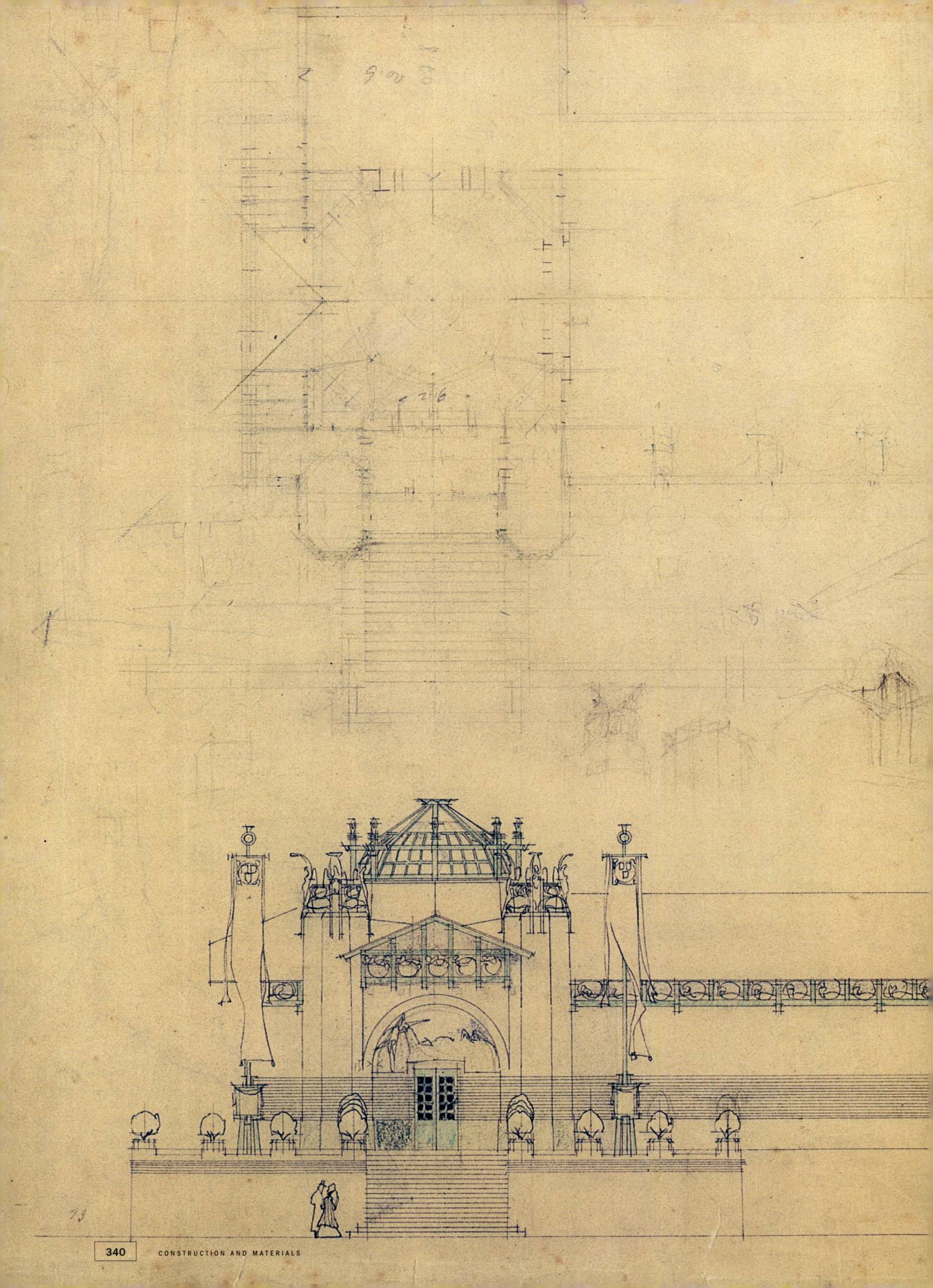

<>349
Mánes pavilion below Kinský gardens in Prague,
sketches of the façades, 1902

CONSTRUCTION AND MATERIALS

correspondence between the Association and the boroughs of Prague and Smíchov (the final demolition order, a request for an extension of the lease, a letter of consent, a letter of thanks). A number of times, Kotěra was forced to intervene in local council discussions, especially after new mayors were appointed. In 1906, Hubáček insisted that the pavilion, built as a temporary one-year structure, be checked for structural faults after five years of its continual operation. The invited expert did not detect any deformation or decay in the construction, and the building was insured again, on the condition that there would be no smoking inside the pavilion, or artificial lighting. The pavilion remained at the foot of Kinský gardens for fifteen years, and never required repairs more substantial than the regular maintenance of its parapets and plastering. During the War the pavilion was not used for its original purpose and, in 1916, Kotěra suggested that it be offered up for sale to the army. However, the pavilion was instead demolished.

Wood was an important building material for Kotěra in his early works, particularly when he was designing exhibition pavilions and family villas (Trmal, Mácha, Fröhlich, Sucharda and Tonder villas). He used it as a plastic and "folkloric" material to construct roofs, gables and half-timber constructions, and for the carved details.

One of these early commissions was a summer residence in the Crimea for Karel Kramář. However, Kotěra maintained his uncompromising creative approach and finally rejected the offer of this prominent client, who was also a close friend. Kotěra, who according to Otakar Novotný *"forced the future owner to think further and beyond his temporary habits [...] and with his own cultivated views discreetly changed his client's way of thinking [...]"*, in this case could not come to an agreement with Mrs Naděžda Kramář, and decided to reject the commission in January 1903: "[...] *I have been thinking again about this matter which used to trouble me earlier and now has become truly pressing. This is a matter of the relationship between the prospective owner and the artist [...] The owner, if he possesses a certain artistic imagination, of course attempts to influence the work. This usually means that he will try to control the artist in charge, who on the other hand seeks to fulfil the task according to his own principles, in his own form. The fact that the artist should comply with the practical demands – the owner's lifestyle, climate, materials, financial and technical means, etc. [...] – is obvious. However, this compliance [...] can only reach a certain limit [...] and if the differences of opinion between the two persist, there are only two possible solutions: either the artist convinces the future owner, or else – they must part".*[2]

The everyday life of the architect-designer was unfortunately dependent on winning commissions, at times also on extracting due fees. Kotěra's insistence on principles, not only in relation to private clients, was probably one of the reasons

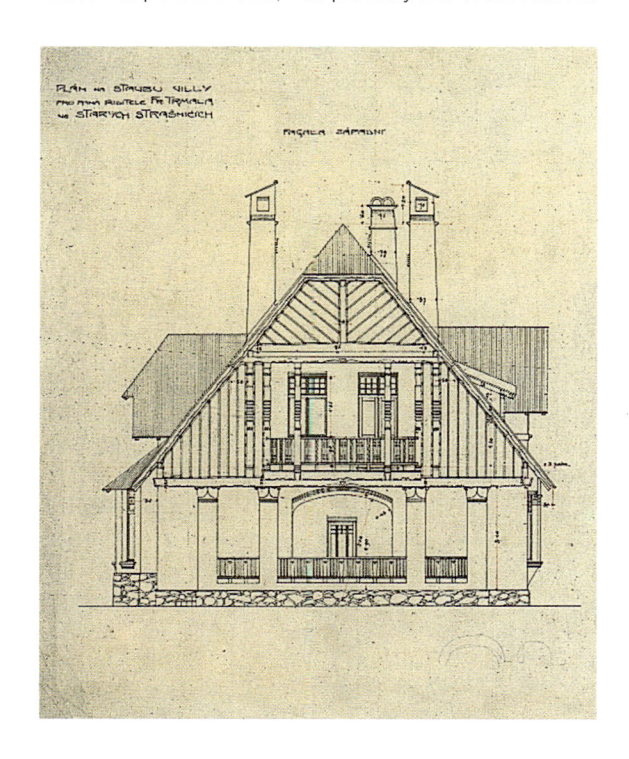

2 ANM, Karel Kramář fund, sign. 23.5336–40.

< 350
Trmal's villa in Prague-Strašnice, façade – technical drawing, 1902–1903
> 351
Peterka's house in Prague, wrought-iron grille – detail, 1899–1900

why some of his quality competition designs (Savings Bank in Hradec Králové, Koruna insurance company building in Prague) were never brought to fruition.

Conversely, Kotěra's collaboration with František Ulrich, Mayor of Hradec Králové, during the years 1895 to 1904 proved exceptionally auspicious. The 1901 commission for the project of the Regional Authorities building, which Kotěra built in 1903–04, marked the beginning of this collaboration. In 1910, the Regional Authorities building and the adjacent hotel passed to the ownership of Josef Urban, its former leaseholder, and Kotěra was commissioned to design a hotel extension. It included a spacious cinema hall for one thousand people, the largest in the country at the time. The Hradec Králové branch of Hollmann Co., Kotěra's regular contractors, built its reinforced concrete ceiling vault and the gallery.

Reportedly, just after the completion of the Regional Authorities building, Mayor Ulrich, who was also chairman of the City Museum's Board of Trustees, approached Kotěra with an offer to design a new museum building for Hradec Králové. Kotěra's correspondence with Ulrich seems to suggest that, in March 1903, Kotěra travelled to Plzeň to visit his friend Škorpil,[3] who was to advise him on the museum's programme. That same year, the museum was allocated a building site on the Elbe embankment, which was to be protected from flooding by the planned regulation of the river. From the very beginning, Kotěra approached the building of the museum, which was ultimately his greatest work, with a care bordering on pedantry, apparent as much in the formulation of the final plans, as in the architect's choice of materials and the organisation of the building work itself. In January 1909, when the foreman's plans scaled at 1:100 were ready, together with the plans of the main details, Kotěra sent the contractor Melcer from Hradec Králové a sample of glazed bricks from the Tomášek kiln, which he intended to use for the museum. That same year in April, after the works on the foundations had already begun, Kotěra wrote the following letter to the Board's secretary: *"In deciding which offer to take, it will be absolutely necessary to disregard the persons involved, and give priority to inexpensive and well executed work. I would like to point out that it will be necessary to contract reputable companies, with which you can be certain that they will not present us with unfounded demands [...] I met with the*

---

3 Josef Škorpil (1856–1931), architect and director of the Museum of Decorative Arts in Plzeň.

PŮDORYS

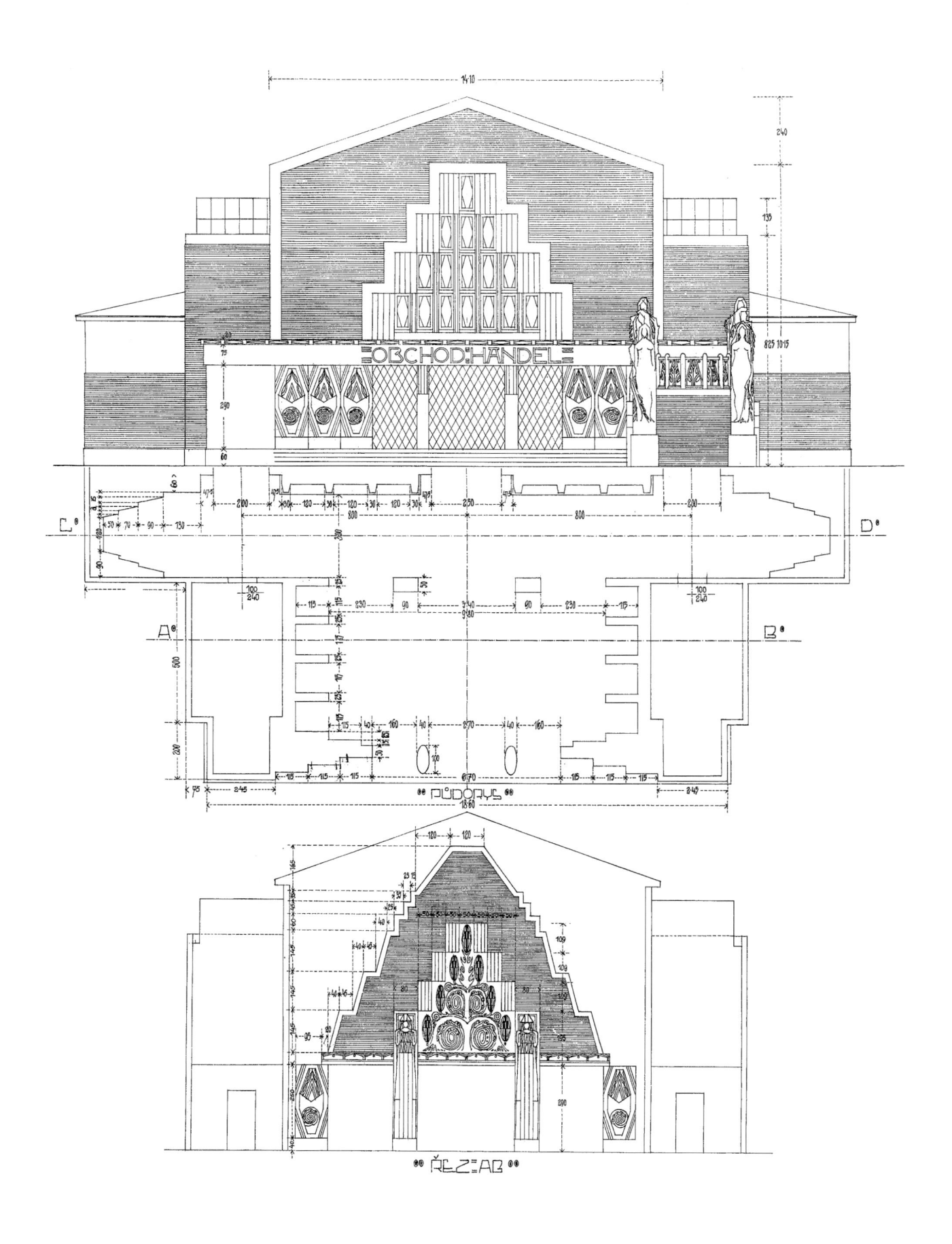

ŘEZ=AB

< 352
Trade and Industry pavilion at the Chamber of Trade and Commerce Exhibition in Prague, technical drawing of the two entrances, 1908
> 353
Design for the pavilion of the Poštorná plant owned by the Prince of Lichtenstein at the World Exhibition in Milan, cross-section, 1905

representative of the Králův Dvůr cement works. He asked for my consent to use their product for the museum. I have no objections against using their cement for the foundations, however I do object to its use for the reinforced concrete [...]".[4]

In laying the concrete foundations underneath the sandstone tiling of the lapidarium in the museum's basement, the engineers had to consider the future backwater level of the regulated Elbe in their calculations. The old fortified bridge across the Elbe near the museum also had to be replaced with a new construction, and Kotěra was approached to assess what work was required. In July 1909, he wrote to Ulrich: "*[...] I looked through the plans of the new bridge across the Elbe, and the designs handed over by the city technical office on the 28th of June 1909. The report is well grounded and its benefits are clear. I can only warmly recommend it to you. I would be glad to sketch the possibilities of its realisation*".[5] The Bromovský-Schulz Co. from Adamov built the new Prague bridge – designed as a riveted arched truss – in 1911–13. Kotěra completed the work, enhancing the design of the bridge with parapets and lamp-posts placed on both sides, and with appealing, small public convenience buildings made of sandstone and concrete.

In the meantime, the main work on the museum building was completed in 1910, including the glazing of the skylights and the reinforced concrete dome, for which the Prague-based Wolf & Štětka Company provided green lozenges made of Antique glass and the popular profiled glass known as "*luxfer*". The installation of the two sculptures of seated figures at the entrance to the museum presented the greatest technical problem during completion in 1911. Iron supplied with threaded pegs was inserted into the armrest of one of the sculptures to support the bronze male figure. The sculptures, made by the Rakovník kiln after a design by Stanislav Sucharda, each weighed 60–70 metric tonnes together with the masonry. The façades, on which the horizontal combed stucco was alternated with exposed bricks, were decorated with glazed decorative details above the entrance, including a lion and coat-of-arms. Concerned about Sucharda's sculptures, Kotěra complained to the central office for the sale of ceramicware in Prague: "*[...] the glazing on both sculptures, which did not turn out that well to begin with, has now changed for the worse. The green glaze has almost turned completely yellow [...] I inspected the building and the tiling, and I must say that the work has been done with extreme negligence [...] you are mistaken in*

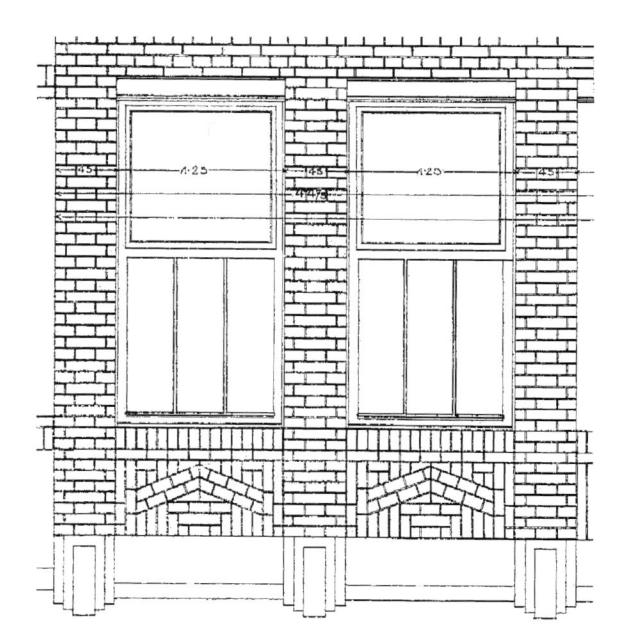

---

[4] Archiv MVČ in Hradec Králové, MPM HK and Literature Archive funds. I would like to thank Jaroslava Pospíšilová for providing this information.
[5] See note 4.

< **354**
Laichter's house in Prague-Vinohrady, façade – detail, 1908–1909
<< **355**
Laichter's house in Prague-Vinohrady, façade – technical drawing, detail, 1908–1909
> **356**
City Museum in Hradec Králové, plaster models of façade motifs, 1909–1913

your suggestion that the unfavourable impression of the two sculptures rests in the fact that the façade is not yet finished, for the building is already complete. The façade will darken in time and the glazes, whose tone is already too light, will become even more conspicuous. The only reason for this is that the colours have not been produced according to the sample, particularly the green [...]".

Kotěra's engineer Pokorný supervised the entire building process and solved most of the everyday building problems with Melcer, the Hradec Králové site manager. Whenever it was possible, this was done in writing, and the surviving letters suggest that Kotěra made a consistent effort to personally supervise the building work. He travelled to Hradec almost every week, however, he ultimately lost his enthusiasm: "*[...] I shall not travel to Hradec for this, and you must understand that I am already losing my patience. My work, and my efforts to complete the building to the best of my abilities, did not meet with the kind of understanding I was anticipating [...] I shall not recommend any more companies to the Board*". Finally, Kotěra ordered the sculptures to be painted over, and commissioned the František Fröhlich Company to do the work. Kotěra also designed a detailed reconstruction of the museum grounds – except for the garden restaurant which the owner of the nearby Urban hotel originally intended to manage. The design included pavement tiling for some of the more prominent sites (such as the sample for the mosaic pavement Kotěra designed for the east side of Eliščino embankment and for Rašínova avenue). The following correspondence from April 1914 testifies that Kotěra was pleased with the results: "*[...] It has already been 11 years since [...] you invited me to take on this project. I was still a young man then, at the beginning of my career and, forgive me for adding, it was not an easy beginning [...] I commenced the work with the enthusiasm of a young man and I have ended it with the prudence which accompanies a more mature age. As strict and self-critical as I wish to be in examining this first larger commission of mine, I can still say with a clear conscience that I used my strengths well and that it is truly one of my best works. I am grateful to you, not only for entrusting me with the work but even more for your arbitration in all matters that followed; as it often happens with such demanding endeavours, these were not always favourable [...]*". In 1922, Kotěra received

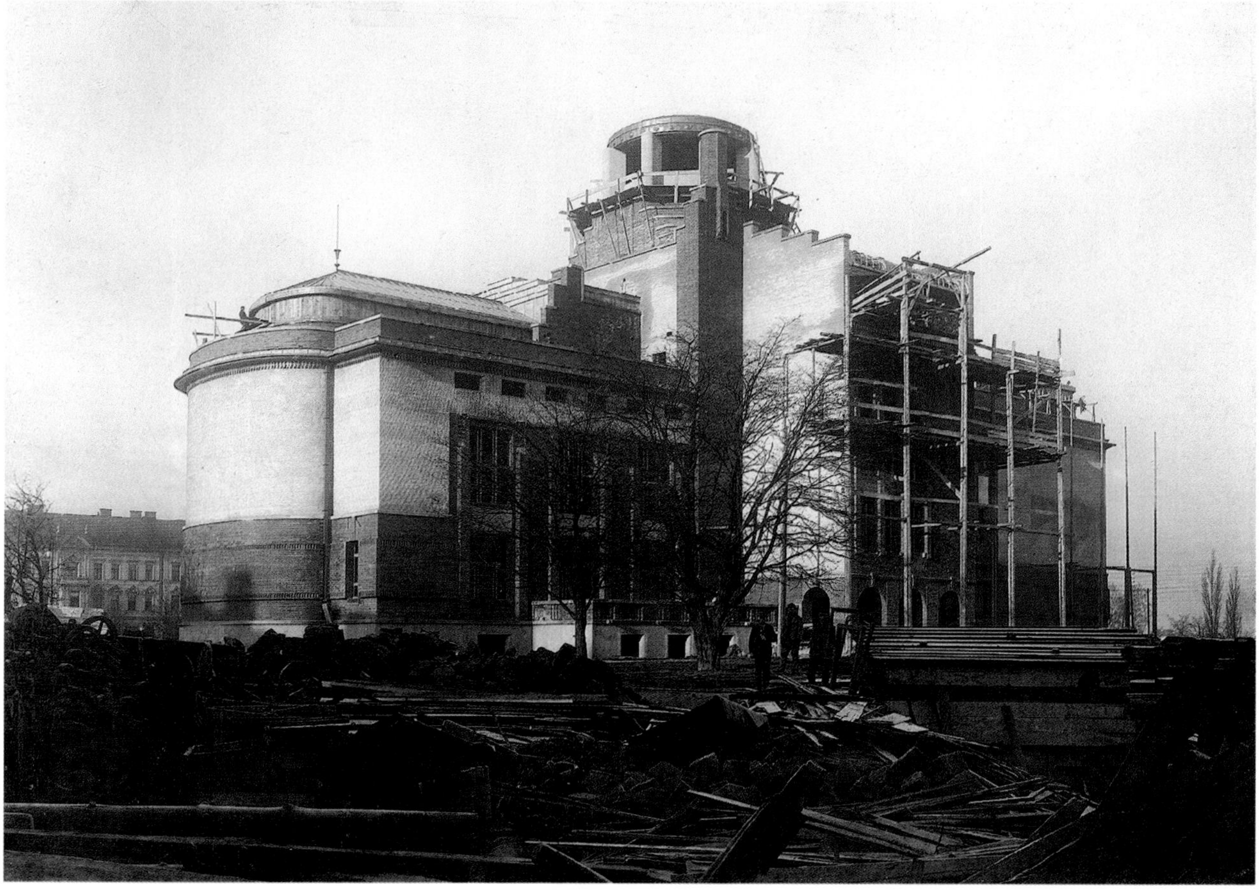

< 357
City Museum in Hradec Králové, view of the construction site, 1910

his last commission from Ulrich, still incorporating the landscaping and urban design of the museum grounds. This was a project for an apartment building whose bevelled outside corners were meant to ensure that the view from the embankment remain undisturbed.

Kotěra was one of the first architects to break down the barrier between the jurisdiction of the building contractor, and that of the architect, traditionally treated as a mere decorator. This phenomenon is well illustrated by the building of National House in Prostějov, which the town hall of this *"Czech garden in Moravia"* decided to commission in the spirit of the Regional Authorities building in Hradec Králové. From a construction point of view, the building work on the project, which commenced in 1905, did not differ in any way from the standard practice of the period. The restaurant and the theatre area were clearly divided and both were covered with iron roofing. Local builders carried out the carcassing works. Specialised firms from Prague, apparently on Kotěra's suggestion, provided the technical facilities and the more demanding exterior and interior decoration for the museum, on which Kotěra collaborated with his colleagues from Prague (Franta Anýž and Křižík provided the light fittings, Antonín Tringler the installations, František Fröhlich undertook the painting, etc.). Clearly, there was a trend to employ mainly Czech companies: the kilns in Rakovník[6] were commissioned to produce the ceramic facing, as well as Sucharda's fountain with its ceramic female figure, instead of the much closer Poštorná works. Otakar Pokorný, Kotěra's colleague and construction engineer, supervised the complex construction work during the three-year-long building process. Kotěra, who always made an effort to personally oversee the quality of the work on his projects, visited Prostějov only five times during the entire period. He relied completely on Pokorný, and recommended him to Prostějov Mayor Horák for the post of town construction engineer: *"[...] I warmly recommend Mr Pokorný's application. I know him to be truly intelligent, extraordinarily hardworking and conscientious. The superhuman effort that he made during the work on the clubhouse is the most telling proof of this. At least one or two assistants are usually involved in such extensive building projects, to aid the foreman, whereas here, Mr Pokorný undertook the work all by himself [...]"*. However, Pokorný later turned down the offer.[7]

In 1905, Kotěra designed another pavilion, for the World Exhibition in Milan, representing the Poštorná tile works owned by Prince of Lichtenstein.[8] All the exterior and interior surfaces of the brick pavilion were envisaged as a *"sample book"* of the factory's products, displaying over 200 types of glazed profiled tiles (the more complex pieces were produced using models), including the entire palette of the colours on offer. The decorative carved ceramic facing of the walls was interlaid with moulded and cast ceramic with relief ornamentation – geometric, vegetative and animal motifs, and themes depicting earthenware production. The ceramic facing of the façade was complemented with floor tiles and mosaic panels, with roof tiles and stoneware curbstones for the plinth. A pergola was placed in front of the staircase leading to the terrace, with a semi-circular fountain decorated with a ceramic female figure. The entrance columns bore a massive

---

[6] The Rakovník-based Kasalovský & Sommerschuh factory, producing fired clay products, mosaic tiles and stoves.

[7] Edith Jeřábková, Prostějov – enkláva české secese na Moravě. Dissertation, UP Olomouc 1995 (manuscript deposited in SOA Prostějov). SOA Prostějov, Archiv města Prostějova, files 425–426.

[8] The factory in Poštorná near Břeclav was founded in 1867. By 1890 it already had over 500 employees and mainly supplied Vienna (glazed flat roofing tiles for the church of St Stephen). In 1907, Prince Johann of Lichtenstein bought the Rakovník factory (founded in 1883) and affiliated it with the Poštorná plant. He appointed former shareholder of the Rakovník factory Emil Sommerschuh (1866–1920) as manager of both factories. The ceramic products from Rakovník were used to furnish the restaurant and wine bar in Municipal House, the coffee-shop in the Imperial Hotel in Prague, the hotel Gellert baths in Budapest and many others.

352 WORKERS' HOUSING COLONIES

< 359
Housing colony for the state railway employees in Louny, 1909, 1913, 1919

Workers' Housing Colonies

PAVEL ŠOPÁK

The workers' housing colonies became a prominent theme in Kotěra's oeuvre after 1910. The rather fervent debate on the subject held between Czech architects and intellectuals in the years prior to the First World War could provide us with some insight into the importance of this issue in Kotěra's time and in contemporary Czech culture in general. Nevertheless, it was only in the early 1920s that this polemic reached a scope and intensity worthy of our attention, at the same time elucidating Kotěra's efforts in this sphere.

The notion of *work* was the focal point which encouraged deliberation on the part of intellectuals, artists and technocrats of the young Czechoslovak Republic. During the early 1920s, urban planner Vladimír Zákrejs wrote: *"Work is what will save us. Difficult, long-term and responsible, it will only become successful if it is led by reason, knowledge and tenacity, the essential principles on which we must rest our actions."*[1] *"The task for the economists, engineers and sociologists of this country* [will be] *to work on the development of a new social order, which* [would bring] *into harmony the justified requests of our times with our present economic situation"*,[2] Rudolf Svoboda concluded in a related text.

The notion of work linked public and private life with politics and economy and was related in a similar manner both to education and culture. It was granted an almost mythical interpretation – in the theoretical concepts of the representatives of technocracy, work was seen as the means to save the world,[3] while in the artistic theories of the early 1920s it had been postulated as the moral corrective of civilisation viewed as a purely material activity. It suffices to recall the definition of art proposed by writer Vladislav Vančura. According to him, art is an *"organisation of work"*, placed in opposition to civilisation, the *"organisation of profit"* with clearly negative connotations.[4] It influenced the themes treated along the civilist line of Czech painting and sculpture of the 1920s, and became a motto for contemporary architecture – it was not by coincidence that the above-mentioned text by Zákrejs was conceived as the leading article of the newly established architectural journal *Stavitel* (Builder).

In its first volumes, the conception of the journal was focused on the topical subject of the period, the question of social housing, building for the classes for whom industrious labour epitomised life. A modest individual house, adjusted in its proportions to accommodate the *"small man"*, appeared as the most credible expression of the ideals of humanity, human dignity and the self-confidence of a free individual within a democratic society. Humanitarian values – and work – these were the pillars on which rested the social, and cultural policies of the Czechoslovak President Tomáš Garrigue Masaryk, who was concerned not only with the establishment of the Czechoslovak Republic but also its placement within a *New Europe*. Another notion – the idea of *home* – entered the same debate, joining work and humanitarian values as the crucial issue in the turbulent post-War atmosphere. From the early 20th century onwards, architects engaged in the theme of home as a complex

---

1 Vladimír Zákrejs, "Organisace práce". *Stavitel* I, 1919–1920, p. 2.
2 Rudolf V. Svoboda, "Technika a sociální péče". *Stavitel* I, 1919–1920, p. 27.
3 Jindřich Fleischner, *Chrám práce*. Praha 1920. – See also: Karel Čapek, Jindřich Fleischner, Chrám práce, in: Karel Čapek, *O umění a kultuře. – Od člověka k člověku (dodatky)*. Praha 1995, pp. 114–119.
4 Vladislav Vančura, "Nové umění". *Host* III, 1923–1924, pp. 119–123.

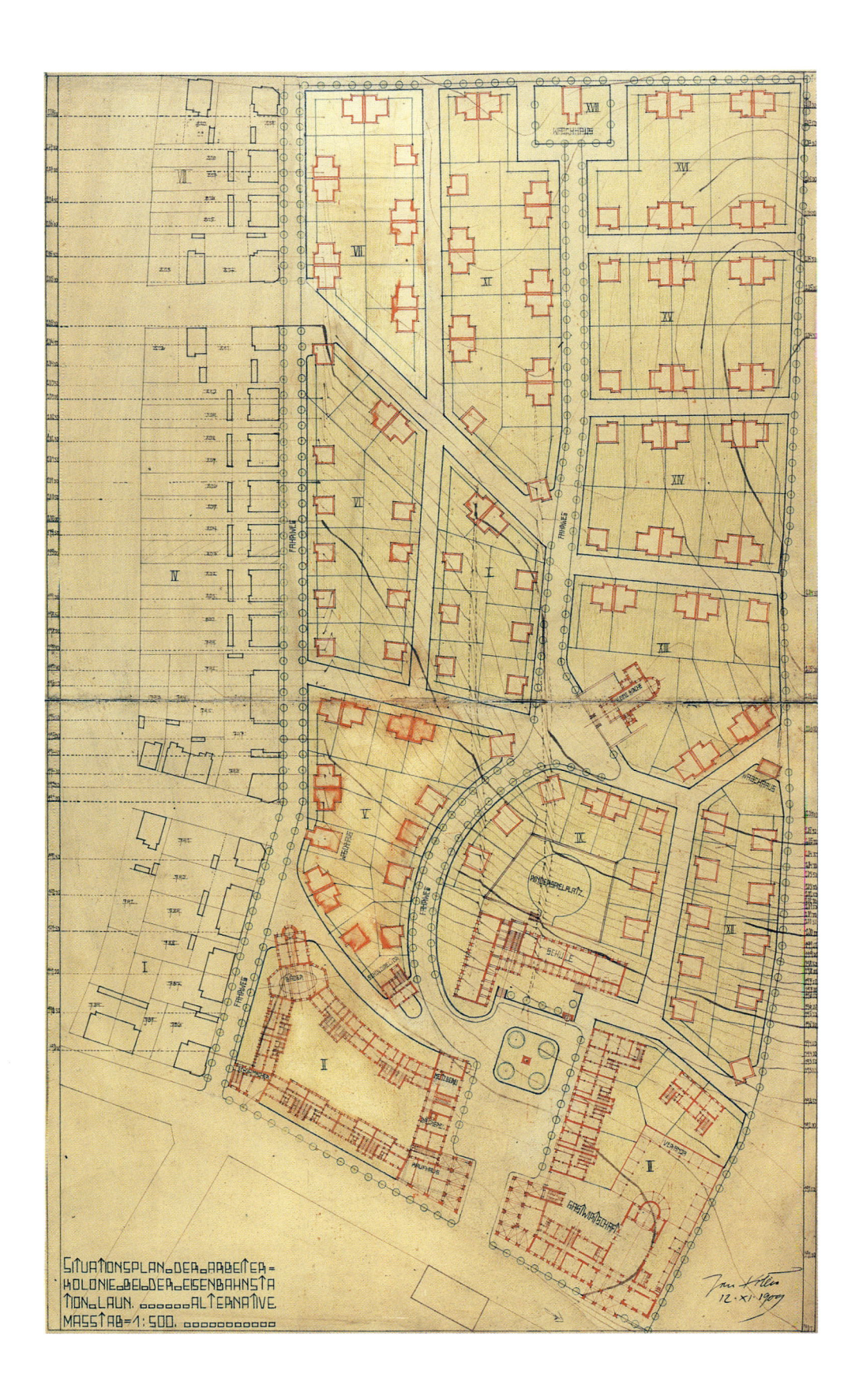

WORKERS' HOUSING COLONIES

> 360
Housing colony for the state railway employees in Louny, layout, 1909

> 361
Housing colony for the state railway employees in Louny, coloured perspective view, 1909

psychological and social entity, both in their theoretical considerations and in their practical projects. They studied the links between man and his natural surroundings and searched for the roots of human identity and its historical conditioning, as expressed in Bohemia – after a model from the German-speaking countries – in the *movement for the protection of the homeland*.

Jan Kotěra's article,[5] summarising his experiences of the preceding decade, occupied a decisive place among a wide spectrum of projects for the dwellings of the less fortunate, printed in the first volumes of *Stavitel*. The journal published reproductions of Kotěra's earlier projects for residential architecture accompanying his short informative text, their conspicuous placement being indicative of Kotěra's authority in matters of residential architecture. In addition, the Building Association which, in collaboration with the Architects' Club, organised a public tender for a project for small labourers' or white-collar workers' homes at the beginning of 1922, nominated Kotěra as honorary chairman of the jury.[6]

Kotěra's designs are best understood in the context of the current reforms of communal living, their reflections in architectural theory and their consequences on the practical work of architects. In the last third of the 19th century, the increasingly high level of industrialisation was followed by a traumatic sense of the inadequacy of available working-class housing. Various housing societies were formed to support the process of finding appropriate solutions to the problem, basing their activities on existing legal measures, mainly the housing law of 8th of July 1902, regulated by a special decree from the Ministries of Finance and Interior dated 7th of January 1903. The implications of this law on

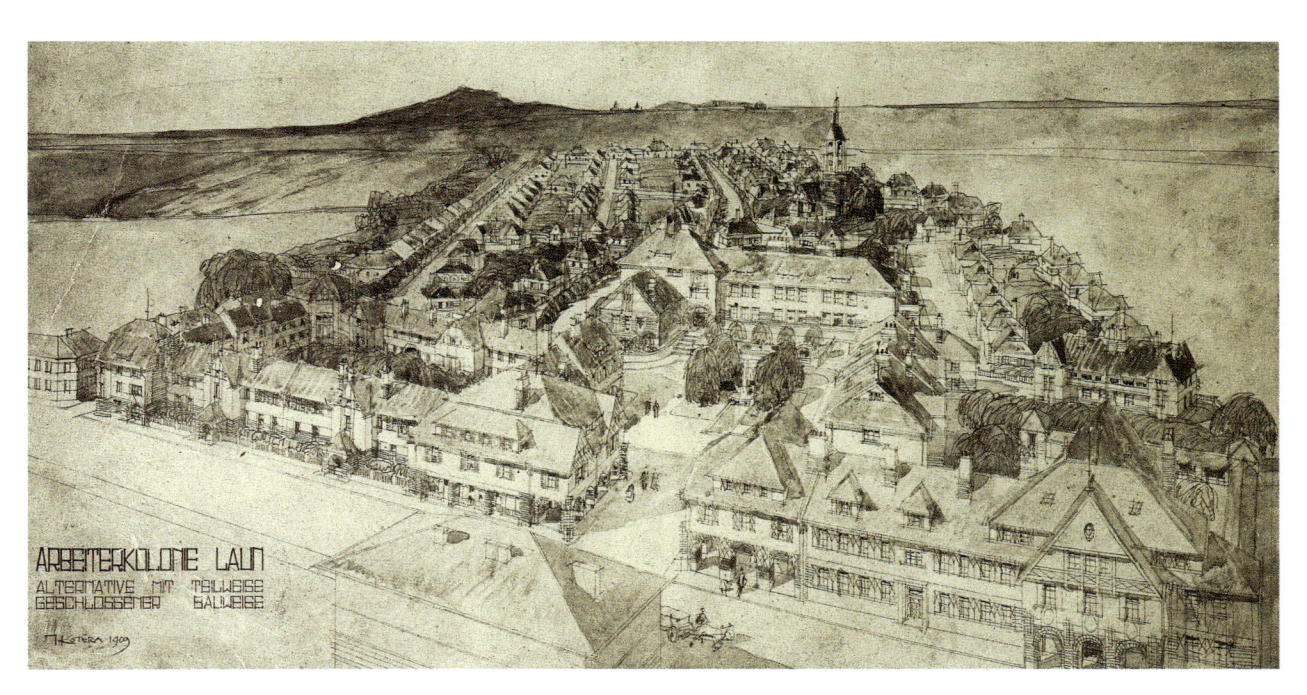

---

[5] Jan Kotěra, "Dělnické kolonie". *Stavitel* II, 1921, nos. 5–6, pp. 65–84. Also published independently.

[6] In the end, Kotěra did not participate in the deliberations of the jury.

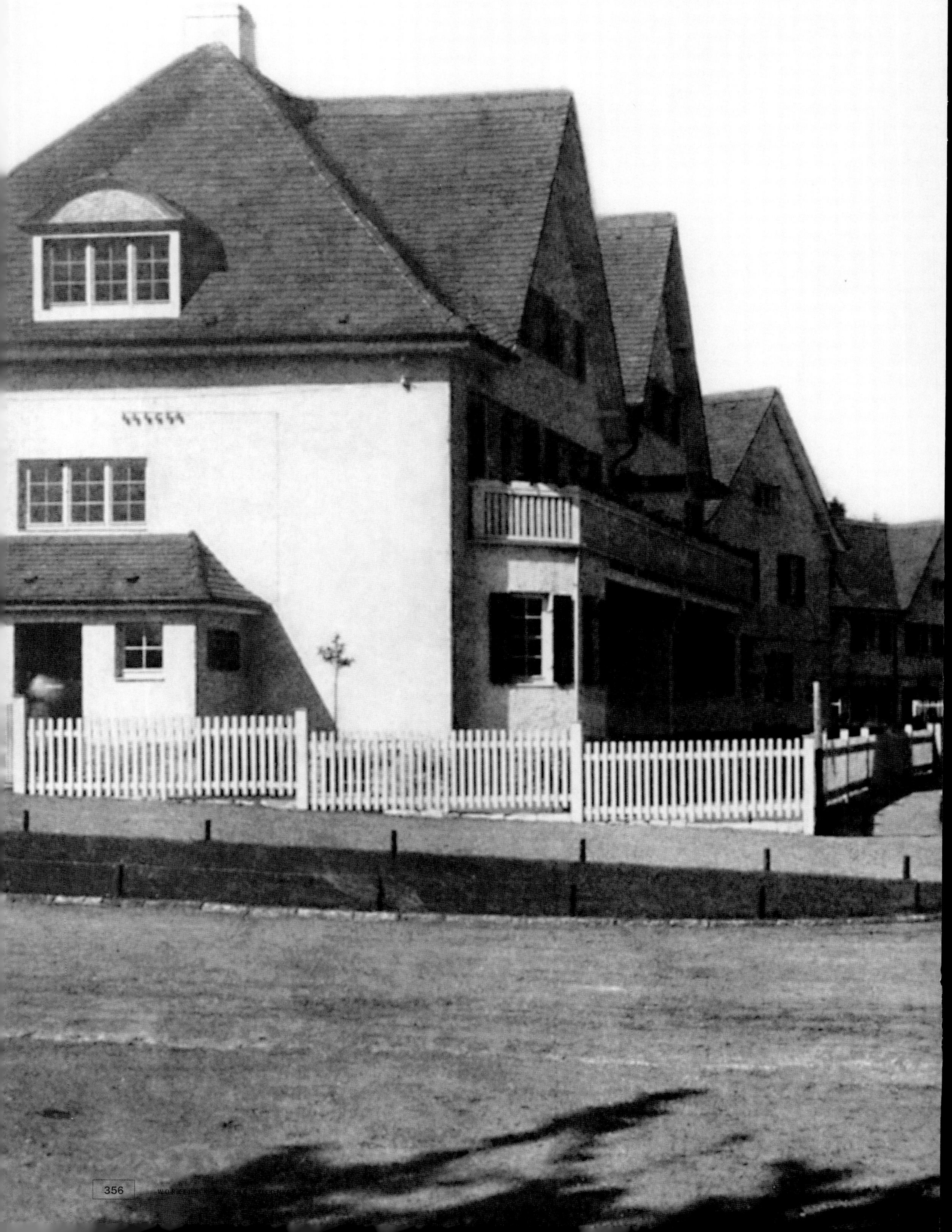

<> **362**
Housing colony for the state railway employees in Louny,
1909, 1913, 1919

the architecture of the housing colonies suggested, in particular, that it was important for these homes to be built as *"open or at least semi-open housing systems"*.[7] Even before the passing of the above-mentioned law, the same prerequisite was emphasised in connection with the revision of the regional housing regulations.[8]

The question then arose as to the new definition of the working-class home. The 1902 Workers' Exhibition in Prague was marked by an attempt to offer new solutions to this question, presenting model housing for workers in the form of a simple one-storeyed house with saddle roof designed by Julius Myslík,[9] confronting an earlier model of the Czech cottage by Antonín Wiehl which was still on display in the Exhibition Grounds after its success at the 1891 Jubilee Exhibition. The two buildings reflected two different models of popular living: the earlier invited a reception of vernacular motifs and folkloric citations, compatible with the atmosphere of late historicism, while the other, created eleven years later, accentuated the utilitarian aspects, only sporadically using various forms of terraced housing. The third concept of the working-class villa as a somewhat reduced model of the representative middle-class house based on the use of a complex formal apparatus, was very well received; however, its high cost made it even less applicable. This last view on public housing was reflected in the journal *Zprávy SIA* (News from the Society of Engineers and Architects), which at the time presented a small number of model working-class villas which had actually been built.[10]

After the birth of the Czechoslovak Republic the issue of public housing was constituted on a new basis. It was founded on the belief that the new political elite would find just solutions for social problems, especially pressing in the aftermath of

---

7 Eduard Srb, *Lidové a levné byty*. Praha 1909, pp. 20–66.
8 Eugen Eislet, *Pásma stavební–zřizovaní ulic*. Praha 1896, p. 8.
9 Eduard Burget – Milan Kudrys, Buď práci čest! První dělnická výstava v Praze 1902. *Dějiny a současnost* 2000, no. 3, p. 21.
10 Eduard Srb (see note 7), pp. 103–108.

> < 363
> Housing colony for the state railway employees in Louny, 1909, 1913, 1919

the First World War, the migration of the country's population, along with inflation and a chronic lack of building materials. This social sentiment stood behind the title of Kotěra's article "Workers' Housing Colonies", even if, in most cases, the houses could not have been defined as working-class dwellings. The idiom of post-War building legislation was similar, with its key housing law, which regulated new building policies, passed on the 11th of March 1921. The aforementioned tender for projects for small labourers' or white-collar workers' homes was actually held as its direct consequence.

In the debate that followed, a wide variety of public housing projects were suggested, consisting in great part in motifs from rural architecture. The most radical position within this movement, with references to English or German examples, was adopted by Otakar Fierlinger who, in view of the current lack of building materials, pleaded for a return to traditional architecture, with houses made of rammed earth and thatched roofing.[11] The radical notion of this *"journey back to the roots"* was reflected in a wooden cottage designed by Oldřich Liska.[12] Nevertheless, the majority of the designs adopted the tradition of rural architecture made of brick.

The English movement for garden towns, together with numerous German examples, exerted a far greater influence and had much more profound consequences on public housing in Bohemia. It was not by coincidence that a text by Raymond Unwin, English reformer of urban thinking, translated by Kamil Roškot, was used to supplement reproductions of Kotěra's workers' housing colonies. The English theory was mirrored in Bohemia through a variety of approaches. Vladimír Zákrejs' writing was underlined by the belief that *" [...] the countryside is the symbol of the love of God and His care for humanity. We must return to the love of God as a species [...] This is why the city must again unite with the village, and a new hope, new life and new culture shall arise from this union."* [13] Jan Kotěra's pragmatic solution, based on the need to respond to the housing situation from within the existing urban structures, rejected Zákrejs' and Fierlinger's social utopianism and their plans for the *"expedient colonisation of the country"*.

Kotěra based his public housing projects on the same generally accepted principle of a house designed for a single or a small number of families. This solution was more in harmony with the exalted atmosphere of the period, coupled with the longing for a prosperous, idyllic dwelling: *"We must be protected inside our modern home [...] as the snail is protected by its shell; the modern house must become our warm, idyllic retreat, hidden behind a low wall or the hedge and trees in our gardens"*.[14] The other type of public housing projects focused on apartment houses which were often stylised into imposing palatial structures, expressing instead the period ideals of human dignity, at the same time a sign of the political self-awareness of social-democrats within public administration. Kotěra was sceptical about the possibility of offering a solution to the housing problem with projects for detached family homes: *"Although the ideal of family life will always be an independent dwelling, surrounded by a sufficient amount of free space, whether it be a garden or field, [...] we must ask ourselves whether this type of architecture is appropriate for the working*

---

[11] Otakar Fierlinger, *Domácí staviva. Příspěvek k osidlování, řešení bytové otázky a ochraně domoviny*. Praha 1920.

[12] Rudolf V. Svoboda, "Dřevený roubený domek obývací v Hradci Králové". *Stavitel* I, 1919–1920, pp. 202–203.

[13] Vladimír Zákrejs, *Zahradní města*. Praha 1913. Unpublished. AA NTM, V. Zákrejs' estate, file 9, folder: Zahradní města – studie ke knize.

[14] Emil Edgar, "Jaké rodinné domky lze dnes stavěti?". *Stavitel* II, 1920–1921, p. 130.

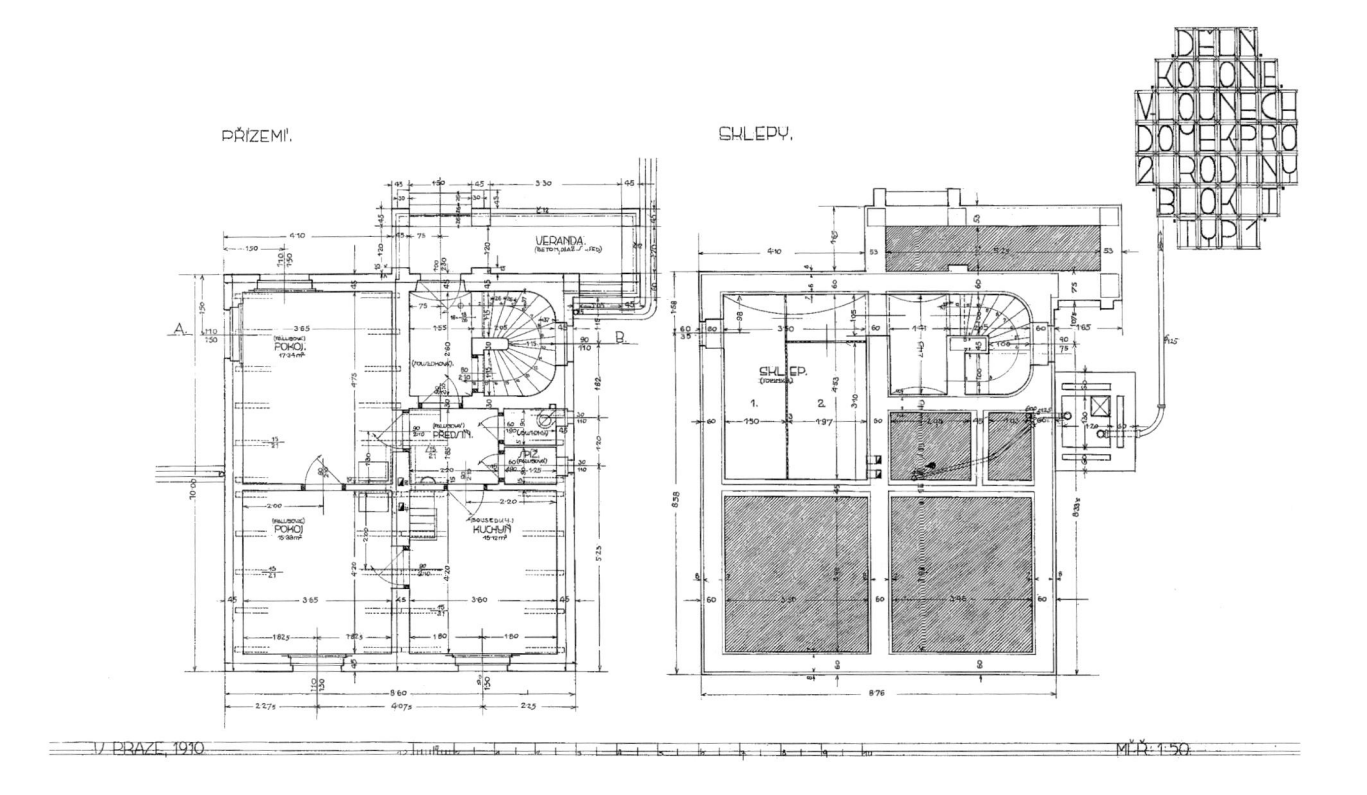

classes, and whether the price of land would allow this to come about".[15]

The housing complex for railway employees in Louny was Kotěra's earliest and most fascinating project for a workers' housing colony. It was chosen to present the architect in a study by K. B. Mádl from 1922[16] and Kotěra described it as his *"dearest work"* in a letter to his Viennese friend Richard Gombrich.[17] The architect situated his new housing colony on a spacious plot next to the highroad leading to Černčice (on what is today Husova třída), between the old colony of terraced family houses dating from 1905 and a wall surrounding the local sugar refinery. Its layout was designed according to two different models. Detached and terraced family houses were arranged higher up around three separate axes and connected via transverse or diagonal paths, while a long street oriented from north to south, curving around the houses and widening into a promenade of avenues lined with trees, became the main communication axis of the entire project. Kotěra used the laundries and the administration building adjacent to a playground as the focal point of his composition. Beyond the undulating terrain was a symmetrical square, its sides enhanced by arcades and a small park with a fountain. The complex was to be completed with restaurants, shops, baths and a social club, with a primary school building set in the hillside as its dominant feature. In his first version, the architect had included a church with a prism-shaped tower, marking the culmination of his composition and symbolising the relatively independent status of the colony within Louny. In the second, alternative version of the project, the church was replaced by a playground. The picturesque and shifting quality of this urban complex reflected the legacy of German or Sittean

---

15 Jan Kotěra (see note 5), p. 65.
16 Karel B. Mádl, *Jan Kotěra*. Praha 1922, pp. 22–23.
17 Rostislav Švácha, "Jan Kotěra". *Domov* XXV, 1985, no. 1, pp. 49–53.

< 364
Housing colony for the state railway employees in Louny, typical house groundplan, block I, type 1
> 365
Housing colony for the state railway employees in Louny, 1909, 1913, 1919

urban planning schemes, even if Kotěra had consciously also adopted the English theory of garden towns.

The First World War halted the building work on this colony, although its final design had been completed back in November 1909. Only the upper part of the colony was built before the War, with paths leading in straight lines, contrary to the design. After the War, Kotěra reworked the lower section, directed towards Husova třída. He replaced the school building with residential houses and, in his plans from 1919–20, designed two blocks of houses for Husova třída, only one of which was finally built. The second, symmetrical block which would have demarcated the square, has remained only on paper.

Kotěra based his designs for two-storey residential houses on nine essential types which differed in the number of apartments on each floor, in the placement of the staircases and balconies, whether they included a loggia or not and whether they were detached or semi-detached houses. The typologically varied houses were linked together via a unified artistic approach: their ground floors were executed in exposed brick, while the walls of the upper floors and the projections were

362 WORKERS' HOUSING COLONIES

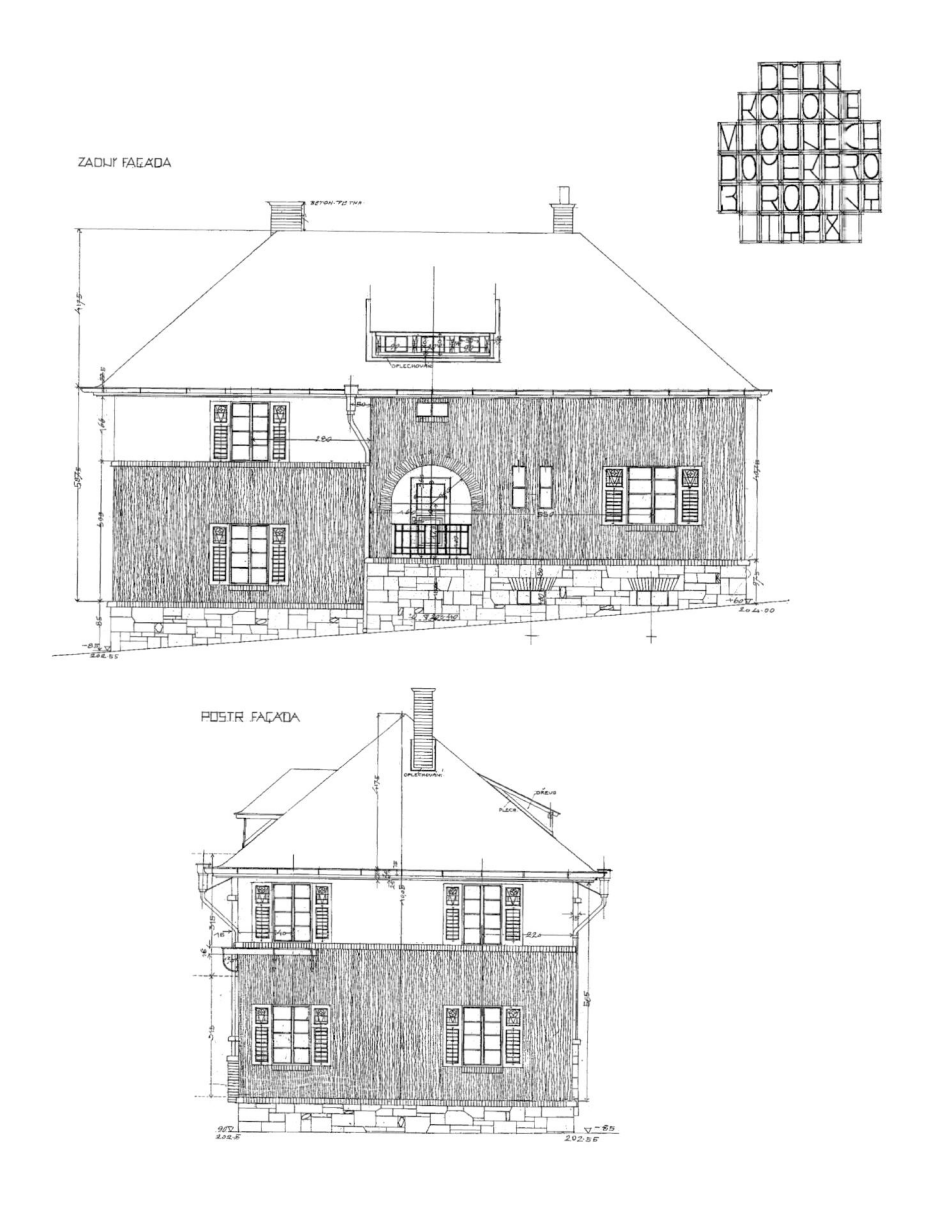

< 366
Housing colony for the state railway employees in Louny,
rear and side façades of a typical house, type X, 1910
> 367
Housing colony for the state railway employees in Louny,
rear and side façades of a typical house, block I, type 3, 1910

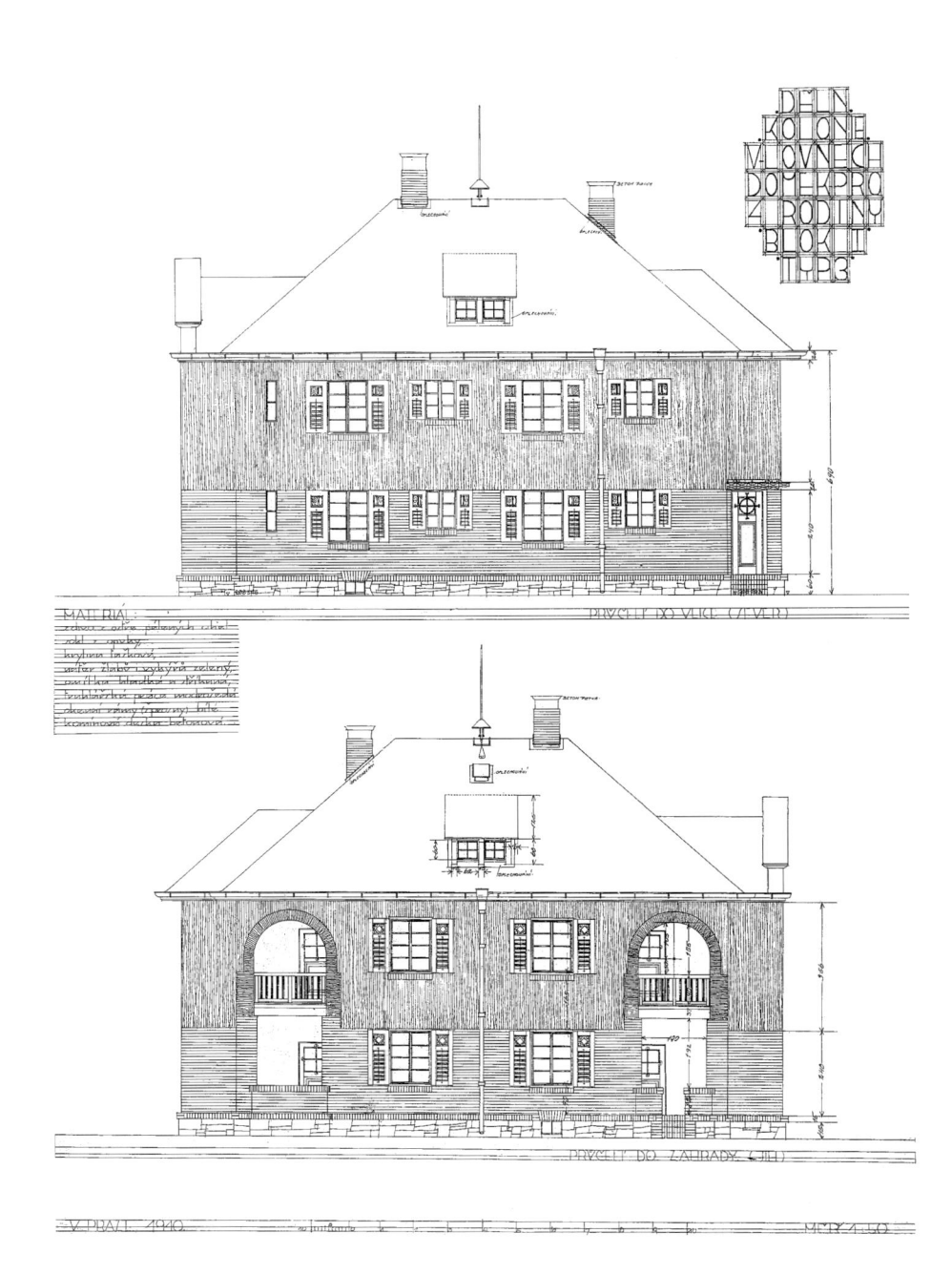

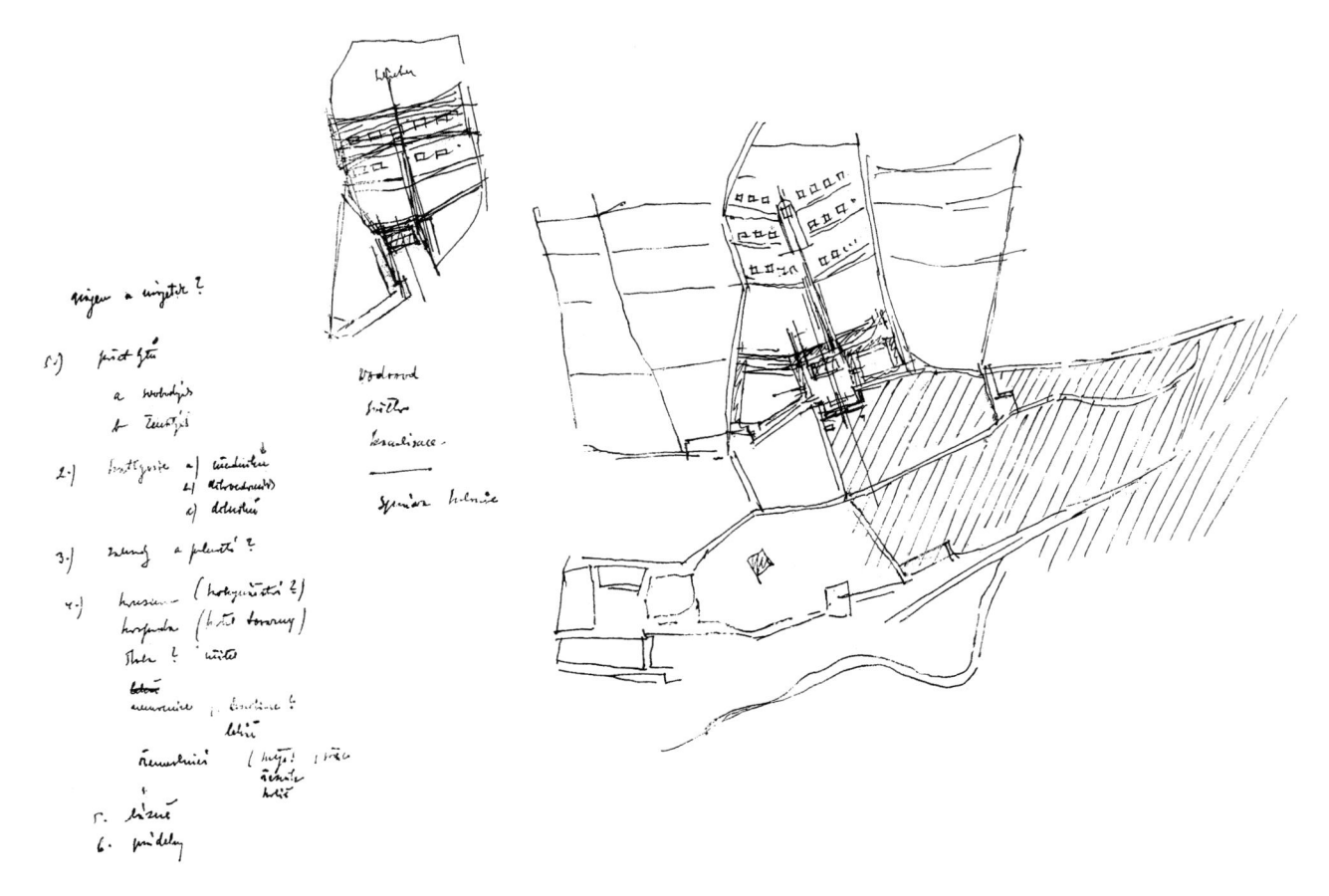

covered in a combination of smooth and coarse plaster, their parapets lined with fired bricks. The pavilion roofs, hipped in the longitudinal sections, were covered in fired tiles and had dormer windows.[18]

If, for his colony in Louny, the intention of the architect was to create a *"coulisse, leaving a large opening with a view onto the upper part of the settlement"*,[19] in the unrealised housing development in Záběhlice, on which Kotěra worked in 1909 and again in 1914–15, the streets were conceived as *"rectilinear and clear-cut"*.[20] Kotěra's formulation appears to be a metaphor of the endeavours of the prospective owner – the initiator of this housing colony. This person was Karel Marek, a railway expert and, for a short period in 1911, minister of public works, for whom the architect built a villa in Holoubkov (1907–09); the residential district was to be used by the employees of the state railway company. The principle which Kotěra adopted enabled the expansion of a future colony into the open terrain of the suburban location. The effect of the design lay in the symmetrical longitudinal and transverse axes, marked by avenues lined with trees. Into these clearly defined frames Kotěra placed his three-storey buildings, whose oblong blocks were bevelled on the corners and in the centre of the façades; he gave them dynamic rectangular windows with rustic partitioning, arched entrance portals and saddle roofs with dormer windows, alternating them with smaller houses with rectangular groundplans. A square with a school and a spa complex were to create the focal point of the residential quarter.

Zlín was the next location for which Kotěra designed a similar settlement. For this project, he found an influential client in the figure of Tomáš Baťa. It is very likely that the discussion about the solutions to the housing problem of the employees

---

18 According to information provided by Karel Vaic from the housing department of Louny Town Hall.
19 Jan Kotěra (see note 5), p. 65.
20 Ibid., p. 66.

< 368
Design of the workers' housing colony for Baťa's company in Zlín, 1918
> 369
Design of the housing colony for railway employees in Záběhlice, perspective view, 1914

of Baťa's factory originated at a time when Kotěra was designing an adaptation of the entrepreneur's home (1911). We can pinpoint the year of the first design to 1915: the sketch which has survived displays a large urban complex, situated south of Baťa's factory and south-west of the old part of Zlín. A group of public buildings, including the colony's administration building, the shop, pub, school, hospital, various services (tradesmen, barber shops) and museum, was oriented towards the factory. A tract of land with only a few sporadic houses spread out from the vertical axis of the complex, symmetrically formed around an honorary courtyard. The chosen spatial concept reflected the view that the worker would spend eight hours at work in the factory and then devote eight hours to his field or garden. The idea of bringing together industrial production with traditional forms of living to which the workers were accustomed proved unrealistic; it was far simpler to obtain groceries and other necessary items in the shops, which led to a reduction in the size of the original plots.[21]

At the beginning of 1918, Kotěra created a different concept, realised only in part. A set of architectural plans indicates the original intention of the architect: he situated residential buildings along the highroad leading to Otrokovice (today's Tomáš Baťa street), their groundplans shaped as elongated rectangles enclosed by projections, alternating with smaller semi-detached houses in pairs and in fours, and situated on the southern side of the rising terrain. However, even in 1918 the architect did not abandon his idea to complete the design

---

21 František Lydie Gahura, "Zlín". *Stavba* 12, 1934–35, no. 9, p. 138.

with a triangular square dominated by a taller building and enclosed by the concave shape of the façades, reminiscent of the design he had already employed in Záběhlice. However, this motif was later abandoned. The only realised part was the main route located further up the hillside, leading in a curve following the configuration of the terrain and forked at both ends. Kotěra situated the (unrealised) service buildings on its intersections – their groundplans reminiscent of the laundry huts from the design of the colony in Louny. This was to form the plan for the composition of the Letná colony, built in part during the following years. It is not easy to reconstruct the course of its construction with certainty – only half of the apartment houses along Tomáš Baťa street were ever built, only to be demolished after the Second World War. Two of the five family houses with mansard roofs (nos. 856, 858) survived, part of an earlier construction phase – known as "Včelín" (Bee-Hive). These were followed by nine simple semi-detached houses with flat roofs which have survived to this day. Built in fours, these buildings were situated on what is today Kotěrova street (nos. 860, 862, 864–868, 870, 875), with smooth plastered fronts interrupted only by the low retaining walls and the continual lines of the windowsills, however, the striking contours of their roofs stand out against the skyline. The construction of the Letná complex continued after Kotěra's death in 1923, adhering to the original urban plan designed by him. Nevertheless, the houses themselves were adapted by František Lydie Gahura, Kotěra's student and architect employed by Tomáš Baťa, who replaced the plastered walls with exposed bricks and thus gave the houses an even simpler form.

Even less is known about the "white-collar" colony at Hradčany, separated from Letná by Březnická street and situated closer to the town. It included five two-storey buildings which with certainty could be ascribed to Kotěra. Based on rectangular groundplans, these houses had high pavilion roofs and were completed with porticos rendered in exposed brick (nos. 640–644). They were clearly derived from buildings of the first type which the architect designed for Louny. According to architect Eduard Staša, the work on this colony began in 1919 and continued after Kotěra's death. Once more, Gahura modified the original types (no. 1274). The buildings were lost in the American air raid on Zlín in November 1944, the only remaining house (no. 640) being demolished in 1992.[22]

Kotěra's project for a housing colony in Králův Dvůr near Beroun was motivated by similar contacts with an influential private investor. In 1908, Kotěra designed a villa in Černošice for the engineer Emil Kratochvíl, director of the local ironworks. That same year, at Kratochvíl's invitation, he designed the plans for a Czech school building in the same town. After strong resistance from the districts allocated to the school, the project designed by the local architect Jaroslav Valečka was chosen instead. Kotěra returned to Králův Dvůr not long after the birth of the independent Czechoslovak Republic, when the management of Králův Dvůr ironworks, together with the local cement factory, decided to build a new workers' housing colony in an effort to reduce the housing crisis in this town. The building plot for the project was chosen on Na Knížecí, between Diber brook and the highroad leading

---

[22] Magistrát města Zlín, Stavební archiv, volumes 640, 870, 1274. – Museum města Zlína, Pozůstalost Eduarda Staši, Kotěrův návrh na stavbu dělnické kolonie firmy T. A. Bati ve Zlíně, plan no. 14 of 28 March 1918. – Eduard Staša, *Kapitolky ze starého Zlína*. Zlín 1991, p. 35. – Pavel Novák, *Zlínská architektura 1900–1950*. Zlín 1993, p. 24–25. – Filip Havliš, "František Lydie Gahura". *Prostor Zlín* VI, 1998, no. 1, p. 18.

< 370
Workers' housing colony for Baťa's company in Zlín,
Včelín residential building, 1918
> 371
Králův Dvůr workers' housing colony, layout, 1920

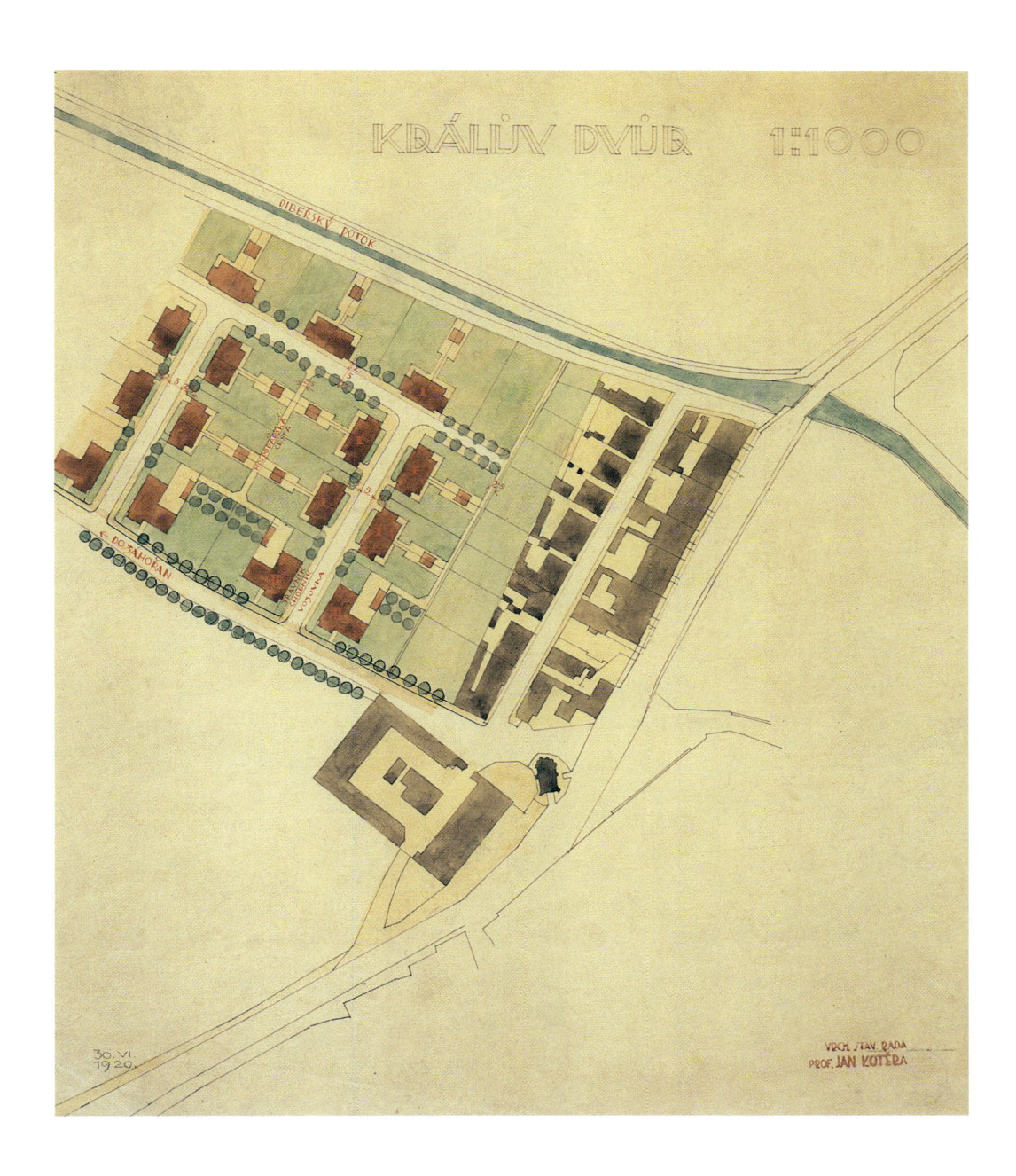

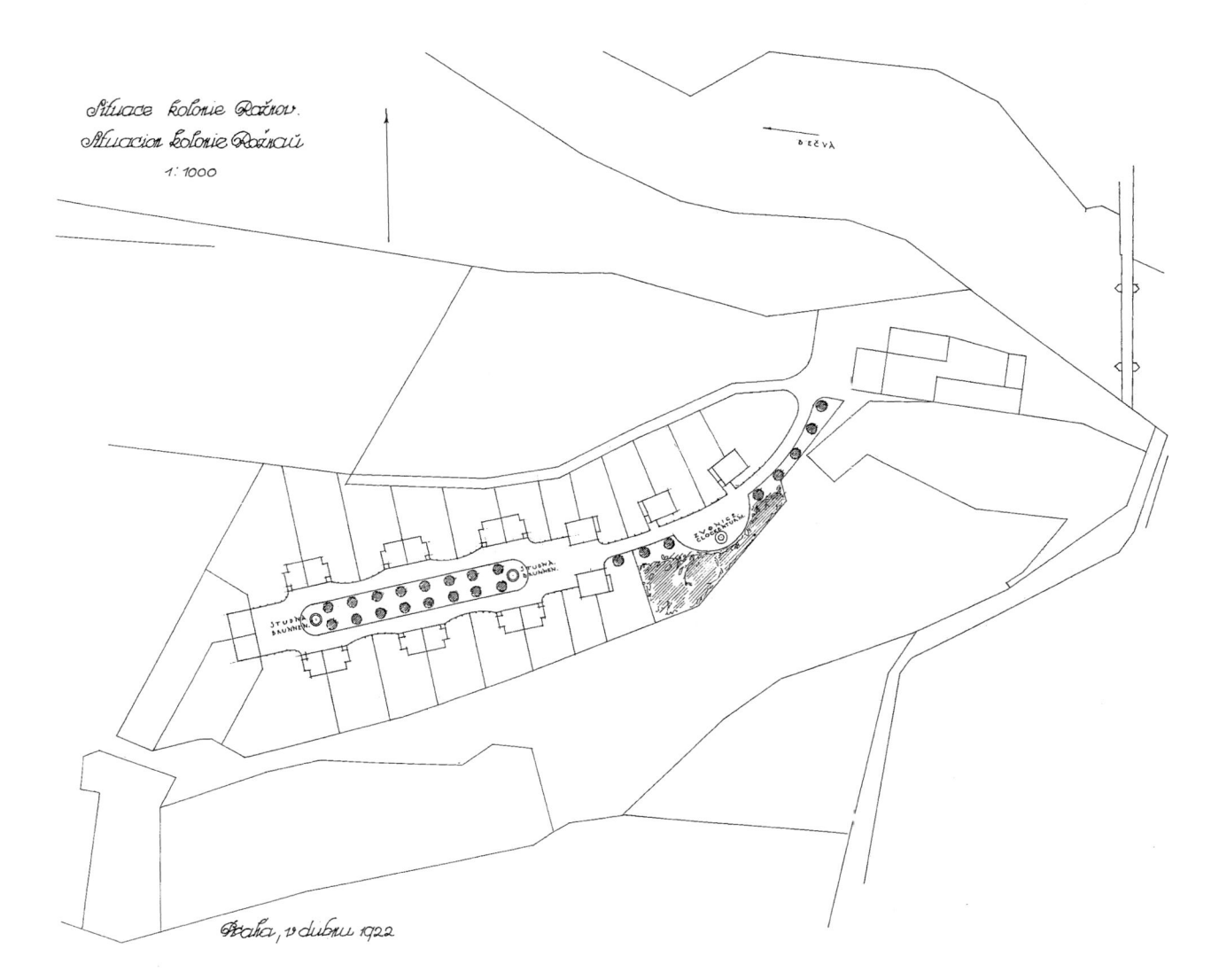

to Zahořany. In 1920, the architect proposed a plan of fifteen houses placed around a square courtyard, its corners supported by L-shaped houses with six rooms on each floor, while all the other houses were planned with four rooms per floor. The inner block was reserved for stables, hen houses and hutches for domestic animals. Although the urban concept formed a typological unit, created with a vision of possible expansion in the future into a larger urban complex, only six pairs of semi-detached houses were built by 1920 (nos. 146–151). These two-storey buildings with rectangular groundplans, their sides enlarged with projections, were designed with symmetrical façades and courtyard loggias with an arched finish on the level of the first floor. The windowsills divided the surface of the façade. The wooden blinds suggested a sense of intimacy, as did the tall, hipped roofs with dormer windows on the central axes of the façades.[23]

The last of Kotěra's projects for housing colonies which was finally built was a complex of pairs of semi-detached houses for pensioners from the Vítkovice mining company in Rožnov pod Radoštěm. This remarkable project, stated as unrealised in earlier literature (sic!), was actually built – on Na Bučiskách, on the south-western outskirts of the town. An arched blind alley was laid between the river Bečva and the

---

[23] Jiří Topinka, "Slavná historie kralodvorských dělnických kolonií". Berounský žurnál 8 July 1999, p. 4.

WORKERS' HOUSING COLONIES

< 372
Housing colony in Rožnov, layout, 1922
> 373
Housing colony in Rožnov, 1922
>> 374
Králův Dvůr workers' housing colony, 1920

steep forested slope of Hradisko hill, two-thirds of its length widened by greenery, with two wells and avenues lined with trees. Ten pairs of semi-detached houses were built during two different phases, between April 1922 and June 1923, and from May 1923 until the spring of the following year, their regulation plans signed by the architect Bohuslav Fuchs.[24] Unlike the original, more economical plans, a rather complex alternative version was built, with fronts widened by projections, smooth façade surfaces with lisene frames and mansard roofs. The strong folklore tradition of the town provided inspiration for the use of vernacular motifs – wooden porches on the sides of each building, several types of dormer windows, wooden soffits on the roofs, as if made from shallow panels, and decorative jamb framing on the windows used in an abbreviated form of folk ornament. Kotěra even completed his urban plan with a small bell tower. The important fact about the Rožnov colony, like the residential quarter of the colony in Louny, is that most of it has survived to this day without a change in character, which is also true of its distance from the adjacent towns and its seemly incorporation into the surrounding countryside.

The group of five residential colonies forms an inconspicuous yet fascinating group in Kotěra's oeuvre. They display a striking variety of urban designs, well incorporated into wider spatial contexts, with houses whose style is a synthesis of vernacular motifs, traditional Biedermeier architecture – a style inducing a sense of intimacy, reliability and the human dimension in architecture, types of English rural dwellings and German *Heimatbaustil*. Kotěra's various treatments of the rewarding theme of the individual dwelling thus found itself – to cite Rádl in his definition of Masaryk's philosophy – *"between the Scylla of utmost sensitivity and the Charybdis of extreme rationality"*.[25] The architect intended to go only so far in order that *"the thrift of today would not become the losses of tomorrow"*;[26] he also chose a style which would respond to the need for the intimacy of one's home, whilst respecting the economic potential of the prospective owner, as well as the legal environment, the European architectural tradition and the formal idiom of modern architecture.

---

24 Státní okresní archiv Vsetín, Archiv města Rožnov nad Radhoštěm fund: file 95.

25 Emanuel Rádl, *T. G. Masaryk. Přednáška ve sdružení pokrokové mládeže v Praze 13. prosince 1918*. Praha 1919, p. 12.
26 Jan Kotěra (see note 5), p. 66.

With his brother Jaroslav, 1893

Jan Kotěra – Biography

18th December 1871 Jan Kotěra was born in Brno as the younger son of Antonín Kotěra, future founder and director of the Czech Business School in Plzeň, and his wife Maria (born Vögel).

1887–1890 studied at the German technical college, School of Engineering in Plzeň.

1890–1894 Kotěra was employed at the architectural design studio of engineer J. F. Freyn in Prague-Smíchov.

1894 Kotěra won second prize in a competition to build a social club in Přelouč, a project he then submitted for the entrance exams at the Academy of Fine Arts in Vienna.

With his parents and brother Jaroslav, 1893

1894–1896 designed a project for the reconstruction of the castle at Červený Hrádek for family friend Baron Jan Mladota of Solopisky.

1894–1897 studied at Otto Wagner's special school of architecture at the Viennese Academy of Fine Arts. Here he met Josef Maria Olbrich, fellow students included Josef Hoffmann (studying in the senior year), Hubert Gessner, Jože Plečnik (both in the year below) and others.

Journal *Der Architekt* began publishing Kotěra's works.

1896 Kotěra won the golden Függer medal for a college project to design royal baths, also a special school award for his project of a parish church.

1893

1897 Kotěra won the Prix de Rome for his final college project – Cap Gris-Nez – for an ideal city at the entrance to a future Calais-Dover tunnel.

☐ Became a member of the Siebener Club in Vienna, later to become active in promoting the new Viennese Secession movement.

☐ Presented his works at an exhibition of the Unity of Fine Arts in the Rudolfinum in Prague.

1898 Kotěra undertook a journey to Italy from February to June, resided in Palazzo Venezia in Rome (where the Austrian Embassy provided studios for the Prix de Rome candidates). He was to visit Italy several times in the future.

☐ Exhibited his college works in Plzeň.

☐ Took up a post at the special school of decorative architecture as successor to Friedrich Ohmann at the Prague School of Applied Arts (his students at the School included Josef Gočár, Otakar Novotný, Bohumil Waigant etc.).

☐ He joined the Mánes Association of Fine Artists.

☐ Took part in the second exhibition of the Mánes Association in the Topič salon with his drawings from Italy and his college work.

1899 Jan Kotěra married Berta Tráznikova. He furnished his own apartment in Jenštejnská street in Prague.

1899– 1900 Kotěra's first important commission – Peterka's house in Prague.

☐ He became editor of the journal *Volné směry* (fourth volume onwards); prepared a special issue devoted to architecture where he published his conceptual statement "On New Art"; illustrations presented modern European and world architecture.

1900 Kotěra oversaw the completion of the exhibition design for the School of Applied Arts at the Paris World Exhibition, begun by Friedrich Ohmann; the design won a silver medal.

☐ His design of a saloon tramcar for the Prague Transport Company manufactured by the Ringhoffer factory in Smíchov and exhibited in Paris won the Grand prix.

☐ Kotěra's first design and installation of an entire exhibition – 3rd exhibition of the Mánes Association.

☐ His daughter Věra was born.

With his future wife Berta, 1895

1902 the publisher Anton Schroll in Vienna published Jan Kotěra's book *My Work and That of My Students*. Both Czech and German versions were published (*Meine und meiner Schüler Arbeiten*).

☐ Design and construction of the Mánes pavilion building at the foot of Kinský gardens together with a design for an exhibition of Auguste Rodin.

☐ His daughter Johana was born.

1902–1903 design and construction of Trmal's villa in Prague-Strašnice.

1903 a visit to Paris.

c. 1904

1904

1903–1904 design and construction of the Regional Authorities building in Hradec Králové.

☐ Kotěra organised and designed the Czech section of the 1904 World Exhibition in St Louis.

☐ Otakar Novotný worked in Kotěra's studio.

1904 his son Miroslav was born.

☐ Design and construction of Stanislav Sucharda's villa in Prague-Bubeneč.

1905 Kotěra travelled to Holland and Belgium together with his students.

☐ Prepared an exhibition of Czech art at the Munich World Exhibition, won the Bavarian Order of St Michael, Third Degree, for this design.

☐ Designed an exhibition of Czech art as part of an exhibition on Austrian art in London in 1906. On the occasion of Kotěra's visit, the Royal Association of British Architects organised a banquet in his honour.

☐ Installation of the Modern Gallery permanent collection in the Wiehl pavilion at the Prague Exhibition Grounds.

1905–1907 design and construction of National House in Prostějov.

1905–1908 Josef Gočár worked in Kotěra's studio.

c. 1905

Wife Berta with children – Hanča, Věrča and Miri, 1906

1906 first project for the City Museum in Hradec Králové (built in 1909–1913).

1906–1907 design and construction of Vršovice waterworks in Prague-Michle.

1907 Kotěra was entrusted with the design of the Law and Theology Faculty building at Czech University in Prague; first design.

☐ Installation of an independent exhibition by the Mánes Association representing Austria (together with the Austrian Hagebund association) at the World Exhibition in Venice.

1907–1909 Pavel Janák worked in Kotěra's studio.

1908 Kotěra co-founded the journal *Styl*; worked as an editor.

☐ Mánes Association Exhibition at the Jubilee Exhibition in Hagebund in Vienna.

☐ Travelled to Opatija for medical treatment.

☐ Travelled to Germany (Darmstadt, Stuttgart, Frankfurt).

1908–1909 design and construction of Laichter's house in Prague.

☐ Design and construction of his own villa and studio in Prague-Vinohrady.

1909 second project for the Czech University buildings.

1909–1913 (–1919) design and construction of the state railway employees' housing colony in Louny.

1910 Kotěra appointed professor at the newly established special school of architecture at the Academy of Fine Arts in Prague (thanks to Tomáš G. Masaryk and Jan Herben). Courses were held in the studio in Kotěra's own villa, which continued to be used for teaching after Kotěra's death, until 1924 (his students here included Josef Štěpánek, Bohuslav Fuchs, František L. Gahura, Jaromír Krejcar, Kamil Roškot, Adolf Benš etc.).

On his departure campaigned for Jože Plečnik to succeed in his post at the School of Applied Arts in Prague.

1910–1911 Kotěra took part in organising the participation of the Mánes Association architects at the International Exhibition of Architecture in Rome in 1911.

c. 1910

1911–1913 design and construction of M. Urbánek's department store, known as the Mozarteum, in Prague.

1912 stayed at a health spa in Karlovy Vary.

1913 Kotěra initiated the founding of the Czech Union of Applied Artists.

☐ Installation of the Austian section at the Munich World Exhibition; Kotěra was awarded the Bavarian Order of St Michael, Second Degree, for his design.

☐ The third project for the university, rejected by Grand Duke Franz Ferdinand; Kotěra worked on a somewhat revised version of the project during the First World War.

☐ Sojourn in Paris.

1913–1915 design and construction of the Lemberger-Gombrich villa in Vienna.

With his son Miroslav, c. 1913

1914 his son Jaroslav was born.

1914–1919 initiated the founding of the Aid Committee for Destitute Artists and took charge of its administration.

1917 Kotěra embarked upon plans for a book on architectural composition.

☐ Signed a petition by fine artists which followed the similar Declaration of Writers sent to Czech members of Parliament appealing for the protection of the interests of the independent Czech nation.

1919 sojourn in Paris, negotiations on the organisation of an exhibition of Czech art in Paris.

1919–1920 design and construction of a separate building for the School of Architecture at the Academy of Fine Arts in Prague (completed by Josef Gočár in 1923–1924).

Fishing, with son Miroslav, 1915

1920 after a decision from the Ministry of Public Works to announce a new tender for the university building, regardless of Kotěra's completed project, the Mánes Association and the Association of Architects responded with a joint petition sent to the Ministries of Education and Public Works and to the daily press; the architects involved in these Associations refused to participate.

1921 Kotěra won the tender for the university building.

☐ Jan Kotěra was awarded (together with Jože Plečnik) the first honorary membership of the Association of Architects.

☐ The journal *Stavitel* published Kotěra's article "Workers' Housing Colonies" as its special supplement.

☐ Journey to Holland with students from the Academy of Fine Arts.

374 JAN KOTĚRA

c. 1920

1921

1922 in collaboration with professors at the Prague Academy of Fine Arts and School of Applied Arts, Kotěra presented a proposal of statutes for a new university, created with the merger of these two institutions; the school was to comprise a fine art faculty and a faculty of applied arts.
☐ Last journey with his students to Rome.
17th of April 1923 Jan Kotěra died after a protracted illness.

1926 a posthumous exhibition of Kotěra's works was organised; heirs and other private owners bequeathed his estate to the Czech Technical Museum (today National Technical Museum) in Prague.

In the course of his career, Jan Kotěra was appointed to the following positions:

Member of the Board of Trustees of the Modern Gallery (1902–1920);
chairman of the Mánes Association (1906, 1907, 1910, 1911, 1916, 1917, 1918); deputy chairman (1905, 1912);
chairman of the Association of Architects, division of the Mánes Association (1908, 1909);
director of the Academy of Fine Arts (1912/1913, 1914/1915, 1915/1916, 1920/1921, 1921/1922);
chairman of the Aid Committee for Destitute Artists (1915–1920);
regional committee advisor for matters of regulation (1910–1921).

Jan Kotěra was also a member of the SČUG Hollar (Association of Czech Graphic Artists), Association of Architects, honorary member of the Fourth Class of the Academy of Arts and Sciences, full member of the Salon d'Automne in Paris, Hagebund association in Vienna.

**Completed buildings
– map of the various locations
within Czech Republic**

- Hronov
- Louny
- Dobruška
- Hradec Králové
- Chrustenice
- Praha
- Kolín
- Nučice
- Radtboř
- Králův Dvůr
- Černošice
- Chrudim
- Vysoké Mýto
- Všenory
- Holoubkov
- Hostišov
- Červený Hrádek
- Kosova Hora
- Bechyně
- Telč
- Jindřichův Hradec
- Třeboň

□ Frýdek-Místek

□ Rožnov

□ Prostějov

□ Zlín

Dr F. Tonder's salon in Prague
1902 DC
part of the furnishings kept in the Museum of Decorative Arts in Prague
S: AA NTM fund no. 21 Jan Kotěra, entry no. 25

Mánes Association pavilion in Prague below Kinský gardens
1902 DC
demolished
S: AA NTM fund no. 21 Jan Kotěra, entry no. 26

Exhibition design for the works of Auguste Rodin in the Mánes Association pavilion
1902 DC
L: M(Mádl), Rodinova výstava. *Zlatá Praha* XIX, 1902, 33, p. 394

Design for the 7th exhibition of the Mánes Association in the Mánes pavilion
1902 DC
L: VII. výstava spolku výtv. umělců Mánes, pohled. *Volné směry* VII, pp. 169, 174, 177

Jiráseks' tomb in the local cemetery in Hronov
1902 DC
S: AA NTM fund no. 21 Jan Kotěra, entry no. 27

Interior design of a study for K. Hoffmeister
1902 DC
S: UPM, inv. no. 73.500–512

Fröhlich's villa in Černošice
1902–1903 DC
Janského 316, Černošice
S: AA NTM fund no. 21 Jan Kotěra, entry no. 28

Mácha's villa in Bechyně
1902–1903 DC
Fučíkova 188, Bechyně
S: AA NTM fund no. 21 Jan Kotěra, entry no. 29

Trmal's villa in Prague-Strašnice
1902–1903 DC
Vilová 91/11, Praha 10
S: AA NTM fund no. 21 Jan Kotěra, entry no. 30

Design for a villa for Dr K. Kramář in the Crimea
1902 DO
S: AA NTM fund no. 21 Jan Kotěra, entry no. 31

Design for an extension of the garden house in Barbo Kristo in the Crimea
1902 DO
S: AA NTM fund no. 21 Jan Kotěra, entry no. 32

Josef Urban's salon in Prague
1903 DC
L: Zdeněk Wirth, *Jan Kotěra 1871–1923*. Obecní dům, Praha 1926

Design for Peisker's family house in Žďár (near Borohrádek)
1903 DO
S: AA NTM fund no. 21 Jan Kotěra, entry no. 33

Competition entry for the monument to Empress Elisabeth in Vienna
1903 DO
S: AA NTM fund no. 21 Jan Kotěra, entry no. 34

Slukov tomb in Olšany cemetery in Prague
1903 DC
S: AA NTM fund no. 21 Jan Kotěra, entry no. 35

Kožíšek tomb in Olšany cemetery in Prague
1903 DC
in collaboration with S. Sucharda
S: AA NTM fund no. 21 Jan Kotěra, entry no. 36

Interior design of an apartment for the Matějček family
1903 DC
S: UPM, inv. no. 31.211

Regional Authorities building in Hradec Králové
1903–1904 DC
Palackého 409, Hradec Králové
S: AA NTM fund no. 21 Jan Kotěra, entry no. 37

Design for an exhibition on Czech art at the 1904 World Exhibition in St Louis
1903 DC
S: AA NTM fund no. 21 Jan Kotěra, entry no. 38

Pumping station in Prague-Braník
1903–1905 DC
Modřanská 229, Praha 4
L: AA NTM fund no. 21 Jan Kotěra, entry no. 60 (see: Vršovice waterworks in Prague-Michle)

Landsberger tomb in the Jewish cemetery in Frýdek
1904 DC
S: AA NTM fund no. 21 Jan Kotěra, entry no. 39

Maydl tomb in Olšany cemetery in Prague
1904 DC
in collaboration with B. Kafka
S: AA NTM fund no. 21 Jan Kotěra, entry no. 40

Perutz tomb in the Jewish cemetery in Prague-Strašnice (JUC. Max Perutz)
1904 DC
S: AA NTM fund no. 21 Jan Kotěra, entry no. 41

Vojan tomb in Olšany cemetery in Prague
1904 DC
in collaboration with S. Sucharda
S: AA NTM fund no. 21 Jan Kotěra, entry no. 42

Design for a small church in Holoubkov
1904 DO
S: AA NTM fund no. 21 Jan Kotěra, entry no. 43

Adaptation of the regional committee conference hall in Jindřichův Hradec
1904 DC
nám. Míru 88/1, Jindřichův Hradec
S: AA NTM fund no. 21 Jan Kotěra, entry no. 45

Design of an extension for the villa of B. Kočí in V Zátiší street
c. 1900–1905 DO
S: UPM, inv. no. 30.994 a,c

Sucharda's villa and studio in Prague-Bubeneč
1904–1907 DC
Slavíčkova 248/6, Praha 6
S: AA NTM v fund no. 21 Jan Kotěra, entry no. 47

Design for the adaptation of the fountain and column of the Holy Trinity in Jindřichův Hradec
c. 1904 DO
S: AA NTM fund no. 21 Jan Kotěra, entry no. 49

Design for the conference hall of the Civic Savings Bank in Prague-Smíchov
1905 DC
Štefánikova 17, Praha 5
S: AA NTM fund no. 21 Jan Kotěra, entry no. 46

Hamerník family tomb in the cemetery in Prague-Liboc
1905 DC
demolished
S: AA NTM fund no. 21 Jan Kotěra, entry no. 50

Design for Elbogen's villa in Prague
1905 DO
S: AA NTM fund no. 21 Jan Kotěra, entry no. 44

Design for the 16th exhibition
of the Mánes Association in the Mánes
pavilon in Prague
1905   DC
S: AA NTM fund no. 21 Jan Kotěra,
entry no. 52

Installation of the Modern Gallery
permanent collection in the Wiehl
pavilon at the Prague Exhibition Grounds
1905   DC
L: Moderní Galerie otevřena. *Máj* III, 36,
19th May 1905, p. 583

Dr F. Tonder's villa in St Gilgen
1905–1906   DC
Lienbachscherweg 2, Nr. 146,
Wolfgangsee, St. Gilgen
S: AA NTM fund no. 21 Jan Kotěra,
entry no. 53

Design for the exhibition pavilion of
the Poštorná ceramics factory owned by
the Prince of Lichtenstein, held in Milan
1905   ?
S: AA NTM fund no. 21 Jan Kotěra,
entry no. 55

Design for Professor Hnátek's waiting
room in Prague
c. 1905   ?
S: AA NTM fund no. 21 Jan Kotěra,
entry no. 56

Installation of the Czech section at an
exhibition on Austrian art in London in
1906
1905–1906   DC
L: Zprávy a poznámky. *Volné směry* X,
1905–1906, p. 77

National House in Prostějov
1905–1907   DC
Vojáčkovo nám. 218, Fr. Hlaváčka 1, 2,
Prostějov
S: AA NTM fund no. 21 Jan Kotěra,
entry no. 54

Regional Authorities building in Nové
Hrady
1906   DO
L: Zdeněk Wirth, *Jan Kotěra 1871–1923*.
Obecní dům, Praha 1926

Groh tomb in Olšany cemetery in Prague
1906   DC
in collaboration with S. Sucharda
S: AA NTM fund no. 21 Jan Kotěra,
entry no. 182

Mráz tomb in Olšany cemetery in Prague
1906   DC
demolished
S: AA NTM fund no. 21 Jan Kotěra,
entry no. 58

Štěpánek tomb in Olšany cemetery
in Prague
1906   DC
S: AA NTM fund no. 21 Jan Kotěra,
entry no. 57

Design for the Ringhoffer factory
presentation at the Milan Exhibition
1906   DC
S: AA NTM fund no. 21 Jan Kotěra,
entry no. 65

Sýkora's house in Chrudim
1906–1907   DC
Fibichova 27, Chrudim
S: AA NTM fund no. 21 Jan Kotěra,
entry no. 59

Vršovice waterworks in Prague-Michle
1906–1907   DC
Baarova 365/5, Praha 4
S: AA NTM fund no. 21 Jan Kotěra,
entry no. 60

City Museum in Hradec Králové
1906–1913   DC
Eliščino nábřeží 465, Hradec Králové
S: AA NTM fund no. 21 Jan Kotěra,
entry no. 61

Furnishings for the Arco coffee-house in Prague
1907 DC
demolished
S: AA NTM fund no. 21 Jan Kotěra, entry no. 66

Design for a garden pavilion for Mr Petschek in Prague-Bubeneč
1907 ?
S: AA NTM fund no. 21 Jan Kotěra, entry no. 67

Kraus' villa in Prague-Bubeneč
1907 DC
Sibiřské nám. 208/5, Praha 6
S: AA NTM fund no. 21 Jan Kotěra, entry no. 68

Design for a study for the Prague Lord Mayor in the Old Town Hall in Prague
1907–1909 DC
Staroměstské nám. 4, Praha 1
S: AA NTM fund no. 21 Jan Kotěra, entry no. 69

First design for the Law and Theology Faculty, Czech University of Charles-Ferdinand in Prague
1907 DO
S: AA NTM fund no. 87, entry no. 1 UNIV

Design for a villa for Dr Záveský
1907 DO
L: Zdeněk Wirth, *Jan Kotěra 1871–1923*. Obecní dům, Praha 1926

Trade and Industry pavilion at the 1908 Jubilee exhibition of the Chamber of Trade and Commerce in Prague
1907–1908 DC
in collaboration with J. Gočár and P. Janák
demolished
S: AA NTM fund no. 21 Jan Kotěra, entry no. 71

Specialised Education Pavilion at the 1908 Jubilee exhibition of the Chamber of Trade and Commerce in Prague
1907–1908 DC
in collaboration with K. Göttlich
demolished
S: AA NTM fund no. 21 Jan Kotěra, entry no. 72

Götz's villa in Chrustenice
1907–1908 DC
Chrustenice 52
S: AA NTM fund no. 21 Jan Kotěra, entry no. 75

Marek's villa in Holoubkov
1907–1910 DC
Holoubkov 123
S: AA NTM fund no. 21 Jan Kotěra, entry no. 70

Design for E. Vojan's villa in Prague
1908 DO
S: AA NTM fund no. 21 Jan Kotěra, entry no. 73

Design for a primary school with an apartment for the headmaster in Králův Dvůr near Beroun
1908 DO
S: AA NTM fund no. 21 Jan Kotěra, entry no. 74

Rubeš tomb in Olšany cemetery in Prague
1908 DC
demolished
S: AA NTM fund no. 21 Jan Kotěra, entry no. 76

Office building in Nučice (Dušníky)
1908 DC
Krahulov 139, Nučice
L: Zdeněk Wirth, *Jan Kotěra 1871–1923*. Obecní dům, Praha 1926

Laichter house (apartment building with publishing house) in Prague-Vinohrady
1908–1909 DC
Chopinova 1543/4, Praha 2
S: AA NTM fund no. 21 Jan Kotěra, entry no. 77

Own villa with studio in Prague-Vinohrady
1908–1909 DC
Hradešínská 1542/6, Praha 10
S: AA NTM fund no. 21 Jan Kotěra,
entry no. 78

Kratochvíl's villa in Černošice
1908–1910 DC
Karlštejnská 282, Černošice
S: AA NTM fund no. 21 Jan Kotěra,
entry no. 79

Design for the building of the Academy
of Music in Prague
1908–1910 DO
S: AA NTM fund no. 21 Jan Kotěra,
entry no. 188

Second design for the Law and Theology
Faculty, Czech University of Charles-
Ferdinand in Prague
1909 DO
S: AA NTM fund no. 87,
entry no. 24 UNIV

Design for the Třeboň waterworks
1909 DC
S: AA NTM fund no. 21 Jan Kotěra,
entry no. 80

Design for the adaptation of the Modern
Gallery building in Stromovka park in
Prague
1909 DC
S: AA NTM fund no. 21 Jan Kotěra,
entry no. 81

Study for the placement of the Modern
Gallery in various locations in Prague
1909 DO
S: AA NTM fund no. 21 Jan Kotěra,
entry no. 92

Kotěra family tomb in Vinohrady
cemetery in Prague
1909 DC
S: AA NTM fund no. 21 Jan Kotěra,
entry no. 83

Design for a forest chapel in Nové Hrady
1909 DO
S: AA NTM fund no. 21 Jan Kotěra,
entry no. 181

Design for the Peppina Villa hotel in Opatija
1909–1910 DO
S: AA NTM fund no. 21 Jan Kotěra,
entry no. 82

The Vojáček memorial in Prostějov
1909–1910 DC
S: AA NTM fund no. 21 Jan Kotěra,
entry no. 89

Charvát's villa in Vysoké Mýto
1909–1911 DC
Rokycanova 247/IV, Vysoké Mýto
S: AA NTM fund no. 21 Jan Kotěra,
entry no. 84

State railway employees' housing colony
in Louny
1909, 1913, 1919 DC
streets: Husova, Bezručova,
Čeňka Zemana, Máchova, Alšova,
Klicperova, Kpt. Jaroše, Dykova,
Kollárova, Nerudova
S: AA NTM fund no. 21 Jan Kotěra,
entry no. 85

Prof K. B. Mádl's apartment furnishings
in Prague
1910 DC
furnishings kept in the Museum
of Decorative Arts in Prague
S: AA NTM fund no. 21 Jan Kotěra,
entry no. 86

Design for a forestry exhibition in Vienna
1910 ?
S: AA NTM fund no. 21 Jan Kotěra,
entry no. 87

Adaptation of Prague bridge
in Hradec Králové
1910 DC
S: AA NTM fund no. 21 Jan Kotěra,
entry no. 88

Reconstruction of the Grand Hotel
(Urban) in Hradec Králové
1910–1911 DC
Československé armády 275,
Hradec Králové
S: AA NTM fund no. 21 Jan Kotěra,
entry no. 90

Reconstruction of Bianca
(L. Bondy's) villa in Prague-Bubeneč
1910–1913 DC
reconstruction: M. Spielmann, 1919
Na seníku 48, Praha 6
S: AA NTM fund no. 21 Jan Kotěra,
entry no. 91

Dr Borůvka's family house in Prague
1910–1911 DC
Mickiewiczova 239/13, Praha 6
S: AA NTM fund no. 21 Jan Kotěra,
entry no. 97

J. Groh's family house in Prague
1910–1911 DC
Mickiewiczova 240/15, Praha 6
S: AA NTM fund no. 21 Jan Kotěra,
entry no. 98

Reconstruction of T. Baťa's family house
in Zlín
1910–1912 DC
Gahurova 292, Zlín
S: AA NTM fund no. 21 Jan Kotěra,
entry no. 96

Competition entry for the Credit Bank
in Hradec Králové
1911 DO
S: AA NTM fund no. 21 Jan Kotěra,
entry no. 93

Competition entry for a multi-purpose
building for the Koruna insurance
company (U Špinků house) in Prague
1911 DO
S: AA NTM fund no. 21 Jan Kotěra,
entry no. 94

Competition entry for a spa building
in Grad
1911 DO
S: AA NTM fund no. 21 Jan Kotěra,
entry no. 95

Competition entry for
the Austro-Hungarian Bank in Vienna
1911 DO
S: AA NTM fund no. 21 Jan Kotěra,
entry no. 101

Design for a hydrotherapeutic institute
and hotel (Vila Triestina) in Lovran
1911 DO
S: AA NTM fund no. 21 Jan Kotěra,
entry no. 102

Reconstruction of the Imperial hotel
in Dubrovnik
1911–1912 DC
M. Blažića 2, Dubrovnik
S: AA NTM fund no. 21 Jan Kotěra,
entry no. 99

New Mandelík family castle in Ratboř
1911–1913 DC
Ratboř 40
S: AA NTM fund no. 21 Jan Kotěra,
entry no. 100

Slavia Bank in Sarajevo
1911–1913 DC
demolished
S: AA NTM fund no. 21 Jan Kotěra,
entry no. 103

Urbánek house (apartment building with
a publishing house specialising
in music – Mozarteum) in Prague
1911–1913 DC
Jungmannova 748/30, Praha 1
S: AA NTM fund no. 21 Jan Kotěra,
entry no. 104

Tichý tomb in Vyšehrad cemetery in Prague
1912 DC
in collaboration with B. Kafka
S: AA NTM fund no. 21 Jan Kotěra,
entry no. 105

Competition entry for a memorial
to Hadzhi Dimitriyev in Slivenec (Bulgaria)
1912   DO
S: AA NTM fund no. 21 Jan Kotěra,
entry no. 106

General Pension Institute in Prague
1912–1914   DC
in collaboration with J. Zasche
Rašínovo nábř. 390/42, Praha 2
S: AA NTM fund no. 21 Jan Kotěra,
entry no. 107

Reconstruction of the old castle owned
by the Mandelík family in Ratboř
1912–1915   DC
Ratboř 1
S: AA NTM fund no. 21 Jan Kotěra,
entry no. 108

Competition entry for the Royal Palace in
Sofia
1912   DO
S: AA NTM fund no. 21 Jan Kotěra,
entry no. 109

Third design for the Law and Theology
Faculty, Czech University of Charles-
Ferdinand in Prague
1913   DO
S: AA NTM fund no. 87, entry UNIV

Competition entry for a monument
to Jan Žižka on Vítkov hill in Prague
1913   DO
in collaboration with J. Štursa
S: AA NTM fund no. 21 Jan Kotěra,
entry no. 110

Design for the Austrian pavilion at
the international exhibition in Glaspalast
in Munich
1913   DC
S: AA NTM fund no. 21 Jan Kotěra,
entry no. 111

Lemberger-Gombrich villa in Vienna
1913–1915   DC
Grinzinger Alee 50–52, Wien
S: AA NTM fund no. 21 Jan Kotěra,
entry no. 112

Design for the Epilepsy Institute
Malovaný lis in Prague-Libeň
1914   DO
S: AA NTM fund no. 21 Jan Kotěra,
entry no. 113

Housing plan for the Heinovka complex
in Prague-Žižkov
1914   DO
S: AA NTM fund no. 21 Jan Kotěra,
entry no. 114

Design for a housing colony for railway
employees in Prague-Záběhlice
1914   DO
S: AA NTM fund no. 21 Jan Kotěra,
entry no. 115

Janoušek tomb in Olšany cemetery
in Prague
1915   DC
in collaboration with J. Štursa
S: AA NTM fund no. 21 Jan Kotěra,
entry no. 116

Design for a monument to Bedřich
Smetana on Žofín island in Prague
1915   DO
in collaboration with J. V. Myslbek
S: AA NTM fund no. 21 Jan Kotěra,
entry no. 117

A. Mandelík tomb in the Jewish cemetery
in Kolín
1915   DC
in collaboration with J. Štursa
S: AA NTM fund no. 21 Jan Kotěra,
entry no. 118

Design for Dr Hácha's tomb
1915   DO
S: AA NTM fund no. 21 Jan Kotěra,
entry no. 119

Design for the adaptation of the library at the Academy of Fine Arts in Prague
1915   DO
S: AA NTM fund no. 21 Jan Kotěra, entry no. 121

Designs for the Law and Theology Faculty, Czech University of Charles-Ferdinand in Prague
1915–1918   DO
S: AA NTM fund no. 87, entry UNIV

Design of M. Pulchart's family house in Solnice
1916   DO
S: AA NTM fund no. 21 Jan Kotěra, entry no. 122

Design for R. Maturová's villa in Prague-Trója
1916   DO
S: AA NTM fund no. 21 Jan Kotěra, entry no. 123

Nosek tomb in Olšany cemetery in Prague
1916   DC
S: AA NTM fund no. 21 Jan Kotěra, entry no. 124

Design of a tomb for Alois Kotěra
1916   DO
S: AA NTM fund no. 21 Jan Kotěra, entry no. 125

Design for a military cemetery in Olšany cemetery in Prague
1916   DO
S: AA NTM fund no. 21 Jan Kotěra, entry no. 126

Design for a military cemetery in Slaný
1916   DO
S: AA NTM fund no. 21 Jan Kotěra, entry no. 127

Design for a war memorial for Nové Hrady in Southern Bohemia
1916   DO
S: AA NTM fund no. 21 Jan Kotěra, entry no. 128

Design for a war memorial for the town of Příbram
1917   DO
S: AA NTM fund no. 21 Jan Kotěra, entry no. 129

Design for a war memorial for the town of Jihlava
1917   DO
S: AA NTM fund no. 21 Jan Kotěra, entry no. 130

Design for the completion of the landing stage by the Šitkovská waterworks in Prague
1917   DO
S: AA NTM fund no. 21 Jan Kotěra, entry no. 131

Design for T. Baťa's library in Zlín
1917   DO
S: AA NTM fund no. 21 Jan Kotěra, entry no. 132

Adaptation of a warehouse façade in Telč, Moravia
1917   DC
Staňkova 215/II, Telč-Podolí
S: AA NTM fund no. 21 Jan Kotěra, entry no. 133

Design for the reconstruction of the Houštky spa near Brandýs nad Labem
1917   DO
S: AA NTM fund no. 21 Jan Kotěra, entry no. 134

Design for a cinema in Zlín
1917   DO
S: AA NTM fund no. 21 Jan Kotěra, entry no. 7

Waldes tomb in the Jewish cemetery in Prague-Strašnice
1917   DC
in collaboration with J. V. Myslbek
S: AA NTM fund no. 21 Jan Kotěra, entry no. 135

Design for the reconstruction
of the gardens of H. Matyáš and
A. Šrenk in Dobruška
1917　DO
S: AA NTM fund no. 21 Jan Kotěra,
entry no. 137

Design for the Sokol gymnasium
in Dobruška
1917　DO
S: AA NTM fund no. 21 Jan Kotěra,
entry no. 138

Design for a memorial plaque to
F. V. Hek on his family house in Dobruška
c. 1917　DO
S: AA NTM fund no. 21 Jan Kotěra,
entry no. 139

Reconstruction of V. Rýdl's family house
in Dobruška
1917–1919　DC
Novoměstská 187, Dobruška
S: AA NTM fund no. 21 Jan Kotěra,
entry no. 136

Workers' housing colony for T. A. Baťa's
company in Zlín
1918　DC
Letná district, Zlín
S: AA NTM fund no. 21 Jan Kotěra,
entry no. 140

Design for the Greif family tomb
1918　DO
S: AA NTM fund no. 21 Jan Kotěra,
entry no. 141

Heveroch tomb in Vinohrady cemetery
in Prague
c. 1918　DC
S: AA NTM fund no. 21 Jan Kotěra,
entry no. 184

Design for T. F. Šimon's villa
in Prague-Bubeneč
1918　DO
S: AA NTM fund no. 21 Jan Kotěra,
entry no. 142

Design for a theatre
in the Sylva-Taroucca palace in Prague
1919　DO
S: AA NTM fund no. 21 Jan Kotěra,
entry no. 143

Design for a family house for
the entrepreneur J. Waldes in Prague
1919　DO
S: AA NTM fund no. 21 Jan Kotěra,
entry no. 145

School of Architecture at the Academy of
Fine Arts in Prague-Bubeneč
1919–1924　DC
U Akademie 172/2, Praha 6
completed by J. Gočár (1923–1924)
S: AA NTM fund no. 21 Jan Kotěra,
entry no. 146

Competition entry for the university
building (codename: Idoneum et simplex)
1920–1921　DO
S: AA NTM fund no. 87, entry UNIV

Competition entry for the Law Faculty
(codename: Ω in red)
1920　DO
S: AA NTM fund no. 87, entry UNIV

Competition entry for the ministerial
buildings in the Petrská district in Prague
1920　DO
S: AA NTM fund no. 21 Jan Kotěra,
entry no. 147

Competition entry for the Prague Credit
Bank on Wenceslas Square in Prague
1920　DO
S: AA NTM fund no. 21 Jan Kotěra,
entry no. 148

Design for the Kopřivnice rail car factory at the automobile exhibition in Prague
1920 DC
S: AA NTM fund no. 21 Jan Kotěra, entry no. 149

Design for the adaptation of the steps in the Schönborn palace gardens in Prague
1920 DO
S: AA NTM fund no. 21 Jan Kotěra, entry no. 150

Laichter tomb in the city cemetery in Dobruška
1920 DC
S: AA NTM fund no. 21 Jan Kotěra, entry no. 152

Design for the building of the management of the Králův Dvůr cement works in Prague-Vinohrady
1920 DO
S: AA NTM fund no. 21 Jan Kotěra, entry no. 153

Workers' housing colony in Králův Dvůr
1920 DC
Jungmannova street, Králův Dvůr
S: AA NTM fund no. 21 Jan Kotěra, entry no. 154

Design of a building for the Ringhoffer factory, Kopřivnice Rail Car Works and Vítkovice Mining Company in Prague-Smíchov
1921 DO
S: AA NTM fund no. 21 Jan Kotěra, entry no. 155

Administration building of the Vítkovice mining and metallurgical company in Prague
1921–1924 DC
Olivova 1419/1, Praha 1
S: AA NTM fund no. 21 Jan Kotěra, entry no. 156

Feldmann tomb in the Jewish cemetery in Kolín
1921 DC
S: AA NTM fund no. 21 Jan Kotěra, entry no. 157

Navrátil family tomb in Vinohrady cemetery in Prague
1921 DC
S: AA NTM fund no. 21 Jan Kotěra, entry no. 158

Competition entry for the Industrial Bank on Na Příkopě street in Prague
1921 DO
S: AA NTM fund no. 21 Jan Kotěra, entry no. 159

Competition entry for the Prague Credit Bank at Na Můstku street in Prague
1921 DO
S: AA NTM fund no. 21 Jan Kotěra, entry no. 160

Design for the reconstruction of the Sokol cinema in Dobruška
1921 DO
S: AA NTM fund no. 21 Jan Kotěra, entry no. 161

Design for Prof Heveroch's waiting room for his practice in Prague
1921 DC
S: AA NTM fund no. 21 Jan Kotěra, entry no. 162

Design for R. Vanický's house in Kostelec nad Orlicí
1921 DO
S: AA NTM fund no. 21 Jan Kotěra, entry no. 163

Design for an adaptation of the presidential apartment in Prague Castle
1921 DO
S: AA NTM fund no. 21 Jan Kotěra, entry no. 164

Štenc villa in Všenory
1921–1922 DC
Brunšov 357
S: AA NTM fund no. 21 Jan Kotěra, entry no. 165

Revised competition entry for the Law Faculty at Charles University
1922 DC
nám. Curieových 7/901, Praha 1
completed by L. Machoň (1926–1931)
S: AA NTM fund no. 87, entry UNIV

Workers' housing colony in Rožnov pod Radhoštěm
1922 DC
Bučiska, Rožnov pod Radhoštěm
S: AA NTM fund no. 21 Jan Kotěra, entry no. 166

Design for K. Vik's family house in Turnov
1922 DO
S: AA NTM fund no. 21 Jan Kotěra, entry no. 167

Schauer's tomb in Olšany cemetery in Prague
1922 DC
in collaboration with O. Španiel
S: AA NTM fund no. 21 Jan Kotěra, entry no. 168

Design for an administrative building for the Ringhoffer factory in Prague-Smíchov
1922 DO
S: AA NTM fund no. 21 Jan Kotěra, entry no. 169

Community houses in Hradec Králové
1922 DC
Palackého, Eliščino nábřeží, Hradec Králové
S: AA NTM fund no. 21 Jan Kotěra, entry no. 170

Design of a family house for C. Bartoň, Petrův dvůr in Náchod
1922 DO
S: AA NTM fund no. 21 Jan Kotěra, entry no. 171

Design for J. Laichter's family house in Dobruška
1922 DO
S: AA NTM fund no. 21 Jan Kotěra, entry no. 172

Design for the City Savings Bank in Kolín
1923 DO
S: AA NTM fund no. 21 Jan Kotěra, entry no. 173

Design for the adaptation of the loft in the villa owned by the entrepreneur Kysela in Prague-Bubeneč
1923 DO
S: AA NTM fund no. 21 Jan Kotěra, entry no. 174

Design for the reconstruction of house no. 1584 for the management of Králův Dvůr cement works in Prague
1922–1923 DC
V Tůních 2, Praha 2
completed by L. Machoň
S: AA NTM fund no. 21 Jan Kotěra, entry no. 179

Literature which confirms Jan Kotěra's attribution is mentioned in the case of designs and buildings for which there is no known documentation or other sources available.

Jan Kotěra's drawings, paintings and prints (landscapes, sketches for ideal architecture, folkloric and historical buildings, portraits of family and friends, caricatures, self-portraits, ex libris, memorials, designs for applied-art objects) are kept both in state institutions (National Gallery, National Technical Museum and Museum of Decorative Arts in Prague, East Bohemian Museum in Hradec Králové) and in private collections.

DC design and construction
DO design only
?   construction uncertain
L   literature
S   source

Exhibitions

1897 – exhibition of the Unity of Fine Arts at the Rudolfinum, Prague
1898 – Exhibition of student works in Plzeň
1898 – Jubilee exhibition of Architecture and Engineering at the Exhibition Grounds in Prague
1898 – second Mánes exhibition in the Topič salon, Prague
1900–1901 – Mánes Association exhibition, Künstlerhaus, Vienna
1904 – 12th members' exhibition of the Mánes Association, Mánes pavilion at the foot of Kinský gardens, Prague
1908 – international exhibition of architecture in Vienna
1909 – Mánes exhibition in Valašské Meziříčí
1911 – Mánes exhibition of architecture at the International Exhibition of Architecture in Rome
1914 – Exhibition of the art and literary circle in Charkov
1913 – Salon d'Automne, Paris
1919 – 51st Mánes exhibition, Kunsthalle, Bern
1921 – Exhibition of the Association of Architects at the Museum of Decorative Arts, Prague
1920 – 53rd exhibition of the Mánes Association members and the 18th exhibition of the Hollar Association, Municipal House, Prague
1921 – Salon d'Automne, Paris
1923 – 68th exhibition of the Mánes Association, Hagebund, Vienna
1926 – Jan Kotěra (1871–1923), 101st exhibition of Mánes, Municipal House, Prague
1943–1944 – exhibition of architectural drawings by Jan Kotěra, Czech Technical Museum, Prague
1972 – exhibition of works by Jan Kotěra, Mánes, Prague; City of Brno House of Art

This list includes exhibitions in which Jan Kotěra participated during his lifetime, and the later retrospectives of his works.

BIBLIOGRAPHY

1. Texts by Jan Kotěra

A. Publications

◻ Jan Kotěra, *Práce mé a mých žáků 1898–1901*. Anton Schroll, undated (1902).

◻ Jan Kotěra, *Dělnické kolonie*. Knihovna Stavitele, vol. 1, Praha 1921.

B. Articles in journals

◻ Jan Kotěra, O novém umění. *Volné směry* IV, 1900, pp. 189–195.

◻ Jan Kotěra, Jože Plečnik. *Volné směry* VI, 1902, pp. 91–106.

◻ Jan Kotěra, Luhačovice. *Volné směry* VIII, 1904, pp. 59–76.

◻ Jan Kotěra, Interieur c. k. uměl.-prům. školy v Praze pro světovou výstavu v St. Louis 1904. *Volné směry* VIII, 1904, pp. 119–141.

◻ Jan Kotěra, Villa JUC. F. Tondra v St. Gilgenu. *Styl* I, 1908–1909, pp. 17, 19–25.

◻ Jan Kotěra, Národní dům v Prostějově. *Styl* I, 1908–1909, pp. 254–284.

◻ Jan Kotěra, Architekt Otto Wagner. *Volné směry* XIX, 1918, pp. 229–230.

◻ Jan Kotěra, Jindřich Prucha. *Volné směry* XIX, 1918, p. 41.

◻ Jan Kotěra, Z řad členů S. V. U. Mánes odešli... *Volné směry* XIX, 1918, p. 41.

◻ Jan Kotěra, Karel Myslbek. *Volné směry* XIX, 1918, p. 41.

◻ Jan Kotěra, Dělnické kolonie. *Stavitel* II, 1920–1921, pp. 65–82.

◻ Jan Kotěra, K návrhům na zastavení Petrského nábřeží budovami ministerskými. *Styl* II (VII), 1921–1922, p. 22, plates XV–XVII.

◻ Jan Kotěra, Data k projektu budovy pro právnickou a theologickou fakultu české university. *Styl* II (VII), 1921–1922, p. 93, plates LIX.–LXXVIII.

◻ Jan Kotěra, Návrhy a provedené stavby Jana Kotěry od roku 1900–1921. *Styl* II (VII), 1921–1922, pp. 94–95.

◻ Jan Kotěra, Z dopisů svému příteli R. G. ve Vídni. *Stavitel* V, 1924, pp. 58–65.

◻ Z dopisů Jana Kotěry z Itálie r. 1898. *Stavitel* V, 1924, pp. 65–67.

◻ Jan Kotěra, Z italských dopisů. S úvodem Josefa Šusty. *Umění* IV, 1931, pp. 115–128, 269–275, 313–316, 356–359.

2. Texts on Jan Kotěra

A. Monographs and catalogues published for various exhibitions

◻ Antonín Matějček, *Jan Kotěra*. Special print from the journal *Der Architekt*. Anton Schroll, 1916.

◻ Karel B. Mádl, *Jan Kotěra*. Jan Štenc, Praha 1922.

◻ Zdeněk Wirth, *Jan Kotěra 1871–1923*. Obecní dům, Praha 1926.

☐ Zdeněk Wirth, *Architektonické kresby Jana Kotěry*. České technické muzeum, Praha 1943.

☐ Otakar Novotný, *Jan Kotěra a jeho doba*. SNKLHU, Praha 1958.

☐ Marie Benešová – Jiří Štursa – Jana Guthová – Jiří Vasiluk, *Jan Kotěra*. Mánes, Praha a Dům umění města Brna 1972.

B. Books / Separate publications

☐ Jaromír Pečírka, (entry) Kotěra Jan, in: *Thieme-Becker*, Leipzig 1907–1950, vol. 21, pp. 348–349.

☐ *Aus der Wagner-Schule*. Supplement to the journal *Der Architekt*. Anton Schroll, 1897.

☐ Academy Architecture, vol. 21, London 1902, 128–131.

☐ Karel. B. Mádl, *Umění včera a dnes*, I, II. Praha 1908.

☐ Zdeněk Wirth – Antonín Matějček, *Česká architektura 1800–1920*. Jan Štenc, Praha 1922, pp. 73–78.

☐ (Ed. Jaromír Krejcar), *L'architecture contemporaine en Tchécoslovaquie*. Praha 1928.

☐ Vilém Dvořák, (entry) Kotěra Jan, in: *Masarykův slovník naučný*, IV, 1929, p. 125.

☐ Karel Teige, *Moderní architektura v Československu*. MSA 2, Odeon, Praha 1930, pp. 44–62.

☐ Jan E. Koula and Co., *Obytný dům dneška*. Družstevní práce, Praha 1931, p. 21.

☐ Pavel Janák, *Sto let obytného domu nájemného v Praze*. Knihovna Stylu, Praha 1933, pp. 12, 13.

☐ Antonín Matějček, *Hlasy světa a domova*. SVU Mánes, Praha 1931, pp. 134–138.

☐ *Padesát let Státní uměleckoprůmyslové školy v Praze 1885–1935*. Jan Štenc, Praha 1935; articles by Jaromír Pečírka, pp. 23–25, 33–36, 39; article by Pavel Janák, pp. 56–58.

☐ Jan E. Koula, *Nová česká architektura a její vývoj v XX. století*. Česká grafická unie, a. s., Praha 1940.

☐ František Lydie Gahura, *Estetika architektury*. Zlín 1945.

☐ Prokop Toman, *Nový slovník československých výtvarných umělců*. Rudolf Ryšavý, Praha 1947, vol. I, pp. 537–538.

☐ *Hans Vollmer's Künstlerlexikon des 20. Jahrhunderts*. Seemann, 1956.

☐ Oldřich Zeman – Jan Kühndel – Jiří Grabmüller, *Národní dům v Prostějově – památka moderní české architektury*. Prostějov 1957.

☐ Felix Haas, *Moderná svetová architektúra*. Bratislava 1966.

☐ Ottokar Uhl, *Moderne Architektur in Wien*. 1965.

☐ Bohuslav Fuchs, *In margine uměleckého odkazu Jana Kotěry*. Dům umění města Brna, 1972.

☐ Bohuslav Syrový, *Architektura*. SNTL, Praha 1972, p. 161.

☐ Marco Pozzetto, *La Scuola di Wagner 1894–1912*. Commo di Trieste, 1975.

☐ *Encyklopedie českého výtvarného umění*. Academia, Praha 1975, pp. 228–229.

☐ Dušan Janoušek, Sedmdesát let prostějovského Národního domu. *Jubilejní XX. Wolkrův Prostějov*, Prostějov 1977, pp. 21–23.

☐ Vladimír Šlapeta, *Moderní architektura v Prostějově 1900–1950*. Regional cultural centre in Prostějov in collaboration with the National Technical Museum in Prague, as a special issue of the journal *Štafeta*, 2, 3 and 4/1977, December 1977.

☐ Pavel Marek – Vladimír Šlapeta, *Národní dům v Prostějově*. Okresní kulturní středisko v Prostějově 1978 (1980, 1987).

☐ Emanuel Poche and Co., *Praha našeho věku*. Panorama, Praha 1978, pp. 20, 25, 26, 28–31, 36–40, 47, 49, 53, 59, 64, 70, 71, 74, 83, 101, 102, 106, 118, 128, 143, 144, 176, 195, 202, 203, 366, 367, 368, 369.

☐ Zora Dvořáková, *Josef Václav Myslbek*. Melantrich, Praha 1979, pp. 177, 192, 225, 232–234, 252, 262, 282, 288, 289, 295, 308.

☐ Felix Haas, *Architektura 20. století*. SPN, Praha 1980.

☐ Jiří Gebrian, *Jan Kotěra a Zlín*. Gottwaldovsko od minulosti k současnosti, vol. 3, OA v Gottwaldově, 1981, pp. 125–147.

☐ Petr Wittlich, *Česká secese*. Odeon, Praha 1982, pp. 51, 57, 62, 123, 154, 155, 158, 159, 174, 175, 176, 177, 187, 230, 235, 240, 263, 264, 282, 284, 319, 320, 324, 325, 329, 333, 355, 364, 370; illustr. 29, 30, 35, 116–120, 134, 142, 143, 146–148, 199, 220–223, 233–237, 273, 274, 314.

☐ Vladimír Šlapeta, (entry) Kotěra Jan, in: *Macmillan Encyclopedia of Architects*. New York 1982, vol. 2, pp. 579–580.

☐ Marie Benešová, *Česká architektura v proměnách dvou století 1780–1980*. SPN, Praha 1984, pp. 243, 247, 248, 249, 250, 251, 252, 254, 257, 258, 259, 260, 261, 278, 285, 291, 292, 416, 420, 427, 434.

☐ Tomáš Vlček, *Praha 1900*. Panorama, Praha 1986, pp. 5, 6, 70, 71, 91, 100, 104, 105, 106, 108, 109, 123, 124, 156, 165, 300.

☐ Alena Kubová – Rostislav Švácha, *Two Architects Between Prague and Vienna. Jan Kotěra und Adolf Loos*. 1991.

☐ Jiří Padrta – Miroslav Lamač, *Skupina výtvarných umělců 1907–1917 (teorie, kritika, polemika)*. Vol. 1, Odeon, Praha 1992.

☐ *Nová encyklopedie českého výtvarného umění*. Academia, Praha 1995, pp. 384–386.

☐ Rostislav Švácha, *Od moderny k funkcionalismu*. Victoria Publishing, Praha 1995, pp. 13, 14, 18, 36, 48, 52, 53, 54, 55, 58, 59, 60, 62, 64, 66, 67, 68, 71, 74, 75, 81, 84, 87, 88, 94, 105, 114, 118, 124, 128, 129, 166, 182, 184, 203, 206, 209, 218, 222, 233, 240, 244, 307, 394, 442, 502, 509, 510, 511, 516, 517, 521, 525, 532, 536, 544, 545, 547, 548, 549.

☐ Pavel Vlček and Co., *Umělecké památky Prahy. Staré Město a Josefov*. Academia, Praha 1996, pp. 495–496.

☐ Rostislav Švacha, (entry) Jan Kotera, in: *Dictionnaire de l'Architecture du XXème siècle*, sous la direction de Jean-Paul Midant. Fernand Hazan/Institut Francais d'Architecture, 1996, pp. 483–484.

☐ Jan E. Svoboda – Zdeněk Lukeš – Ester Havlová, *Praha 1891–1918*. Libri, Praha 1997, pp. 12, 14, 36, 41, 74, 75, 83, 102, 110, 128, 129 133, 182, 183, 186, 188, 201, 218, 242, 253, 254, 258.

☐ Růžena Baťková and Co., *Umělecké památky Prahy. Nové Město a Vyšehrad*. Academia, Praha 1998, pp. 273, 314, 426, 441, 530, 600, 631, 655.

☐ Pavel Vlček and Co., *Umělecké památky Prahy. Pražský hrad a Hradčany*. Academia, Praha 2000, pp. 184, 441, 455.

☐ Vladimír Šlapeta, (entry) Kotera Jan, in: *Dizionario dell Architettura del XX secolo a cura di Carlo Olmo*. Umberto Allemandi 2001, vol. 3, pp. 473–474.

C. Articles in journals and newspapers

☐ Das Schloss Roth – Hrádek in Böhmen. *Der Architekt* I, 1895, pp. 33, 35, plate 53.

☐ Projecte für ein Miethaus im VI. Bezirk. *Der Architekt* I, 1895, p. 55, plates 91, 92.

☐ Concurenz um den Fügerpreis: Fürstliches Schwimmbad. *Der Architekt* II, 1896, p. 47, plate 83.

☐ Studie für eine Pfarrkirche. *Der Architekt* II, 1896, p. 47, plate 86.

☐ Der Architekt, Supplementheft: Aus der Wagnerschule. *Ver Sacrum* I, 1898, p. 25.

☐ Grabgevölbe für die Familie des Freiherren Mladota in Cerveny Hradek. *Der Architekt* IV, 1898, plate 88.

☐ Jan Herben, Druhá výstava spolku Mánes. *Čas* XII, 1898, p. 775.

☐ Jan Herben, Z Wagnerovy školy. *Čas* XII, 1898, p. 501.

☐ Nabob, jemuž na nějakém milionku nesejde... *Zlatá Praha* XV, 1898.

☐ Prager Salon. *Politik*, 25th June 1898.

☐ Karel B. Mádl, K užší konkurenci na budovu nádraží... *Volné směry* III, 1898–1899, p. 315.

☐ Karel B. Mádl, Ein moderner Architekt. *Politik*, 1st January 1899.

☐ Façade eines bemalten Eckhauses für Pilsen. *Der Architekt* V, 1899, 3, p. 16, plate 19.

☐ Karel B. Mádl, Příchozí umění. *Volné směry* III, 1899, pp. 117–142.

☐ Façade eines Hauses am Wenzelsplatz im Prag. *Der Architekt* VI, 1900, p. 2, plate 4.

☐ Výstava c. k. umělecko-průmyslové školy pražské na světové výstavě v Paříži roku 1900. *Volné směry* V, 1901, pp. 71–85.

☐ Karel B. Mádl, Husův pomník. *Volné směry* V, 1901, pp. 50–69.

☐ Gebaude für die Rodin Ausstellung in Prag. *Der Architekt*, VIII, 1902, p. 38. M(Mádl), Rodinova výstava. *Zlatá Praha* XIX, 1902, 33, p. 394.

☐ Literatur: Jan Kotěra: Meine und meiner Schüler Arbeiten. 1898–1901. *Der Architekt* IX, 1903, p. 26.

☐ Studio Talk, Prague. *The Studio* XXVII, 1903, pp. 141–145.

☐ České umění reprezentováno bude. *Volné směry* VIII, 1904, p. 142.

☐ 1. června zahájena byla... *Volné směry* IX, 1905, p. 190.

☐ Zdeněk Wirth, Okresní dům v Hradci Králové. *Volné směry* X, 1906, pp. 297–299.

- Studio Talk, Prague. *The Studio* XXXI, 1904, pp. 83–86.

- Hermann Muthesius, Die Wohnung Kunst auf der Weltausstellung in St. Louis. *Deutsche Kunst und decoration*, XV, 1904–1905, pp. 218–221.

- Karel B. Mádl, Dvě divadla. *Národní listy* XLVII, 1907, 339, 8th December 1907, p. 13.

- Pražské záležitosti. *Styl* I, 1909, p. 116.

- Poznámky k č. 9. Monumentální architektura 1908–1910. *Styl* II, 1910, p. 110.

- G., Jubilejní výstava v Praze. *Styl* I, 1909, pp. 189–190.

- Profesor Jan Kotěra – Prag. *Moderne Bauformen* IX, 1910, pp. 441–447.

- Recent Designs in Domestic Architecture. *The Studio* LVII, 1912, pp. 313–315.

- Studio Talk, Munich, At this Year's International Art Exhibition... *The Studio* LX, 1913, pp. 236–237.

- Japanese revue Keushiku Sekhai (Architectural World), 1913.

- Museum in Königgrätz. *Berliner Architekturwelt* XVI, 1914, p. 356.

- Otakar Novotný, Architektura symbolická, pomník a Žižkův pomník. *Volné směry* XVIII, 1915, p. 88.

- Antonín Matějček, Jan Kotěra. *Der Architekt – Bildende Kunst* I/XXI, Wiener Monatshefte verenigt, 1916–1918, pp. 109–122.

- Vlastislav Hofman, O dalším vývoji naší moderní architektury. *Volné směry* XIX, 1918, pp. 193–207.

- Ministerské budovy na nábřeží Svatopetrském. *Stavitel* I, 1919–1920, p. 201.

- Česká architektura. *Stavitel* I, 1919–1920, p. 204.

- Antonín Kotek, Česká architektura. *Stavitelské listy* XVI, 1920, pp. 81, 132.

- K soutěži na právnickou fakultu vypsané ministerstvem veřejných prací. *Stavitel* II, 1920–1921, p. 16.

- Další poznámka k soutěži na právnickou fakultu. *Stavitel* II, 1920–1921, p. 62.

- Výsledek soutěže na stavbu české university v Praze u Čechova mostu. *Stavitel* II, 1920–1921, p. 138.

- Soutěž na stavbu universitních budov... *Stavitel* II, 1920–1921, p. 138.

- Otakar Novotný, Kotěrova universita. *Styl* I (VI), 1920–1921, p. 76.

- Bauten von Jan Kotěra. Oberbaurat, Professor der Kunstakademie Prag. *Der Baumeister* XIX, , 1921, 2, pp. 1–8.

- Ladislav Machoň, Jan Kotěra padesátníkem. *Národní listy*, 18th December 1921.

- Studio Talk, Prague, Professor Jan Kotěra... *The Studio* LXXXII, 1921, pp. 236–237.

- Kotěrova universita. *Stavitel* III, 1921–1922, p. VI.

- Návrhy a provedené stavby Jana Kotěry od roku 1900–1921. *Styl* II (VII), 1921–1922, pp. 94–95.

- Kotěra a Moderní galerie. *Stavitel* III, 1921–1922, pp. VI–V.

- Vilém Dvořák, Dvacet let proti proudu. *Styl* II (VII), 1921–1922, 9–10, pp. 88–93.

- Pavel Janák, K jubileu Jana Kotěry. *Styl* II (VII), 1921–1922, pp. 87–88.

- Antonín Matějček, Prof. Jan Kotěra padesátníkem. *Stavitel* III, 1921–1922, pp. 1–6.

- Otakar Novotný, Jan Kotěra v roce 1921. *Volné směry* XXI, 1921–1922, pp. 207–208.

- Zdeněk Wirth, Česká moderní architektura. *Styl* II (VII), 1921–1922, pp. 1–2.

- Emil Edgar(?), Architekt Jan Kotěra padesátníkem. *Kámen* III, 1922, vol. 3, p. 6.

- Za profesorem Janem Kotěrou. *Stavitel* IV, 1922–1923, pp. 78–81.

- Die neuen Monumentalbauten der Prager Karls-Universität. *Prager Presse*, 11th March 1923, p. 4.

- Vilém Dvořák, Za Janem Kotěrou. *Zlatá Praha* XL, 1923, 12.

- Vilém Dvořák, Za Janem Kotěrou neboli osud českého umělce. *Národní kultura* II, 1923, 4.

- Vilém Dvořák, Za profesorem Janem Kotěrou. *Tribuna*, 18th April 1923.

- E., Jan Kotěra. *Stavba* II, 1923, 2, p. 17.

- Emil Edgar, Jan Kotěra mrtev. *Kámen* IV, 1923, pp. 82–83.

- Bohuslav Fuchs, Vzpomínka na Jana Kotěru. *Drobné umění* IV, 1923, pp. 93, 111.

- Jaroslav Hilbert, Architekt Jan Kotěra. *Venkov*, 18th April 1923.

- Vlastimil Hofman, Za architektem Janem Kotěrou. *Tribuna*, 19th April 1923.

- Josef Chochol, Jan Kotěra. *Časopis československých architektů* XXII, 1923, pp. 165–171.

- Pavel Janák, Jan Kotěra, umělec a organisátor čes. umění. *Výtvarná práce* II, 1923, pp. 134–135.

- Klub architektů v Praze, Pro vysokou školu architektury. *Stavba* II, 1923, 2, p. 8.

- Jaromír Krejcar, Jan Kotěra. *Stavba* II, 1923, 2, pp. 4–7.

- Fritz Lehmann, Jan Kotěra. *Prager Tagblatt*, 18th April 1923.

- Antonín Matějček, Jan Kotěra. *Národní politika,* 18th April 1923; reprinted in: A. Matějček, *Hlasy světa a domova*. SVÚ Mánes, Praha 1931, pp. 134–138.

- Antonín František V. Mokrý, Jan Kotěra. *Právo lidu*, 28th April 1923.

- Jaromír Pečírka, Jan Kotěra. *Prager Presse* III, 18th April 1923.

- F. Obrtel, Kotěra v Prostějově. *Venkov*, 20th April 1923.

- Karel Polívka, Jan Kotěra. *Časopis československých architektů* XXII, 1923, pp. 65–66.

- J. Rössler, Jan Kotěra. *Stavitelské listy* XIX, 1923, pp. 108–109.

- J. K. Říha, Za Janem Kotěrou. *Stavba* II, 1923, 2, pp. 1–4.

- Václav Vilém Štech, Jan Kotěra. *České slovo*, 18th April 1923.

- Zdeněk Wirth, Jan Kotěra. *České slovo*, 18th April 1923.

- František Žákavec, Jan Kotěra. *Národní listy*, 17th April 1923, evening edition.

- Jan Kotěra. *Volné směry* XXII, 1923–1924, insert preceding p. 81.

- Vilém Dvořák, Za Janem Kotěrou. *Styl* IV (IX), 1923–1924, p. 3.

- Josef Svoboda, Prof. Jan Kotěra a nové tvoření výtvarně-stavební. *Elegantní Praha* II, 1923–1925, pp. 12–13.

- Jan Kotěra. *Stavitel* V, 1924, p. 57.

- Památník architektu Janu Kotěrovi. *Výtvarná práce* III, 1924, pp. 247–249.

- Pavel Janák, Učitel bydlení. *Výtvarná práce* III, 1924, pp. 168–190.

- J(Jíra), Jan Kotěra. *Národní osvobození* I, 25. 7. 1924, p. 5.

- R-ce (editorial), Vila Bianca. *Stavitel* V, 1924, p. 68.

- R-ce (editorial), Spořitelna v Kolíně. *Stavitel* V, 1924, p. 68.

- Zastavovací plán pro stavbu dělnické kolonie firmy T. a A. Baťa ve Zlíně. *Stavitel* VI, 1925, p. 62.

- Budova Vítkovického horního a hutního těžařstva. *Stavitel* VI, 1925, pp. 115–118.

- Výstava Jana Kotěry. *Stavitel* VI, 1925, pp. 159–160.

- Oldřich Starý, Česká moderní architektura. *Stavba* IV, 1925–26, pp. 154, 155, 160, 161, 162, 183, 186, 187, 188, 190, 192.

- Karel Teige, Posmrtná výstava Jana Kotěry. *Stavba* IV, 1925–1926, pp. 90–93.

- Zdeněk Wirth, Jan Kotěra. *Styl* VI (XI), 1925–1926, pp. 147–155.

- Kotěrův návrh na královský palác v Sofii. *Styl* VI (XI), 1925–1926, pp. 37–38.

- Souborná výstava díla profesora Jana Kotěry. *Výtvarná práce* IV, 1926, pp. 201–202.

- František X. Harlas, Výstava Jana Kotěry v Obecním domě. *Národní politika*, 16th January 1926.

- Jaroslav Hilbert, V Kotěrově výstavě. *Venkov*, 24th January 1926.

- Pavel Janák, Čtvrt století. *Volné směry* XXXIV, 1926, pp. 100–105, 110.

- J. R. M. (Marek), Jan Kotěra, malíř. *Národní listy*, 22nd January 1926.

- Ke Kotěrově výstavě. *Volné směry* XXIV, 1926, pp. 97–99.

- J. R. Marek, Jan Kotěra, malíř. *Národní listy*, (22nd January 1926).

- Bohumil Markalous, Sociálně-etické poslání architektovo. Po výstavě Jana Kotěry. *Stavitel* VII, 1926, pp. 17–19.

- Bohumil Markalous, Souborná výstava architekta Jana Kotěry I. *Právo lidu*, 20th January 1926.

- Bohumil Markalous, Souborná výstava architekta Jana Kotěry II. *Právo lidu*, 21st January 1926.

- Antonín Matějček, Stavební plastika Jana Štursy. *Výtvarná práce* IV, 1926, pp. 4–7, 10, 11, 14, 15, 18.

- Nikodem, Souborná výstava životního díla Jana Kotěry. *Národní osvobození* III, 21st January 1926, p. 3.

- Arne Novák, Tragika architektova. *Lidové noviny*, 10th January 1926.

- Otakar Novotný, Prameny Kotěrova díla. *Výtvarná práce* IV, 1926, pp. 301–318.

- Oskar Schürer, Kotěrova výstava v Obecním domě. *Tribuna* VIII, (22nd January 1926).

- F. X. Šalda, Příklad. *Tvorba* II, 1926, 8, pp. 137–138; reprinted in: F. X. Šalda, O *umění*. Československý spisovatel, Praha 1955, pp. 609–611.

- Max Urban, Jan Kotěra. *Národní listy*, 15th January 1926.

- Max Urban, Kotěrovy universitní budovy. *Národní listy*, 24th January 1926.

- Karel Herain, Ulrichův Hradec Králové. *Umění* III, 1930, pp. 300–302, 304–323, 328–335, 338, 340, 342–344, 346, 348, 354.

- Josef Šusta, Z italských dopisů Jana Kotěry (vzpomínkový úvod). *Umění* IV, 1931, pp. 112–114.

- Desáté výročí smrti architekta Jana Kotěry… *Umění* VI, 1933, p. 340.

- Hrobky a náhrobky Kotěrovy. *Kámen* III, 1933, 3, p. 5.

- Oldřich Starý, Jan Kotěra. *Čítanka průmyslníků*, 1939, pp. 242–243.

- J. S. Svoboda, Jan Kotěra. *Národní listy*, 16th April 1933.

- Václav Vilém Štech, K desátému výročí úmrtí Jana Kotěry, *České slovo*, 16th April 1933.

- Zdeněk Wirth, Jan Kotěra kreslíř. *Umění* XV, 1943–1944, pp. 253–270.

- Ladislav Machoň, Jan Kotěra. *Praha v týdnu* IV, 1943, 50, pp. 4–5.

- V. Drchal, Výročí Jana Kotěry. *Technika a život* XIX, 1948, p. 122.

- Oldřich Starý, Pětadvacet let od smrti Jana Kotěry (17. IV. 1923). *Architektura ČSR* VII, 1948, p. 82.

- Zdeněk Wirth, Otakar Novotný, Jan Kotěra a jeho doba. *Umění* VII, 1959, pp. 173–174.

- Hans Ankwicz von Kleehoven, Die Anfänge der Wiener Seccesion, in: *Alte und Moderne Kunst*, 1960, pp. 6–10.

- Jan E. Koula, Rodinný dům jako pionýr nové architektury. *Architektura ČSSR* XXVIII, 1969, pp. 524, 526, 527.

- Vítězslav Procházka, Jan Kotěra – osobnost stále aktuální. *Umění a řemesla*, 1971, 4, pp. 58–59.

- Jiří Tywoniak, Jan Kotěra a Červený Hrádek u Sedlčan. *Sedlčanský sborník*, 1971, pp. 110–120.

- Jaroslav Liska, Kotěrovy umělecké začátky. *Československý architekt* XVIII, 1972, 1, p. 4.

- Marie Benešová, Jan Kotěra. *Architektura ČSR* XXXI, 1972, 8, pp. 392–400.

- Vladimír Šlapeta, Národní dům v Prostějově. *Štafeta* IX, 1977, 4, pp. 8–10.

- Jan Michl, Výstava architektonického díla Jana Novotného. *Umění* XXIX, 1981, pp. 81–83.

- Vladimír Šlapeta, Česká meziválečná architektura z hlediska mezinárodních vztahů. *Umění* XXIX, 1981, p. 309.

- Rostislav Švácha, Jan Kotěra. *Domov* XXV, 1985, 1, pp. 49–53.

- Pavel Zatloukal, Wagnerova škola v Praze. *Umění* XXXIII, 1985, p. 469.

- Rostislav Švácha, Poznámky ke Kotěrovu muzeu. *Umění* XXXIV, 1986, pp. 171-179.

- Zdeněk Lukeš, Jan Kotěra. *Umění a řemesla*, 1988, 3, pp. 25-31.

- Eduard Staša, Vila Tomáše Bati ve Zlíně. *Tep*, 10th August 1990.

- Pavel Zatloukal, Baťova zlínská vila. *Architekt* XXII, 1991, 12, p. 4.

- Pavel Zatloukal, Baťova zlínská vila. *Zlínský funkcionalismus*. Sborník příspěvků sympozia pořádaného u příležitosti 100. výročí F. L. Gahury a 90. narozenin VI. Karfíka. Státní galerie ve Zlíně, 1991, pp. 58-61.

- Eduard Staša, Starozlínské vzpomínání - o jedné vile na Čepkově. *Zlínské noviny*, 9th December 1994.

- František L. Gahura, Vzpomínky. *Architekt*, 1995, 4-5, pp. 13-14.

- Jiří Šetlík, Uměleckoprůmyslová škola v Praze 1885-1995. *Umění a řemesla*, 1995, 2, p. 2.

- Edith Jeřábková, K ideovým aspektům Kotěrova Národního domu v Prostějově. *Umění* XLIV, 1996, pp. 411-424.

- Jindřich Vybíral, Jan Kotěra - Medailon. *Architekt*, 1996, 26, p. 49-51.

- Jan Stach, Neznámá historie. *Telčské listy*, 1996, 6.

- Politika Obecního domu. *Ateliér*, 1997, 9, p. 12; reprinted in: Rostislav Švácha, Politika Obecního domu. *Architekt* XLIII, 1997, 14-15 (July), pp. 73-74.

- Jindřich Vybíral, Druhý život Jana Kotěry. *Dějiny a současnost* XIX, 1997, 3, pp. 35-37.

D. Exhibition catalogues

- *Výstava architektury členů Mánesa*. Obecní dům, Praha prosinec 1930.

- Zdeněk Wirth, *Výstava za novou architekturu*. Umělecko-průmyslové museum, Praha květen-září 1940. Jan Štenc, Dr. Eduard Grégr a syn, Praha 1940, pp. 15, 40, 47.

- Collected authors, *Česká secese, umění 1900*. Exhibition catalogue, Alšova jihočeská galerie, Hluboká n. Vltavou, 1966.

- Tsechische Kunst 1878-1914. Auf dem Weg in die Moderne (ed. J. Kotalík, B. Krimmel). Darmstadt 1984.

- Vladimír Šlapeta, *Czech Functionalism 1918-1938*. Architectural Association exhibition catalogue, London 1987.

- Milena B. Lamarová - Vladimír Šlapeta - Petr Wittlich - Jiří Šetlík - Josef Kroutvor - Olga Herbenová - François Burkhardt - Alessandro Mendini, *Český kubismus. Architektura a design 1910-1925*. Vitra Design Museum, Weil am Rheim 1991, pp. 8, 23, 34, 35, 38, 42, 45, 48, 52, 53, 80, 88.

- Zdeněk Lukeš - Damjan Prelovšek - Tomáš Valena, *Josip Plečnik - architekt Pražského hradu*. Správa Pražského hradu, Praha 1996, pp. 28, 29, 30, 34, 36, 89, 90, 91, 100, 101, 126, 134, 141, 213, 259, 367, 368, 508, 511, 512, 514, 517, 518, 519, 534, 539, 568.

- Petr Wittlich and Co., *Důvěrný prostor/Nová dálka. Umění pražské secese*. Obecní dům, Praha 1997, pp. 49, 82, 83, 99, 202, 204, 205, 206, 212, 213, 215, 216, 217, 221, 222, 223, 234, 236, 237, 239, 244, 252, 256, 264.

- Rostislav Švácha, Jan Kotěra et ses élèves. *Prague Art Nouveau*. Métamorphoses d'un style. Prague - Gent 1998, pp. 172-187.

☐ Collected authors, *Prague 1900, Poetry and ecstasy*. Van Gogh Museum, Amsterdam, 1999.

☐ Rostislav Švácha, Obnova Markovy vily od Jana Kotěry, *Stavba* IV, 2001, pp. 66–69.

Kotěra's work was also presented in the following publications:
L'Amour de l'art, Architektura ČSSR, Der Architekt, L'Architecture vivante, Architectural Review, Baumeister, Bildende Kunst, Český svět, Interieur, Moderne Bauformen, Stavba, Stavitel, Styl, The Studio, Umění, Ver Sacrum, Volné směry, Výtvarná práce, Zlatá Praha, Život

This bibliography is based on an inventory of literature compiled by staff at the Prague National Technical Museum, headed by Petr Krajčí, a project supported by a grant from the Ministry of Culture of the Czech Republic. Vladimír Šlapeta and Radmila Kreuzziegerová completed the inventory.

Index

A

Agrest Diana 60

Amberg Anna-Lisa 24

AMSTERDAM 117, 145

— stock-exchange building (Berlage H. P.) 24, **25**, 141

Amsterdam school 157, 219

Anýž Franta 307, 349

D'Aronco Raimondo 16

Arts and Crafts 16

B

Bahr Hermann 154

Baillie-Scott Mackay Hugh **15**, 16, 125, 175

Balšánek Antonín 60, 95, 119, 153, 181

Bauer Leopold 16, 60, 74, 117, 147

Bauhaus 154

BECHYNĚ

— Mácha's villa 17, **19**, 91, **103**, 105, 106, 124, 125, **127**, 342

Behrens Peter 10, 24, 31, 42, 141, 154, 169, 231, 336

Bendelmayer Bedřich 116

Bendelmayer & Červenka Co. 284

Beneš Eduard 253

Benešová Marie 9

Benš Adolf 44

Berlage Hendrik Petrus 24, **25**, **67**, 117, 119, 141, 142, 145, 146, 147, 148, 153, 154, 157, 161, 165, 169, 195, 219, 235, 237, 316

BERLIN 42, 79, 80, 189, 231, 303, 336

— AEG turbine hall (Behrens P.) 154

Bernini Gianlorenzo 146

Bílek František 67, 249, 260, 262

Blažej Ladislav 30

Boccioni Umberto 195

Böhm Ottokar 95, 116

Bondy Léon 203, 223, 350

Bötticher Karl 57, 58, 60

Bourdelle Emile Antoine 267, 268

Bráf Antonín 60

Bromovský & Schulz Co. 346

BRUSSELS

— Maison Tassel (Horta V.) 87, **93**, 121

BUFFALO

— Larkin Building (Wright F. L.) 23

Bukovina Regional Railway 321, 337

Burget Eduard 358

Burian Emil František 195

Bůžek Karel 66, 67

Bydžovská Lenka 55, 241, 242

C

Calais – Dover (project) 14, **83**, 85

Carlyle Thomas 70

Carrà Carlo 195

Carrier David 65

Cézanne Paul 270

Chadraba Rudolf 153

Chochol Josef 15, 21, 24, 25, 44, 141, 154, 157, 204

CHRUSTENICE

— Götz's villa 145, 164, **165**, 165, 171

Cmunt O. 31

COLOGNE

— German Werkbund Exhibition 31, 35, 158, 246, 336

Crane Walter 16

Cuc František 116

Czech Union of Applied Artists 35, 245, 253

Č

Čapek Karel 353

Čapek-Chod Václav Matěj 252

Čenkov Emanuel **243**

ČERNOŠICE

— Fröhlich's villa **103**, 106, 125, **127**, 131, 342

— Kratochvíl's villa **143**, 147, 164, 165, **167**, 171, 366

Černý František M. 30, 42

Červený Hrádek castle 11, 74, **75**, 96

D

Dal Co Francesco 154

DARMSTADT

— Mathildenhöhe artists'colony 24, 91, **93**, 119, 123, 154, 155

Dietz von Weidenberg Friedrich **75**

Dlabač Alois 96, 100

DOBRUŠKA

— Laichter's house 213

— Laichter tomb 314, 321

— Rýdl's house 209, 213, 223, **225**

Domečka Ludvík 148

DOUBRAVKA NEAR PLZEŇ

— Church of St George **95**, 101

Dryák Alois 97, 247

Dudok Willem Marinus 30

DÜSSELDORF 31, 253

Dvořák Karel 321

Dvořák Vilém 69, 142

E

Eck Jindřich 116
Edgar Emil 304, 359
Eiselt Eugen 358
Elbogen family **119**, **305**, 306, **309**, **311**, 321
Engel Antonín 34, 305
Engelmüller Ferdinand 258
d'Este, Grand Duke Franz Ferdinand 37, 70, 235

F

Fabiani Max 11, 63, 74, 78, 145
Fanta Josef 34, 61, 67, 68, 98, 117, 242, 252, 280
Feuerstein Bedřich **149**, 254
Fiedler Conrad 57
Fierlinger Ottokar 30, 31, 359
Fleischner Jindřich **149**, 154, 353
Foehr Adolf 116
Fojtík Pavel 327, 336
Fragner Jaroslav 21
Freyn Josef 11, 73
Fröhlich František 125, 347, 349
FRÝDEK
— Landsberger tomb **303**, 307, 314
Fuchs Bohuslav 9, 42, 44, 142, 147, 235, 369

G

Gahura František Lydie 31, 64, 145, 146, 237, 365, 366
Gandelsonas Mario 60
Gessner Hubert 11, 95, 116, 145, 242
Gmeiner Astrid 35
Gočár Josef 16, 21, 25, 30, 34, 42, 146, 149, 151, 157, **169**, 169, **187**, 201, 204, 206, 210, **211**, 223, 263, 284, 293
Gombrich Ernst 231

Gombrich Richard 63, 66, 99, 100, 121, 131, 154, 155, 231, 252, 305, 360
Göttlich Karel 31
GRAD
— spa building 31, **43**
Graf Otto Antonia 11, 73
Gratama Jan 145
Grebeníčková Růžena 153
Greif Karel 319
Groh Josef 148, 314
Gropius Walter 17, 154
Guimard Hector 16, 336
Gutfreund Otto 262, 268
Guthová Jana 9

H

Hácha Emil 38, **51**, 205, 209, 318, **325**
Hackl Alois **75**
Hankar Paul 16
Hansen Theofil E. von 13, 98
Harlas František X. 60, 66, 116
Hasenauer Carl von 11, 13, 73, 74
Hausen Marika 24
Havliš Filip 366
Hellméssen Antonín 284
HELSINKI
— central railway station (Saarinen E.) 24
Herain Karel 149
Herben Jan 68, 125, 148, 242
Herben, Mrs Olga 283
Herčík Ferdinand **243**
Heveroch Antonín 242, 291, 292, 293, **299**, 319
Heveroch, Mrs Kamila **261**, 292, 293, **299**, **301**
Hevesi Ludwig 92
Hilbert Jaroslav 66, 67
HLÁSNÁ TŘEBÁŇ 42
Hlava Jaroslav 235

Hlávka Josef 121
Hofbauer Arnošt **243**
Hoffmann Josef 10, **11**, 11, 13, 14, 16, **17**, 17, 25, 31, 42, 74, 79, 91, 95, 125, 145, 146, 147, 157, 165, 219, 231
Hofman Vlastislav 157, 204, 262
Hoffmeister Karel 281, **285**, **287**, 291
Högg, G. 304
Hollmann & Co. 343, 350
HOLOUBKOV
— church 101
— Marek's villa 25, 145, 164, 165, **167**, 171, 291, 315, 364
Honzík Karel 42
Horák Josef 349
Horejc Jaroslav 181, 262, 268, **269**, 281, 319
Horneková Jana 268
Horta Victor 16, 87, **93**, 121, 146
HOSTIŠOV
— Herben's house 101, 125, 131, 148
Houdek A. 314
Howard Ebenezer 31
HRADEC KRÁLOVÉ 30, 95, 116, 151, 279, 290, 343, 346, 347, 359
— City Museum 10, 24, **27**, **29**, **31**, 37, 116, **147**, 148, **151**, 151, 153, 154, 158, **180**, **181**, 181, **183**, 183, **185**, **187**, 191, 212, 223, 235, 249, 263, **267**, 267, 268, 270, 272, **277**, 284, 287, **289**, 290, **291**, 291, 292, 315, 343, **347**, **349**, 350
— Grand Hotel Urban 31, 156, 190, **191**, 191, 195, 268, **269**, 270, 284, 343, 347, 350
— Prague bridge 31, **39**, **41**, 158, 191
— Regional Authorities building 20, **23**, **107**, 116, 117, 119, 125, 148, 191, 270, **275**, 284, **287**, 343, 347, 350

— Savings Bank 31, **43**, 343

Hrausky Andrej 93

HRONOV

   — Jirásek tomb 307

Hubáček František 339, 342

Hübschmann (Hypšman) Bohumil 203, 212

Hudeček Antonín 67, 151, 245

Hynais Vojtěch 68

I

Infeld Adolf von 87

J

Janák Pavel 20, 25, 31, 34, 35, 39, 44, 60, 62, 70, 99, 141, 146, 157, 169, 201, 204, 206, 209, 210, 223, 262, 284, 292, 293

Jelínek Hanuš 253

Jeřábková Edith 155, 349

JIHLAVA

   — war memorial 207, 262

JINDŘICHŮV HRADEC

   — conference hall 284, 291

Jiránek Josef 116

Jiránek Miloš 15, **243**

Jurkovič Dušan 11, 17, 106, 116, 125

Justich Jiří 95, 328

K

Kafka Bohumil 137, 262, 314, 316, 318

Kainradl Leo 11

Kalvoda Antonín 321

Kaňka Miroslav 307

Karasimeonoff Stefan **75**

Kastner Jan 92, 281, 284

Kavalír František 117

Kestranek Hans 63, 66

Kick Friedrich 11

KILMACOLM

   — Hill House (Mackintosh C. R.) - **20**

KLADNO

   — Town Hall 96

Klerk Michel de

Klenka of Vlastimil Richard **243**

Klika Miloš 242

Klingenstein Emil 306

Klopfer Paul 22

Klouček Celda 284

Klusáček Karel 242

Knüpfer Beneš 14

KOLÍN

   Jewish cemetery

      — Feldmann tomb 321

      — Mandelík tomb 318

Kós Károly 125

KOSOVA HORA

   — vault of Mladota of Solopisky **303**, 305

Košťál František 290

Kotalík Jiří 149, 281

Kotěra Alois 319, **325**

Koula Jan 96, 100, 106, 117, 280

Koželj J. 93

Krajči Petr 73

KRÁLŮV DVŮR

   — workers' housing colony 30, 366, **367**, **369**

   — primary school with headmaster's apartment 31, **37**, 366

Kramář, Karel and Naděžda 61, 62, 342

Krásný František 95, 96, 97, 99

Kratochvíl Emil 165, 366

Krejcar Jaromír 30, 34, 42, 44, 70, 71, 171, 189, 339

Kress Karel 350

Kreuzziegerová Radmila 64, 66

Kroutvor Josef 86

Kruft Walter H. 57, 76

Kříženecký Rudolf 96

Křižík Co. 327, 349

Kubiček Alois 30, 31,

Kubišta Bohumil 237

Kudrys Milan 358

Kuipers Evert Johannes 142

Kurzweil Max 11

Kvapil Jaroslav 22, **63**, 137

Kvasnička Vilém 212

Kysela František 22, 119, 137, 175, 267, 268, **273**, 281

L

Laichter Jan 13, 16, 30, 142, 148, 175, 177, 319

Lajta Béla 177

Laudel Heidrun C. 58, 74

Lenderová Zdena 287

Letarouilly Paul 86

Letzel Jan 116

Liderhaus Kamil **75**

Lichtwark Alfred 62

Linert Stanislav 327, 331, 336

Liska Oldřich 359

LONDON

   — exhibition on Austrian art 252, **255**

   — Whitechapel Art Gallery (Townsend H. C.) **15**, 16, 123

Loos Adolf 10, 13, 30, 57, 75, 141, 147, 156, 242

Losos Ludvík 328, 329

LOUNY

   — workers' housing colony 30, 85, 154, 165, 171, 209, **353**, **355**, **357**, **359**, 360, **361**, **363**, 364, 366, 369

LJUBLJANA 42, 68

Ludwig Alois **75**

Luhačovice spa 17, 62, 279

Lukeš Zdeněk 96, 99

Lützeler Heinrich 66, 68